Spirit and the Obligation of Social Flesh

Spirit and the Obligation of Social Flesh

A Secular Theology for the Global City

Sharon V. Betcher

FORDHAM UNIVERSITY PRESS

NEW YORK 2014

A version of chapter 6, "Take My Yoga upon You: A Spiritual *Pli*
for the Global City," was published in *Polydoxy: Theology of
Multiplicity and Relation*, edited by Catherine Keller and Laurel
Schneider (London and New York: Routledge, 2010) (ISBN
978-0-415-78136-7).

Fordham University Press has no responsibility for the persistence or accuracy of URLs for external or third-party Internet
websites referred to in this publication and does not guarantee
that any content on such websites is, or will remain, accurate or
appropriate.

Fordham University Press also publishes its books in a variety of
electronic formats. Some content that appears in print may not
be available in electronic books.

Library of Congress Cataloging-in-Publication Data

Betcher, Sharon V., 1956–
  Spirit and the obligation of social flesh : a secular theology for
the global city / Sharon V. Betcher. — First edition.
      pages cm
  Includes bibliographical references and index.
  ISBN 978-0-8232-5390-6 (cloth : alk. paper) —
ISBN 978-0-8232-5391-3 (pbk. : alk. paper)   1. Globalization—
Religious aspects.   2. Cities and towns— Religious
aspects.   I. Title.
  BL65.G55B48 2014
  202.09173'2—dc23

                                                    2013006699

Printed in the United States of America

16 15 14   5 4 3 2 1

First edition

For Sallie and Janet,
my theological colleagues

CONTENTS

ACKNOWLEDGMENTS

This book began with a question opened up among colleagues at Vancouver School of Theology: What would a school of theology be and do in a city that dreamed of being the greenest city on earth by 2020? That's a worthy dream for a city, and it has been a fascinating challenge to think theologically beside such a worthy dream for human habitat. I am grateful to my colleagues Gerald Hobbs and Sallie McFague, who first birthed the question in a meeting of the History and Theology division.

My deep appreciation goes to the students in the various courses offered in response to discerning this theological niche—Sandra, Debra, Ann, Brother Shane, Shannon, Jessica, David, Carmen, Caroline, Jeanette, Paul, Alisdair, Min Goo, Karen, Cecilia, Aaron, Will, Jangwon, Leslie, Geoff, Kat, and Hee Tae. Students have challenged me to see the city through many different sets of eyes—of indigeneity; of rural-to-urban immigration; of international migration; of class, sex, and gender; of religious hybridity—if also through the lens of popular culture, often the discursive lingua franca of the city. Special thanks to Clara King, who served as project coordinator and research assistant through the earliest phases of this project. Kerri Mesner, Min Goo Kang, Maryann Amor, Will Ferrey, and Midori E. Hartman provided invaluable research assistance and helped coordinate a number of public forums that evolved out of this question. Their company and the fact that we also found occasions for laughter made the venture into the question of theology in and for the city an artery of curiosity for one born and raised to—and still suffering some nostalgia for—subsistence farming. Thanks again to editor Bud Bynack and to the Transdisciplinary

Theology Colloquium of Drew University, through the invitations to which several of these chapters first emerged.

svb
May 1, 2012

A version of chapter 1, "Crip/tography: Of Karma and Cosmopolis," was published in *Planetary Loves: Spivak, Postcoloniality, and Theology*, edited by Stephen D. Moore and Mayra Rivera (New York: Fordham University Press, 2011).

Introduction

> That is God. . . . A shout in the street.
>
> —JAMES JOYCE, *Ulysses*

Within the next decade or two, two-thirds of humanity's seven billion persons (and counting) will be urbanized—often housed in megacities of millions of human inhabitants. Every day on the Asian continent, 137,000 persons migrate from the countryside to cities, and every year, the country of India "needs to build the equivalent of a city of Chicago . . . to provide enough commercial and residential space for its migrants."[1] Already, 76 percent of the North American populace is urban—80 percent of Canada, when it is factored outside U.S. statistics; fewer than 2 percent of the population of North Americans in this postindustrial society remain engaged in agricultural production.

In 1950, only New York City and Tokyo had populations of more than ten million people. By 2010, there were already twenty such megacities— cities such as Lagos, Mexico City, Mumbai, Shanghai, Jakarta, Los Angeles, São Paulo, Buenos Aires, and Cairo. Demographers expect that by 2015, there will be 59 cities with populations between one million and five million in Africa alone, 65 such cities in Latin America and the Caribbean, and 253 in Asia.[2] The overwhelming majority of net additions to the human population—88 percent of the growth from 2000 to 2030—will be urban dwellers in low-income and medium-income countries. Even those who do not live in cities cannot but feel the pull of them—on their children's media/ted dreams, on their finances, on their lands and bodies, through depopulation with its accompanying shortages of skills and capital, through the gutting of generational belonging, as well as of elder wisdom and the wisdom that comes from contact with the natural environment.

Spirit and the Obligation of Social Flesh: A Secular Theology for the Global City assumes the urbanization of humanity as the context for spiritually motivated, philosophical reflection on the role that Spirit can play in an urbanized and secular world. As the theologian Harvey Cox put it, "We must learn to live in cities or we will not survive."[3] In *The Secular City*, his pivotal and still shockingly bold challenge issued to Christian theology in 1965, daring it to wake up and to leave behind its nostalgia for the town-based parish, Cox suggested that the shape of our life—what he then re-ferred to as "the technological metropolis" (4–5, 19)—shifts both the form of theology and our vocation, redirecting our passional desires to "'the *saeculum*,' this world of change" (19). While the third millennium arrived with derision regarding modernity's secularization thesis, given the seem-ing prairie fires of religious voices raised across all of earth's continents, Christianity—in the cosmopolitan zones of northern Europe and the coastal zones of North America—is, as theologian Gordon Lynch put it, nonetheless in "near terminal decline."[4] This volume assumes Cox's sense that "authentic secularity," bearing a rhizomatic relationship to Christian-ity (*Secular City*, 20–21), demands respect for plural views, but as theologian Catherine Keller writes, "pluralism is not enough."[5] Situated in the cosmo-politan zone, amidst rapidly emergent urbanism across all continents of the planet, this volume assumes that the secular, including the need to work with and through religious plurality—and while noting that the secular is ever to be distinguished from secularism—can be lived religiously so as "to frame with [one's] neighbor a common life suitable to the . . . city" (Cox, *Secular City*, 121).

Arguments abound as to whether the exponential growth of our ur-ban habitat is good or bad news. Urbanism—a boon of creativity and knowledge—is credited with lifting humanity out of poverty and occasioning an increase in the overall quality of life, including reductions in infant mortality and in malnutrition, accompanied by greater access to education and culture, as well as by that most underrated system, the one sustaining human health: sanitation.[6] And urbanism may be the greenest option for the planet amidst human population growth, argue others, including Edward Glaeser and David Owen, inasmuch as it allows for smaller scales of living—greater proximity to one another, as well as to work, thus making public transportation feasible while decreasing demands on natural resources.[7] Indeed, New York City, construed in terms of density and resource use, may be the greenest of cities in North America—even as its ecological footprint still extends far beyond its assumed city limits.[8] Others, however, such as journalist-activist Mike Davis, warn that urbanism is generating cities of millions of people who are destitute, without purpose, disconnected, and unrelated—either forced into slums or pushed into a decaying economic and urban infrastructure. As Davis writes in *Planet of Slums*, "The price of this new urban order . . . will be increasing inequality within and between cities of different sizes and economic specializations."[9] For most of the world now (in contrast with how urbanization came about in North America over the past hundred and fifty years), "urbanization progresses without industrialization," and that spells "urbanization as favelization"—that is, by way of the creation of barrios, shanty towns, and socioeconomic and racial ghettos.[10] And because "arrival cities," the landing pads for recent urban immigrants, require loose and creative energies to transform themselves into places of desire, creative entrepreneurship in such places—Ciudad Juarez, for example—can veer into criminal ventures that uncannily borrow the generative infrastructure of capitalism. As Ciudad Juarez's infamous nickname, "Murder City," exemplifies, the city then becomes differently and privately militarized.[11]

Consequently, some of us perhaps are more "modest witnesses," as historian of science Donna Haraway might put it, of urbanism's uplift—"suspicious, implicated, knowing, ignorant, worried, and hopeful."[12] We enjoy the roominess of difference, the art of habitat, and access via education to economic activity, while being simultaneously aware of the loss of generational thickness, the loss of circles of belonging and psychic wellness, and the multiplication of the ways in which bodies may become overly stimulated and anxious, thus ill, in the urban hive. Christopher Flavin of Worldwatch Institute captures a certain ambivalent, appreciative, if urgent realism for thinking through urbanism: "Urban centers are hubs simultaneously of breathtaking artistic innovation and some of the world's most abject and disgraceful poverty. They are the dynamos of the world economy but also the breeding grounds for alienation, religious extremism and other sources of local and global insecurity."[13]

Owing to the ways in which urbanism can disperse kith and kin (a quality that may itself be sometimes desirable) and to the ways in which economics actually opens up not only the jet stream of workflow, but also pluralist understandings of the world, persons can become unstrung, both relationally and in terms of life rituals. Urban studies theorist Leonie Sandercock, thinking of the rapidity with which cities worldwide become multiethnic, multiracial stewpots, especially today, insists that "fear is as great a threat to the future stability of cities and regions as the much more talked about economic forces."[14] And Flavin notes, "The battles against our greatest global problems, from unemployment and HIV infections to water shortages, terrorism and climate change, will be largely won—or lost—in the world's cities." "It is particularly ironic," he concludes, and we might wryly agree, "that the battle to save the world's remaining healthy ecosystems will be won or lost not in the tropical forests or coral reefs that are threatened but on the streets of the most unnatural landscapes on the planet."[15]

Of Planetarity and Cosmopolis

At stake here is the figuration of the possibilities of human life that Gayatri Spivak has called *planetarity*, as opposed to the "globalization" so often invoked these days. In place of "the imposition of the same system of exchange everywhere," based on the figuration of the earth as an "abstract ball covered in latitudes and longitudes, cut by virtual lines . . . now drawn by the requirements of Geographical Information Systems," a figuration of the world now as a "gridwork of electronic capital," subject to our control, planetarity asks that "we imagine ourselves as planetary subjects rather than global agents." "The planet is a species of alterity," Spivak writes, "belonging to another system and yet we inhabit it, on loan." If indeed "to be human is to be intended toward the other," and if "we provide for ourselves transcendental figurations of what we think of this animating gift"— "names of alterity" such as "nation, god, nature"—we open ourselves to "what is above and beyond our own reach," what is "not continuous with us," even as it is "not, indeed, specifically discontinuous." To think in terms of planetarity is thus to open oneself "to embrace an inexhaustible taxonomy . . . including but not identical with the whole range of human universals."[16]

To think in terms of planetarity offers ways to situate oneself in a positive manner in such relations of alterity, to seize the opportunities for spiritual and material growth and well-being that they offer, and the urbanization of the world, with its best of all possible imagined formations, cosmopolis, provides for the occasion and the imperative for doing so. Cosmopolis is, explains Sandercock, a utopian state of mind and a practice—the dream of a multicultural city wherein genuine differences are cultivated, through the practice of inclusive justice as need be, toward togetherness and common destiny.[17] Jane M. Jacobs reminds us that cosmopolitanism, the effort to generate a common urban lifeworld, appears as an origami of enfolded alterity, carrying memorial patterns of colonial habits, if not animosities: "In contemporary cities people connected by imperial histories are thrust together in assemblages barely predictable, and often guarded against, during the inaugural phases of colonialism. Often enough this is a meeting not simply augmented by imperialism, but still regulated by its constructs of difference and privilege."[18] The challenge to our urban social becoming is to envision ways in which this situation becomes supportive of life, not destructive of it.

Hopes for a humane existence and for planetary well-being, whether negotiating climate change, or access to water, or possible dreams of a good life after "oil," will need to be worked out in relation to today's worldwide centripetal pull toward urban dwelling. Whereas "the enormous social and political changes of the previous two centuries" in the West stemmed from mass urbanization accompanied by industrialization,[19] today, planetwide urbanization occurs conversely without that grid of work, without industrialization. In an urbanizing world increasingly produced by the abstractions of capital movements, a planetary, rather than a global, orientation offers hope that we can find the resources necessary to make life worth living in the world that we help emerge. Theology can and should provide the grounding for a cosmopolitanism that makes that orientation possible.

A Theology for Seculars

In the city today, theology turns "secular."[20] *Seculars*, a term that developed in medieval Europe, were uncloistered religious persons who carried their spiritual passion and sense of an obligated life into temporal concerns, specifically, their daily circumambulations of the city. In a moment not wholly unlike our own (that is, as urban centers swelled with the onset of the European profit economy), seculars lived in the city, on behalf of the city, but by way of alternative values and attitudes that challenged the materialism and isolation of urban life. The spiritual crisis of the medieval commercial age "was seen in a growing discordance between new economic and social realities," historian Lester Little tells us. "Life in the new profit economy raised acute problems involving impersonalism, money, and moral uncertainty," problems that "a traditional, initially unresponsive, clergy and theology" did not address.[21] As early capitalism was occasioning poverty, homelessness, and the displacement of the aging, of "commoners" (peasants who had been on feudal lands), and the sick, seculars—often born among the aristocratic class and as likely to be women as men—worked their care for the city singularly by setting up confraternities (not unlike today's Catholic Worker Houses) that, over time, became hospitals, leprosariums, schools, places of retreat, and spaces for performing various ritual services, such as funerals.

But today, too, spiritual practices can be created that will humanize and renew cities, these amassing hives of humanity—sowing trust where there is fear, posing alternative forms of beauty to those advancing the aesthetics of capitalism, offering friendship and neighborliness.[22] As theologian Philip Sheldrake asserts, spirituality is "not confined to the inner life of the Christian community but includes the practice of *everyday* living in the heart of the world of human places."[23] Seculars do today admit with John Caputo that we have "lost all communications from On High."[24] And secular persons humbly admit that religions are venturous human constructs, since, as philosopher Richard Kearney remarks in *Anatheism: Returning to God after God*, "there is no God's-eye view of things available to us" (xv).

Seculars might thus seem to be stuck on the *virgule* between theism and atheism. The Christian theology brought to voice here observes the psychic full stop brought by "lost . . . communications from On High." A certain cultural frame has reached its obsolescence, even as anguish marks this loss. It is, as philosopher Jean-Luc Nancy puts it, the occasion of a "loss of sense" that simultaneously recoils with a "sense of loss."[25] And yet, if disorienting, this loss neither voids the devoted life nor interferes with the possibility—as Dietrich Bonhoeffer already surmised in the midst of the past century—of a practice of felicity, of a "religionless religion." In this, I wager with Kearney that "it is only if one concedes that one knows virtually nothing about God that one can begin to recover the presence of holiness in the flesh of ordinary existence" (*Anatheism*, 5). Such devotion proceeds by becoming vulnerable to others,[26] by regenerating social flesh.

Social Flesh

Social flesh, a phrase coined by Chris Beasley and Carol Bacchi, names "an ethico-political ideal" that "highlights human *embodied* interdependence."[27] Inherently, it emphasizes "the *mutual* reliance of people across the globe on social space, infrastructure and resources" and so invites us to rethink the ground of interdependence—not from within contemporary economies of subject and state, but by posing a philosophical concept that levels neoliberal assumptions now informing sociality and its related political networks ("Envisaging a New Politics," 280). It challenges atomistic individualism, its assumption of the accidental quality of relations and its inherent hierarchy of worth, and so contrarily asserts the development of social virtues attendant on our embodied coexistence (ibid., 285). Life, in fact, "requires social support and political and economic conditions that enable it to continue, in order for that life to be livable. An 'ontology of individualism' is not capable of recognizing the precariousness of life."[28] As 2012 U.S. Democratic Senate candidate for Massachusetts Elizabeth Warren famously insisted, "nobody in this country got rich on his own."[29] Social flesh acknowledges that "we are all . . . receivers of socially generated goods and services"

(Beasley and Bacchi, "Envisaging a New Politics," 293). By emphasizing the social nature of flesh and the interdependent physicality of social life, the ideal challenges "the privileging of normative over 'other' bodies" and undercuts the *noblesse oblige* that grants some an aura of benevolent superiority by marking others as needy (ibid.). Social flesh philosophically grounds the foundational nature of our interdependence and so may be worked to generate practices that care for and are cultivated with attention to this interdependence.[30] In relationship to urbanism, one hopes that thinking about social flesh might lead to what I will term *corporeal generosity* and forbearance in the global city, a way and a place for us to be and become together.

By putting into question "the social privilege that produces inequitable vulnerability and the associated need for altruism" (Beasley and Bacchi, "Envisaging a New Politics," 293), the ideal of social flesh simultaneously problematizes "the differential distribution of precarity."[31] *Precarity* names, first of all, the existential fragility into which we each have been born.[32] As philosopher Judith Butler puts it, "We are social beings from the start, dependent on what is outside ourselves, on others, on institutions, and on sustained and sustainable environments, and so are, in this sense, precarious."[33] In a world of becoming (figured not just ontologically, but politically), life has always been precarious. Venturing this insight as an ontological and existential category, in *Precarious Life: The Powers of Mourning and Violence*, Butler's reflections on the trauma of 9/11, she probes the interdependent nature of social flesh: "This fundamental dependency on anonymous others is not a condition that I can will away." Further, "No security measure will foreclose this dependency" and "no violent act of sovereignty will rid the world of this fact" (xii). Her existential reflection on ontological vulnerability twists suddenly, as she recognizes the social construction of normative human morphologies and the complementary deployment of violence suffered by those disqualified, deemed, in one way or another, "invalid," into an analytic intervention in the "restrictive conception of the human." In other words, even within our regime of cultural knowledge, in how we have come to understand "the human subject," we encounter always and already social and political precaritization—what Butler calls "the derealization of the 'Other,'" a derealization that first numbs and then conditions the ethicopolitical conscience (ibid., 33).[34]

Flesh presents us with "a primary vulnerability to others, one that one cannot will away without ceasing to be human" (Butler, *Precarious Life*, xiv). As bodies, we are therefore always uncomfortably inside out, or "outside ourselves." Flesh leaves us not only vulnerable to the other, but vulnerable "to a sudden address from [the other] that we cannot preempt" (ibid., 27, 29). The skin line does not so much protectively seam us in corporeality as create an unavoidable fold of insecured vulnerability—and where so, pain and suffering, these saturating affects, will also likely seep into us.

Consequently, in *Precarious Life* Butler begins to suggest a practicable ethics for social flesh. Thinking with Emmanuel Levinas, she hints at a philosophical practice of nonviolence to be situated in proximity to the fear and anxiety of this tenuous, porous tissue we inhabit—not in any way presuming the eradication of aggression, but so as to navigate (like one skilled in martial arts) the strong emotional tides of fear, sorrow, sympathy, and anxiety without spinning these energies into murderous action, without exacting injury. "To grieve, and to make grief into a resource for politics, is not to be resigned to inaction, but it may be understood as the slow process by which we develop a point of identification with suffering itself" (30), she writes. She explains:

> We all live with this particular vulnerability . . . a vulnerability to a sudden address from elsewhere that we cannot preempt. . . . Mindfulness of this vulnerability can become the basis of claims for non-military political solutions. . . . We cannot, however, will away this vulnerability. We must attend to it, even abide by it, as we begin to think about what politics might be implied by staying with the thought of corporeal vulnerability itself. (29)

Even "dominant forms of representation can and must be disrupted," she advises, "for something about the precariousness of life to be apprehended" (xvii–xviii). While Butler clearly had in mind at that post-9/11 moment "the media representations of the faces of the 'enemy'" (xviii), I have in mind the socially construed "bodies in pain" loosed on city streets, the abject ones marked *disabled* (and I include under that term poverty, homelessness, illness, disease, the supposed "ruin" of our cities).[35]

Thus, "we are beings who are, of necessity, exposed to one another in our vulnerability and singularity," Butler writes of our social flesh in *Giving an Account of Oneself*, and "our political situation consists in . . . learning how best to handle and to honor this constant and necessary exposure" (31–32). Butler consequently sketches a practice of ethics that involves both psychoanalytic transference (the bodily offering of what psychologist Donald Winnicott termed "a holding environment") and what a religious practitioner might call *kenosis*—a radical openness to the other.

Calling into question humanist anthropology, that is, "the man of reason" (Genevieve Lloyd) and his "bill of rights," Butler writes, again working with Levinas, "Responsibility emerges as a consequence of being subject to the unwilled address of the other," as a consequence of this "persecution" of autonomous subjectivity (*Giving an Account*, 85). In regard to this latter kenotic aspect, she writes: "If violence is the act by which a subject seeks to reinstall its mastery and unity, then nonviolence may well follow from living the persistent challenge to egoic mastery that our obligations to the other induce and require" (ibid., 64). Here then we have the beginnings of a ritual, a practice that philosophically understands the renunciation of anesthetizing metaphysics (and, implicitly, theodicy) and therefore a nonviolent way of living into ethical responsibility along the skin line.

I myself have been nurtured in and through—and this text will evidence that it has been sourced from—Christianity's ancient, though not always obvious or normatively dominant, love of the flesh. In his essay "On the Flesh of Christ," the third-century father Tertullian explained that God "will love the flesh which is, so very closely and in so many ways, [God's] neighbor—although infirm . . . although disordered . . . although not honorable. . . . although ruined, although sinful. . . . although condemned."[36] Scholar of late antiquities Virginia Burrus, her work ranging across the third-century world of Christian writers, concludes that flesh became "the site of a deliberately offensive, explicitly countercultural faith."[37]

Thinking with and from flesh makes alterity central, even in relation to the self and one's body, if also in regard to cultural expectations regarding wholeness and wholesomeness, and also, therefore, allows us to talk about what metaphysics has often hidden from the sociocultural agenda, what we know to be true of lives—pain, difficulty, disease, transience, aging, error, and corporeal limit, if even also the epiphanies and critical insights that come with illness, interruption, and encounter. Metaphysics, as the philosopher Gianni Vattimo puts it, results precisely from the refusal to metabolize pain.[38]

"Flesh," as Butler has put it, names a "precarious . . . vulnerability to the other" *(Precarious Life*, 29). Consequently, because flesh is social, the vulnerability, anxiety, fear, disgust, dread, and shame that haunt flesh can be borrowed by cultural technologies such as the politics of health,[39] or by the civilizing or militarizing politics of fear. Equally, flesh recognizes—as if the metaphysical God held outside of our cognition the "animal" behavior that we actually find within ourselves—the temptations to aggression, even the pleasure in toying with aggression, given the uncomfortable torsions and tensions of difference within social flesh. When thought in this location, Spirit, then, has everything to do with aspiring to a passionate equanimity, replete with infinite mercy, in relation to one another.

Spirit in a Theology for Seculars

Spirit is a theopoetic locus that, given the dream of cosmopolis, enables us to "stand over the cracks of intelligibility and there . . . think."[40] Religions offer an alternative horizon of value or "worth"-ship, another way of being in the world, and *Spirit* has consequently named a concern for how we spend our energies in the world—for example, returning good for ill and loving neighbors or even enemies as ourselves. Religions can be culturally uncomfortable, because religions situate us—agonistically—between two economies: what is culturally available and what is sometimes called then the "divine economy," the horizon of religious ideals. The spiritual life can consequently feel a bit more like Jacob wrestling the angel (Genesis 32:22–32) than like serene placidity, since it occasions locating our lives with an alternative horizon of value to what we have become habituated to on a daily basis. Spirit—in something of an apocalyptic (that is, "unveiling") relation to human reason—can be felt as a certain gravity, an exuding, exceeding obligation binding bodies back toward one another. In this way, assuming the life of a secular expressly does not mean assuming rationalism as an absolute.[41]

Such a sense of Spirit is to be distinguished from Hegel's Spirit/ually infinitized world, since in a "world . . . composed of heterogeneous force fields,"[42] that is, in a pluriverse, "[t]hings are 'with' one another in many ways, but nothing includes everything, or dominates over everything"; a pluriverse is "strung-along, not rounded in and closed."[43] As theorist William E. Connolly explains in *A World of Becoming*, "The operation of multiple tiers of becoming in a world without a higher purpose amplifies the need to act with dispatch . . . in particular situations of stress. The fact that we are not consummate agents in such a world, combined with the human tendency to hubris, means that we must work to cultivate wisdom under these very circumstances" (7). In that vein, I will speak of Spirit as a necessary "prosthesis," an aid that might help us advance toward spacious and fearless empathy, toward forbearance amid messy entanglements. As practicable disciplines, religions—or "philosophies," such as Advaita Vedanta and Buddhism—develop social muscles, such as freedom from reactivity, not always recognized by culture at large.

While sourced from Christianity, *Spirit and the Obligation of Social Flesh: A Secular Theology for the Global City* also limns ascetic, Vedic, and Buddhist practices and thought, and such practices and thought have long found a home in North American culture, literary as well as popular.[44] Yoga might be the most recognizable, recent influx, but Advaitan ("nondual") Vedantic thought, within which the universe and the sacred as also the person and nature are co-implicated (or nondual), helped shape the thought of nineteenth-century American Transcendentalists, including Emerson, Whitman, and Thoreau, its perspective informing their emphasis on ecological spirituality as well as their underlying desire for an embodied, in-the-world spirituality.

Although such nature transcendentalism, the default religious ethos of progressive America, tends to further an emotional power of attachment to place in general (not to be dismissed, given contemporary social dislocation), such ecospirituality refuses, as most transcendentalist traditions have, to think the human habitat we name *urbanism*.[45] Transcendentalism can be in love with purity and wholeness, can fall into amnesia of the colonial history of place and idealistically turn its back on the juiciness of flesh.[46] Vedic thought, in its American circuits, has married well with the individualism generated within the West. But urbanism today presents humans with new challenges, such as learning to form attachments amid difference or learning to think beyond kin and kind. This is not necessarily to suggest that Advaitan Vedantic thought does not have the philosophical and practicable resources for the contemporary situation, but to challenge persons who let individual well-being—in the name of "health"—be the end-all and be-all of the "spiritual, but not religious" life.[47]

If such religious accents undoubtedly have called likewise on the desire of Christians, forces internal to Christian theology have also been shaping its own coming out, its "dis/enclosure."[48] Christianity's own reclamation of nondual thought has been most assiduously fostered within process theologies (informed by the philosophy of Alfred North Whitehead and theologically furthered by John Cobb, Jr., as well as by Catherine Keller, Jay McDaniel, and Rita Brock), within mystical, contemplative strains, and within philosophically honed theologies that propose to think "faith without religion" (Kearney, *Anatheism*, 4). Nonetheless, amidst urbanism and across the northern and coastal swathes of North America, progressive Christianity has been moving outside the walls of institutions. Recognizing that "secularism" can then become the default position for persons who have formed a deep love of nature, whose sense of the sacred abides, who wish that "theology" would "matter" more than Christian dogma has seemed to allow, who have grown frustrated with institutions, sometimes because of and sometimes apart from their failure to deal intellectually with the death of the transcendent and omnipotent God, *Spirit and the Obligation of Social Flesh: A Secular Theology for the Global City* tries to speak into this amorphous community of cultural "protest/ants."

"Spiritual bankruptcy," as John Cobb, Jr., points out, may not be just an issue of institutional Christianity (as any number of us might charge), but can also become the condition of any one of us thrown back on our own resources amidst the pace of contemporary life. "Secularizing is essential to the relevance of the [Christian] church to the current problems," writes Cobb, pointing toward progressive Christians' appreciation of the wisdom of the scientist, the philosopher, the political strategist. But as Cobb so carefully parses, there's a difference between "secularizing and assimilating to a secularist culture," which in its Western incarnation has been materialist and encouraging of self-interest.[49] While Cobb thus argues for an affective theism, for many such as political theorist William Connolly, who like Cobb critiques the absolutism within secular rationalism, as for others of us, theism may not be intellectually viable.

So how do we continue to nurture spiritual values, another economy of life, when we have been cut loose from the resources of institutions? I ask that as an open question, although this book is an attempt at offering some reflective wisdom to the loose and amorphous open field of seculars, including newly secular Christians and persons of irresolvably "partial faiths." (John McClure uses this term affirmatively to designate those of us educated in or otherwise arriving at appreciation for being able to see with and through plural and diverse religious metaphysics, which we then refuse to resolve into either a singular amalgam or by reversion to cradle traditions.[50]) What follows is meant to offer, as Richard Kearney has suggested in his *Anatheism*, "a small intellectual agora" (xiii). Here might additionally gather those aspiring to the new forms of urban monasticism (seculars in the most original sense perhaps) as well as persons "spiritual but not religious" wanting to hone their spiritual endeavor analytically; the intellectually honed who philosophically find themselves concerned about the absolutism of rationalism and who want a more complex, even sometimes mystically informed secularism; those—such as Quakers, Unitarians, and some Advaitans—who insist "no guru, no path, no method," as well as persons in the field of urban studies, some of whom take spirituality seriously as a possible constructive force of the city.

Crip Epistemology, or Urbanism through the Lens of Disability Studies

What prepares us to meet the troubles that lie ahead in cities—for the ways in which economic downturns impact our urban dreaming, or ecological backlash transforms climates and sea levels? How will we, bottle-fed on idealism, live with passionate attachment in a less than ideal world? To cultivate devotion to the world will require that we learn to catch ourselves in all of the various and diverse fits of indignation and patterns of disgust that we spew against life. Because of this, the critically examined life of the contemporary urbanite is here worked through the analytic corpus of disability studies—especially insomuch as it might make possible both the affective navigation of the founding resentment against precariousness and open out the diverse angles and degrees of precarity in the city to the embrace of social flesh and the prosthetic enablement of Spirit. It is an approach that I will call *crip/tography*.

The appearance of "disability" within a culture "tells us of a culture's sociability," its fundamental capacity to have people live together, as disability theorist Henri-Jacques Stiker notes.[51] Urbanism, in its architectural modes as well as in its social expectations, has been thought through the neoclassical, "normative," model of the human—a disposition that creates exclusions in geography and architecture comparable to what this presumed "universal" does within the human community. In that neoclassical model, "disability" names one long-standing social "derealization of the 'Other.'" It marks a point at which the social quality of flesh and the physical nature of interdependence has been disavowed, refused. Culling out "disabled" individuals is a management strategy that unloads social interdependence by "in-valid/ating" certain persons' human worth, setting them outside the commons of social flesh. While women, ethnics, and those of diverse sexualities have challenged and entered the humanist book of life (though not in any complete way that has led to social and economic equality), disability—the perceived somatic "lack" that engendered woman as deficient male and black as degenerate human—remains the undeconstructed keystone of modernity.

But of course, disability has a longer aesthetic history, a history of deeply embedded resentment against the precariousness of life itself. By creating the set-aside named "disabilities," society shields its eyes from the vulnerability of birth and the risk of becoming; it always already buffers the existential conditions of precariousness by marginalizing certain bodies and excluding them from the pool of aesthetic value. For these reasons, I bring the critical lens of disabilities studies to bear on the life of the city, using its focus to examine the fear that isolates urbanites from the embraces of social flesh.

Urbanism during North American industrialization has privileged the sovereign subject with agential willfulness, efficiency of motion, able to commute intention to effect, spatially insulated, autonomous, seemingly responsible, moving in bubbles of prestige, and has disdained bodies associated with disease or pain as unsavory, ugly, stupid, lacking integrity, and/or discordant. One of the dominant Western urban narratives, the "narrative of ambition," informs, even more intensely amidst postindustrial consumer capitalism, the "anxious display of status"[52] while excluding bodies that struggle for survival. This "taste"—and its hidden distaste— for bodies, this control of who may appear in public and whose lives are forfeitable, also effectively carves out urban territories of not necessarily constructive difference. In the chapters that follow, I will crip/tographically survey the effects of this *habitus*, such as civic valorizations that "hide the homeless" not only in preparation for the Olympics, but so as to appear an ideal, global city for tourism, for investment by the global elite.[53] After all, "Disability is spatially as well as socially constructed."[54]

By viewing urbanism through the lens of disability studies, I hope to contribute to a redress of the neoliberal chasms that exist architecturally and geographically as well as subjectively within urbanism—whether that chasm is between "private affluence" and the "public squalor" it denounces, or between "consumers and the destitute," these effects of Social Darwinist and humanist refusals of mutual responsibility, of social flesh.[55] As disabilities theorist Tobin Siebers notes, the aesthetics of disqualification, which "invalid/ate" the disabled (and *aesthetics* as used here means "to feel by means of one's senses"[56]) transpire "when we turn a corner and find ourselves face to face with another body." So, I ask, what "rite" of readiness prepares us for the affective "heat of everyday encounters between bodies . . . when feelings of attraction and repulsion surge forth with embarrassing immediacy, fierceness and clarity?"[57] How then do we dance the "ballet of the good sidewalk"—that choreography of the sidewalk that makes for life and holds the promise of urbanism on a daily basis?[58] What "rites of passage" make sharing of this everyday world and our urban neighborhoods possible among bodies with whom we do not always share taste, smell, or cultural resonance?

But if one also assumes disability as a locus for engaging the world of becoming, does not theology itself become something inimical in this turn toward an energetic materialism?[59] To be sure, disability studies expressly releases many of the traces of what a theological worldview has presumed: there will be no transcendental telos, no promise of salvation, no fix, no redemption. Or, as disabilities theorist Petra Kuppers puts it, "no origin story, no diasporic experience . . . no patrilinear descent, no matriarch, no heteronormative narrative that duplicates itself into the future." In fact, there is among persons disabled "no necessary family resemblance." Disability, in fact, "describes nothing shared: no one form of embodiment or orientation to the world." Because "disability is an individuating experience, one in which difference, in its many forms, becomes experiential as a category function . . . we mostly have to make our families ourselves, choose our community."[60] So are not disability studies and theology ill-disposed to each other? Thinking about it from another direction, however, what would theology be and do among the damned and damaged, in the winter of the worn-out and wrecked relics of commodity capitalism? In the "ruins?" Such questions of life in the post-apocalyptic metropolis already play heavily through popular culture, especially the literary imagination.

This spiritual-philosophical exercise assumes as background the criticism and landscape of the death of God theologies, the work of those who critiqued theology while keeping their eyes on the Holocaust and Hiroshima, those who paid attention to God "in the ruins," in other words.[61] Disabilities theologian Nancy Eiesland broke into the sociosymbolic life of classic Christian theology and offered a counterprojection of its SuperMan God: "I saw God," she recalls of her own dream sequence, "in a sip-puff wheelchair. . . . Not an omnipotent, self-sufficient God, but neither a pitiable, suffering servant. In this moment, I beheld God as a survivor." Later, with the scarred hands and feet of the resurrected figure of Jesus in mind, she continues: "Here is God as survivor . . . a simple, unself-pitying, honest body, for whom the limits of power are palpable but not tragic." Such symbolic innovation, Eiesland hoped, would allow Christians to "recognize . . . the incarnate Christ in the image of those judged 'not feasible,' 'unemployable,' with 'questionable quality of life.'"[62] "Christians do not have an able-bodied God as their primal image," writes Rebecca Chopp, appreciatively reflecting upon Eiesland's imagistic offering, but rather find "grace through a broken body."[63] Eiesland's image echoes Dietrich Bonhoeffer's evocation of a "suffering God"[64] and the more recent images from "weak theologies" of a God emptied into the flesh of the world, and so suggests the potentially catalyzing intersection of disability, postcolonial, and radical or recent theologies that have undertaken to give accounts of religion following "the death of God."[65]

To find a place of equanimity, of deep love and insight about the world, humanity, and our urban situation, will require the navigation of disgust, fear, and pain otherwise than by encultured avoidance, will require the "cripping" of urbanely assumed Platonic notions of beauty. In this work, I consequently speak of embracing and being embraced by social flesh as the generation of corporeal generosity, of learning "freedom" as a depth of nonreactive spirit amidst fear, of forbearance amidst existential disappointment, of sharing the burden of pain, one of the most cumbersome dimensions of precarity in the West, given our Berlin Wall between pain and pleasure, and the consequent way in which pain deposits bodies into no-go zones of cities. Further, corporeal generosity will open aesthetics beyond the conforming rubric of rigid symmetry.

Developing corporeal generosity requires the ability to work with affects, the region of the sentient interface that serves as the basis for analytic reflection, for the intellectual enterprise. Changing our aesthetic beliefs about the world, including how we become wise with and to the ways of fear, requires some practiced interface with the affects—with gut feelings, with lightning-quick impulses, with regions of the brain such as the amygdala. So, for example: No person of liberal persuasion is personally in favor of poverty or homelessness, these forms of precarity; yet nothing is so well affected by today's economy as the chasm opened "between the exalted, gluttonous classes with their linguistic refinements and perfumed pretensions and the indigent masses for whom life [is] an hourly scramble for survival."[66] Our participation in that economy requires certain affective occlusions that become intellectual occlusions, things hidden, at points, even from our good will. Those affective occlusions likely have been scaled toward the promotion of moral or civil rectitude more than toward the corporeal generosity of what love seemingly promises.

William Connolly, in *Why I Am Not a Secularist*, has suggested that people's blithe unawareness of such repressions has to do with the way in which "the secular presentation of public space encourages [persons] to ignore or degrade the *visceral* register of subjectivity and intersubjectivity" (163; emphasis added). Secular space in the West presumes an implicit Kantian notion of "common sense" itself banked upon "the metaphysical idea of an inscrutable supersensible realm" and consequent moral purity (ibid., 174). Like its religious transcendental twin, Western secularism, banked upon Hegelian idealism, assumes an implicit metaphysics of presence that it uses as the referent for adjudicating what it construes as common sense.[67] In order to break with this neoliberal ethos and become attendant to social flesh, Connolly invites us beyond assuming that "quest for a whole, secure, centered, transcendental way of being" and to "work on ourselves, privately and publicly," so as "to participate in an ethos of engagement that rises above the demands for wholeness and purity in public life" (*Why I Am Not a Secularist*, 161). In other words, cosmopolitans can retrain our "gut brain" so as to develop our affective intelligence, our intellect for alliance: "Since thinking operates on several registers of being, and because each register is invested with a set of feelings or intensities, to change your thinking is to modify to some degree the sensibility in which it is set" (ibid., 148). In this text, I consequently dig into the somatic economies vitalizing our bodies in order that we might work the next stage of civil rights, this recreation of social flesh, into our own street choreography and, by extension, into our way of crafting the shelter of life we name *the city*.[68]

A kind of disaffected rationalism—assumed as epistemological lens in the scientific laboratory—has often equally substituted for "belief" within Christian theology:[69] "In this self-imposed modesty, which has ecclesial sanction and imposes a prohibition on the mystical [or feeling] self, there lurks perhaps one of the difficulties central to modern Protestantism," German theologian Dorothee Soelle insists. "Its defensive stance toward the emotions turns the enormously fetishized 'faith' into a nonexistential category; that is, into something essentially made-up, 'fictional, contrived.'" Yet, she concludes, "The repulsion of experience, as well as the fear of engaging it, represents a kind of spiritual suicide."[70] That theology, seeking foundational security on the scale of mathematical principles, nonetheless assumes the locus of disaffected rationalism may have considerable bearing on how nonfunctional Christianity has been judged to be in the northern reaches of the Western hemisphere today.[71]

To speak of our brain as the outcropping of sentient feeling, of our intellect as enfolding our sensible interdependence with the world, would also suggest that theology be worked affectively, as a matter of the heart. Here I celebrate, through constructive interreligious and philosophical analytics, the wisdom of Christianity's ancient psychologies—the wisdom that knows it takes practice, years of practice, to become free and available, without fear, disgust, or aversion, and with compassionate love, to one another, as well as the wisdom that knows we are not free until we in fact serve the neighbor. *Theology* is the name of an art—often an incantatory poetics, but equally here a cultivated way of feeling the world by means of one's senses, of cultivating the senses toward corporeal generosity, entrustment to life, and forbearance with one another.[72] Theology might consequently work with a political theorist such as Connolly to create an affective intelligence that can "hold . . . body and soul together at street level."[73]

In this work, I try to imagine how affective intelligence, specifically, corporeal generosity and forbearance weighted toward the practice of "felicity in history," as philosopher Luce Irigaray puts it,[74] might effect change within the urban street ballet and, by extension then, within the character of political life, of urban geography and architecture. Visual art—from street theatre to public art installations—works to swerve assumptions, to break open presumptions. Politics, disabilities theorist Petra Kuppers likewise insists, does not simply transpire as policy change, but is embodied so as to address the shared life force. That is, politics begins with the intercorporeal—hence, Kuppers's own reach for "social sculpture" for an unhinged time.[75] I hope to loose persons who, beginning to develop practices for dealing with fear, disgust, and pain, might—moving along the corridors of urbanism—offer the embrace of interdependence and other aspects of social flesh. Inasmuch as we are liberated into social flesh, such practices have not so much to do with "helping the crip and the needy" as with recognizing that our liberation is bound up with one another.[76]

Crip/tography and Urban Aesthetics in a World of Becoming

I've called the performative choreography of one who has assumed the careful work of an examined life for moving along the corridors of global cities *crip/tography*.[77] As a metaphor, crip/tography employs "disability" as a lens for hermeneutically engaging the city, for opening out its aesthetics and analytically assessing its affects. "Disability" is the trope that continues to "establish differences between human beings not as acceptable or valuable variations but as dangerous deviations."[78] While disability has served in the modern period as "'the master trope of human disqualification'" (again, even underlying modern notions of gender as well as race and class),[79] in the Western university and for the public more generally, disability is considered a topic of marginal relevance. That would suggest that we have not yet wholly deconstructed— and are unwilling to relent— belief in and the willingness to posit others as inferior. As disabilities theorist Tobin Siebers puts it, "The continued existence of the practice of interpreting disability as deviance rather than as human variation reveals a shocking conclusion hard to accept in this day and age. . . . Disability [thus] represents at this moment in time the final frontier of justifiable human inferiority."[80] Oddly, our North American world can both smartly insist upon evolutionary cosmology, which necessarily assumes morphological variation within place and across time, and yet reassure itself of its comfortably classic taste by resort to this categorical disqualification—that is, "disability."

Crip/tography consequently assumes the epistemological lens of disability theory to map the social geography, architecture, and aesthetics of urban life. Disability theory provides us with an angle of vision that can help us analyze one of the most serious fractures in globalization and therefore urbanization—the aesthetic aspect of capitalism, including its corresponding repressions in "civility," in what is thought to make a city livable, in the conversations concerning beauty, from high fashion to the ideal tourist snapshot of the city itself and the economics that circulate both.

The "dis-ing" of "disability" has to do with the affective interface, with psychological refusals—of pain, of flesh, of finitude—in those who would presume to be normative—those who have already submitted themselves to the biopolitics of health. Even for me, having now lived with a mobility impairment (an amputation of the left leg, which is not prosthetically remediated) for nineteen years, it has come as something of a shock to recognize that the "Downtown Eastside" of Vancouver, the poorest postal code area in Canada, is populated by bodies we might otherwise label "disabled." Here is a social amassing of bodies, a social enclosure, that cannot be accounted for by hard-luck stories of individuals. And yet if that is the most obvious social and economic "refus/al," even those who pass as "normal" may carry on the streets of the city reservoirs of psychic pain occasioned by dislocation, relational truncations, and modernity's razing of traditions without easy resort to their reconstruction.

Crip/tography thus pays disciplined attention to the choreography of our urbanized bodies in hopes of producing the social and psychic ruptures that engender detachment from normativity—from the fear-laden agenda of such constructions of beauty and civility. Jean-Luc Nancy observes that creation of the world of justice, of "being-in-common" with one another, requires nothing other, can be measured by nothing other, than being exposed to one another.[81] But structured exclusions create ways and means of avoidance. That's where religious wisdom can be brought to bear as an analytic intervention within our affective intelligence. Crip/tography remembers—in and through constructive engagement with Buddhist practices—the cripped iconography of Christian religious aesthetics, for example, the "beautiful Savior" who, having "no form or majesty" that we should desire, was "despised and rejected" (Isaiah 53).

In addition to the analysis of the choreography of bodies in the cosmopolis, crip/tography is also a mapping of the physical and psychological space in which that choreography occurs. The choreography of "the inappropriate/d other," to use Donna Haraway's term, can reveal the forces at work in the contemporary city that position both the normative and its others—both position them physically and "out them in their place." Crip/tography as cartography thus can map out both lines of force and avenues of resistance within the city, locating sites where feeling can open out with and for the other, sites where pain and our empathic engagement of it can yet validate the nature of human life.

Crip/tography understood in this double sense thus puts theology on location on the streets of our cities. In this way, it reclaims, for seculars today, the notion of "seculars" generated in the Middle Ages of Europe—persons who turned aside from the enclosure of monasteries and made care of the city their own work. While progressive Christians call for theologies more relevant to our cultural situation, for an ecclesial form that moves us outside the parish structure, crip/tography proposes a Christianity that is analytically honed and affectively practicable, that is conversant with the diverse religious communities of the city, as well as with popular culture. It spells out a form of "mendicancy" to breach the retaining walls of civility in the global city (which have, as sociologist Sharon Zukin argues, encrypted fear), to breach "security" walls of neoliberalism.

Crip/tography—this nomad theospirituality for everyday life—is not so much a project of "saving the world," or "saving souls," or even for saving the vulnerable other, as it is for learning to live precarious life with the deepest sense of devotion and faithfulness possible. We might call crip/tography a *preterite* spirituality—a theology for seculars indeed. Borrowing Calvinist terminology, in his literary corpus Thomas Pynchon imaginatively considers the "prete⁻ites"—those who are rejected or passed over. For Pynchon, the religious setting is American secular culture, the preterites being those excluded and anonymous, in terms of social organization, and, in that way, "cut off from grace."[82] A preterite spirituality—and in this one finds resonance with learning to live disability, which releases the realm of ideals, fantastical eschatologies, and redemption—"foster[s] dispositions that reflect a sense of human limitation." Preterite spiritual communities "make no claims to be the first, 'prefigurative' flowerings of emancipated modes of being," but instead "are dedicated to local efforts at survival, self-transformation, and face-to-face service."[83] These make no promise of radical transformation, no claim to purity (ecological, ideological, economic, Platonic, or spiritual), but instead celebrate a shared kinship of all souls who escape from or refuse to recognize class or gender by simply, rather, honoring friendship, who are critically awake to existence, self-forgetting and generous, trained toward patience amidst the quotidian over the long term, toward freedom and responsibility through self-reflection.[84] A reminder is well in order that our sociocultural worlds can fall into the trap of illusions, delusions, the dreams of Caesars, just as individuals can, and must learn ever and again the teachings of impermanence, mutability, and transience. Crip/tography attempts to analyze the aesthetics and affects that allow aspects of that sociocultural delusion to persist.

Crip/tography is finally an approach based on Spirit's generosity, its empathic breadth, that redresses fear, advances neighbor love, and encourages each of us to bear another's pain. Crip/tography reminds us yet again that to become human it is not necessary to become whole, but to attend to the call of the other—and thus to become just, to practice love, pardon, tenderness, mercy, welcome, respect, compassion, solidarity, and communion among all our relations.

Accordingly, chapter 1 elaborates the concept of crip/tography, mapping the lines of force, psychosocial and economic, that have produced the aestheticization of fear in the global city within the regime of late capitalism under the rubric of enforcing "civility," determining a social geography, a physical environment, and a choreography of bodies there based on recoil from the other and from responsibility to the call of the other. Proposing to renegotiate the values of urban civility, it begins the task of envisioning ways in which a reconceived understanding of Spirit, within the Christian tradition of the eucharist and beyond it, can lead to practices that can serve as a counterforce to these alienating and destructive forces and towards loosing the dream of cosmopolis.

As a way to approach such practices, chapter 2 examines more comprehensively the role that the aestheticization of fear plays in the daily life of the global city, examining the role that conceptions of beauty play in structuring the urban environment, especially in the cosmopolitan glam zone and within the choreography of bodies there. As a prolegomena to the practices for the embracing of social flesh developed in the next two chapters, chapter 2 also articulates a conception of beauty informed by the reality of disability and the insights of disability studies regarding the pain and fragility of existence.

Chapter 3 opens by surveying responses to the aestheticization of fear, with the goal of beginning to develop ways to assist us in answering the call to carry the pain of the other, drawing on both Christian and non-Christian traditions and practices, from Christology and "God in pain" theologies to the Buddhist practice of *tonglen*, or breathing through pain, and the theology or epistemology of the cross articulated by Martin Luther. It also critically examines the theological and metaphysical assumptions that have interfered with practices that further the embrace of social flesh and the work of those who, like Simone Weil, have explored the basis of those practices.

Chapter 4 further elaborates on ways to embrace social flesh, here by drawing on practices and traditions within and beyond Christianity for confronting the fears of death, disease, and impermanence that encounters with disability, in particular, can spark. Here I argue that a recuperation of and meditation on the grotesque at the heart of Christian iconography can further the forbearance and corporeal generosity necessary to and characteristic of the embrace of social flesh.

Chapter 5 broadens the perspective to prepare for chapter 6's vision of the prospects for a life in global cities informed by Spirit as a prosthesis enabling the embrace of social flesh. Chapter 5 surveys the reasons for the widespread aversions of the flesh for which "disability" serves as the master trope, and it articulates an alternative vision in which disability can be seen instead as a master trope for life itself—not in the tired theological sense of the "brokenness" of original sin, but a positive sense, as openness to the prosthesis that Spirit offers.

Chapter 6 celebrates that promise as the promise for life in cosmopolis. Drawing together the conceptual strands articulated in the preceding chapters, it develops a conception of Spirit as an immanence that enfolds us and bring us into relations of forbearance and corporeal generosity, as enabling, in other words, the practices of social flesh amidst the differences of life in cosmopolis and the pains that life brings. "As a prosthesis capacitates the body, Spirit capacitates our belief in the world, enables the mutual submission—or entrustment—of flesh one to another," as I write there. It thus offers a path—a theology for seculars—by which we all can go forward together in cosmopolis.

ONE

Crip/tography

> Suppose we raise the possibility of a God who belongs not to the fixed
> order of presence, but to the (dis)order of the deconstruction of
> presence . . . [and] in favor of a paradigm where . . . sovereign power slips
> out of favor? Suppose . . . that the event that is sheltered in the name of
> God does not belong to the order of power and presence, but rather
> withdraws from the world in order to station him or herself [Godself]
> with everything that the world despises? Suppose we think of God as
> someone who prowls the streets and disturbs the peace of . . . Christen-
> dom? Suppose we imagine God as a street person with a definite body
> odor, like Lord Shiva living as a beggar?
>
> —JOHN CAPUTO, *The Weakness of God*

> The human being is human in answer to an "outside call."
>
> —GAYATRI CHAKRAVORTY SPIVAK, "Righting Wrongs"

Rockefeller Center, Christmas 1999

We know that we will soon be moving to the other edge of the continent,
and we want her to have the enchanted memory of skating at night under
the Christmas tree at Rockefeller Center. After waiting in line for two and
a half hours, my daughter Sarah, along with her friend and my partner Jeff,
take to the skating rink. I make my way to a glass concourse at rink level that
should allow me to build my own memory—that of watching my daughter
set against the jeweled night lights of the city, dusted with the twinkle of
snowflake, enfolded in this celebration of humanity turned, by the touch of
frost and holiday celebration, toward the warmth of one another.

But this is Rudy Giuliani's New York after the first bombing of the
World Trade Center towers and at the time of the cleanup of unwanted
bodies that can clutter the aesthetic appeal of the streets and therefore

26

undermine the economic profitability of a global city, these glam zones of culture and cosmopolitanism, and my body easily slides off the mark of civility.[1] There being no benches, I sit on the floor of the rink-level concourse as tight against the window as I can squeeze and there slip into the bittersweet mesmerization of trying, as a benchwarmer in this situation, to absorb the pleasure of those on the ice. A security guard breaks into my reverie: "Move, or you will be charged with loitering" is the message I receive through the exchange we conduct in our versions of English, mine still Midwestern, as distinct from his, that of a recent immigrant: one recent immigrant, with his own ill fit into the straitjacket of civility (and trying to access the economic circuit through that newly created and often ironically immigrant-based "security" industry), forced to confront the fact that my body won't stay upright and mobile. "I just want to watch my twelve-year-old daughter skate," I protest. "Look at me," I say, insisting that he take in the disability, the crutches. "I can't join her on the ice. Please let me watch." "Crutches? As likely pipe bombs. How would I know? Please move. I don't want to lose my job; I can't risk it," he counters. Between the irony of his surveillance of my lack of compliance with civility and our mutual empathy, we are caught, finally working out a deal that I can stay ten minutes (only!); he will look the other way, but if I hear him whistle, it's a warning that I need to move immediately, because his supervisor will have spotted this infraction. We strike a deal, try to come to solidarity below the radar of civility, which each of us in our own way threatens.

"Picture the world in motion," theologian Ray Bakke invites us: "the southern hemisphere is coming north, east is coming west, and on all six continents migrations are to the city."[2] Indeed, "globalization as urbanization," postcolonial theorist Gayatri Spivak adds, "seems one of the least speculative strands in the thinking of globalization."[3] Given "the general drive for order, cleanliness and beauty, which Freud put at the center of the civilizing project . . . it is only a small exaggeration to say that cities are us, and we are cities," here at the dawn of the twenty-first century, suggests philosopher and culture critic Mark Kingwell.[4] Spivak adds her agreement: Everywhere across the planet, "we can *see* cities exploding their spatial outlines and virtualizing into nexuses of telecommunication." "That," Spivak dryly notes, "is the canonical account of globalization." But, warns Spivak, catching us romanticizing the glass and twinkles, the thick of the crowds, such visibility can lull us into not perceiving "the invisible power lines that make and unmake the visible." To get at the latter, she advises, "requires archaeology, genealogy."[5] Here I assume her challenge toward an archaeology of the invisible power lines of global cities. Aspirations for planetary well-being and conviviality (Paul Gilroy) must today be asserted by swerving such trajectories. After opening out the gestural articulations of civility, Spivak's renovation of western anthropology—her suggestion that "the human being is human in answer to an 'outside call'"[6]—will be assumed as key to a soulful choreography hoping to counter urban grids of fear.

As the doubly loaded scene I've described at Rockefeller Center suggests, in what Spivak calls "globalicities,"[7] those invisible power lines that make and unmake the visible cross and spark in sites where the colonial work of "civilizing"—of sorting bodies into publically acceptable appearances, coupled with the assumption of their regularity, rationality, productivity, symmetry, and independence—has not dropped off the agenda in this age of globalization. In the postcolonial metropolis, colonialism lingers on in the choreography of bodies within our urban geography, where that "racism that is not really ethnic but biological" sorts bodies.[8] It does so as the shadow of cosmopolitan civility.[9] Because theology, like many of the humanist disciplines, has yet to begin thinking "from site rather than text,"[10] I both map the site of the postcolonial city and examine the choreography of bodies as they perform along the invisible power lines that such a mapping makes visible.

The current that electrifies the urban landscape and powers the imposition of urban civility is an affective response to the other—specifically, fear of the other and its reactive aestheticization in a biologized ideal. As global cities increasingly re-create themselves as "experience museums" of culture and the cultured, civility not only dispenses with bodies burdened with difference, but continues to colonize and collapse the space within which such bodies might take their place.[11] The age of decolonization, from the 1960s to the 1970s, when the decolonized began rushing like flood waters toward their colonial metropoles, was also "a watershed in the institutionalization of urban fear," as the sociologist Sharon Zukin puts it.[12] In former colonies worldwide, wherever the myth of development took hold, there followed a certain primal anxiety about "lack," a postcolonial version of the colonial missions to redress "degeneracy." But the colonial mission had a similar metropolitan history—specifically, the rehabilitating of disability. Disability, like presumed degeneracy, marks those who have not managed to become or to stay self-sovereign, who have failed the privatized work of managing the mutable body as bounded territory, of preserving order, and both the presence of the disabled and the urban in-migration of formerly colonized persons can loose a psychic storm surge of dread upon mere visual encounter.

"Empire" has recently been able to incorporate the "ethnic" computation of difference in earlier stages of colonialism by capitalizing on it.[13] But colonialism's "'computation of normalities' and 'degrees of deviancy' from the white norm"—this standard for measuring bodies fit for civilization, based upon their being categorically proper—remains in effect.[14] The bodies of the urban homeless are, in this regard, comparable to those marked "disabled," and indeed these categories significantly overlap each other. Social research suggests that "disorder—like crime—is caused by conditions like poverty and a lack of trust between neighbors" and that so-called civility legislation, such as that prohibiting homeless persons from frequenting parks—even prohibiting benches, as I discovered—does not reduce, but simply displaces, the homeless population. However, citizens, under the auspices of securing the city, prefer enacting civic ordinances that restrict which bodies will be allowed in public space, especially in its decorous zones—the city center of fashion, the sites of tourism, and the neighborhoods of the rich.[15]

The economies of global cities—as in, for example, the young nation of America following the Civil War, when prosthetics were cosmetically deployed to project a national image of virility and vitality—depend upon sequestering bodies presumably burdened with this biologized difference.[16] Given that "profit maximization, rather than the fulfillment of social needs, is the leading motive of the private land economy that produces most of the built environment of capitalist cities," disabled persons find ourselves hemmed in, landlocked.[17] The analysis of disabled bodies as unproductive has been built into spatial, geographical impediments, thus "perpetuating the dominance of 'able-bodied' persons."[18]

But this equally extends to aesthetics: The emergence of a consumer economy has been tied to "a vision of satisfaction that could become available to those prepared to reshape themselves," notes urban studies and disabilities theorist Harlan Hahn. As urbanization developed, image became the medium for negotiating the interface with strangers—hence the role of advertising, as persons attempted to fit themselves into a community of strangers. "In cities that were supposed to be havens of heterogeneity," Hahn concludes, "influences promoting conformity may have imposed an even more severe burden on visibly disabled men and women than in the rural environs that had flourished prior to the so-called industrial revolution."[19] And while Don Mitchell's analysis of the "annihilating economy" has been worked up from outrage over anti-homeless laws, disability experience resonates with his assessment that "what is at work . . . at the urban scale . . . is the implementation . . . of a regulatory regime—and its ideological justification—appropriate to the globalizing neoliberal political economy." What emerges as the supposedly public space of the globalized city resembles instead an idealized landscape, Mitchell notes, "a privatized view suitable only from the passive gaze of the privileged," substituted "for the (often uncomfortable and troublesome) heterogeneous interactions of urban life."[20] As global cities come to depend on the culture industry (replacing former industrial cores), the "aestheticization of fear" thus becomes a major civic strategy for determining who belongs on the streets of global cities.[21] The aesthetics of civic space remain limned with dread of the biologized other, and the choreography of civility, along with its mapping of civic space,[22] is one of the lines of force where humanism continues to work a colonial agenda.[23]

I use the word *crip/tography* to name the cartography that helps us see the invisible power lines that make and unmake the visible world of global cities and the choreography of how bodies are to behave in that world. If both disabled persons, as defined by reference to the fit, economically productive body of earlier industrial capitalism and of the aesthetically, acceptable body of consumer capitalism, and the postcolonial find themselves surveilled "for fear of . . . ," cities such as New York also hold out the possibility, as Jane M. Jacobs notes, of unraveling imperial trajectories.[24] Hence, the hope of cosmopolis, of mongrel cities, of cities where diversity, plurality, and heterogeneity can prevail without fear.[25]

In mapping the dream of cosmopolis as well as palpating the problems and possibilities of the dance of bodies within global cities, crip/tography attempts to elaborate a postcolonial theology in and for life in the global city. In doing so, it attempts to think *crip*, like *queer*, not as "a positivity but

as a positionality, a location or strategically marginal position from which
to resist the norm." Crip/tography assumes (as did Foucault) that "progressive politics does not require a vision, but an awareness of the intolerable
and an historical analysis that informs political strategies."²⁶ What I have
been calling *civility* not only deploys power lines that displace bodies loaded
with difference, but configures urban space accordingly.²⁷ Crip/tography
pays disciplined attention to this geography and choreography of our
urbanized bodies in hope of producing the social and psychic ruptures that
engender detachment from normativity. A theology based on crip/tography
seeks religious passion disciplined into practices that might—like the mad
monks of Myanmar²⁸—break through the restraints of civility.

Donna Haraway, like Gayatri Spivak, urges us to "set aside the Enlightenment figures of coherent and masterful subjectivity, the bearers of rights,
holders of property in the self," Haraway herself encouraging us to think
beyond humanism by thinking with "brokenness," and more specifically,
by recalling Jesus as a historical grotesque. Interpolated through Isaiah's
figuration of the suffering servant-slave, Jesus emerges as related to colonialism's "inappropriate/d others."²⁹ If Christianity might recall itself
to the cripped iconography at its heart as the possibility for a spreading
rhizome of bodies among whom "*eros* and *thanatos* no longer agree to be
compliantly contradictory," this might lead toward a practice of navigating
civility otherwise. Resetting Jesus into the tableaux stretching from the
cripped Jacob to today's "inappropriate/d others" already displaces the now
failed or failing relationship of liberal theology with culture by assuming
with Yvonne Sherwood that "the Bible is in some respects radically other to
the modern project of the care and growth of the self,"³⁰ contesting the
modernist portraiture of Jesus as "vital, pure and busy" healer set over
against the "miserable wash of humanity" at the heart of colonial mission.³¹
In so doing it may also allow for the passional renegotiation of civility among
those otherwise straitjacketed into globalizing culture's body politic.

Renegotiating Civility

Civility is of course a highly valorized term, and in most discourses, a
highly valued quality. However, civility, as I have been discussing it, also

constitutes what Spivak has called an "enabling violation." In that respect, it resembles another highly valorized term: *human rights*. "The idea of human rights," Spivak among others has argued, "may carry within itself the agenda of a kind of Social Darwinism." She continues in a sarcastic note: "The fittest must shoulder the burden of righting the wrongs of the unfit—and [thus emerges] the possibility of an alibi. Only a 'kind of' Social Darwinism, of course. Just as 'the white man's burden,' undertaking to civilize and develop, was only 'a kind of' oppression. It would be silly to footnote the scholarship that has shown that the latter may have been an alibi for economic, military, and political intervention." She concludes: "I am of course troubled by the use of Human Rights as an alibi for interventions of various sorts. But its so-called European provenance is for me in the same category as the 'enabling violation' of the production of the colonial subject."[32]

"Civility" is the same kind of enabling violation in the production of the contemporary metropolitan subject, and just as Spivak declares that "one cannot write off the righting of wrongs," one of course cannot simply "write off" a value and a practice such as civility. Instead, as she says, "the enablement must be used even as the violation is renegotiated."[33] The task is to renegotiate civility as enabling all inhabitants of cosmopolis to carry on "heterogeneous interactions of urban life" without resort to the violation of the biologized other.

Cities exist "as human settlements in which strangers are likely to meet," Richard Sennett explained in *The Fall of Public Man* in 1976, when cities were gripped by the first wave of the current institutionalization of fear. Such meetings in turn call "for a rather special and sophisticated type of skill," or rather, as Zygmunt Bauman adds, "a whole family of skills," which Sennett listed under the rubric of civility.[34] Civility, according to Sennett, might be defined as that "activity which protects people from each other and yet allows them to enjoy each other's company." In this way, civility "shield[s] others from being burdened with oneself." "Wearing a mask" becomes the epitome of civility, since "masks permit pure sociability, detached from the circumstances of power, malaise, and private feelings of those who wear them."[35] Equally, however, civility—a psychosocial line of force—protects the transcendent plane of value, the growth-capitalist scale of valuing unlimited potential, innumerable opportunities, and unencumbered ability.

If we immediately recognize the choreography to which Sennett refers, we can also, recalling the scene at Rockefeller Center, contemplate how this line of force we call "civility," this expectation that we shield each other from the burden of ourselves, might negatively affect what Spivak, in "Righting Wrongs," calls the "imperative to responsibility." The globalized world, she insists, "must be filled with the more robust imperative to responsibility that capitalist social productivity was obliged to destroy" (533). Consequently, Spivak charges us with something of a religious responsibility—that of "suturing the lost cultural imperative to responsibility" into the human rights agenda (ibid.). This ethical imperative, she insists, must be established at the heart of our understanding of the subject and prior to humanism (537, 545). For a religious person, Spivak's anthropological starting point— "the human being is human in answer to an 'outside call'" (545)—carries an intriguingly strong theological impulse—the concept of *vocare*, to be called.

I am intrigued, given Spivak's provocation, to think back to the story of Cain and Abel (Genesis 4), a tight theological hub from which spins out the biblical narrative addressing the first or original sin (that is, fratricide, at least in some accounts), the founding of the city, and the haunting question, "Am I my brother/sister's keeper?" Not only does the modern city "represent a masked structure of dependence on various 'elsewheres,'" for example, dependence on agricultural lands, as well as on nonadjacent industrial zones and *maquiladoras*,[36] the modern city equally allows us—by encouraging the mask of civility—to avoid carrying the burden of the other. The temptation to secure our own well-being by capitalist accumulation, to become invulnerable to interdependence by building the infrastructure of the city, also allows us to avoid being our brother and sister's "keeper." Daily, we face the temptation to refuse recognition to the face of the other. In this vein, civility protects the practice of the rights and freedoms of the sovereign self, but avoids negotiating our interdependence, avoids carrying the burden of the other, of welcoming his or her difference.

For those of us trained within the mythos of humanism, the recognition that our valorization of and efforts at the practice of civility have been based upon a repression by abjection of the burden of difference and have thus enforced this apartheid of bodies—the recognition that our humanist posture has been and thus remains limned with colonialism as we walk the streets of the city—can be a difficult admission. Theologically more troublesome, however, is the insight that this apartheid might well have to do with the order of the body generated within Protestantism: "Capitalism could not make sense, it could not be the social organization for accomplishing certain types of material labor, if the disciplining of the body in Protestant terms did not already make sense," writes Janet Jakobsen, recalling the insights of Max Weber.[37] Self-sovereignty has crept willy-nilly into our notions of religious subjectivity. If we crip that posture, if we bend it to the call of the other, then the religious subject might affirm with Spivak that "to be human is to be called by the other." "We are obligated to respond to our environment and other people in ways that open up rather than close off the possibility of response," suggests Kelly Oliver, echoing Spivak.[38] Assuming such a theological anthropology might begin to break with the lines of force hemming us into this liberal choreography of civility.

Let me demonstrate how this can work. Vancouverites emerge like moles to the few hours of sunlight breaking open life in the rainforest. On one such morning, I make my way to Capers Organic Grocery and Deli, where I'm something of a regular. (Cripped bodies often require the interdependence of face-to-face relations, and I consequently regularize my habits so as to become known.) On the corner of Fourth and Vine, the other regulars (street people, whom Capers does not restrict) greet me—without my professional garb and therefore without my passable mask—as "the professor," with a touch of admiration and a bit of ironic laughter. (To be disabled is to share an affinity with street persons, and I am, after all, an uncivil body inside the civility of academia.) Capers Deli presents one with an interesting cross section of life in the global city. Émigrés of former British colonies enter North America through our port; Vancouver has one of the highest immigration rates among cities on this planet. Behind the deli counter, I am consequently likely to meet up with someone whose original professional status outranks my own, but who cannot get relicensed in this country, with a Sikh forced into the food industry; or with a street person from the Downtown Eastside in recovery and job retraining; or, owing to our informal status as an international gay refuge, with an M-to-F tranny. Shanti from Singapore often teaches me about non-Western traditions, such as roasting goats and making oil lamps for Diwali.

But today, there's a new presence in deli prep—Indo-Canadian, I think. And when she spots me twelve deep in the lineup for the comfort of tea and a muffin on this damp and dripping morning, she gasps and nearly drops her pans. Sure that I have yet again been fixed in the stare, the horrific clench of fear that keeps my disabled body tenuously on the edge of civil acceptance, I grow stone cold, psychically suck myself in. (I, you see, have the body that can bring the world to a standstill. Almost, but not quite the picture of civility: "You have one leg," the most common utterance after the gasp. Duh, I know; but the onlooker seems to be just now getting used to the idea.) But no: her energies surge toward me not as fear, but as—could it be?—a force of reverence. I am apparently an honored guest, the last who will be first. And then without any command of English, she moves the twelve others aside, shaming them with her finger. I'm embarrassed, shocked, amazed.

Could Christians and cosmopolitans all learn to practice this capaciousness of being bent toward because called by the other? The other twelve were not intending to be mean, just aiming to give me the cloak of civil decency, that is, tolerant inclusion, by making no fuss about my difference in their lineup. But she has just shown me an energy, born of spiritual passion, that might breach the retaining walls of all of these different zones set up by the command force of civility in the global city. Whereas liberalism has typically gotten stuck enforcing "decency theologies,"[39] here, the naturalized ethos of the city was burst by something like an imperative to responsibility, to a value not civilly scripted. Here at least was something that related humans once again to the mystery of the ineffable in a way that provoked the promise of another economy of value, another way of mapping human relations in the city, another choreography of relations there.[40]

Crip/tography maps such locations and such gestures amidst the social pressures of civility. Like the industrious Jack and Jill, who went up the hill to fetch water, my body, too, was born under the regime of self-sovereignty demanded by capitalist economy, within which we treat ability like a piece of property for enclosure. But I broke my crown and had a falling out with that notion of self-sovereignty. Civility, by protecting us from the burden of the other, of the degenerat/ing body, keeps this sense of self-sovereignty in play with and through the aestheticization of fear. However we name the alternative, be it "planetarity," as does Gayatri Spivak, or "conviviality," as does the postcolonial scholar Paul Gilroy from amidst the mongrel city of London, this sovereign self must be fissured, fractured, by something like religious passion. Salman Rushdie in *Midnight's Children*, and Inosh Arani in *The Cripple and His Talisman*, like Haraway and like other postcolonial authors, hold before us the iconography of the broken body as figural map of the postcolonial. Because the en/crip/tion of pain exposes self-sovereignty as illusion, it is the crip who may figurally open out the way for going "post/al" in cosmopolis. Given the ways in which civility plays upon the aestheticization of fear, Christianity—"the practices of others made odd"[41]—can be lived crip/tographically, as a geography of resistance. Geographies of resistance don't necessarily seek to "mirror geographies of domination," but rather to uncouple from domination by creating and making available alternative spatialities.[42]

Having delved into "the rubric of civility" so as to consider how this psychology of liberal humanism already assumes a strategy for managing the burden of difference,[43] I consider reweaving social flesh through ritual practice. In that vein, I turn to two theological venues which might be heard to share my concern for renegotiating this colonially limned line of force named civility. Neither theologian abides the Freudian Berlin Wall segregating pain from pleasure—and hence neither withholds either pain or pleasure from religious passion; both eschew the modern calculus of loss/gain and thus move with passion into agentially unsafe scenes. In these ways, both challenge a civil and controlled Christianity which has seen itself "as the comforter, resolver, or even eliminator of suffering."[44] Graham Ward situates his theological proposal, *Cities of God*, as an express attempt to counter cultural individualism (a posture civility does assume) with an ontology of participation, an ontology which Ward insists will be good news for "the brokenness of bodies in postmodernity": "'This is my body' announces, for the Christian, the scandal of both crucifixion and resurrection, both a dying-to-self-positing and an incorporation into the city of God. Here is announced a theology for the disabled, the sick, the racked, the torn, the diseased, the pained" (*Cities of God*, 81; 96). I will next take as theological midrash the contemporary novel *Broken for You* by Stephanie

Kallos, which assumes as an epigraph "the fracture," the narrative of blessing at the heart of Christian eucharistic ritual, i.e., "He took Bread, . . . brake it, and gave it to his disciples, saying, Take, eat, this is my Body, which is given for you" (*Broken for You*, v). Kallos's novelistic re-imagination of the negotiation of a life economy sets out from her intuition that the breaking open of the body, even if by pain and disease, enables the passional capaciousness exemplified by the deli-prep assistant.

Amidst these analyses, I turn to think with and through biblical exegesis and theological analysis of how eucharist, this *sacramentum* or "oath of loyalty" taken among cripped bodies, might have been released as anticolonial commentary or strategy about the ancient city, thus inviting our own re-imagination.[45] Sacrifice, as a rite, founded the ancient city; it was understood to secure the well-being of the city.[46] That fact dares us to read ourselves into Christianity's iconic embrace of the body pivoted upon "the fracture," this mimetic retort to the ancient, imperial economy of well-being in the city. "God's new order"—ever and again imaged as contagious (like mustard seeds) and contaminating (like yeast)—"is about the reclamation of human space as the arena for economic and social justice," is about challenging the valorization "of people, places and activities," challenging "the value placed upon them by the cultic leaders, their urban masters, or their Roman overlords," theologian Andrew Davey insists.[47] If "the ancient city was founded on sacrifice," then Christian sacrament might have been suggesting a mimetically resistive wisdom—given its own location and "oath taking" among imperially displaced, dislocated, and iconically cripped bodies.

The Eucharist of Inappropriate/d Others

Generosity—a "desire to redistribute"—does not necessarily, Spivak reminds us, flow or even trickle down from the well-laden table; it "is not the unproblematic consequence of a well-fed society" ("Righting Wrongs," 534). The heart of those ensconced as self-sovereign turns rather, Sennett advises, toward narcissism: "narcissism is now mobilized in social relations by a culture deprived of belief in the public and ruled by intimate feeling as a measure of the meaning of reality." Indeed, "[n]arcissism is the Protestant ethic of modern times," Sennett charges, obviously adverting to, by escalating, Max Weber's intuition that Protestantism supplied capitalism with an amenable anthropology.[48] If "worldly asceticism" erased sociability and turned subjective impulse inward, today's cult of narcissism borrowed that initial structure of ascetic distance from society, but now makes subjective feeling an obsessive—even if doomed-to-fail (since narcissistic desire can never be sated)—index of well-being.[49] Publicly eulogized as "enlightened self-interest" and made normative, this sense of cultured subjectivity, a privatized and inflated subjective individualism, closed in upon its own feelings and ravenous for experience, discriminates itself from class/ified or biologized difference. The self—gone missing from public sociality, but immersed in culture consumption—practices sovereignty over the body in a manner similar to the stance it assumes toward property rights, toward the right to capitalize on property, to geographically map the city.[50] With the advance of capitalist globalization, those bodies that do not similarly hold property "privately"—private property being asserted as neoliberal realism and common law regarding the global city—literally cannot take place: "When capital is believed to have no need for any particular place [as has been true within the myth of capital in network society], then cities do what they can to make themselves attractive to capital. . . . 'Quality of life' laws [like that to which I was subjected in Guiliani's New York City]—making urban areas attractive to footloose capital and to mid-to-upper classes—annihilate the space of those who do not own property, who have no legal right to place."[51] Recognizing then that even those of liberal vision are "obliged to admit that there is no continuous line from rights to responsibilities" (Spivak, "Righting Wrongs," 535), Christians and other cosmopolitans might agree with Spivak that "the only way to make these sweeping changes" into a postproductive economy is "to take seriously the necessary but impossible task to construct a collectivity among the dispensers of bounty as well as the victims of oppression" (537), to angle subjectivity toward the call of the other.[52] Within Christian life, such an economy of solidarity, the economy of Spirit, has been practiced through eucharist.

CAN CRIPS PARTICIPATE?

"Activating a dormant ethical imperative," Spivak advises, requires that "one enters ritual practice transgressively . . . as a hacker enters software"

("Righting Wrongs," 544, 559). It is thus on the ritual site of the eucharist that Graham Ward situates his theological proposal, *Cities of God*, an express attempt, under the banner of "radical orthodoxy," to recall Christians to this heuristic ritual for living out an "ontology of participation"[53]— Ward's version of suturing responsibility into humanist subjectivity. Where "cities become variants on the theme-park, reorganized as sites for consumption, sites for the satisfaction of endless desire" (*Cities of God*, 56), "where the "social [becomes] the cultural" (61), we require another kind of theological response, Ward writes (62). The line of force which Ward particularly addresses is desire, since the body is the principal site for the operation of contemporary power (76). According to Ward, an adequate Christian response to the atomism of Western culture (which appears as his primary culture complaint) has to include "a strong doctrine of participation" so as "to undermine the social atomism which contemporary cyberspace, global cities, and new forms of mobile, short term 'employment' . . . develop" (74). "The Christian theology outlined in [*Cities of God*]," Ward writes, "starts from what it is to be called by God as an embodied soul to participate in Christ's body" (77). In this way, he assumes Christian subjectivity must "start . . . with the collective," not the individual (2), stressing participation and interdependence—hence, the eucharist as map of desire. Ward circles around the question, "What kind of bodies is Christianity concerned with . . . if . . . this eucharistic and Christic body informs all other understandings of 'body'?" (83).[54] However, at this juncture, I can only concur with Marcella Althaus-Reid's assessment that "radical orthodoxy . . . fails to take into account the epistemological plateau of the excluded."[55]

I worry that Ward has not really hacked the eucharist, not paid sufficient attention to fissuring open the sovereign self. Ward asserts that the iconic status of the body of Jesus "is configured through an identification with the suffering of the body," eventuating in an economy of desire that is no longer libidinal, but experienced as mourning.[56] However, the modern subject has always been something of a "wounded identity," Wendy Brown warns, mourning an ideal, a lost transcendent, which has made it conducive to capitalism.[57]

Further, I am suspicious of Ward's presumption to cultural resistance by mere oppositionalism. Christ, explains John S. Dunne, in *The City of the*

Gods, stands in a long line of savior-kings, ruling over an eternal city (135). In Roman imperial iconography, it was the emperor who carried a vision of worldwide peace, sufficiency, and reconciliation, just as do today's globalizing forces. And Ward well knows that "sacrifice founded the ancient city."[58] We might instead ask how the eucharist, itself an ancient rite affiliated with sacrifice, might mimetically generate an *alternative* choreography among subjugated bodies, distinct from imperial theology. Where ancient emperor cults appreciated the self-composed, sober, civil self, we ask, what might have been loosed by putting the body of a torture victim—a crip, a grotesque—iconographically on the throne of that savior-king, the emperor?[59]

Whatever differences are marked by "disability" and its cognate resonance with the biologized "waste" of globalization, they "defy assimilation."[60] Justice construed as "a matter of distributing benefits produced by mutual cooperation among those capable of contributing" will never arrive among those seen as en/crip/ted on today's city streets. Crips, disabilities ethicist Anita Silvers insists, rather require something "like a project for engendering trust," where trust implies "accepting one's vulnerability to another . . . in the confidence that such exposure of vulnerability will not be used to harm the other."[61] Trust might here then be said to be an extension of responsibility insomuch as it holds open the call of the other.[62] But while the disembedding technologies of modernity have required trust in hard and soft infrastructure technologies, these dry up human social trust.[63] Fear—including its aesthetic modes—needs to be redressed not so much by participation, as Ward would have it, as by a trust culture.

"Christianity," Ward contends, quoting Michel de Certeau, "was founded upon the loss of a body—the loss of the body of Jesus Christ, compounded with the loss of the 'body' of Israel, of a 'nation' and its genealogy" (*Cities of God*, 92). "It is the loss," Ward then concludes, "which prepares the way for the mystical." Correcting himself, Ward explains: "Rather than loss, I wish to speak of 'displacement' . . . the displacement of the one, archetypal body, which engenders a transcorporeality in which the body of Christ is mapped onto and shot like a watermark through physical bodies, social bodies, institutional bodies, ecclesial bodies, sacramental bodies" (93). But what shall we make of this Christic wound that allows for its own disappearance, a wounded body made more spiritually capacious because it is displaced? As one with some experience of bearing what for this culture appears as stigmata, I wonder how this torture victim, this victim of imperial power, this uncivil grotesque (Isaiah 53), comes to be so easily disappeared and what that disappearance effects. The colonized, the body—visually fixed as hemorrhaging, bleeding, stigmatic, as Franz Fanon first suggested—can never disappear, can never pretend to transparency. Rather, our bodies circulate outside invested desire, with civility patrolling any allowance of/for their desire. As Zygmunt Bauman, among others, persistently points out, for the bodies of those who are "absentee landlords" and in the cult/ure of public appearance, disappearance or transparency is the norm of power. Thus Ward's dispersion of the wounded body, its "translocationality,"[64] unwittingly serves not the broken bodies of postmodernity, as he had hoped, but the absentee landlord class who live an absence of presence to relational accountability.

What might emerge, I wonder, if we rather figurally remembered here the stigmatic, because colonized, body that resisted cultural power's disappearing act? Might our responsibility to the call of the other here begin to cross through cultural apartheid? Rather than analogical idealization (because vision we have, but no practiced paths opening out therefrom), the iconography of the inappropriate/d other can instead promote a geography of resistance opening off from feeling with and for the wound of the other, a geography of assuming pain, and our empathic engagement, as of the nature of human life. The model of self-sovereignty avoids and Ward's proposal skirts precisely such an empathic interdependence—as if we could find the muscle named "responsibility" by shutting our eyes.[65]

To reread Christian iconography as decisively cripped—as engaging "wounds" that refuse displacement—can open out a different and suggestive possibility: Isaiah 53, the poem we call "The Song of the Suffering Servant" and the basis for the medieval painting *The Man of Sorrows*, constitutes the greatest hypertext for our synoptic passion narratives. Traditionally, Isaiah's suffering servant, when conflated with Jesus as victim of Roman torture tactics, has lent itself to atonement theories. Feminist theologians have accused such theologies of perpetuating abusive relationships by embracing justification through the actions of a vicarious sufferer. Yet the servant songs of Deutero-Isaiah, composed within and/or consequent to the exile of Judah in Babylon, could be read to expose imperial conditions, not to legitimate them: to expose the powers that occasion the enslaving or colonizing of subjugated peoples, manifest in/as physical torture, hobbling, humiliation, and shame.

Indeed, what is fundamental about the poem is not the question of figural identity, a question of which cultic hero is being talked about here—Moses, Israel itself, or Jesus—but rather "the reader's response and reaction to the figure of the ["dis'd"] servant."[66] "He grew up before the Lord like a young plant whose roots are in parched ground; he had no beauty, no majesty to draw our eyes, no grace to make us delight in him; his form, disfigured, lost all the likeness of man, his beauty changed beyond human semblance. He was despised, shunned by people, a man who suffered, no stranger to sickness, like one from whom people turn away their gaze. He was despised, and we held him of no account."[67] "We," the readers, are drawn in so as to admit our personal and/or cultural disgust toward the disfigured one, that being the gate to our own ethical retooling—passing from aversion through critical self-examination. The poem reads best, as scholar David J. A. Clines has argued, as a liturgical passage of meditative confession that cuts through the aesthetic naturalization of disgust and our metaphysical justifications for a person's suffering or grotesque profile: "Surely he has borne our infirmities . . . yet we accounted him stricken by God" (verse 4). As Clines puts it, "The force of verses 4–5 lies entirely in the contrast between what 'we' believed was the source of . . . suffering (God) and what was in fact its sources ('our sins')."[68] Like the meditative engagement of an icon, this narrative passage works to transform the attitude of the reader—moving through aversion toward self-recognition, both in terms of accepting appropriate culpability in ethical offloading and for the projectional, judgmental declaration of naming someone as a "misfit."

The text presumes something like cultural or personal insight therapy, the modern approach to psychological and behavioral dysfunction aimed at developing self-awareness and understanding of one's own affective life, cutting through the gravity of cultural impulse, the presumption to know the disgusting when one sees it, so as to access the deeper insight that it was our risk, culpability, or life *ressentiment* she or he was bearing.[69] "The poem's very lack of specificity," Clines argues, "refuses to let it be tied down to one spot on the globe or frozen in history: it opens up the possibility that the poem can become true in a variety of circumstances—that is its work."[70] "If we see the Man of Sorrows not (or not only) as Christ but as an unidentified suffering individual," we have a liturgical passage for working through disgust.[71] It is a poetic passage also taken up in visual arts that can guide one's iconographic meditation. In fact, the artist Van Gogh, a more faithful and less ideologically fixed reader than Christians have been, sketched—on the basis of the consequent song of the suffering female servant/slave, Isaiah 54—*Sorrow*, depicting a street prostitute, whom he met and took in and whose daughter he then adopted into the household.[72] Recognition occasioned by the analytic incision of Isaiah 53 or its iconographic variation can be the pinch on consciousness that initiates one on the path of ethical nonharming, for suddenly one hears, in the words of Isaiah, an ethical deconstruction of any metaphysical "naturalization" or theistic legitimation of disability.

Upon rereading, then, Isaiah 53 suggests not vicarious suffering, but a therapeutic ritual:[73] "Surely he has borne our griefs and carried our sorrows; yet we accounted him stricken." Rather than justifying vicarious suffering, it exposes the mechanism of social scapegoating. Isaiah 53 invites persons to confront the relations occasioning exclusion and rejects the shame that others are attempting to impose on the humiliated. Like disability or the biologizing of difference, ringed by the aestheticization of fear, projecting suffering onto another obscures our participation in the distorted relations of empire. Isaiah 53, read as the de/crip/tion of the in/valid, might thus also occasion a confession of the ways in which we presume upon "the philanthropy of the poor."[74]

"Following Jesus, the torture victim, means daily negotiation of Roman power," observes biblical scholar Warren Carter.[75] The salvific potential of proclaiming the cross, as Neil Elliott explains, was the exposure of unjust and terrorizing political relations that then could be identified and collectively resisted.[76] Similarly, the Pauline instructions on the need to discern the body of the crucified Christ at the eucharist: If persons joined themselves to the body of Christ and still lived unrighteously with others, they were participating in the same systems of judgment and condemnation that

crucified Jesus (1 Corinthians 11:23–26).[77] Such discernment might be lived
in relation to the subalterns of our culture—as crip/tographic iconography,
as a locus for a geography of resistance.

OF SPLINTERED GLAZES, HAIRLINE FRACTURES, CRACKS, AND OTHER PREREQUISITES OF INTIMACY

If literature occupies that other, often officially unacknowledged theological venue in the West, Stephanie Kallos's novel *Broken for You* might offer
us not so much a vision of new humanity as a suggestion for living the fractures of human life as possible spiritual path.[78] Margaret Hughes, the pro-
tagonist of the novel, has been encrypted within her 15,000-square-foot
Seattle-based mausoleum of a mansion since the death of her eight-year-old
son and her consequent divorce from her husband. For decades then, the
seventy-five-year-old has tended the porcelain and art glass collections
gathered in by her father—these, the ill-gotten wealth of a man who dealt
with the Nazis to procure stolen Jewish goods during World War Two. As
if the sins of the father were visited upon the child, Margaret develops an
astrocytoma—a star-shaped, incurable malignant tumor of the brain. But
now leveraging illness as a chance to break with old habits, that choreography of a life tending but "the objects of my affection," she invites in one
melancholic boarder after another to disorder the isolating decorum of her
wealth—first, Wanda, the orphaned dramaturge, chasing an impossible
love; then stolid and asexual Susan, a nursing assistant; next Bruce, the ca-
terer become community cook, seeking gay refuge, and so on—the handy-
man, a gardener, a lover. Born from her "fracture" and theirs—in a way that
echoes the medieval Christological concept of "wound become womb," but
without disappearing the historied hurt, is an adoptive family—including,
with thanks to a turkey baster, a second generation, Bruce and Susan's little
Augie.

As individual lives fracture, the members of this adoptive family hold
and redeem one another. Gathering energy from their shared accountability, they finally even invent a ritual of atonement to loose the palpable guilt
exuding from the porcelain collections, none of the pieces ever returnable.
Inverting the horror of Krystallnacht, "when bodies had been shattered
but things had not" (Kallos, *Broken for You*, 313), each soup tureen will

break its silence and tell its family history, even if invented—each goblet, each figurine, each egg coddler and saucer. Visitors to the mansion as well as family members, each having held him/herself accountable to history's horror in the telling of such an invented story, smash each plate, each vase, each teacup in turn, redeeming the fragments as mosaic tiles for Wanda's art.

This adoptive community, taking shape here in the literary imagination, resonates with Foucault's queer geography of resistance by adoption,[79] and with Spivak's sensibilities for turning the bearer of rights towards collectivity. Spirit adoption, one of the earliest strategic practices of Christianity within the conditions of empire (which tends to strew bodies hither and yon and make genealogies impossible), was a redemption strategy for mortal bodies (Romans 8).[80] Far from promising grace to overly moralistic and guilt-ridden consciences, the apostle Paul connected Spirit to the liberation of history's humiliated—from political oppression into economic mutuality, from the relational alienation induced by urban in-migration and slavery into sociocommunal, ecclesial belonging. Disrupting the power plays of empire, its land grab and its legalized terrorizing of the poor, Spirit opened solidarity among those the empire humiliated, and threaded transcendence, if also "history," through them.

But Kallos's text appears intriguingly to address itself to "the bearers of right," to those in that crypt of sovereign selfhood, even if at the top of the proverbial ladder, and seeks to redress not just atomization (as did Ward), but the dehumanization of wealth,[81] the social ills accruing amidst the affluent. "The rise in aggregate wealth has not," qualitative studies have insisted, "raised reported subjective well-being"; rather, wealth—presenting us with the ways and means to insure ourselves against the vicissitudes, fluctuations, and volatilities of interdependence—has "coincided with an epidemic expansion of mental-health disorders."[82] Economist Avner Offer, presenting study after study in *The Challenge of Affluence*, asks us to consider the correlation between material abundance and a wide range of social and personal disorders—family breakdown, child and youth anxiety, addiction, crime, declining social trust and, often among youth, "attachment disorders" (340). Seen from the psychic inside out, affluence—as a way of embargoing ourselves against interdependence—not only undermines social commitment, but psychic well-being: "Strong materialistic values were associated with a pervasive undermining of well-being, from low life satisfaction and happiness, to depression and anxiety, physical problems such as headaches, personality disorders, narcissism and antisocial behavior" (351). That modernity chose to relate us through the cash nexus alone makes this a social, not one-to-one, correlation. Kallos seems intuitively to catch us in that condition.

Consider Kallos's work, then, a training manual in breaking with "the objects of [our] affection" so as to move away from "sentiment," which she describes as "ascribing a value to something above and beyond what its value is to God" (*Broken for You*, 367), towards relational embeddedness and the love of a mortal and transient life. Kallos, moving momentarily into the voice of the spiritual director, instructs: "Look . . . at the faces and bodies of people you love. The explicit beauty that comes not from smoothness of skin or neutrality of expression, but from the web of experience that has left its mark. Each face, each body is its own living fossilized record. A record of cats, combatants, difficult births; of accidents, cruelties, blessings . . . [T]hese records are what render your beloved beautiful" (367). You see, Kallos writes at one point, "We're worth more broken" (348).

Wounds, breaking through the solid encryptions of social civility, here become capacious because of their invitation for deterritorialization of the body. Illness breaks open the tacit infrastructure of the real, of the normal, of what is presumed to make life meaningful, of what is of value, even of how we articulate health. (From an alternative position, "health" might well be indexed to humane practice—not to the perfection of the boundaries of the body.) Echoing Spivak's sensibilities that the only way "to persuade global finance and world trade to jettison the culture of economic growth" would be "to take seriously the necessary but impossible task to construct a collectivity among the dispensers of bounty as well as the victims of oppression" ("Righting Wrongs," 536–37), Kallos tracks the passing of capitalist inheritance into the collective of cripped bodies adopted into a household.

Introducing Spirit into Crip/tography

David Harvey reads globalization as the lines of force moving through bodies: "[B]oiled down to its simplest determinations, globalization is about the socio-spatial relations between billions of individuals."[83] By deconstructing the lines of force yoking civility and the politics of public appearance, I have tried to analyze the ways in which the forces of globalization in late capitalism in global cities have choreographed our relations in the global city under a regime dominated by the aestheticization of fear, of fear of the other. As a method of resistance, as a counterforce to these forces, I have found in physical and in sociopsychic suffering something like the possibilities of a spiritual practice. With the psychic and physical shearing of my health crisis has also come something of a shift in the register of a life, of consciousness. Perhaps this shouldn't be surprising if "spiritual waking arrives ever as the dis/abling of the ableist dream."[84] As Ward's account of religious subjectivity also recognizes, there is not "a spectrum with pain at one extreme and pleasure at the other." Rather, religious accounts have historically "appealed to experiences which are simultaneously both painful and consummately beatific." If "the mystic's cry of ecstasy, the mathematician's speechless awe at the dark spaces between the stars, the exquisite intellectual confession of what is beautiful sheers towards the edge of the tremendum," and if "each testify to experiences that exceed the neat categorization, the spectrum extremities, of pain and pleasure,"[85] becoming disabled or falling ill could sometimes serve as something like the slap of a Zen master.

By suggesting that we live our fissures and fractures "like the Zen tea box broken in a hundred places"[86]—in other words, as a spiritual discipline toward deterritorialization from our existing ideological regime—I mean to point toward the discipline of attentively spending one's energies and learning to open spaces of time for retreat; the discipline of not following the veins of envy, jealousy, hatred, anger; the discipline of releasing the romantic harmonies of life, those presumed harmonies not after all unrelated to the power and punishment of judgment; the practice of sympathy for the other who startles and flees in fear from my en/crip/tion (their fear cannot be but of their own humble contours of flesh); the practice of re-entering the geography of a life trusting that if I should slip, fall, become "landlocked" by failure of crutch or wheelchair, someone will actually be humane. I am learning to trust myself again to human interdependence, a risk from which wealth is an insulator. The recognition of the meagerness and volatility of ego; the blessing of the crack through which one begins to recognize the ideological power lines of a culture; the reminder of life transpiring before the ineffable; an awareness of a resplendent plenitude out of which I can at times manage to live mindfully: in regard to all of these, I here claim nothing more than situated knowledge. Anyone can cultivate subjective fractures that tumble us from the transcendental cult of public appearance.

But I now find myself in a bit of quandary: If Christianity is dead or in "near-terminal decline," are we left with the values and valorizations of rationalism?[87] Even Spivak intimates, when reading Kant, that she could understand that something like a God supplement would help us imagine "responsibility" toward subalterns: "this name ['God'] may be seen as *a* name of the radical alterity that the self as 'the narrative center of gravity' is programmed to imagine in an ethics of responsibility."[88] How, then, do we conceive of a name for this supplement without falling into the egoic traps that rationalism has set for us? For now, I hold this place in Christian theology with the concept, with the whisper, of "Spirit": "A notion of 'post-colonial spirit' can engender postcolonial theology," Mark Lewis Taylor submits, and I concur.[89] "Spirit," Mircea Eliade found, digging into the texts of Hebrew prophets and priests (Genesis, Ezekiel, Isaiah), was first developed as a sacred metaphor during times of catastrophic dislocation, when religious persons were exiled from their sacred lands. If, with exile, "space threatened to become permanently emptied of meaning," Hebrew prophets suggestively constructed "Spirit" as the placeholder spelling "the potential sacrality of all spaces," even "the decentralized spaces of [peoples'] exile."[90] To be sure, Spirit would come in colonial time to reign over a regime of accruing land, with Spirit then linked into the voracious dialectic delivering the primitive into the civilized. But such colonial choreography of imperial sovereignty need not be construed as inherent to Spirit. So let Spirit name this other economy of passion—the choice to live "out of a desire beyond one's immediate control for a good one cannot fully know for others who are quite different."[91] Spirit, a capacitating prosthesis, a way to make the world hospitable, has a generosity of presence.[92] And Spirit assumes, as civility does not, to carry "the burden" of the other. Crip/tography assumes this generosity of Spirit, assumes that Christic iconography can invite us to such spacious and fearless empathy, that ancient rituals such as eucharist and adoption can play with our imaginations still. Given that "fear is as great a threat to the future stability of cities and regions as the much more talked about economic forces,"[93] crip/tography maps the terrain for a new choreography among bodies moving along the corridors of cosmopolis.

"Fearful Symmetry": Between Theological Aesthetics and Global Economics

> There is no exquisite beauty . . . without some strangeness in the proportion.
>
> —EDGAR ALLAN POE, "Ligeia"

Global cities, economically disconnected from nation-state and bioregion, are the architectural outcropping of economic globalization.[1] Not all cities inhabited by millions of human bodies will be counted as global cities; global cities bedazzle with their culture production, skyscapes of human architectural genius, and consumer markets nestled into the basin of nature's womb. Think of Vancouver, gateway to the Pacific, with its emerging vertical downtown of glass-walled condominiums, packed in the downtown core at a density to rival that of Hong Kong (an architectural phenomenon itself called *Vancouverism*[2]), mirrored in its oceanic basin and dwarfed by its backdrop of mountains. This emergent "City of Glass"[3] becomes all the more attractive as First Nations indigeneity bleeds into its art and rituals.

Not only do the arts seem to be one of the primary human practices pulling persons into the orbit of the city; today "the look and feel of cities reflect decisions . . . on uses of aesthetic power," observes urban sociologist Sharon Zukin in *The Cultures of Cities* (7). With the demise of manufacturing and industrial sectors and the emergence of the financial sectors, "cultural production seem[s] to be more and more what cities [are] about" (viii). In such an aesthetic economy, global cities create themselves as an "organizational commodity,"[4] as desirable stage sets for the play of the transnational financial elite, for tourism. So when Zukin says that in the symbolic economy of cities "fear has been aestheticized" (*Cultures of Cities*, 2), she means that fear is also now articulated through our notions of beauty and our related notions of civic well-being, of urban space, of the choreography of bodies moving within this space.

Because the economic viability of global cities depends upon this theater of culture, depends upon generating the urban core of the city as itself an "experience museum," these cities surveil themselves, aiming toward cultured desirability: "Every effort to rearrange space in the city is also an attempt at visual representation," writes Zukin (*Cultures of Cities*, 24). Global cities—with "livability" indexed to tasteful, cultured beauty— shape and tone, nip and tuck themselves—via gentrification, civil city legislation, and downtown-core densification. Equally, glass corridors of office and condominium complexes mirror back aerobically perfect bodies, and assert, given that clean specular surface, a transparency of being (evidence that we are not teeming with disease and darkness),[5] so as to attract economic transactions. For global cities, economics moves aesthetically.

Theologies committed to postcolonial conscientization need to consider global cities as key praxistic sites, because these cities operate as economic command centers.[6] Further, in order to critique the economies of global cities, postcolonial theologies will need to engage aesthetics. It is the way fear and disgust have been affectively enfolded in the aestheticization of urban space and of the movement of its inhabitants that I want to explore more deeply here.

Beauty and Justice

"Beauty" has been conceptually forwarded in contemporary literature and theology not just as a function of capital, but as a yearning arriving both with and after modernity. Something seems to be whispering up from the deep of at least the Western unconscious, perhaps a yearning for sensory aliveness, as bookshelves are lined with literary and theological titles striving to engage beauty.[7] Inasmuch as beauty broaches something universal (or might we say "public?"), as Kant advised, and not merely private, beauty may signal our uptake of hope for a renewed public, even for a public trust.[8] Given that we have been living what Jacques Lacan called "the ego's era," beauty, with its inherent tendency to undermine self-interest and thus to stimulate the political imagination,[9] may yet—we seem to be hoping with Dostoevsky—save us.[10]

In her manifesto *On Beauty and Being Just*, Elaine Scarry has argued that "beauty . . . intensifie[s] the pressure we feel to repair existing [ethical] injuries" (57). In other words, beauty incites an "impulse toward . . . distribution" (6). It impels us towards justice. This transpires, Scarry instructs us, in three ways. First, that "something is . . . beautiful is bound up with an urge to protect it, or act on its behalf" (80). Second, our attention having been given involuntarily to a particular that is beautiful, we will voluntarily extend such heightened attention "to other persons or things" (67; 81). And finally, having beheld beauty, the "beholder . . . often seeks to bring new beauty into the world" (88). And yet, if I may speak as "theologian in residence" within a global city, nothing so much opens up sharp social polarizations within these cities as the resort to aesthetics, the call of the beautiful.

If the city is "a site of spectacle and bedazzlement," then "economy and culture are not categories that can be held apart."[11] And nothing will so much divide the global city as the line between aesthetically invested cultural production and what such cities deem unsightly. Indeed, "cities dominated by tourism enterprises," Lily Hoffman, Susan Fainstein and Dennis Judd report, "are characterized by a hierarchical, coordinated, standardized control of nearly all aspects of the tourist experience."[12] But what controls the experience of those who visit the global city controls the experience of those who are visited. When we consider the politics of beauty as it "takes place," under the economic and therefore political agenda driving global cities, "culture . . . controls cities. . . . The look and feel of cities reflect decisions about what—and who—should be visible and what should not, on concepts of order and disorder, and on uses of aesthetic power" (Zukin, *Cultures of Cities*, 1, 7). When we place this discourse of beauty within the politics of global cities, what emerges might be less resonant with William

Blake's awed reverence for the tiger's eye burning in "the forests of the night" than with a truly "fear-ful symmetry."[13]

So if we are to accept Scarry's thesis that beauty impels or propels justice, we will need to analyze what appears to be a certain schematic disarticulation of "the impulse to distribute" built into global-city aesthetics: the aestheticization of fear. Mike Davis, who notes an "obsession with physical security systems and collaterally, with the architectural policing of social boundaries . . . at the street level," seems to concur.[14] Zygmunt Bauman likewise supports such a conclusion:

> The state, having founded its *raison d'etre* and its claim to citizen's obedience on the promise to protect its subjects against threats to their existence, but no longer able to deliver on its promise . . . or able responsibly to reaffirm it in view of the fast globalizing and increasingly extraterritorial markets, is obliged to shift the emphasis of "fear protection" from dangers to social security to the dangers to personal security. It then "subsidiarizes" the battle against fears "down" to the realm of individually run and managed "life politics" while . . . contracting out the supply of battle weapons to the consumer markets.[15]

As aesthetics becomes a ruling norm of development within global cities, "urban glamour zones," most frequently positioned in the downtown core, emerge as set over against and in exclusion of others, the transnational migrants, "the poorly paid . . . service workers who tend to the needs of the professionals," but live "on the other side of the global city/globalization divide."[16]

More broadly, those on the other side of that divide are the "disabled," in all the senses in which "disability" can be construed. "We . . . take the form of our surroundings," the philosopher Ernst Bloch once observed.[17] And so because the "modern city lives by the straight line," as Le Corbusier put it,[18] and because "'great thoroughfares'" would by means of "the mere visibility . . . of the 'civilized,' . . . improve the 'normally degraded,'" the bourgeois body assumes the vertical axis.[19] Because there is "a tight connection between geographic place and assumptions about normative behavior,"[20] disability here can be recognized as a geographic construction—the result of "being out of place," being a "mis-fit." Disability constitutes a geospatial transgression within this particular social construction of place and bourgeois body.[21] The central structure of Holt Renfrew, one of the toniest stores in Vancouver's shopping district, is built with a glass-enclosed escalator rising three stories—reminiscent of grand staircases. But obviously my wheelchair-bound body is not at this point one that is allowed to appear. Comparably, cashiers and bank tellers, working at counters that do not even allow them a line of vision to espy me waiting in my wheelchair, interact on a daily basis only with the "upright." Who is allowed to appear, who is felt to belong, will affect the shaping of social space, just as social space will, in turn, affect the bearing of body.[22]

Within global cities, the socioeconomic role of aesthetics has "sharpened inequality," writes Zukin (*Cultures of Cities*, 169). In regard to the aesthetic control of cities, she concludes, "Sharper social polarizations . . . arise from restructured urban economies. . . . These social divisions are held in place by greater state surveillance and policing, making the city more like the panoptican prison" (ibid., 112).[23] Aesthetics within global cities have become something like an imperial presumption operating at the higher economic strata of globalization and within civic leadership as it tries to woo and win the attention of an international, itinerant financial elite. As global cities themselves assume the role of culture generation (a perhaps not-unnecessary consideration, given their diasporic residents), aesthetics has come to function nonetheless as something like "the Augustan Program of Cultural Renewal" instituted after the Battle of Actium (31 B.C.E.). "The power of visual imagery was by no means the least of the forces that propelled Rome into the world of Hellenistic culture and contributed to the dissolution of the old Republican order," historian Paul Zanker explains, describing how the city became the canvas of imperial ideology. By deploying a "superabundance of new imagery," coordinated in the edifices of new sanctuaries, memorials, theaters, and other public buildings, "through didactic arrangements and constant repetition and combination of the limited number of new symbols, along with the dramatic highlighting of facades, statues and paintings, even the uneducated viewer was indoctrinated in the new visual program."[24]

Not all cities holding multiple millions of inhabitants accrue global city status; the term *global cities* demarcates those that operate as *aesthetic* capitals. Indeed, "global cities now increasingly coordinate global *class* processes."[25] So the phenomenon of "global cities" marks always already an exclusion. And the exclusion within this "presumption to beauty" seems to pivot precisely upon what Scarry hoped might link beauty with justice—fairness.

"A single word, 'fairness,' is used both in referring to the loveliness of countenance and in referring to the ethical requirement for 'being fair,' 'playing fair,' and 'fair distribution,'" Scarry notes (*On Beauty*, 91). But in thinking through this singular schema, Scarry reverts to yet another nominal singularity suggestive of the pact between these two senses of beauty— *symmetry*, which Scarry identifies as "the single most enduringly recognized attribute" of beauty. Symmetry—the balanced proportions of the fair or seemly—likewise characterizes distributional justice as John Rawls defines it: "a symmetry of everyone's relation to each other" (*On Beauty*, 96, 93). Shaking off the thought that these might be but analogies and backing up her argument by resort to Augustine's surmise that "beautiful things please by proportion," she arrives at a "much stronger formulation": "The very symmetry of beauty . . . leads us to, or somehow assists us in discovering, the symmetry that eventually comes into place in the realm of justice; . . . beautiful things . . . hold steadily visible the manifest good of equality and balance" (98, 97). To be sure, Scarry acknowledges, "the surfaces of the world are aesthetically uneven," taking us here for a walk when suddenly we are dropped through a sensory rabbit hole or become enraptured by bird song or buttercup. Even along the roadway of uneven aesthetic surfaces, however, Scarry still insists upon linking beauty with its key Platonic attribute: "Folded into the uneven aesthetic surfaces of the world is a pressure toward social equality. It comes from the object's symmetry" (110).

Disability is defined precisely by its lack of "aesthetic symmetry,"[26] and one marked categorically "disabled" recognizes this love of symmetry as one of our most modern structures of exclusion. While aesthetic symmetry has been asserted as a cross-culturally consistent, biological preference,[27] and as a foundational assumption for good art, I, along with disabilities theorists Sharon Snyder and David Mitchell, worry, ethically speaking, about a eugenic impulse in this capture of deviation by the character of "symmetry." Snyder and Mitchell worry, in fact, that eugenics as a "hegemonic formation is not yet over." Rather than being over and past, it can "lurk . . . like a social phantasm just below the surface, determining standards, manner and parameters of our cultural, political and intellectual debate about embodied differences."[28] "Symmetry," even in or especially in the name of beauty, already aestheticizes fear.

To get a morphological reading of what this means for bodies, think of the faking scandal at the opening ceremony of the Beijing Olympics, where Lin Miaoke, the girl with the red dress, pigtails bouncing from perfectly balanced placement atop her head, already an advertising sensation in China, was revealed to be merely lip-synching the "Hymn to the Mother-land." The seven-year-old with the perfect voice, Yang Peiyi, who actually did the singing, was considered "unsuited" for the lead role because of her buck teeth.[29] "The main consideration was the national interest," said the event's musical director. "The child on the screen should be flawless in image, in her internal feelings, and in her expression." That this should not be written off as nothing more than Chinese nationalism was brought home the next day when, in an interview, John Furlong, chair of the Van-couver Olympics, would not exclude the possibility that something similar might take place at the 2010 Winter Olympics.[30] While philosopher Alfred North Whitehead surmised that "truth is the conformation of appearance to reality" and is in that way a contribution to beauty,[31] "the fair" in the age of image not need be true—nor can it, in a process-philosophical sense, then be beautiful. Symmetry, the presumed primary attribute of beauty here, becomes a fearsome measure or standard of belonging.

"Aesthetic Anxiety" and the Structuring of Urban Space

Aesthetic judgments and values shape the geography of the global city (wherein "city" is not a marketplace, but a culture) and the choreography of the bodies that inhabit it another way: by determining not just who fits and who is a misfit, but the space in which they circulate and who has access to it. In the global city, the aesthetic demand for the fair of face has been, so-ciologically speaking, linked to "the privatization of public space" (Zukin, *Cultures of Cities*, 1), even to "a new class war" (Davis, "From *City of Quartz*," 325). Public culture, Zukin reminds us, has traditionally been "a process of negotiating images that are accepted by large numbers of people" (*Cultures of Cities*, 10). She explains:

> Public culture is socially constructed on the micro-level . . . by the many social encounters that make up daily life in the streets, shops and parks—the spaces in which we experience public life in cities. The right to be in these spaces, to use them in certain ways, to invest them with a sense of our selves and our communities—to claim them as ours and to be claimed in turn by them—make up a constantly changing public culture. (ibid., 11)

But public culture within global cities has run up against two major arterial constrictions—the construction of pseudopublic spaces, upscale malls and culture acropolises such as Vancouver's Yaletown or Robson Street, and the economically motivated, civic control of public spaces such as downtown sidewalks and parks. The "ballet of the good sidewalk," upon which Jane Jacobs saw the hope or decline of our great cities pivot, has become restricted and regulated.[32] Often, in fact, the good sidewalk has been replaced by the corridors of "sumptuary malls," where our circumambulatory ballet is performed under the protective gaze of private security forces (Davis, "From *City of Quartz*," 324, 325). Frederick Law Olmstead, architect of North America's public realm and the father of New York City's Central Park, "conceived public landscapes and parks" as zones for intentionally "mixing classes and ethnicities in common . . . recreations and enjoyments," generating thereby the American *polis*, if not also supplying a social safety valve for class struggle (ibid., 325). Today, however, "the cultural power to create an image, to frame a vision, of the city has become more important as publics have become more mobile and diverse, and traditional institutions—both social classes and political parties—have become less relevant mechanisms of expressing identity," Zukin advises us. In that way, the public operates quite differently than Olmstead hoped. "By accepting these spaces without questioning their representations of urban life," Zukin warns, "we risk succumbing to a visually seductive, privatized public culture" (*Cultures of Cities*, 2–3).

"Place marketing,"[33] in which New York becomes the "Big Apple" and Minneapolis the "Mini Apple" and Las Vegas "The Strip," is something analogically like what the Augustan image makers did. As global cities increasingly use "city culture" as an economic base, as "entertainment," public spaces—including city streets—are "no longer open to the public without conditions,"[34] whether those are conditions set into civic codes requiring the homeless to be vacated to a nondecorous zone of the city or whether the class politics itself enacts, by the pressure of image or the stimulation of fantasy, its own conditions such that, as Zanker has noted of Augustan Rome, even the uneducated viewer can read the inhibiting signs. To the aesthetic immodesty of disability, we have added as casualties the messiness of a more vital and democratic citizenry, the breadth of a heterogeneous public.[35]

Of Beauty and the Venus de Milo

One might consequently be tempted to dismiss Scarry's thesis linking beauty with justice, given what Davis refers to as the "Manichean" move of "conscious[ly] 'hardening' . . . the city surface against the poor" ("From *City of Quartz*," 328) effected within the aesthetic politics that governs the global city. But the aesthetics within our own commodity involvement as well as religion's often ignored aesthetic commitment and indeed recent civil rights campaigns, for example, "Black is Beautiful," might at least remind us of the motivational, constructive, and even ethically powerful quality of beauty. Indeed, liberation theologian Ivone Gebara insists on the importance of beauty for its ameliorative quality: "My ecofeminism is pregnant with the staunch conviction that beauty is important in healing people."[36]

One could consequently mount a significant argument for why the discourse on beauty might be important, including beauty's capacity simply to give pleasure; to bind us humans socially, not as egos, but below our mindless chatter, to each other and to the cosmos; to revitalize the moral imagination, to generate (as Kant hoped) a revitalized public.[37] Further, considering that beauty forces us to move below analytic intellect to affect and therefore to begin to think together nature, culture, and soul or sentient body— thus, to think place, which Christian theology has been reluctant to do. But in terms of city culture more particularly, surely we learned the lesson from the Pruitt-Igoe Housing complex in St. Louis, and also from Cabrini Green, in Chicago: Lack of attention to beauty creates the humanly uninhabitable.[38]

There are therefore good reasons to value aesthetic affects in the global city. Neither as a person with lower-class roots nor as a person living with a disability do I find myself reluctant to speak and live an economy of beauty. I grew up in a subsistence-farming economy that lived for nothing so much as for beauty—beauty informing the decision not to clear-cut the black walnut trees, though good money would have been welcomed, as much as it set the daily news agenda around the dinner table, whether the story of the fox spotted on the north forty acres or the strawberry gems lying dew-bathed on golden straw. And yet as subsistence farmers, we were caught in a paradox of diverse economies of beauty: even in this outlying zone of Minnesota's Twin Cities, the stylistic disarticulations enforced by poverty were deemed ugly. And nothing so much rings in my guts as the class-inflected, childhood taunt "ugly and stupid" set off by the wearing of obviously outdated and hand-me-down clothing.

The same rings true with disability: I woke from trauma to the hum of the refrigerator, the chirp of the common sparrow, sun-drenched heaviness, and the Muzak-spun voice of Louis Armstrong singing "It's a Wonderful World." Yet if I find any number of reasons to celebrate beauty, if I admit that even in this condition, my eye is drawn to the art of the body, in the larger cultural milieu I am apparently supposed to volunteer for the position of the grotesque, the monstrous, or for cultural satirist of the emperor's court. As a child of rural poverty, and now as disabled, I have found the economy of beauty quick to the tongue and, where the impulse to distribute moves garden goods or home-cooked meals or hospitality, quick to the hand. But culture's discourse moves awkwardly around me, a seeming Medusa-like threat, a contagion force of life's humiliations. And I have learned again likewise to patrol myself as just "ugly and stupid."

As I see it, social and economic exclusion of persons with disabilities—and also, I might add, of those with evident lower-class roots—has itself been strongly linked to "aesthetic anxiety,"[39] and that anxiety has been defined specifically, at least as related to disability, as a "lack of symmetry." Social fear, especially of the mutuality of influence, the cross-"contamination" of relational ontology, and a will to control hides itself within the attribution of symmetry as foundational to beauty. And would this not then prevent the coexistence of radical diverse morphologies of well-being, while also legitimating a certain social complacency?[40] Even then, or at the very least, legitimating an impediment to the path of empathy in the face of pain? Modernity's Berlin Wall established between pain and pleasure so shapes beauty as to decouple the human body as beautiful from its relation to fragility, corporeality, pain, the animal body, the call of the other—from the embrace of social flesh, in all its aesthetically pleasant and unpleasant dimensions—all of which "affect us against our will," as, ironically, Kant insisted beauty would.

Work in disabilities studies, especially in its coincidence with postcolonial theory, allows us to open up the symbolic economy that consciously attempts and rhetorically asserts its responsibility to secure the city, that does so through that increasing class polarization, "class" itself being an aesthetic affective designation. Disability—the mark of asymmetry, of disfiguration, of corporeal restriction and limitation—has been "the keystone in the edifice of bodily based inferiority rationales built up since the late eighteenth century."[41] But rather than prove out again the social exclusion of persons so categorized, disability theory here can help us stretch, maybe even breach, the Platonic, idealist relation to beauty that has been embedded in urban architecture and somatic expectation. To do so is to concur with by expanding upon the insight of theologian Alejandro Garcia-Rivera, who asserts that "only a cultural aesthetics which can face up to suffering, even find its aesthetic force" in suffering, "could adequately describe Hispanic and Latin American experience."[42] And it is to confront Western culture with the Romantic and eugenic notion of beauty that has come down to us in consumer capitalism and its contemporary mega-mall, the global city. After all, "The Kantian association of beauty with otherness"—the association of beauty with what "refuses human measure," with things that "assert . . . their own unique form," that remind a person that "other things exist beyond his/her control" and so pull one into "a plural universe"—did not, owing to National Socialism, survive World War Two.[43]

Disabilities theorist Tobin Siebers—with Kant well in mind and disability a lived experience—suggests rather that at least in these last two centuries, beauty has had a weakening relationship with the idealist attribute of symmetry, that beauty within the art world, even in the face of the eugenics practiced in the name of health over the past two centuries, has been increasingly limned with disability.[44] Tracing what he calls "disability aesthetics" by rehearsing the presence in art history of statuary such as the Venus de Milo, his claim is that "good art incorporates disability . . . works of art for which the argument of superiority is made tend to claim disability" ("Disability Aesthetics," 65). The beautiful "presents us with a view unconstrained by the powers that control modern subjectivity." Artworks surprise us with their "lack of mastery," and so "escape our control in order to be experienced as beautiful" (ibid., 39). Siebers arrives at his notion of "authentic" art by first assuming that aesthetics "posits the human body and its affective relation to other bodies as foundational to the appearance of the beautiful." In that vein, he concurs with Edgar Allan Poe, who claimed (contrary to Scarry's invocation of Platonic symmetry) that "there is no exquisite beauty . . . without some strangeness in the proportion."[45]

"Good art," in Siebers' sense of it, refuses to be defined by "harmony, bodily integrity and health"; it leaves behind idealism's doctrine of disinterestedness—the "ideal invented in the eighteenth century but very much alive today" that "separates the pleasures of art from . . . the body" and its underlying corporeal emotions ("Disability Aesthetics," 71; 63–64). An idealist will read Kant's claim that "beauty is disinterested" not as an invitation—as I might wish—to spiritual detachment (that is, as an offer of spaciousness to the presence and influence of otherness in a relationally entangled world),[46] but as an occasion for affective or emotional disarticulation, for objectification. Need one draw the connections that link this aesthetic commitment and the facial plane and somatic bearing of today's "imperial" images, especially within fashion photography, with the refusal of the public ballet of the sidewalk? Disinterestedness—disinterest resembling the elite demeanor of a body—disarticulates interdependence ("Disability Aesthetics," 63–67). In Siebers's essay, we have once again run up against that structure of exclusion that Zukin characterized as the aestheticization of fear. A distinct phobia swerves beauty into the path of disinterestedness, which is then hermeneutically and architecturally assumed. "To change life . . . we must first change space," urban sociologist Henri Lefebvre observed.[47] I would add, to change life, we must first change aesthetic beliefs.

Tragic Beauty

The history of "good" art, Siebers asserts, explicitly explores "the fragility of the human body" and in so doing "expands the spectrum of humanity that we will accept among us" ("Disability Aesthetics," 63, 64, 67). This thought echoes philosophers Gilles Deleuze and Felix Guattari's reading of Kant, for whom "the stiff regularity of geometric shapes" and "the functional symmetry of organic forms" was "ultimately boring."[48] Guattari consequently defines art as "an activity of unframing, of rupturing sense" so as to occasion "a reinvention of the subject itself."[49] "The beautiful's singularity means that it has an internal coherence which cannot be assessed in terms of a transcendent concept," Stephen O'Connell counsels us.[50] That global cities now protect the disinterested ideal by establishing increasing spatial insulation in the name of personal security suggests that an alternative practice of beauty, one incorporating "disability aesthetics," might articulate the political community of the global city otherwise. And that further, that tendency to reach for a transcendent concept as an anchor of beauty, if even of the city, must itself be aesthetically deconstructed.

RELIGIOUS DREAMS AND THE CITY

Changing our aesthetic beliefs about the world involves not only how we decorate and move in our own bodies, but what we imagine as good, habitable places. Today most of humanity in tracking ineffable mystery will not meet up with William Blake's tiger in "the forests of the night," but will have to make our way in the urban jungle—any number of us, within the particular ethos we now name global cities. Yet thinking the gleam of the tiger's eye within the urban jungles of global cities, the home of the majority of humanity in this century, presents theology with something of a conundrum. In fact, thinking the flash of transcendence within the landscape of any city presents theology, whether American transcendentalism or Christian theology, with several dilemmas. While transcendentalism tended to reify nature as a zone of uninterrupted, humanly uninhabited wilds, modern theology, in terms of Christian thought, expressly splits time from place, valorizing time—in terms of history, eschatology, and kairos—as the dimension of the sacred while a/voiding an epistemology of place, despite the Hebrew testament's emphasis upon the land as a central sacred unit.[51] Further, in terms of place, the city itself has been, as Susan Brooks Thistlethwaite observes, a religiously ambiguous zone for Christian theology.[52] Indeed the axial religions in their entirety, replete with a preference for the locus of transcendence at a lofty remove from the world, were born, philosopher Karl Jaspers tells us, among an ancient urban elite, who bemoaned the "seemingly insoluble problems of urbanization." At that time, Jaspers continues, urban rulers, lacking confidence in human social life and repudiating dependence on nature, allied themselves with the transcendental beyond.[53]

Cities consequently have been theologically engendered and debased—as, for example, the infamous Rome, "whore of Babylon" (Rev. 18) or, earlier, Sodom, the city of corruption (Gen. 13–19). Or, conversely, cities have been held before humanity as utopia. Think, for example, of the heavenly city of Jerusalem of Isaiah 60–62 and of Revelation 21, or Athens, the city of enlightenment, democracy, and reason. But such urban utopias as Athens have been infamously achieved, as any scholar of early democracy might well recall, by employing structures of exclusion. Athens ascribed citizenship only to propertied and free males. Comparably, philosopher Gilles Deleuze reads the apocalyptic vision of the New Jerusalem, its streets lined with precious stones, as an embodiment of panoptical oppression—a mimetic replay of Babylon's totalitarian regime, which has generated, as iterated within and through Christianity, a system of judgmental power; that is, "The New Jerusalem, with its wall and its great street of glass, is an architectural terror," owing to its pre-programmed "self-glorification" and its "installation of an ultimate judiciary and moral power." After all, "only those who are written in the Lamb's book of life" enter there.[54]

So the city—despite there being nothing else in human history so much a sign of our human drive towards the arts and sociality (or what Edward Soja calls *synoikismos*[55])—remains in religious thought either debased, or, like ancient Athens or envisioned Zion, inhabitable only through the practice of exclusion. Referred out of context to a transcendent elsewhere, the issues of urbanization, including human social life therein, have been marked as religiously intractable—a denigration that serves the urban ruling core who, "through economics of scarcity and political totalitarianism, seek to exploit the image of the city as fundamentally corrupt (and hence not redeemable)."[56]

Thinking cosmopolis as site of our "possible good"—as an energy nexus within which we must learn to live sustainably, including by evidencing human conviviality—might then equally be yoked to thinking transcendence or sacrality otherwise (here I use *transcendence* to mark that which we might reverence). At this point in our human history with the earth, it appears that we will find our way as a species on this planet, learning to walk "the beauty way"[57]—or not—within the spatial geography of cities. Our challenge will be to find reverence and meaning not only in the mountains and the outback, but within "the city of glass." We need to think transcendence as something more than a nature (as wild-ness) mysticism (to which we are prone in the Pacific Northwest), since this tends to situate ecological "protest/antism" in a righteous, if praxistically empty lament emphasizing the distance between a romanticized nature and a debased city. Comparably, we need a transcendence that can help us parse the global resource divide that cuts through the economic core of global cities. We need to know the pull of an ineffable beauty that might interrupt the economic overdetermination of global cities, a beauty that swerves the chic social posturing that celebrates the city, but only by excluding the underclass and the out-classed (often the regional agricultural and migrant workers on whom the city depends for food, one of the city's most necessary, if conspicuously overlooked, arteries[58]).

INTERIOR DESIGN

"The world in which we live is increasingly something of our own creation," Warren Magnusson reminds us, "and it is this feature, more than the presence of dense clumps of buildings, that makes urbanism as a way of life so different from what went before."[59] But if so, then we must become equally ethical artists of place, insists moral geographer Robert Sacks: "Place"—even as we interweave it with nature and nature's amplifying energies—"is something we construct. . . . Our place creation cannot only change reality, but also expand or contract it," can "enrich or impoverish reality." Sacks presents us with two criteria for place creation that resonate with Siebers's "disability aesthetics": "We should create places that expand our awareness of reality, and we should create places that increase the variety and complexity of reality."[60] "Places, like people," advises Sacks, can "specialize in virtues." And this ethical climate of a place "can affect our psychological condition and our political and economic relations," including whether or not we give into the self-interest bound up in capitalism today.[61]

At least some trajectories of Christian theology would include disability aesthetics and its relation to the fragility of flesh, because Christian theology has consistently yoked beauty not only to creation, but to cross. (Think of how the first chapter of Genesis with its refrain to beauty, "and God saw that it was good," was composed amid the geopolitical storm of postexilic life and its sufferings. Or think of the hymn "Beautiful Savior" and its awareness of the crucifixion of life.) These sites of beauty and suffering are not to be severed in their informing of one another, with cross as obvious evidence of the frayed beauty of earth and of a love willing passionately to persist with it. Beauty in Christian theology is not then an Arcadian romance, but points toward an existential exquisiteness of the great open in full view—a view nonetheless of suffering and pain.

In Christian aesthetics disability might even be the common mean, the norm: what happened to me happens to bodies in a lifetime. "Becoming flesh," as teachings on incarnation provoke us to do, might keep beauty true to sentience and undeterred by pain and fear of it. But that would mean that my porpoiselike, single-pod, undulating belly dance of mobility, my exotic bird dance performed with samurai-competency on sticks and resembling the martial art of jodo aikido, must be at least a candidate for beauty—and not automatically assigned to the category "grotesque." (Imagine what generosity that breaching of our culturally trained eye might open out!) "The embodied difference of beauty," Kant suggested, opens us to be moved against our own will, even so far as to renounce our way with it.[62] In this vein, feminist liberation theologian Ivone Gebara reminds us that "the beauty that will save us is, above all, not pretty."[63]

An intriguing resonance with Siebers's thought might be found within Augustine's description of beauty within the heavenly city, scholar of late antiquities Virginia Burrus advises. Assessing the broken and beloved bodies of the martyrs, Augustine's surmise of beauty is caught up in a paradox. Claiming that "not a hair of your head will perish," Augustine insists upon the resurrection of the body as restorative while yet equally insisting upon the beauty of the memorial wounds: "In the kingdom of God we want to see on their bodies the scars of the wounds which they suffered for Christ's name . . . For in those wounds there will be no deformity, but only dignity, and the beauty of their valour will shine out, a beauty in the body and yet not of the body" (*City of God* 22.19).[64] Of such ruminations,

Burrus concludes that for Augustine, "beauty lies precisely in the stigmatized, the marked, body—the body that is both lacking and excessive, but never simply 'whole.' It is in the stigma, Augustine suggests, that we perceive not just flesh but a 'life' and thus also that we perceive transcendence, or 'God.'"[65] Burrus further explains: "It is in the stigma of the other that there is disclosed a beauty—a superfluous, unnecessary beauty" that, as Augustine emphasizes, "draws us irresistibly into a spiral of desire and doxology. 'There we shall be still and see; we shall see and we shall love; we shall love and we shall praise.'"[66]

Aware of the fragility of evolutionary emergence, the process philosophy of Alfred North Whitehead likewise evoked beauty in terms resonant with Siebers's disability aesthetic: Because all beings are "brought into existence through . . . a movement of emergence, which involves and includes adventure and striving, overcoming," process philosophy asserts that "the truly beautiful is always . . . tragic." Indeed, for process philosophy, beauty is "nothing other, nothing less, nothing more than a disclosure of the divine activity" at the heart of the cosmos—that is, God more particularly as the "[l]ove [that] bears all things." For process theology "the world" has no ontological unity of its own; rather, what sympathetically holds in relationships that we call "world" (or "nature," or "chaosmos") is, in process terms, God. And God in God's consequent nature—that is, "God as influenced and affected by [the] creation"[67]—may be simply known as "tragic beauty."[68] In something like a Buddhist act of *tonglen*, God, the Empathic Heart of the chaosmos, breathes in so as to carry the pain, breathes out empathy.

And yet tragic beauty may be not so much a transcendence "out there" as a name for the locus of our calling. To name God "tragic beauty," to identify God with the beauty of the earth, has to do with our own practice of moving empathically through pain toward renewed love of the earth with eyes wide open. Christians empathically metabolize the fragility of existence, breathing—borrowing, as I will argue in the next chapter, the practice of tonglen—through pain a beauty other than that foreclosed and disarticulated by fear, breathing through the rigid security cordons of symmetry. Moving Deleuzean insights toward theological conversation, Roland Faber writes: "Aesthetic reality . . . indicates not something that exists but that . . . insists."[69] This holy "insistence" opens out an ethical wake the width of jazzlike improvisations; it leads us, as Catherine Keller puts it, "to decide for the most heterogeneous width of relations that I in my edgy fini-tude can embrace."[70]

When we assume a disability aesthetic that practices "ethical width" rather than exclusion, that aesthetic might draw up next to the insights of Jewish poet T. Carmi for ritual mobilization. Carmi writes of the proverbial heav-enly gates which, during the High Holy Days of Yom Kippur, are opened their widest. These wide-open gates, the image of the width of God's mercy and of the welcome extended to bodies in the heavenly city of Jerusalem, symbolically link transcendence to our practice of place, for example, "city gates." Further, we might imagine this as embodied spiritual practice, since *gates of heaven* is, a practitioner instructed me, another name for the heart chakra, which can slam shut without a way to metabolize fear:

> The day is fading.
> The gate is swinging shut.
> Oh, what a terrible cry!
> Can't you hear it?
> Open it! Open it!
> Someone is trapped in the gate.[71]

If beauty were not so much about enforcing symmetry as welcoming (in the words of Charles Darwin) "endless forms most beautiful,"[72] we would be well on our way to cosmopolis, that dream of a mongrel city.[73]

Breathing through the Pain: Engaging the Cross as *Tonglen*, Taking to the Streets as Mendicants

> The asymmetrical forgetting of generosity at the foundation of social injustice depends on the asymmetrical evaluation of different bodies.
>
> —ROSLYN DIPROSE, *Corporeal Generosity*

China Mieville, in his recent novel *The City and the City* (2009), imagines a city split by something of a demilitarized zone. While the inhabitants of these cities flow through each other, while the cities inhabit shared space, persons in Beszel and Ul Qoma each have their own language, gestures— indeed their own maps of the city, their own distinct names for spatially identical zones; and, most intriguingly, they have learned a way of "unseeing" each other. The DMZ has, in other words, been articulated by distinguishing persons' speech, their body carriage, their enculturation of the body, their psyche. If citizens of one side should attempt to "cross," to acknowledge lives from the other side, officers of "the Breach" step in to reenforce their unseeing. It is a science fiction novel, one says; one wants this vision of the city to be a dystopic warning (playing as it does between impulses of rabid nationalism versus unificationist policies within cities, as powers of the nation-states wane). Or, at the least, let it be about Berlin of twenty years ago . . . or Jerusalem.

Insight wakes slowly through the miasmic fog of liberal disbelief: We already live this split city. For "[t]he city exists as a series of doubles. . . . We discover that inside the city there is always another city."[1]

To inhabit the city, any city of the West, at least, assumes adopting practices of unseeing. Don't meet the eyes of the stranger on the street, this country kid was told when moving to the Mini Apple (Minneapolis). Don't stare, a mother warns her child, biting out her warning between clenched jaws as the child drags against the tether of her arm, trying to assess the morphological difference I pose to human community. Don't look: It's a message we've all learned—to avoid the body sleeping in the doorway, on the heating grate. Well-trained, unseeing indifference: It's said to be a mode of survival, necessary for life in the city.[2]

Exiting my favorite bookstore, I pull on my cloak of invisibility. His face turns toward mine seeking the recognition I'm trying to withhold. He's looking for change, and something about the juxtaposition of our mutually abject bodies throws us for a blink of a second into shared territory. I catch his eyes, then something more, which forces me to look away: The cartilage of the tip of his nose has been burned off, is encrusted with sores from snorting. My inability to hold his flesh in loving mindfulness, given our shared territory, tears through me, a body that can go breach, that can pretend to both sides of the divide between us. In his appeal for recognition and my failure, I'm cross-examined: Should persons religious find comfort in this casual survival wisdom, this habituated indifference? For whom is it urban survival wisdom? From what does indifference shield me . . . or what, when I'm on the other side of the divide, does it avoid in me?

The Tale of Two Cities

This traumatic divide within today's global cities, these "glam" cities of culture, pivots upon the refusal to metabolize pain—"disability" being both a trope and the lived condition thereof.[3] *Disability* names a class of refus/al. "Disability subjection," Susan Schweik reminds us, "is deployed and embedded, ideologically and structurally, in classed . . . capitalist social relations" such that "in the history of begging, as (almost) everywhere, 'disability history' and 'poor people's history' profoundly intertwine."[4] As philosopher Roslyn Diprose observes, "The asymmetrical forgetting of generosity at the foundations of social injustice depends on the asymmetrical evaluation of different bodies."[5]

Such divides between "the city and the city" (Mieville) form around visceral, visual abjection—not simply as the effects of individual poverty and addiction. Raw statistics indicating that up to 85 percent of homeless persons have been categorized as "disabled" or have "chronic health problems" support this claim.[6] Take Chris Hedges's description of Camden, New Jersey, known as "the second most dangerous city in America": "Camden is where those discarded as human refuse are dumped, along with the physical refuse of postindustrial America."[7] As a response to the aestheticization of fear, disability abjection is a psychic aversion or revulsion to bodies presumed to be in pain, held as much in metaphysics as in the psychotheology or psychocosmology of an individual who holds his/her breath, who convulses in the somatoscape of pain.[8]

Freud—and the Western world after him—have assumed that "pleasure is opposed to pain, that only gratification is pleasurable."[9] But "suffering," explains neurologist Antonio Damasio, is meant to "put us on notice" that not all is well with the world. Human survival, Damasio continues, depends upon sensitivity to pain: "Suffering offers us the best protection for survival, since it increases the probability that individuals will heed pain signals and act to avert their source or correct their consequences. . . . It is difficult to imagine that individuals and societies governed by the seeking of pleasure, as much as or more so than by the avoidance of pain, can survive at all."[10] With no God any longer demanding "good Samaritan" obligations and maybe only a vague common sense encouraging such, even Christianity seems to have jettisoned suffering in the work of incarnating love and creating justice, despite taking the body in pain as its central icon—that is, the body of Jesus, the imperial torture victim; and along with suffering Christians seem to have jettisoned meditative practices for working as pain bearers.[11]

Breathing through Pain: Christology and Tonglen

Given Western urban patterns of withholding generosity when confronted by the abject body,[12] I propose rethinking Christology as a practice inter-

polated through Buddhist *tonglen*, a meditative practice for extending loving kindness through the aversions of fear and pain. "To be a truly just
society," theorist David Morris concludes, we need "to construct a new
understanding of pain: an understanding that did not disavow but rather
accepted and transformed the tendency in pain to isolate the individual."[13]
Infusing Christian imagery with the meditative breath practices and affective wisdom of tonglen can do that. Tonglen reworks habits of aversion and
thereby capacitates love of the flesh by refusing the pain/pleasure divide.[14]
Its practices are proximate enough to Christianity's own historic deployment of "Jesus as a grotesque"[15] and Luther's recovery of an atonement
theory called "the sweet exchange" that these can be regenerated for our
urban situation. In this way, Christians as well as other cosmopolitans can
be invited to live as the medieval seculars did, but in a postmodern world,
with an "attitude of mendicancy" interruptive of the aesthetic circuits of
capitalism on city streets.[16] As an alternative to steely, cold indifference,
inhabitants of the cosmopolis can be invited to recuperate pain for moral,
ethical affective insight. Or to put it bluntly: I'm drawn to rethink "vicarious" or "substitutionary atonement" as a way to retrain cosmopolitan psyches
toward bodies that suffer, that are in pain.

*It was all rather unprofessional, I suppose. Evan was young—a surgical resi-
dent from Columbia Presbyterian—and something had shaken him awake. He'd
been sleeping in the residents' on-call room when the moment before his phone rang
he startled awake—with just an impression of something looming. He was the first
surgeon on the scene, the first to recognize that the thirty-seven-year-old woman
in good health with a sprained ankle was dying, that my left leg was already dead,
that the absence of a spike in temperature—and the actual depression in body
temperature—meant not well-being, but death. For three days as I lay between
death and life (my partner juggling attention to me with care of our then five-
year-old), Evan slept beside me, pulling chairs and cots next to my bed in the ICU,
holding my hand. When finally I was conscious enough to register visual impres-
sions, I didn't see him as much as recognize him among a group of five surgeons
and additional personnel in the operating room. I know I know him; I feel the energy
between us. I call him by a look; he's the one I want for comfort, for reassurance.
He's the one who carries my nightmares—yes, literally. Having been so close, the
psychic intimacy does not shut down after three days, when his colleagues interrupt
his watch and send him home to New York City. That's when it begins: He wakes*

with my nightmares, the nightmares that if I fall asleep again I will this time lose the other leg. Before he starts his shift, he will reach under the covers to check the temperature of my right foot. Sometimes he will drive back to the hospital from New York City, because he can't sleep. It's our deal: He shakes with my terror just so that I can eke out a few more bytes of energy to stave off the massive infection.

This chapter is owed to those, like Evan, who carried me through trauma, to persons who dared to step out of their skins and carry my life: Enid, the nursing assistant, who cradled my head at night and sang lullabies; Hope, my primary care nurse; and David and Asher, who were my transports to all seventeen surgeries. Asher, a skinhead, and David, a recent Israeli immigrant, decided that their cooperative relationship was what was keeping me alive against horrendous odds. Or at least their relationship just *might be* keeping me alive, and so they chose not to jinx it. They carefully scanned the surgery roster, called each other and juggled schedules to stay beside me—not just during the first three critical, in-hospital months with fourteen surgeries, but with several post-trauma resections over the next nine months. Then there was Jasmine, a nurse, whose eye gaze carried me through a surgical procedure that would otherwise have doused me with yet more amnesia-laden anesthesia, a surgery the preparation for which would have cost me nutritionally at a point when I was protein malnourished. These individuals carried my pain in ways far beyond what their jobs required. They taught me, each in his or her own unique way, "vicarious atonement"—that we can answer the call to shoulder the pain of and with another human. They caught my attention because this is not the story we tell publicly about pain, but it could be.

I am consequently attempting to rethink what it might mean to "believ[e] in the world" (as Deleuze puts it) or "love the world as God has loved it" (as Christianity has asserted) as a call to carry the pain of the other, to bear pain with the other—hence, the attitude of mendicancy. Inasmuch as the interpolation of Christology with and through Tibetan Buddhist tonglen might also move us beyond the need to parse Christian theology along the theism/nontheism divide, I am hoping to open out a kind of lively, improvisational mendicant catholicity for a devoted, urban life. Spirituality, asserts Philip Sheldrake, is "not confined to the inner life of the Christian community but includes the practice of *everyday* living in the heart of the world of human places."[17] Elsewhere he writes, "The meaning and future of human cities is one of the most critical spiritual, not simply social, economic or planning issues of our time."[18]

Take as a genealogical case study of living with and bearing the pain of the other—of the enfolding embrace of social flesh—the *mendicant*, a term that, etymologically, roots itself in the morphology of disability, that is, "physical defect," and the social expectation for such a person's livelihood by resort to begging, a practice now unwelcome in the city, on the street.[19] Religious historian Stephen Munzer observes that in Christianity, triadic bonds linking beggar, God, and almsgiver were once stronger than they are now. "In the high Middle Ages, the . . . poor begged in trust and hope that God, through others, would aid them. At the same time, those who responded to these pleas for aid drew their justification from the gospels and from the traditions of the church. . . . Because God was understood to bless both the begging and the giving . . . a bond existed between mendicant and almsgiver." To underline this point, Munzer adds: "Indeed each had something to offer. The almsgiver offered material aid and, in turn, received spiritual benefits . . . a blessing from the poor beggar."[20] The mendicant in this way challenged the instantiation of mere economic value; s/he had something more valuable to give than the alms received—blessing.

The religious practice of austerity, of poverty (as within monasticism) might well have developed as imitative of, if not self-identical with, the practice of the mendicants, with those who, because of physical challenges, resorted to begging. Families often tithed disabled persons to the church. (Some historians suggest that Hildegard von Bingen, for example, may have been so tithed.) This is obviously not to argue that persons disabled continue to be reduced to begging; rather, I wish to wake us to the loss of this sheath of religious respect, even authority, that had previously been afforded bodies in pain, a respect and authority that Orientalism now confers on the crimson-robed monks who have begun walking my Kitsilano neighborhood, placing them in a completely different category from the disabled and homeless sleeping next to buildings and in parks.[21] They are seen as figures purporting transformative wisdom. In the ruin of God and with monastics today blissfully distinguished from suffering bodies, this "neighbor love" for "mendicants" clearly must be worked out anew. This seems especially true in the Pacific Northwest, where North American Christendom first folded under, where the modern flight from relational bonds coincides with the invitation to do something entirely new. Here any form of "altruism"—let alone intimacy with pain—has difficulty gaining traction.[22]

Protestant Spiritual Anthropology and Anesthetization by Metaphysics

In global cities, this avoidance of altruism and intimacy with pain, too, is a consequence of the aestheticization of fear, an avoidance that both metaphysics and religion have abetted. In the article "Suffering in Theory," Cleo McNelly Kearns has said, "Suffering is in some respects highly contagious, and it can at times be caught, so to speak, simply by entering its sphere" (61). And Margrit Shildrick observes, "It is above all the lack or loss of control that provokes anxiety, and the association with any body that exemplifies that quality is fraught with danger."[23] And yet, she continues, "It is not so much that the body of the other is horrifying in and of itself (though it may be), but that it will enter into the space of my own body and effect the very transformations that would disturb my claim to autonomous selfhood." That the gravitous affect of pain seeps through tissue makes flesh simply "dreadful." In the end, "a mere phenomenological understanding of our embodied subjectivity"—as interflesh, as shared, "as dependent on an interface with a world of others mediated through the senses," does not necessarily mitigate that anxiety.[24] While ontological claims that we are only ever "given over" to one another,[25] that we "interare," as Thich Nhat Hanh puts it, can be important, these will not necessarily mitigate our fear of the vulnerability of flesh, for the "contagious quality of suffering" remains to "trouble our movement toward the sufferer" (Kearns, "Suffering in Theory," 61).

Hyped with fear, including the fear of coming to touch upon pain, disease, and suffering, how do we not simply retreat to the protection of kin and kind, as if these were even available to us amidst globalization as urbanization?[26] Traditionally, religions have considered pain to be infinitely shareable, and have worked with pain as something like a tool for the transformation of self and world, writes religious scholar Ariel Glucklich. "In fact," Glucklich observes in *Sacred Pain: Hurting the Body for the Sake of the Soul*, "the phenomenon of shared pain is extremely pervasive" among religions, and within Christianity particularly (30). Among considerations of other religious paths, he points to how "the vicarious property of physical suffering stands at the center of Christian life," though reminding us that "the shared-pain model transcends Christology and mysticism" (28–29, 32).[27]

However, Western culture and especially Protestantism have turned away from the spiritual and psychological value of shared pain and vicarious suffering. "Our culture—the modern, western, industrial, technological world—has succeeded in persuading us that pain is simply and entirely a medical problem" to be redressed by each individual with his/her professionals, yet it is "less our pain than our culture . . . that draws us irresistibly toward the medicine cabinet," cultural theorist David Morris prods. "Our biochemistry is inextricably bound up with personal and cultural meanings that we carve out of pain," he continues, such that pain arrives only ever "shaped or modified by . . . specific human cultures." "Pain," he concludes, "is never the sole creation of our anatomy and physiology. It emerges only at the intersection of bodies, minds and cultures."[28] That *cultural* contour of pain we find difficult to understand, amidst our determined individualism and materialism. In other words, "pain" is inherently a symptom of our always already socially shared flesh, a symptom demanding interpretation of our shared life, even while we assiduously avoid others we projectively presume to be in pain.

Christians, too, have been caught up in capitalism's eugenic, Romantic ethos. Protestants have tended to resent those who intrude on the neutrality of external space, to resent especially "the visibility of indecent pain," sociologist Richard Sennett observes. In *The Conscience of the Eye: The Social Life of Cities*, he argues that even the "impersonal milieu," the "blandness" or "neutrality" of our modern cities is owed to the sense of human subjectivity released by the Protestant Reformation—of a human who carries "the essence of self and God" *internally* while libidinally neutralizing the body along the skin line and, by extension, neutralizing the outside world: "One can deal with the outside in purely instrumental, manipulative terms, since nothing outside 'really' matters" (46).[29] Obsessed with inner spiritual struggle, Sennett argues, the Protestant wishes the outside world to be neutral, placid, effaced. "Obsessive inner struggle" leaves the self dispositioned with "a deep hostility toward the needs of others," with "a resentment of their very presence." "This hostility marks now the way the homeless or mentally disturbed are seen on the streets; they are resented because they . . . are visible. The very sight of their need is an intrusion upon the self" (45). Ethically speaking, Protestants have detached their cultural values from their sentient interface and turned "value" or worth into a "floating mental operation" (xi). So at the root of our/Protestant ineptitude in the street ballet of the good city sidewalk, Sennett surmises, is Christian, especially Protestant, spirituality or spiritual anthropology. This residue of Protestantism tends to inform the very nature of cosmopolitanism still.

The Protestant desire for a neutral outside, a pain-free world, also no doubt reflects a Western metaphysics that refuses pain any sense of reality, any meaningful role in the life of an individual or culture—except perhaps as personally torturous so as to produce repentance, self-surrender (Sennett, *Conscience of the Eye*, 42, 45–46). In classic Christian tradition, substitutionary or vicarious atonement—the belief that Jesus died in our place, for our guilt, to satisfy the debt of our sins against God's honor—has presumed to rescue persons, by stoic repression here and postponement to an afterlife, from this broken world of transience, finitude, and mortality into the absolutely real of eternity, where there will be, presumably, no tears, no death. Doctrines of this ilk make pain an indication of sin, of moral failure, and give evidence of a power-truth regime beyond this world. In other words, they place authority beyond suspicion, but endorse sociopolitical normativity and the torturous individualization of pain.

A metaphysics that refuses to metabolize pain, as Sennett points out, shows through our annoyance with all that would dare interrupt our aesthetic cityscape. But "pain," philosopher Gianni Vattimo insists, "is the very essence of metaphysics." Again, in his words, "there is no metaphysics except the metaphysics of pain." That is, metaphysics is the way we have dealt with pain in the West. "The Hegelian dialectic is probably the furthest point reached by the western metaphysics of pain," he notes. "It emphatically asserts that 'reality' is positive despite our mode of perceiving it; the fact that we suffer indicates not that there is something 'amiss' in

Being, only that we are mistaken to think that there is." Vattimo adds that this essentially Christian, Hegelian metaphysics "informs and conditions many of the practical and medical ways of treating pain" today—for example, as private (confessional) relations with a physician, how much pain-killer will be administered, the tendency to treat depression with pharmaceutical rather than analytic therapy, and so on.[30] "The battle against pain . . . has only one limit," Vattimo concludes,

> and that is solidarity with others, the assumption of our own finitude that commands us not to yield to hubris and not to become overbearing, as do those who absolutize themselves and so lay themselves open to all the violent implications of metaphysics, including resentment at not being immortal and the particular intensity with which pain of any kind afflicts them—for to them it can only appear to be something mysteriously directed at them by an inscrutable and baleful power.[31]

If our work is to live with pain in such a way that it does not sever or cut insurmountable chasms through the city but might support the emergence of social flesh,[32] Christian practice is challenged to move beyond these existentialist scenarios.

In the same way that Sennett challenged Protestants' tendency to neutralize the street ballet, Gilles Deleuze has reproached the philosopher Immanuel Kant "for granting priority to harmonious recognition over perplexing feelings of intensities" which equally seems to me like the attitude of cosmopolitans toward bodies bearing the dominant representation of "in pain." Avoiding perplexing feelings derives from a Romantic inclination toward the world, like that developed by Hegel. "For Deleuze, [Kant's] transcendental subjectivity"—the humanist figural complement to that Romantic inclination—"functions always as repression of the world of intensities." The modernist subject has had no way to navigate the tide of feelings, especially nonharmonious, disjunct, or agonistic affective torques. To become ethically responsive to pain and ethically creative of justice and the civic commons, we need to find some navigational mechanism, some pedagogy, for navigating "the world of intensities." On the other hand, just as "disease" became the dread name of the anxiety of mutual influence on nineteenth-century streets, as the fear of contagion and the contagion of fear became part of the urban experience, perhaps what scares us most as

we move through urban streets today is the "creative open-endedness toward new constellations" to which living at the level of affective intensity
would also thereby open us.[33]

Invocations of "Spirit," whether through energetic monisms, like that at
play in Hegelian idealism, or in Cartesian dualism, have tended heretofore
to generate a certain sociocultural Teflon around the flesh. "Spirit," in the
self-crafting project of contemporary spirit/ualities, often stands in for
"higher consciousness," "a higher, more perfect, decontaminated flesh, a
flesh that has been insulated against the possibility of being itself consumed."[34] Whether by evocation of Spirit, in this way, or by lament of an
ontologically "broken" world, we induce a psychoneural circuit of aversion
to suffering and pain in the world around us. Bluntly, theodicy—cathection
to a good, to a God, beyond the world—pushes suffering into rationalization, rather than into practices that enable us to bear it.[35] Because metaphysics treats all pain and suffering as oppression, as an offense against life,
persons push to the margins bodies that have been culturally freighted
with pain.[36] Thus, resort to either theodicy or metaphysics anesthetizes
pain so as to stabilize our anxious aversion to flesh. Consequently, religions
can depart from metaphysics (as poststructuralist scholars have counseled)
only if they differently calibrate pain.[37]

Curiously, the metaphysics by which this steeling of Spirit against flesh
has transpired has been theologically and philosophically as well as widely,
publicly, and popularly discredited since the time of Nietzsche. Nietzsche
"aroused moral and aesthetic revulsion towards the notion of God" that
had at least until his time underwritten "the whole system of Christian
life,"[38] but this metaphysical story of pain, whereby God somewhat sadisti-
cally enjoyed either the crucifixion of his own Son or the punitive pain laid
upon human existence, or both, also has been challenged by simple popu-
list disaffection, as well as by theistically invested reconstructions by philosophers such as Franz Rosenzweig, political theologians such as Jurgen
Moltmann and Dorothee Soelle, and first-generation and second-generation
feminist theologians. Such a metaphysics was redrafted in Dietrich Bonhoeffer's "religionless religion," which insisted, at the same time, that we
overcome the childish need not to suffer. Bonhoeffer, in fact, suggested
that the Christian is a pain bearer—one who stands beside God in God's
hour of need.[39] Jewish philosopher Emmanuel Levinas likewise has insisted

that "the project of explaining and justifying suffering in this world by a metaphysical order, a good beyond the world with an order that compensates for suffering, is"—consequent to the Holocaust, the Gulag, Hiroshima, and Cambodia—"impossible."[40]

But if so, why this avoidance of another in pain among Christians and other cosmopolitans? No system of thought has been thoroughly deconstructed, theologian Amy Hollywood seems to suggest through her reading of Judith Butler, until the choreography of the body itself has been redirected.[41] In other words, a metaphysics is never simply ideationally held, but is always psychosocially carried. Metaphysics, as Rosenzweig noted, "deals with suffering by disregarding the particularity of the sufferer."[42] So idealist metaphysics has been lived as a "protective" hardness, a contracture of the heart or a holding of the breath, including the construal of the self as interiority, often especially through the legitimizing of "spirituality."

Given such involution, we no longer view the body on the street as a scene of demand for giving and receiving acknowledgement. Commenting on the thought of Deleuze and Guattari, Ian Buchanan has noted,

> The involuted body cannot do anything, but expand the gap between itself and its capabilities, because capabilities are lines leading outward from the body and what it is doing is drawing everything inward. An irrevocable hardening takes place. . . . To be active one must . . . aspire to increase the affects of the body. The more ways the body can be affected, the more force it has.[43]

To deconstruct metaphysics requires some form of practice to deal affectively with the anxiety that otherwise is reinvigorated when the subjective Teflon supplied by metaphysics is worn away. It requires some way of navigating the responsibility to think ethically in the presence of the other, to generate "the formation of new compounds."[44] It requires us, as Levinas suspected, to deal differently with the pain of the neighbor: "When theodicy and its master narrative becomes impossible, we discover that the justification of my neighbor's suffering is a scandal: perhaps the more profound violence," Levinas writes.[45] In other words, razing the scaffolds of rationalization within metaphysics and theodicy requires, in the end, just this question: How do we carry our neighbor's pain? "Who finally takes on the suffering of others," Levinas asks, "if not the being who says 'me'?"[46]

If we are to move beyond metaphysical rationalizations for "the asymmetrical evaluation of different bodies" and our consequent subjective indifference, how might we—Christians, whether theists or not, as well as cosmopolitans more generally—come to bear with one another in cultural labor and procreative justice this condition of life, our social flesh? Hermann Cohen, the teacher of mid-twentieth-century Jewish philosopher Franz Rosenzweig, pointed toward the need to rethink poverty, what he called "the essential form of human suffering," which has been, I would remind us, historically virtually synonymous with disability. Poverty, Cohen contended, is the site where the "physicality of pain is refracted through sociality," thus constituting "the problem that religion must always face."[47] Religion must prevent this form of social suffering from being effaced from humanity's affective consciousness.[48] Because the human is human only when "in and for one another," poverty, Cohen insisted, is *an actual feeling.*" That is, it must never be, for religious persons particularly, merely a social fact, a statistic, a category, a rational negotiation. Poverty, Cohen goes on to say, "is laid hold of and must be grasped *as a prevalent fact of consciousness,* as one that fills the whole human consciousness and has a role in determining all other proceedings and activities."[49] If we humans, who are human only insomuch as we belong to one another, cannot feel the pain of poverty pressing upon our own consciousness, we have already, in Cohen's terms, evacuated our religious dimension.

The failure of religion is a failure of social feeling for the human family, because religion, Cohen implies, is itself the feeling of and for kindred souls. In his words, "only social suffering is a spiritual suffering."[50] Where turned over to statistics, poverty is rationalized, and humanity compounds suffering by the failure to engage religious consciousness, to practice fellow feeling. In a sense, Cohen points to the lie of the objectification and rationalization of the other, here "the poor," also "the disabled," and points toward the conviction wherein Judaism and Christianity speak of humanity's kinship by underscoring this as an aspect of active, affective consciousness. Buddhism speaks likewise of interdependent co-arising—which is not something only philosophically touted, but equally cultivated in the mindful body. Yet (dare one say it here?) North Americans have been, in the past half century, more anesthetized against the burdens of pain in others, than mindful of them.[51] How can we learn to grasp suffering as a fact of consciousness and practice the economy of obligation, the relational politics, the vulnerable communion of the flesh? How can we, bottle-fed on idealism, live with passionate attachment in a less than ideal world? How will we live among bodies with whom we do not always share taste, smell, political opinion, or religious ideology, with whom we do not share knowing, psychic or cultural, resonance?

"The Pain of God": Social Flesh and Bodily Practices

Theology has responded to such questions posed by this Western cultural phase of the mid-twentieth century and after with theologies of "the pain of God," among which is counted Dorothee Soelle's classic text, *Suffering* (1975). In Christian theology "the idea that God cannot suffer, accepted virtually as axiomatic in Christian theology from the early Greek Fathers until the nineteenth century," was in the twentieth century "progressively abandoned."[52] The "pain of God" theologies explicitly attempted to reverse the anesthetization, this affective somnambulance, of Western culture, but they arrived just after the discrediting of "God"—after the human atrocities of the Holocaust and Hiroshima had discredited any proposals for an all-determining God, a critique that these pain of God theologies also assumed. Likewise, the emergence of these theologies of the pain of God coincided with the valorization of science, its agenda to end suffering as we've known it, to save us even the pain of labor—hence, "labor-saving technologies." So although the theology of the pain of God came to the fore within North America and Northern Europe during the 1960s to 1980s, these theologies, including the radical "death of God" theologies, never became normative for Christian communities. In the process of ignoring the pain of God, we walked away, I fear, from our souls, our affective feeling of kinship with one another, contributing to the emergence of what Julia Kristeva has called "a new malady of the soul";[53] for as Blaise Pascal suggested, "the greatest sickness is insensibility."[54] Since our world situation seems to require a pedagogy for pain, we need to assess how the theology of the pain of God proposed to heal metaphysical anestheticization.

SOELLE'S PRACTICE FOR TAKING LEAVE OF NARCISSISTIC HOPE

Dorothee Soelle's *Suffering* forwarded a theology of the pain of God in and for Western middle-class persons, among whom were Christians who had been characterized as "the presence of absence"[55] during the Holocaust and then again during the strafing and bombing of Vietnam. In her later work, *The Silent Cry: Mysticism and Resistance* (2001), Soelle articulates her lifelong cosmological stance, which she identifies as "mysticism." Mysticism, in her view, simply lifts the experiences that all religious teaching addresses (whether liberation, peace, faith, redemption) "out of the abstractness of religious doctrine and frees them for feeling, experience, and certainty." For Soelle, in other words, *mysticism* appears to refer to the restoration of an *affective* relation of religious faith to all experience—what we might to-day call a practice-able path; *mysticism* names her refusal to pivot faith upon what Luther sought to secure for himself, an "objective foundation," *sola scriptura*, which she claims freezes passion, feeling (*Silent Cry*, 86). She ex-plains: "In the self-imposed modesty" of "intellectual acceptance, which then passes for 'belief'" and "which has ecclesial sanction and imposes a prohibition on the mystical self," the feeling self, "there lurks, perhaps one of the difficulties central to modern Protestantism. Its defensive stance to-ward the emotions turns the enormously fetishized 'faith' into a nonexis-tential category; that is, into something essentially made-up, 'fictional, contrived.'" And she concludes, "The repulsion of experience, as well as the fear of engaging it, represents a kind of spiritual suicide" (ibid., 18). In re-prising an affectively lively faith, she writes appreciatively of Thomas Muntzer's Counter-Reformation aspiration "that people become free from fear": "For the sake of the fear of God, they are to let go of the fear of crea-tures that rules in all of us. . . . The worst fear of creatures is the fear of the authorities wherein people are kept dependent. Imprisoned in it, people cannot fear God. They remain locked in worries for their naked existence and lose their relationship to God over their fear of humans" (Soelle, *Suf-fering*, 87). Soelle positions faith in relation to what we might today call a mindful interface with daily life.

In a similar vein, Soelle reads the Christian gospels as training lessons for the passions: "The passion narratives are not objective accounts; rather they were written for our instruction. We recognize in them our opportu-

nities to relate ourselves to the one enduring the blows and our own
opportunities to suffer in a human way" (*Suffering*, 139).

Contrary to the way in which liberal Christianities today continue along
the recuperative "historical Jesus" trajectory, Soelle wrote that "as pure
history the story about Jesus has no overarching significance." In fact, she
notes that making "a heroic figure out of Jesus" can all too easily sustain
"the apathy-ideal" (*Suffering*, 82).[56] The passion accounts are "only understood and appropriated when [their] continuation is understood" and appropriated within our own lives, for "the truth of the passion account
is that Jesus' experience . . . is not . . . unique." It "can befall anyone" (ibid.,
139, 82). Indeed, quite contrary to the mid-twentieth-century mood prevailing when she wrote, Soelle insisted that "even the smoothest life one
can imagine" must come to accept some measure of pain without casting
it into fatalism. With poetic insight, she reminded us that "[t]he way from
Gethsemane to Golgatha is a taking leave of narcissistic hope" (ibid., 88–
89, 147). Contrary to modern fantasies, love of the world requires a pedagogy for pain. That's what the pain of God theologies, epitomized here by
Soelle, seemed to propose: "The prerequisite for acceptance" of reality "is a
deeper love . . . a love that avoids placing conditions on reality," since "God
is the symbol for our unending capacity to love." Love for the world, for life,
so cultivated, pulses, touches, tones, and informs any and every affliction
such that even "the affirmation of suffering is part of the great yes to life as
a whole and not, as it sometimes can appear, the sole and decisive affirmation behind which the affirmation of life disappears entirely" (ibid., 92, 108).

The passion accounts begin a process of transference for us whereby
loving "the God who is in pain," standing by God in God's hour of need,
grief, or suffering, we begin to open ourselves to feel with the world, to
love the world in the reality of its extremes, its finitude and fallibleness. In
this way, in Soelle's words, "suffering becomes our passion, in the double
sense of that word." She explains: Each "act of suffering is an exercise. . . .
We work with the suffering. We perceive, we express ourselves, we
weep. . . . Nothing can be learned from suffering unless it is worked
through" (*Suffering*, 25–26). And we thereby begin to grow the depth of self
some religious persons have called "the soul." Having, through transference, lovingly fallen for and felt with a "God in pain"—in the words of
Marcella Althaus-Reid, for a "Jesus born of an untouchable woman" and

hence constituting something of "a waste-God or a contaminated Messiah"—results in a different cultural economy of tact or touch, of propriety and property, given that "an economy is a reflection of human exchanges and affections and the law or discipline of these exchanges."[57] Theologies of the pain of God address the anesthetized, saving us by restoring us to feeling with the world. In other words, theologies of the pain of God will not keep us "clean and proper," since "the divine economy is alternative to the path of industry, production."[58] Then again, "those who are free from suffering" or "who are incapable of suffering" do not tend to "work on the abolition of social conditions which of necessity produce suffering," Soelle observes, and she concludes: "Only those who themselves are suffering will work for the abolition of conditions under which people are exposed to senseless, patently unnecessary suffering" (Soelle, *Suffering*, 2–3).

Ironically, far from handing us a giant eraser for pain, as modernity itself promised, pain of God theologies liberate life by teaching the anesthetized to suffer. For Soelle, the only way we might become the presence of those who love the world enough to protest injustice would be by learning to suffer—quite a challenging counter-trajectory to the modernist ethos, given the titillating technological and economic promises of "a better life."

While I share Soelle's sensibility, I will be working toward a more consciously devoted meditative practice for embracing social flesh by constructively working between Christian passions and Buddhist tonglen. Learning to suffer is not easy, given the aestheticization of fear and the anesthetization of pain by everything from religion and metaphysics to medical technology. If our own better life today is yoked to regenerating social flesh, beginning with healing the divide between "the city and the city," doing so will require learning how to move through fear and pain, including its contagion, so as to live beyond the enclosure of relations to kin and kind. We need a discerning way to work with pain—as moral compass, as survival wisdom, to lift new subjectivities into the practice of justice.

"ATTACHING OURSELVES TO THE ALL"

Yet metaphysical anesthetization has not been unique to Christianity and remains as contemporary as it has been classic. For example, in his two most popular books, *The Power of Now: A Guide to Spiritual Enlightenment* (1999) and *A New Earth: Awakening to Your Life's Purpose* (2005), Eckhart Tolle, a popular spiritual guru, can be heard to endorse just such an affective disconnect with pain when encouraging persons to "rise above" the "pain-body" (*Power of Now*, 21).[59] Tolle, like many these days, proceeds in search of a spiritual path that feels, phenomenologically speaking, authentic—that is, that is feelingfully at home with the body in the world, rather than being abstractly rational and belief-oriented. He reads broadly across multiple wisdom traditions (Buddhism, Taoism, Christian mysticism, and Western philosophy) and synthesizes and repackages what he calls "perennial" spiritual wisdom—"that one timeless spiritual teaching, the essence of all religions" (ibid., 10).[60] What he carves out has been called "an inquisitive phenomenology of consciousness" that bears great resemblance to Hinduism and Buddhism.[61]

Yet Tolle's claims rely upon several assumptions and inferences that appear problematically to play into—rather than to resist—the metaphysical project of the West and its avoidance of persons in pain. Tolle has created a metaphysics that precludes the vulnerabilities of flesh.[62] He offers, for example, that "as there are no problems in the Now, there is no illness either." Indeed, "the world is only a reflection" (*Power of Now*, 217). When he claims that right thinking might banish aging (ibid., 102), one begins to suspect a kind of infinitizing of consciousness that overwhelms the here and now.

By contrast, rather than urge one to "rise above" the pain-body, twentieth-century philosopher Simone Weil took the world itself as the orientation for her lived "self": "We should identify ourselves with the universe itself. . . . Let the whole universe be for me, in relation to my body, what the stick of a blind man is in relation to his hand. His sensibility really no longer resides in his hand, but at the end of the stick."[63] Rather than ascetic inurement or transcendence, Weil proposes an immanentalist passage through the world that moves alongside and through the abjection of bodies in pain.[64]

In both of his books,[65] "Tolle is asking and answering the question of why the human race always gives in to concupiscence, seeking for the one what was for the good of all," and his answer is that "the first step down the slippery slope was the isolation of the ego itself, the withdrawing of one's hand from the grasp of one's neighbor's to form a clenching, selfish fist."[66] The second chapter of Tolle's *The Power of Now* contains, not surprisingly, a section entitled "Consciousness: The Way Out of Pain," and his subsequent volume, *A New Earth*, even more concertedly asserts "rising above" the pain-body, but now as a liberative path for "defy[ing] the gravitational pull of materialism and materiality" (*New Earth*, 5–6). The meditative work of "rising above the pain body" aims, in other words, to bring about a shift in cultural consciousness via transcendentalism: "At the heart of the new consciousness lies the transcendence of thought, the newfound ability of rising above thought, of realizing a dimension within yourself that is infinitely more vast than thought," he explains (ibid., 21).[67]

Pain, for Tolle, is the primordial emotion—an existential anxiety or fear, coupled with abandonment and incompleteness—that amasses itself, locks up and saturates other energies of the body when one over identifies with Western culture's model of the self. Apart from the path of liberation, one becomes overly self-conscious and consequently ego-driven (*Power of Now*, 28). "Negative thinking" as well as "any emotionally painful experience can be used as food by the pain-body." More summarily, "The pain-body is an addiction to unhappiness" (*New Earth*, 144–45). In the same way that psychological energies become locked in the neuromusculature, producing samskaras that yoga practice unlocks, the mind can lock on memories, traumas, hurts, and, given the medical discipline of the body, pathologies, thereby identifying with them.

The path of liberation from the pain-body, according to Tolle, thus proceeds by separating one's consciousness of self from the pain-body as the only filter of experience (*New Earth*, 162, 165). This distantiation within the self opens upon what Tolle calls "Presence" (166). Later in the book he speaks of identifying with Presence as hidden purpose in the cosmos, as consciousness of "the deeper perfection that is inherent in life itself" (213), and becoming one with the Now such that, borrowing the philosophy of Krishnamurti, "I don't mind what happens" (198).

Tolle here appears to be paraphrasing the Vedic teaching regarding the self, or *atman*, since in the philosophy of Advaita Vedanta, as scholar Elliot Deutsch explains in a book of that title, the goal of the liberative or wisdom path is to realize that "atman is Brahman"—to know that one's truest self is of the soul of Brahman, the Absolute, as distinct, say, from the ego-invested, habitual notion of self—"the pain-body." "Ātman," Deutsch continues, "is that pure, undifferentiated self-shining consciousness, timeless, spaceless, and unthinkable, that is not-different from Brahman and that underlies and supports the individual human person. . . . It is a supreme power of awareness, transcendent to ordinary sense-mental consciousness, aware only of the Oneness of being. . . . It is the infinite richness of spiritual being" (*Advaita Vedānta*, 48). Atman, this "highest" form of self, participates in the nondual ground of Reality, of Brahman. For Advaita Vedanta, "in the depth of my being . . . then, I am not-different from Reality: the depth of my being, which is not 'mine,' is Reality" (ibid., 50). Consequently, "The central concern of Advaita Vedānta is to establish the oneness of Reality and to lead the human being to a realization of it. Any difference in essence between [the hu]man and Reality must be erroneous, for one who knows [her/]himself knows Reality, and this self-knowledge is a 'saving' knowledge" (47). In the same vein, Tolle writes: "The joy of Being, which is the only true happiness, cannot come to you through any form, possession, achievement, person or event. . . . That joy . . . emanates from the formless dimension within you, from consciousness itself and thus is one with who you are." "Formless consciousness," Tolle contends, is "the essence of who you are" (*New Earth*, 214, 219).

Precisely such teaching has come to serve—within Hinduism and within some nonengaged forms of Buddhism—as a legitimation for an elitist transcendentalism, aloof from the world, and therefore unattentive to other sentient beings. The Cascadian basin in which Tolle lives and writes has, as a spiritual default setting, a nature transcendentalism complicit with Western, urban, middle-to-upper-class culture, if with an ecological ideal. Dalit ("untouchables") theologian Moses Penumaka says of the Advaita philosopher Shankara's resolve to seek the union of the self (atman) with the highest reality, the Absolute (Brahman), "The result is that the suffering of oppressed untouchables and other lower castes is dubbed unreal."[68] Anantanand Rambachan, also a contemporary scholar of Advaita Vedanta, has been likewise critical of it on this point; in *The Advaita Worldview* he insists that while the teachings can be philosophically interpreted to support compassionate, inclusive, and just community, "this will not occur . . . until the

Advaita tradition positively asserts the value of the world and human existence within it" (111).

As his reference to illness illustrates, at some points Tolle seems covertly to oppose the promise of liberative enlightenment—typically translated as *bliss*—to the lived flesh, to sorrows, ills, unhappiness.[69] Such transcendentalism as Tolle here forwards—or at the least into which he plays—needs to be as seriously critiqued as classic Christianity has been. This critique must include an assessment of how identification of atman with Brahman can become an immortality project and thus also—as Kant claimed in regard to Christian pursuit of immortality—an ego project.

Tolle insists that he is in the end describing "the way of the cross": "We are concerned with nothing else here" (*Power of Now*, 223). Having suffered death of the ego, "all judgment and all negativity dissolve," he promises. "There can be no subject-object relationship here, no duality, no you and God," he explains, concluding that "God-realization is the most natural thing there is" (224).[70]

Tolle subtly retains the egocentrism of selfhood—its selfish concern with its own essence—in the very logic and vocabulary of transcendence, which leaps directly from the individual self to the essence of reality without ever acknowledging or dealing with the reality of others. But as Advaita Vedanta scholar Rambachan explains, atman—my highest self—is "the self of all" (*Advaita Worldview*, 41). Consequently "in the most profound dimension of [one's] being [one] is no longer the 'individual' . . . but . . . is Reality itself" (Deutsch, *Advaita Vedānta*, 65). By transferring one's sense of self to atman, Tolle's disciples can admit the transience of the individual self even while staying inured to the existence of others. However, as Rambachan puts it, "the knowledge of the indivisibility of the self, properly understood, leads to a deeper identity and affinity with all. . . . The result of self-knowledge, in other words, is an empathetic way of being" (*Advaita Worldview*, 109–10).

Simone Weil's reading of atman, by contrast, shows the liberative path as assuming—carrying—the shared flesh of a shared world. "The highest *yogi*" is, as Rambachan puts it, "the one who, because of knowing the truth of the self, owns the pain and suffering of others as his[/her] own" (*Advaita Worldview*, 109–10). And Weil herself, suspecting the transcendental temptation implicit in the path she had followed, declared: "We do not become detached, we change our attachment. We must attach ourselves to the all."[71] Far from jettisoning pain, from avoiding persons mired in all-too-real social "negativities," as Tolle's approach suggests, Weil, like Soelle, invites us into passion for life—a path that liberates us by offering us solidarity with others.

SPIRIT AS PROSTHESIS OF HUMAN SENSIBILITIES

As I'm attempting from a theological point of view, Weil wished to construct a philosophy of bodily practices that "might break open the human perspective and free it from a history of mediocre moral and religious conditioning," as Ann Pirruccello has described.[72] Seeing the habitual self as "first and foremost a way of reading the world," Weil contended that the "crucial requirement for going beyond a mediocre life is to undergo a shift in the everyday interpretive mode."[73] Inspired by the conceptual image of atman, of the self as contiguous with the universe, and by an apprenticeship in industrial tool use, Weil suggested that one could transcend one's own perspectives and projects by extending one's sensibility like a prosthesis or tool, an extension of the self through which to sense the world "in such a way that I no longer locate myself and my well-being in my (biological) body."[74] As Pirruccello has noted, Weil believed that transferring one's sense of consciousness to the universe's "impartial order of things" is "the key to cultivating a new moral and spiritual sensibility"; "human sensibilities can extend into situations, objects, texts, actions: we can learn to 'read through'" these prosthetic extensions "to obtain additional interpretations and experiences instead of being limited solely to what is most immediate." Inasmuch as the universe becomes the prosthesis of the self, like the stick of a blind man, "This renunciation of the ego allows one to 'see' what the moral dimension of necessity demands." Sensibility employed as a prosthesis, Weil hoped, would break through egoic conditioning of our desires, motives, actions, and thoughts and the self-referencing quality of our daily readings or "takes" on the world and our lives so that we might be passionally present "to love the world just as it is, rather than for what it provides a sense of ego."[75]

This same point Weil worked from various directions. For example, she shared with Spinoza a suspicion of human agential willfulness.[76] The philosopher returned humans to a certain weightiness or gravity—if not precisely of the earth, to sheer immanence, to "act from necessity," as Weil put it in *Gravity and Grace* (39), amidst the non-chosen encounters of a mundane life as loci of the spiritual practice of "corporeal generosity." As with her reflections on atman, here too she prayed "that our being should one day become wholly sensitive in every part to this obedience that is the substance of matter . . . , that a new sense . . . be formed in us to enable us to hear the universe as the vibration of the word of God."[77] Weil contended that humans, enculturated from birth, must, through a practice of the "decreation" of self (that is, through the deconstruction of directed activity, of goal orientation, of purposefulness), shed the skins of autonomous being so as to develop spiritual skillfulness.[78] Decreation, she wrote, is "an undoing of the creature in us—that creature enclosed in self and defined by self."[79] As the poet Anne Carson imaginatively interprets Weil, that self gets in the way of the "creation that God loves—/*mountains and sea and the years after*—/blue simple horizon of all care./ World as it is when I am not there."[80] Weil herself put the sentiment in prayer form: "May the self disappear in such a way that Christ can help our neighbour through the medium of our soul and body" (*Gravity and Grace*, 40). Consequently, our soulfulness—counterbalanced by God or "supernature"—felt as something of a force of gravity upon the affects, emerges, under Weil's eyes, as something like an animal instinctiveness, as, for example, an animal-like urge to put food in the hungry mouth—not as an act of will, which would be the practice of sovereign self, but through unlearning the human rational blockages, letting compassion as a force of gravity pull us into intercorporeal generosity.[81] Indeed, "freedom of will" became for Weil "a mark of imperfection . . . a failure fully to appreciate what my situation demands of me."[82] As Weil's appreciative contemporary reader Alyda Faber puts it, "to love the world as it is in its deep afflictions and beauty" requires a "difficult attention to particular suffering human beings," given that love's meaning enters our bodies through suffering and joy.[83]

Becoming a prosthesis of world feeling, thus kenotically releasing the self, then helping "our neighbour through the medium of our soul and body"—such spiritual practice begins by opening up the self that pain can collapse, while mindfully staying present to the world. In humanity's release of egoicly guarded autonomy, in letting the harness of finitude constrain us, Weil saw humanity's emergent soulfulness, our growth into a covenant of trust. As scholar David Cockburn explains the direction of Weil's soulful practice, "Nature is the source of everything that flows from my body . . . in the sense that what I do flows from a situation in the world that provides a compelling reason for doing it."[84] Or as Thich Nhat Hanh, an engaged Buddhist, has put the point, "We are only alive when we live the life of the world, and so live the sufferings and joys of others."[85] Soelle summarizes Weil's perspective: "The Christian faith relates to suffering not merely as remover or consoler. It offers no 'supernatural remedy for suffering' but strives for 'a supernatural use for it'" (*Suffering*, 155)—whether breaking through egoic fortresses, strengthening the resolve to love, or developing the agility of passionate equanimity, our ability to stay with the world. In some measure, to love the world as God has loved it will mean breathing in and through its pain.

Herb was sixty-seven and just weeks from his death when I first met him. His forty-four-year-old daughter, like him, also had cancer and would die within the following year. Both had likely contracted cancer through their twenty-four-year-long residence in a Minneapolis suburb whose water had been contaminated by the operations of a nearby creosote plant. As the new parish pastor, I went to his home to get acquainted, already having been informed that Herb was not (despite his membership) a church person, that Christianity was not much loved by Herb. When I arrived, another member of the congregation, a former missionary to China, was already with Herb, urging him to "pray God spare his life." Herb, having apparently "made the world his body," as Weil would have it, quite serenely responded: "I will not use prayer for selfish purposes, to jump the queue to get God's attention. I will only ever take my place among all persons who today will die of hunger."

Sweet Exchange: Christology and Tonglen as Affective Practice

A culture's fear of pain, its lack of wisdom for how to navigate pain, becomes—I am contending—projected as a dominant representation, a marginalization of persons placed outside of the reach of justice. Such "unreformed bodies" pose in their own way a "security threat," the threat of "mutual influence." It is not just that the abject other might need me, but that I might be "touched" by this abject other, that pain should touch me. Contact aggravates the riptide of abjection and awakens consciousness to "a disavowed vulnerability," vulnerability to pain and to proximal ethical reflection, to ethical responsibility.[86] Razing such a dominant representation (that is, of "ruined humanity") implies differently negotiating the social flesh that culture has rejected when sealing off pain.

The anesthetization of pain does not relate simply then to certain bodies, but has become an inadmissible moral knowledge culture-wide: "Cognition depends upon our biochemical lives"—our feeling states, that is—"capturing the interactions with the environment to stay linked to practical agency and reality. . . . By making present our connectedness with the world and our fellow beings, feeling states help us find our way."[87] To mind the earth, given the effects of global climate change, as to mind the neighbor, given the swell of urbanization, requires learning again to think through pain as an aspect of our moral and political agency.

To be sure, "attention to affliction"—especially in the swirl and swelter of suffering—"is a miracle like walking on water . . . a near impossibility."[88] And yet, only those who can summon such attention can then mobilize suffering into voice, and might then have the possibility of working out new ligatures of justice, since bearing with inchoate suffering is, as political theorist William Connolly insists, the first step towards political voice and the opening of new forms of justice.[89] Retraining ourselves so as to traverse aversion, anxiety, and fear with ethical presence of mind will best be remediated, advises Franz Rosenzweig, through ritual, if also including art.[90]

Pedagogies for Pain

Responsiveness to pain does move us into an anxious, inchoate zone, a place below already established parameters and norms, a place within which we must sound out social and political sensibilities, possibilities. It moves us into an interstitial place that calls for the "cultivation of critical generosity," remembering that "the admirable possibilities of being outstrip . . . the corporeal capacity of any particular individual or culture to embody them all."[91] Might we now, renouncing the reach of metaphysics, which have used "God" as a way to turn from anxiety and the responsibility to think ethically,[92] generate a practice for stilling the storm of fear, for carrying inchoate pain into active justice practice?

I would argue that we can, if, instead of assuming the crucifixion of Jesus as an ontologically unique moment within a historically realist perspective and therefore a metaphysical truth to be believed toward salvation (that is, toward the "anesthetizing of pain"), we read Christianity as a practice that allows suffering to speak. Nietzsche engaged "philosophy as spiritual practice" and suggested that within such ascetic, aesthetic practice, the cross evidences the extent to which love goes with the world—"even through this"—this pain, injustice, suffering, and affliction.[93] That also might be taken to be Luther's point: "the historical event in question" within Martin Luther's earlier theology of the cross was not necessarily or only the crucifixion of Jesus; rather, the drama of these events offered a way of living through the suffering and perplexing intensities facing each individual. Further, faith moves through the affective aversions of worldly intensities so as to occasion a "truer" cosmological vision and a "truer" compass of love: "A person may understand all of creation, and in so doing look at the aspects of God revealed in creation. . . . But, claims Luther, a person may actually reach full understanding of the hidden things of God by looking at suffering and the cross."[94] In other words, only by breathing through the sting of death, the grip of fear, do we come into genuine love of the world.

"'Suffering and the cross' mark the places . . . where God [continually] makes Godself known" for Luther, because love moves—without avoidance—through these gross obstructions.[95] "This mystical love is different from forms of Christian transcendence that seek a final end to suffering, from platonically inflected contemplation that seeks the invulnerability of communion with Ideas, or from Stoic tranquility that transmutes suffering in the transcendence of finite attachments," argues Nietzsche scholar Tyler Roberts. "This love," he explains, "does not resist suffering in general, or condemn life because it suffers; it resists . . . the deadening that results from the inability to bear suffering. . . . Love as compassion bears the suffering of oneself and others."[96] If Christianity might again be lived as a philosophy of desire, then desire that seeks to love the world and therefore finds beauty in it will move through the aversiveness of pain and suffering—neither being Romantically ignorant of the yowling hurt of pain and the aching whelp of suffering nor holding these as resentment against life itself.

I'm motivated by Nietzsche's conversion of Luther's theology into a spiritual, philosophical practice to dig underneath dominant atonement theories to suggest that through comparative religious conversation, Christianity might well have developed or, despite general metaphysical anesthetization, can yet develop several pedagogies for pain. The passion narratives can set in motion a "mindfulness" practice (even Paul urged Christians toward such, i.e., "Have this mind among yourselves"; see Philippians 2) like the Buddhist practice of tonglen, which simply means "taking in" pain and suffering and "sending out" well-being and happiness. Understanding and practicing tonglen can help move Christianity's culturally normative relation with pain out of its metaphysical enframement through world resentment. Tonglen, explains one of its most popular contemporary practitioners, Pema Chodron, is "a method for connecting with suffering" and works specifically on moving breath through the occlusions that suffering brings, for example, the clench of fear and the roiling nausea of aversion.[97] By means of a comparative theological approach, I hope to redevelop Christology as an affective practice comparable to Buddhist tonglen for breathing through so as to transcend the culturally dominant pain-pleasure dualism, and in this way to become morally, ethically responsive to pain, because love calls us to bear with, to redeem, the suffering of the other.

"THE SWEET EXCHANGE"

Tonglen is the breathing in of the pain of another, the breathing out—or blessing of the other—with one's own joy and well-being.[98] The "taking and sending" breaths of Buddhist tonglen might as readily summon up an ancient Christian view of the atonement known as "the sweet exchange." Luther's theology of the cross was itself an interpretive innovation on this "sweet" or "happy exchange"—a patristic atonement theory, based on 2 Corinthians 5:21, "For our sake he became sin who knew no sin, so that we might become the righteousness of God" This theology was first posed in the *Epistle to Diognetus* in the second century: "O sweet exchange, O the incomprehensible work of God, O the unexpected benefits; that the sinfulness of many should be hidden in one righteous man, while the righteousness of one should justify many that are sinners."[99] The concept of the "sweet exchange" celebrated the communication of attributes (*communicatio idiomatum*), or as Luther succinctly explained, "We get what is divine and God gets what is human."[100] Just as Jesus carried the guilt load of the sinner, the meditative practitioner of tonglen aspires altruistically to lift or carry the weight of suffering from the person or being in pain. As Geshe Chekhawa, the twelfth-century tonglen master in Tibet put it, "Give all profit and gain to others, Take all loss and defeat on yourself." The breathing practice of tonglen is considered to be the practical, affective application of this saying.[101] For each tradition, Christian and Buddhist, the heartfelt concern of one person moves him or her to vicariously carry the suffering of another.

Luther described the sweet exchange in this way: "By this fortunate exchange with us [Jesus] took upon Himself our sinful person and granted us His innocent and victorious Person. Clothed and dressed in this, we are freed from the curse of the Law, because Christ Himself voluntarily became a curse for us."[102] Luther's innovation on this sweet exchange model of atonement sits somewhere between Anselm's "vicarious satisfaction" model, in which God appears grievously consumed with slights to God's own honor,[103] and "substitutionary atonement," the general theology of the Reformation era. "On the penal substitution model, typical of the Reformation but found already as early as Athanasius, Jesus on the cross through his perfect obedience and/or by suffering the punishment due violators of the law, fulfills the law's terms and exempts human sinners from penalties otherwise owed."[104] While we can assume that Luther likely conflated the "happy exchange" with the more punitive, penal "substitutionary atonement" model,[105] one might well here judiciously argue Luther against himself to loosen this historic conflation: Not only does this substitutionary model corset God into notions of penal justice, without room, in the end, to practice "infinite mercy" or forgiveness, but it also belittles God by making holy wisdom too consistent with worldly reason, with the "deficient psychology" of scholastic rationalism, which Luther famously ab-whored, if you get my pun.[106]

Unraveling the twines of this conflation so as to let the "sweet exchange" be carried on its own merits might well be read as the intent of two recent feminist Christological reflections. In "Incarnation, Cross, and Sacrifice,"

Kathryn Tanner names her reconstructive reclamation "an incarnational model of atonement," but one hears the inference of the sweet exchange when she writes that "God saves by assuming the life of suffering and death" (39, 43).[107] "It is in virtue of the incarnation that humanity is saved—first the humanity of Christ himself and then through him that of every other human being," Tanner explains. As she continues, one picks up the way in which it is precisely the straining negativities of existence that have for her been redressed through this fortunate exchange: "The humanity of Christ (and united with Christ our humanity) is purified, healed, and elevated—saved from sin and its effects (anxiety, fear, conflict and death)—as a consequence of the very incarnation through which the life-giving powers of God's own nature are brought to bear on human life in the predicament of sin" (41). Tanner and I share hopes, I might suggest, for a felicitous practice by which humanity, suffering from fear, anxiety, isolation, conflict, humiliation, and betrayal, can be incited toward living with one another, toward entrustment to life, toward world attachment—that is, toward loving the world as God has loved it ("Incarnation, Cross, and Sacrifice," 46).

While Cleo McNelly Kearns, working with the psychoanalytic philosophy of Julia Kristeva, deals more specifically with the subjective location of *simul justus et peccator*, "at the same time sinner and redeemed," that is opened up by the practice of Luther's deployment of "sweet exchange," she, too, recognizes that Luther "offers one major intervention on suffering in the Christian tradition" ("Suffering in Theory," 65, 67). Kearns explains: "Luther deals with suffering by means of a participatory work of the imagination," a "form of identification" that "he calls the theology of the cross. This spiritual practice entails regarding and speaking of suffering, particularly the public sufferings of crucifixion, as in itself a healing modality not only in the life of Jesus but in the life of the believer as well. . . . The theology of the cross . . . suggests that there is . . . a way of traversing suffering" (ibid., 67). With Kearns, we come closer to engaging Luther's theology of the cross as an affective practice of exchange that resembles that of tonglen.

Tonglen developed within Tibetan Buddhism,[108] and it has been popularized through Sogyal Rinpoche's *Tibetan Book of Living and Dying* (1993) and Lama Surya Das's *Awaken the Buddha Within: Tibetan Wisdom for the*

Western World (1998), as well as more recently by Pema Chodron, a student of Chogyam Trongpa Rinpoche.[109] A form of meditation that accepts the cosmological view that "life is suffering" (not in a tragic vein, but so as to refuse the immature, if instinctive, pain/pleasure divide), tonglen serves as skill training for a way of being in the world in which one begins to develop a limitless, fearless, and unbiased compassion toward all creation. In the practice of tonglen, "We breathe in what is painful and unwanted with the sincere wish that we and others could be free of suffering." After settling one's heart and mind in one's first breaths, within the spacious, unconditional openness or compassion called *alaya*, meditative practitioners in consequent stages practice breathing through the aversive aspects of pain by imagining thick, heavy, hot smoke, then breathing out the qualities of fresh, cool air and light until they become ready to approach bodies in pain.[110] One's own daily aches, interruptions, and sorrows become meaningful training ground within tonglen practice for extending compassion—considered inherently and infinitely available in the cosmos—to all living beings without exception.[111] Only by overcoming revulsion and fear can we be truly alive with the world, Buddhism maintains. Only as we have found ways of navigating through sufferings can we awaken to life as infinitely precious.[112] As Sogyal Rinpoche has said, awareness of mortality, of this edge of sentience, helps us to cultivate "a burning, almost heartbreaking sense of the fragility and preciousness of each moment and each being; from this can grow a deep, clear, limitless compassion for all beings" (*Tibetan Book of Living and Dying*, 191). As Linda Holler puts it, such guided spiritual practices may "heal breaches in sentience [or "social flesh"] . . . and open us to feelings of compassion and empathy."[113]

SPIRIT AS REFUGE, AS LOCUS OF NONDUALITY

Tonglen practice begins by affectively locating oneself in mindful relation to the open, the alaya, the space of all compassion. Breathing in, breathing out, one rests back into what a Lutheran theologian might call "corporeal generosity" or grace, or even simply "Spirit," as Kearns observed of Luther's identificatory transposition (*Suffering in Theory*, 68). Spirit might be described as a locus of passionate equanimity, of extensively infinite mercy, such that—in a way comparable to tonglen's grounding of a person in alaya—to "take refuge" in Spirit opens out space beyond the clench of fear, the catch of aversion.[114] By or through the affective bond of faith, Luther transfers his sense of gravity away from ego (or "self") and to Spirit (thus, also to "neighbor") as an alternative locus of value.[115]

Tonglen, Chodron claims, affectively dissolves the dualistic distinction between good and bad by breathing through the obstruction, borne of fear, that we form around pain.[116] Faith, for Luther, Rudolph Otto asserted decades ago, might comparably have been an "affective" bond, an affective disposition or location, not merely the rationalist, propositional posture that later modernity was to effect.[117] "Mere credence could not justify," explains theologian Brian Gerrish in a more systematically strident vein. "Saving or justifying faith," he continues, "is a commitment which effects a [psychic] 'union' with Christ."[118] Living faith affectively amidst a world alive with vitalities could well have cradled Nietzsche's own emergence, his own movement "beyond good and evil." That Spirit might have been for Luther—as tonglen is said to be—something like an affective "offering of space," a spaciousness for engaging world intensities while yielding neither to flights of fear nor fantasy,[119] suggests something of the locus for and benefits of a nondual philosophy today.

Nevertheless, given both the increasing penitential nature of ecclesial rituals and the developing juridical and penal system, it may not be surprising that Luther's reflections on the "happy exchange" seem to indulge a certain unrelentingly obsessive egocentricity. As individuals began to cut loose from familial, feudal, and ecclesial expectations, the weight of conscience undoubtedly mounted. Luther's earliest reflections on the sweet exchange thus seem to allow him to conceive of a Christ of infinite mercy as a personal introject, as the medicine of his critical self-analysis, even if intensely overexacting: "By this fortunate exchange with us He took upon Himself our sinful person and granted us His innocent and victorious Person. Clothed and dressed in this, we are freed from the curse of the Law." "Therefore," Luther continues, "beware, as you place your sins in your conscience, that you do not panic, but freely place them on Christ," who "'has borne our iniquities.'"[120]

By contrast, tonglen, like other kenotic practices, acknowledges the work of unraveling the selfish pattern of ego so as to open out a completely new way of being.[121] Ego, Buddhism has maintained, not only founds and guards the pain/pleasure divide (which Freud accurately described, but to which he also unfortunately then gave cultural legitimacy), but itself represents a locked state of suffering. "Normally we don't want to give away our happiness, nor do we want to take on another person's suffering; but this not-wanting," Buddhist practitioner Christine Longaker instructs us, "is the voice of our selfish ego." "Following our ego's commands all the time," Longaker warns, "keeps us trapped in cycles of hope and frustration, fear and disappointment."[122] "Self-grasping creates self-cherishing," Sogyal Rinpoche counsels, noting that it is from self-cherishing that aversion to suffering, nervous anxiety, and fear develop. Mistaking "what is in our ego's self-interest" for "what is in our ultimate interest" can thus be considered the source of all suffering (Rinpoche, *Tibetan Book of Living and Dying*, 194, 193). Buddhism consequently urges persons to love ourselves—as well as others—from within the spacious openness or corporeal generosity prior to enframing, prior—in a Deleuzean sense—to judgment.

For Luther in regard to the self, sweet or happy exchange names the way in which "God" breathes through one's own abject, shame-faced, and guilt-prone accounting of the self so as to breathe into the self grace and forgiveness—these deep energies of corporeal generosity.[123] For Luther, Christians know God first through the cross or not at all, as the God who empathically carries and thus continues to breathe through humiliation, through suffering, through pain, so us to stay in solidarity with us. "There is, then, in this theology" of the cross, Kearns observes,

> a potential transformation of suffering in the temporal dimension, in the sense that it can be changed from within—by the very act of recognizing the mortality to which it so painfully draws attention, and yet embracing, witnessing, and speaking back to it. This transformation is effected by a linking of the abject subject with the name of the Other, a linking in which the subject is upheld not by righteous distance from his or her suffering, not by stoic self-sufficiency, nor by counter-charge, nor even by confession, but rather by the gift of the Spirit. (*Suffering in Theory*, 68)

LIVING FLESH WITHOUT REPROACH

Luther's theology of the cross, as Kearns intuits, allows us to live the ambivalence of flesh without reproach, to live deeply into this reversible fold, appreciative of the mortal life, frankly unsurprised by our mortal tissue or human behavior, and so therefore to begin smartly to maneuver the social structures of sin that can otherwise capitalize upon psychic abjection, even or especially our abjection of bodies in pain, our own body or the bodies of others. Putting the point more directly, in the article "Luther and Shankara" theologian Moses P. P. Penumaka writes, "God takes finitude into the divine life" (253). This does not so much inure us to suffering as allow us a locus—introjective, imaginative, as is the nature of psyche—in which to engage the world affectively or feelingly, including its sufferings.

While recognizing humanity's tendency to be foreclosed with guilt, incapacitated by shame, riddled with anxiety, and to shamefully capitalize upon structures of injustice, Luther embraced the finite world as ultimate reality. And as with Luther's Christology and Buddhism, so also with Advaita Vedanta. Penumaka finds in Luther's renovation of the happy exchange atonement model a way to amend Advaita philosophy's Brahmanic tendency to rise above the pain body. "A healthy soteriology in the context of Indian spirituality—a Dalit soteriology," Penumaka concludes, "could benefit from Luther's exchange of attributes, because the mundane sufferings of humble people are [through it] dignified by receiving a place in God's reality" ("Luther and Shankara," 252).

Unlike the Advaitic philosophy of Shankara, in which identification with the Absolute "strips away all finitude," for Luther, the sweet exchange reverses even ultimate reality: "The incarnation includes taking into the divine life the attributes of human daily life, e.g., injustice, suffering and death," such that these "become constitutive of . . . ultimate reality" (Penumaka, "Luther and Shankara," 260). "This," Penumaka confides to us, "constitutes a kind of metaphysical reversal. What an Advaita philosopher might dub maya or non-reality now becomes valorized . . . because ultimate reality absorbs it" (ibid.). God has emptied God's self into the world, assumed the world, such that humans can now move through suffering, pain, anxiety, fear, turmoil, conflict, aversion, even the injustice often effected against those who will work to generate new forms of justice, because God has breathed through them. The affective ventilation of suffering, by introjecting God into the flesh of the world, allows Luther to embrace finitude as ultimate reality.

"WHO FINALLY TAKES ON THE SUFFERING OF OTHERS,
IF NOT THE BEING WHO SAYS 'ME'?"

While Luther no doubt connected salvation to a metaphysical version of substitutionary atonement in ways that I would not and could not, I would nonetheless endorse the ways in which he would have us remain radically, wildly open to the world, love staying affectively present to this. Indeed, it has been more recently maintained by theologians such as Marit Trelstad that Luther imagined his Christology not so much as a "theology" of the cross (as a metaphysical thesis or foundation), but as an active epistemology. Inasmuch as Luther maintained that "God is seen only through the cross," Trelstad suggests that "Luther's . . . epistemology of the cross . . . receives its correct context as a means by which one knows God and the world through the lens of suffering and thus may live one's Christian faith responsibly."[124] Luther maintained this knowledge through suffering to be "a deep . . . form of knowing God that challenges the structures of our world," as a path toward engagement with our neighbor's suffering, as a practice to be carried with us.[125] Comparably, tonglen—with and through breath work—works through false barriers of discrimination.

In Luther's earliest commentary on Galatians, we can witness how Luther himself used this epistemology of the cross to suggest that "there is no distinction between rich and poor, handsome and ugly, citizen and farmer."[126] That Jesus carried the social and psychic weight of abjection, guilt, and humiliation led Luther at one point, with rhetorical flourish, to arraign Jesus for "adultery,"[127] just as elsewhere he called Jesus the worst sinner of the whole world. Luther's point, however, was that when we meet up with one whom we, in our righteous egoism, would mark as adulterer, the epistemology of the cross challenges us to greet that person with "infinite mercy," inasmuch as God already carries the social weight of reproach. The "sweet exchange" becomes here a basis for social affiliation, for rejecting legalism and all its rationalizations, for moving through abjection, humiliation, and shame so as affectively to extend infinite mercy.

In his *Treatise on Christian Liberty*, Luther speaks of the happy or fortunate exchange with nuptial imagery—the wedding of Christ and the felicitous soul, making them one flesh. Where Christ becomes sinner or adulterer through his very fleshy solidarity, where Christ steps into the solidarity of friendship even to the point of persecution and crucifixion, the other person carries no abject taint or stain (2 Cor. 5:21). The epistemology of the cross thus serves as a projective imaginative lens for living through the abject breaches that humanity would otherwise carve into sociality. "The face of the abject other," Kearns has written, describing the thought of Levinas, "obligates more fundamentally than any words, stances, or fantasies of redemption can address." Suffering obligates us to assume an affective practice of compassion or infinite mercy, "prior to any religious, esthetic, or political prospects or consolations" (Kearns, "Suffering in Theory," 58). We can hear this protopractice within Luther's epistemology of the cross if we breathe through our own late-modernist, metaphysical, and hypercapitalist aesthetic aversion to pain.

Christological theology, it would seem to me, thus belongs not in the house of modern reason but in the circuit of the midst of life, in the circuit of love's incarnate becoming, where we are challenged to keep faith with life—without resentment, even amidst pain, and without illusions. Practicing the sweet exchange of "vicarious" or "substitutionary atonement" becomes an act of breathing through our fear, anxiety, humiliation, dread, even hatred of others and wishing them well. If we might today speak of "vicarious atonement" or "substitutionary atonement," then it would be of this nature: the breathing in or carrying of one another's suffering. As Levinas asked, putting forth a similar point, "Who finally takes on the suffering of others, if not the being who says 'Me'?"[128]

Substitutionary atonement thus names an act, even in the face of injustice, of choosing to love the other, of breathing in the disgust, the anxiety, the hatred of the other, the humiliation set in motion by the other, which must swell up from the other's own fear of mortal life, then breathing out: in the name of peace, wishing the other well.

For many of us (and here I would include philosophical theologians such as Gianni Vattimo and Jean-Luc Nancy as much as intellectually disaffected Christians at large), the metaphysics that has classically informed theism has been riddled with fault lines, irreparably cracked—even as we continue to see ourselves as faithful practitioners. To be sure, one doesn't want to ignore the power of projection that can inform Christological atonement theories—the power of, for example, seeing the abject other as

Christ so that one can approach in order to serve. Even tonglen at points borrows projection so as to cut through severe aversion: When one cannot bring oneself to carry the pain of an enemy, one superimposes the projection of a friend, of a person upon whom one has already successful practiced tonglen.

But a theism that presumes to have accomplished this for us does not show us how this infuses, enthuses, our being. Such an insight into Christology dawned on the nineteenth-century German theologian and philosopher Friedrich Schleiermacher: "He cannot have done so in our place in the sense that we are thereby relieved from the necessity of fulfilling it."[129] In other words, Schleiermacher was suspicious of the ways in which Christological models "render humans utterly passive and hence undermine our responsibility."[130] Further, the metaphysical theism that has informed Christianity has aggravated our disarticulation of the moral compass of pain by insisting on obedience to an outside source. A love that opens out through the riptides of revulsion—breathing in, breathing out—so as to find beauty in the fragile and vulnerable tissues of flesh, even that krumped by social injustice, can recircuit transcendence—as generosity—in the city. A religion that does not have a pedagogy for pain not only aggravates the abjection splitting cities, but could well choose its own evolutionary elimination, given the multiple and various scenarios of global climate change, the growth of a planet of slums, the end of oil.

Seculars as Mendicants in Cosmopolis

In the city today, our own habituated revulsions are valorized as the urban survival wisdom of indifference. "Your disgust for them is filthier than their sore," the seventeenth-century Japanese Zen master Bankei told a student who was convulsed by disgust at the presence of beggars with leprosy who had come to the community seeking refuge.[131] Street persons, I have suggested, are on the street not merely because of bad luck, misfortune, lack of skills, addictions, or poverty, but because they have been socially marked with refus/al. We need analytically to see this amassing of bodies as the socioeconomic generation of a class, to consider the likelihood that even theology has operated with an unconscious, unanalyzed class assumption. I've consequently been recuperating pedagogies for pain, which might help us confront our disgust reactions and so respond with generosity, sympathy, and compassion.

Given the "disability abjection" lodged in the bourgeois subject, and given the ways in which economic globalization as urbanization creates a class of "refuse," the ways in which economics uses "disability abjection" to screen out "wasted lives,"[132] breathing through pain interpolates one onto the street differently, enabling new forms of justice to emerge and making different patterns of urbanization possible. A tonglen-informed Christology, when loosed on city streets, in our daily street ballet, can begin to deconstruct class-based aesthetics of fear—the aversion to pain that splits human solidarity, that avoids neighbor love, that declines sacrificial renunciation of the self for the other, that creates the scenario Mieville has referred to as "the city and the city." Or at the least, I hope to disrupt glassy-eyed indifference to bodies on the street, to open sympathetic pores, and to invigorate sympathetic impulses to challenge the sadistic impulses within civil city crudities.

In this vein, *mendicant* might now name the role played by those who have learned from the pedagogy of pain and who practice compassion for the suffering of others, who practice the embrace of social flesh. It might name the modern-day role of the "seculars." Able to think beyond the clench of fear, able to move through aversion, and therefore in touch with deep corporeal generosity, mendicants as seculars engage an alternative economic vision of the city. Susan Palwick, a contemporary science fiction writer, engages possible framings of such mendicancy in *The Necessary Beggar*.[133] Her text—a *midrash*, Palwick acknowledges, on a homily she heard on the Parable of the Wedding Banquet—looses the imagination of a relation with beggars that ascribes to them sacred power, as did ancient and as do non-Western traditions of mendicancy. The ascription of sacred power to street persons, the power to bless and to forgive, assumes at base the humility of shared kinship among all humanity—a kinship that urban "unseeing" avoids. Mendicants in attitude would cultivate—through our own Christological aversion therapy—the loving gaze, the presenting of oneself, in all humility, as kin. At the least, let mendicancy of attitude assume in relation to the other that, as Vattimo has written, "whoever suffers or has suffered deserves respect for this . . . especially for this."[134]

In Gandiffri, "the Land of Gifts," a world of Palwick's active imagination, every young adult, prior to admission to the temple and as a reminder of civic responsibility, serves a year of mendicancy, "a year when s/he must live by generosity and grace" (*Necessary Beggar*, 20, 146). In preparation for the year, each must search out and then meditate upon a prayer carpet—each carpet uniquely spun of colors representing the warp and woof of the cosmic Elements (145). The year of service comes to an end when the mendicant is chosen off the street by a couple who plan to marry. For one week prior to the wedding, the couple take the mendicant home and feast and dress the mendicant as a reminder of their responsibility to the rest of the world, of the hospitality that parents must show their children (who all arrive as squalling strangers), and, insomuch as partners receive each other as gifts, they display gratitude by lavishing gifts on the mendicants. The wedding itself, which will be performed by the mendicant, appears as something of a reverse potlatch—all of the gifts are handed over to the mendicant so as to remind the couple that gifts of the self are the most prized, to remind all that generosity founds life (19). As the wedding ceremony begins, the mendicant offers absolution as s/he has done also when receiving alms: "For what you have given me, your errors and those of all your kin are forgiven. For charity heals shortcoming and kindness heals carelessness" (20). In Palwick's imagined ritual system of mendicancy, the human community learns to be biomimetic: to give to one another what is needed, just as the cosmos does. Only the falling of humans into patterns of self-centered concern, of personal enclosure, precludes the flow of cosmic generosity within the human community (153, 154). Palwick's vision helps us imagine at the least a practice of hospitality to that populous of the city structurally excluded by "disability abjection." It begins to move us into a work of compassion that does not pretend to "help less fortunate persons," but rather to engage one another as kin—and so to recognize our temptation to withdraw from the urban commons, to become too comfortable among our own kin and kind, to recognize how our enclosures in kin and kind interrupt the flow of cosmic generosity, create chasms in social flesh; and so to seek, as mendicant, our own forgiveness.

But in a broader vein, by invoking "an attitude of mendicancy," I am not proposing, I hope it will be clear, to develop the "disabled subject" as a virtuous mendicant or trying to bear down upon beggars with incitements of "cleanliness" and "poverty is next to godliness." Rather, I'm suggesting that the citizen, the cosmopolitan, the secular, the Christian (again, theist or not) assume the location of mendicant. Historically speaking, mendicants arose as an active force of the sacred in the city, especially where population growth outstripped the resources of parish structures. Today, not only does the lack of resources challenge parish structures, but Christians and other cosmopolitans seek practices loosened from these institutional structures. Some form of "walking practice," such as mendicancy, can fill that need. The structure of the city—this form of human existence that Aquinas viewed as the most complete of human communities—has everything to do, at this point in human history, with the well-being of the planet, with the creative possibilities of the human species, with our sheer survival.[135] Cities, the historian Joel Kotkin explains, have always performed three critical functions—providing security, hosting a commercial market, and creating sacred space expressed through sacred buildings, but also incorporating in the city's very structure a vision of human existence. (Even the final chapter of the biblical Book of Revelations imagines a city with no need for a temple, but still sees the city as sacred enterprise.[136]) In the wake of twentieth-century urban planning, and also in the wake of modernity's impact on religions themselves, sacred buildings have increasingly been replaced with glass towers reaching toward a skyward transcendence: "glass skyscrapers would rise like crystals, clean and transparent," generating a "'fantastic, almost mystic city . . . a vertical city.'"[137] The shaping of the modern city did not simply aspire to strip those cities of sacred buildings, however, but sought to "eliminate anything that reinforced public life and so undercut likewise the dimension of the city as itself sacred space, the vital ground of the human commons.[138] Where Christianity must now find an "operationalizable form," a model of practice, even for the secular, something beyond the parish structure, mendicants can be its presence in and on behalf of the city.

FOUR

In the Ruin of God

I see you are on crutches. I trust it's only temporary then, yes? Below the hem of my thigh-length designer black jacket hangs the ravaged emptiness of nothing to see. It screams, too much to take in. Comments on the tips of their tongues trail into absurdity: *Will it get better then? It is temporary, then, yes?* All of life is, yes.

—SHARON BETCHER

There will be no . . . enforcement or extension of rights without human dispositions, moods, and cultural ensembles hospitable to these effects.

—JANE BENNETT, *Vibrant Matter*

To encounter somatic and cognitive variations among the human community can leave some persons anxious, uneasy, queasy. In particular, "a disabled body is supposedly a body in pain," explains disabilities theorist Tobin Siebers, and pain, he continues, "represents for most people . . . an affront to human dignity."[1] Cultural ideologies, including religions, have borrowed the power of such affects to prop up transcendental projects such as wholeness, perfect knowing, and purity of practice or doing. Instead, I've proposed meditatively breathing through pain, our own and that of others, taking in and breathing out all that we might fear so as to break through the religious, metaphysical, and/or cultural constructedness, even legitimation, of our revulsions against flesh. I want here to propose another practice for widening the heart, for growing our affective intelligence, for promoting the embrace of social flesh.

Insomuch as "disability" is only ever an aesthetic judgment against life, meditatively engaging the affects of disability can help us "to work ourselves free—to the extent possible—of entrenched presuppositions and theoretical totalities, keep ourselves open to the future by refusing the certainty that theories and epistemic foundations always promise . . . , given that whatever presses for closure, finality, assurance presses also for an end to vitality, is contempt for life."[2] Disability occasions the psychic reassessment of the order or laws of nature, and of the affective core that has allowed such resentment against life as is held in "naturalism" or "theism" to build. Since in a world of becoming there will be no assurance of health, security, and/or wholeness, reactions of revulsion or disgust at encounters with disability can be seen as a symptom of underlying resentment against life owing to the inclusion of pain, suffering, and vulnerability in a world of becoming. We might admit, then, that "disability" is a psychic dispossession, a resentment in the heart of and thus in the eye of the beholder. In addressing the emotions at the root of our reactions to disablement and to the pain, suffering, and vulnerability we all share, I will be leaning implicitly, if not always overtly, upon traditions and practices as diverse and as similar as the Christian suffering servant of Isaiah 53 and Buddhist practices of corpse meditation to work toward "the 'let-down of repulsiveness'" as over against building up "structures, organizations," by engorging and legitimating the "powers of horror," as Julia Kristeva calls them.[3]

By bringing persons close to flesh, one is reminded of the basic passage of a world of becoming, and we thus can begin to break through the Western effort to standardize the body, to value and offer status only to bodies so tightly normalized. The Buddhist practice of corpse meditation is one way this arduous breakthrough has been accomplished. Corpse meditation, one of the most challenging of practices in the Buddhist repertoire, invites us to crawl under the fence of our cultural rationalizations, categorizations, and organization of the body so as to recognize that what we find repulsive, the horror that we seize upon, is as constructed as are our notions of beauty. In this way, we might affectively work through our repulsions and those upon whom we project them. Whether meditation is focused on "thirty-two parts of the body" or on a corpse, the Buddhist practice of corpse meditation involves "visualizing revolting aspects of the body in death and dismemberment in order to work through and imagine differently many of the issues confronting us." That is, "You see bodily ooze. . . . The body splits open into intestines. . . . Liver, kidney, intestines, the stomach, you can see it all." Thus, "With this sensational faculty of seeing in deep meditation, the mind's eye . . . rubs itself into the gory aspects of embodied existence, brushing up against an insight into their composition."[4] Such practiced forbearance, bringing nonjudgment into a cultivated appreciation (I might hope) for a "world of becoming," is but preparation for "the studied exposure of our mutual vulnerability."[5]

Meditation on the body in this way, as Alan Klima notes, basically familiarizes us with what philosopher Julia Kristeva has named the "abject"—with our loathings, with what occasions our felt repugnance, with what leaves us retching, like muck and sewage, sweat, death and decay: "As in true theater, without makeup or masks, refuse and corpses *show me* what I permanently thrust aside in order to live." "Abjection is above all ambiguity," Kristeva goes on to explain, "because, while releasing a hold, it does not radically cut off the subject from what threatens it—on the contrary, abjection acknowledges it to be in perpetual danger."[6] Persons who relate to abjection by attempting to create boundaries of purity or exclusion cut wide swathes across the city, features that we have crip/tographically mapped, especially in terms of class creation, which in turn affects even the availability of civil protection. Indeed, even general urban landscaping is done with an eye toward removing the supposedly revolting passage of decay.

However, as I see it, corpse meditation, which has been aligned primarily with the fear of death, of spoliation, of transience, must be ratcheted up or modified in order to redress the living menace that "disability" poses to so many. To access what I have argued is primarily an emotional and affective concern, a psychic disposition, within the concept of disability (and within its related colonial categories, race and class)[7] and what William Connolly has conceptualized as a micropolitics of the self in and for "an ethos of engagement that rises above the demands for wholeness and purity in public life,"[8] I wish consciously to float a figuration within Christianity that Christianity itself has seemingly wanted to repress—the grotesque at the heart of Christian iconography.[9] Through meditative practices in relation to the grotesque, I hope we can retrain ourselves to traverse with ethical presence of mind what otherwise makes us "aesthetically nervous," as postcolonial-disabilities theorist Ato Quayson puts it. In other words, I imagine "crip/tography" as leading to an urban iconographic practice of mindfulness, meditatively breathing through all that we might dare to label and categorically dismiss as disgusting, like "disability," so as to break through the cultural constructedness of our revulsions.

Just as corpse meditation prepares us to love flesh, and thus the world and its others, without escaping into idealism or nihilism, the innovation on corpse meditation I propose here, an engagement with grotesque imagery, may, I hope, begin to dig into the entrenched affects that occasion our clinging to fixity, surety, security, good order, natural law, or divine plan. Perhaps most surprisingly (though not if you've ever been party to the bawdy humor of crips . . . or Lutherans), crip/tography here charts a path of "overflowing laughter."[10]

"Garden State": To Be Human in a World of "Human Nature"

And yet a world of becoming may not today be as innocent as even Charles Darwin proposed. Ironically and lamentably, the little "Garden State" of New Jersey, for example, has become a major outpost of Big Pharma and petroleum. In the wake of federal clean water legislation in the United States in the 1970s, recognition came that this tiny state on the Eastern Seaboard sported the greatest number of toxic clean-up sites of any of the fifty states. Did the superbug of group A beta-hemolytic strep, which occasioned massive infection, complete organ shut-down, and the loss of my left leg, brew somewhere, somehow in that local stew? Or in the general atmosphere of antibiotic overuse in North America? Or was my susceptibility to the bacteria simply due, as one doctor suggested, to "cumulative stress," that collective term for keeping pace with the Western world? No one knows, of course.

But it is just as likely that what lowered the immune defenses of my body transpired in my years of living among rolling hills and bucolic pasture-lands where grazed our Holsteins, along a tributary stream of the Mississippi River, under the puff of cumulus cloud and bright blue sky of southeastern Minnesota summers. Within the year after the traumatic infection and amputation of my left leg, I had yet another surgery—the removal of the right lobe of my thyroid, which it had been discovered (during intubation as I was put on life-support) was enlarged, hardened, and wrapped around the esophagus; because it refused to show itself as "cold or hot," as cancerous or not, surgery was ordered as soon as I could tolerate it. Nearly simultaneous with that culminating surgery came the disclosure— secured by news media through the Freedom of Information Act—that these precious heritage scenes of subsistence farming, so drawing on my nostalgia still, might have been unwittingly seeded with atomic particulate from the Nevada tests sites carried by winds over the Dakotas and Minnesota, then consumed along with raw cows' milk by babies born in the mid to late 1950s. Well it could have been a compromised thyroid that left me open to infection.

As a farm kid, I was educated by the birth of calves and sows' litters, tornadoes, lightning strikes, and the archaeology of rocks to the rugged, ragged lurches and bumps of a natural life. Becoming disabled is but one artery of being human in a world of becoming that is not always as orderly and predictable as sunrise and sunset. I've consequently often likened what transpired in my particular case to the impersonal toppling of a grain wagon by a wind shear. And yet, there may not be an absence of human causality in what occasioned my Garden State–variety disability. Bodies are ecologically related to place, but locale—whether due to prevailing winds or our own jetstream of career pursuits—is never any longer simple or innocent for any of us. And nature, we're learning yet again, is hardly itself agentially or teleologically singular, let alone when atomically or pharmaceutically seeded or petrochemically aggravated. In trying to make the world safe (whether by attempting to rid ourselves of bacteria through antibiotic usage, or by addressing our anxiety-riddled relation with "bugs" by creating antibacterial soaps, or by developing nuclear power that salts clouds with atomic contaminants that incidentally rain down on pastoral scenes of Holstein cows grazing on the lands of subsistence farmers), humanity now must begin to acknowledge its responsibility for that which has been among its worst, longstanding fears, "disability" as monstrosity.

Reflecting on the Union Carbide disaster in Bhopal in 1984, postcolonial theorist Ato Quayson notes rightly that there are "worrisome links between global capitalism and local disabilities": "Viewed through a wider lens of social structures and international formations, disability," as we encounter it today, "ceases being an individual affliction to be borne silently by the person with an impairment." Rather, "the dominance and indeed proliferation of certain impairments can be directly linked to social systems."[11] Quayson's claim, of course, extends beyond that of discursive social construction, into international economics and the leveraging of poor governments by finance. For just such reasons, Indra Sinha imaginatively sets his novel *Animal's People* in Khaufpur ("Terror Town," in Urdu), the novel itself being something of an ethical challenge to the Union Carbide disaster at the pesticide factory in Bhopal on December 3, 1984.

The narrator, known as Animal, another of "midnight's children,"[12] is gathered up from amidst the debris of the explosion in the slums and taken in by "Ma," a member of the French Catholic women religious, until his development brings not only morphological maturation but the onset of somatic and psychological disabilities related to his having breathed in the noxious gases. As his spine twists with severe scoliosis, forcing him to walk on all fours, voices assail him, the skin of his hands hardens, callouses, and cracks, and his shoulders widen; and, now "bottoms up," he simultaneously loses (from the perspective of "the Eyes," his beholders) and revokes "the distinction between a 'human . . .' and 'animal'" (*Animal's People*, 1). Queering the name *Animal* flung at him by children, his ass-level—as distinct from eye-level—view of the world not only occasions his own journey through self-disgust, but his awareness of this DMZ set among humans: "Instantly you become all solemn," he says to onlooking, readerly Eyes, ". . . like you were in the presence of the lord of death" (4). Turning his own abject eye outward, he rages at his onlookers, aware that "no one looks inside" (11). Irreligious—who was to say whether a child orphaned that night was Muslim or Hindu? What would religion even mean to one who has been committed, by history, to live with nothing but the power of nothing? Who lives, as "animal," positively outside most religious and naturalist ontologies?—refused and refusing the boundaries of that picket fence named morality, he—whose buttocks stands in for his face—is gloriously bawdy, irreverent, and reduced to shitting on the railroad tracks like the rest of the slum tenants, if that *is* really such a reduction.

"Look Ellie Doctoress," Animal says to the doctor of good will without borders, "You foreigners talk as if the sight of a bum is the worst thing in the world, doesn't everyone crap? . . . There's a lot to be said for communal shitting. For a start the camaraderie . . . It's about the only opportunity you get to unload a piece of your mind. You can bitch and moan about the unfairness of the world. You can spout philosophies. . . . The rich are condemned to shit alone" (154). Animal knows us: Disgust indulged wraps us in individual estates, the patrolled territories of "the body," now so easily—given our exaggerated demeanor—gullible to capital interests and investments.

In one planetary span, neoliberal ideology (that turbine now driving globalization) ekes out disability zones, cities of posthuman "animals," via "slow violence."[13] Animal, of course, stands in for the thousands of persons displaced from or dislocated in relation to the global capitalist economy, and Sinha's postcolonial novel "draws attention precisely to the uneven relations of power that persist" between local contexts and readers who enjoy the commodities circulated through the global markets.[14] Yet as my Garden State variety of disability suggests, this slow violence should not be taken as only a "Third World issue." Although ever and again "the body" of elite culture does try, consciously or not, to dispose of its risk elsewhere than in its own backyard—not without certain successes (as Bhopal reminds us)—ultimately, in a finite planetary system, such attempts constitute a planning fallacy. Animal is a reminder of every person's "radically changed"—ecological, temporal—"nature."[15] A world of becoming today circulates human ignorance, lack of foresight, and injustice, such that disability can arrive as something other than evolutionary varieties most wonderful. Given that we are living in an epoch that some earth scientists have begun to call the Anthropocene—that phase of the earth's history within which the impact of human culture on all planetary systems has become significant—resentment against life, against a world of becoming, can become equally resentment of one another and cynicism in the political arena.[16]

In the face of "becoming disabled" at this time in planetary history, one can, admittedly, both resent the open ontology of world becoming and despair of humanity itself. Within the Anthropocene, learning to love "human nature" may be among the greatest challenges. The healing of moral melancholy and cynicism, so necessary for making our way in an urban world, especially as postapocalyptic scenarios like Fukushima and Bhopal already transpire, may be brought about by loosing this resentment against life encrypted in "disability," since today disability carries even this weight of "human nature." Continuing to survive during the Anthropocene, this epoch of Human Nature, will itself require meditative arts of the self to open the heart beyond the recoils of disgust and the clench of anger. To live we may need to learn what I have learned from my mentors in the disability community: To agree to live is already to agree to forgive and to forbear.

Ascetic Practice as Cultural Resistance: Putting Disgust to Work

Simone Weil, in her aphorisms in a section of *Gravity and Grace* titled "The Mysticism of Work," proposes "the use of disgust," even that connected with manual labor, for spiritual practice. She asks, "Why has there never been a mystic, workman or peasant, to write on the use to be made of disgust for work" in training the self? Then she observes: "Our souls fly from this disgust which is so often there, ever threatening, and try to hide it from themselves by reacting vegetatively." She concludes: "Disgust in all its forms is one of the most precious trials . . . a ladder by which to rise."[17] As Weil saw it, as if meditating on Psalm 22:14, "For [God] did not despise or abhor the affliction of the afflicted," working with disgust can bring us to the cusp of the sacred. This she sees as the epitome of the holy: to hold even what has revulsed us, those we find abject (for Weil, the afflicted), without judgment. In some ways, this philosophical practice of "break[ing] open the human perspective" on disgust and "free[ing] it from its history of mediocre moral and religious conditioning" might, retrospectively, be said to be central to her own work, even as she wonders why no one precisely has taken up the challenge.[18]

Affliction, which I have yoked here with the affect of disgust and with the psychic symptom of "disability," was for Weil a decisive epistemological locus. In *"Dancer in the Dark*: Affliction and the Aesthetic of Attention," theologian Alyda Faber describes Weil's approach: "Through affliction, the world of necessity 'enters' our bodies and souls: we realize that we humans belong to an impersonal world," that "we do not create or control the world, not even this intimate perplexing world that we call 'I'" (87). "A loving attention to the real," Faber writes, summarizing Weil's philosophy, "renounces habitual consolations: that suffering will be redeemed, that ultimately nothing will be lost, that affliction strikes the sinful or careless or weak." Weil's vision, Faber concludes, was one of soulfulness that by "renouncing claims to well being" could "free us to consent to what is, to experience . . . both the shocks of affliction and shocks of beauty," without seeking redemption from or in them (88).

But if Weil's rhetorical lament regarding the dearth of spiritual, philosophical practices for traversing disgust appropriately reads the rarity of neomonastic or ascetic, philosophical arts in twentieth-century Christianity, what we today call "grotesque realism" might not have been as far away from ancient Christian thought as it now seems to us. The fifth-century *Life of Syncletica*, as retold by contemporary scholar of late antiquity Virginia Burrus in her *Saving Shame*, appears itself as something like a narrative version of corpse mediation. Both well-born and beautiful, Syncletica steps outside accessible economies into the life of a Christian ascetic, and, in the end, teaches her psychological athleticism on behalf of the soul, using her three and a half years of terminal illness to "confound the distinction between living body and putrefying corpse" (*Saving Shame*, 105). Burrus herself reached for the *Life of Syncletica* as illustrative of her thesis that ancient Christians "converted [shame] into a defiant shamelessness, giving rise to a performatively queered identity that retrieves dignity without aspiring to honor" (*Saving Shame*, 8). Insomuch as the ascetic him/herself represents a "combatant . . . in the spectacles of the [public] arena," this "performance of a shamed and shameless identity opens up hitherto closed spaces, challenges prevailing assumptions, and thereby creates new social and political possibilities" (ibid., 36, 43). Of Syncletica's *Life*, Burrus concludes: "To the extent that the reader . . . is overwhelmed . . . by the nauseating sight, stench, and even taste of her corrupting flesh . . . we ourselves 'become as if one' with what we are made capable of imagining" (ibid., 107). *The Life of Syncletica*, in other words, is a technology for living the flesh "with the generative power of an excessive self-humbling that offers in exchange for the sacrifice of face" in relation to culture "a joyous opening of the subject within grace" (ibid., 8). Comparably, within Buddhist corpse meditation, practitioners are instructed first to become intimate with hair, nails, teeth, and skin (all dead matter), then to spend as much time as possible around a dying or dead body, holding it mindfully in all its visceral gore "until there is no longer any divide between the image 'out there' or 'in here'" in an effort to derail the fear of death, hence one's attachments, from emotionally obstructing one's engagement with life.[19] Thus, "meditating on death one overcomes death";[20] death loses its sting, its stronghold, and we come to live in grace. In this way, as even Erasmus put it, "death is the mother of spiritual life."[21]

Similarly, the seventh-century *Life of Symeon the Fool*, if not exactly inviting imitation of the sixth-century monk for whom it was named, might nevertheless have served as a teaching tale for urban practitioners. Symeon, after thirty years of ascetic practice in the desert, returns to the city as something of a performance artist in his own self-directed street theater— flirting with prostitutes, consuming raw meat and huge amounts of beans, occasioning farting and even defecating in public. "Symeon's queer shame-lessness," Burrus explains, "has . . . shamed the shamers by exposing the arbitrary tyranny of every naturalized social convention. Symeon . . . throws in his lot with those who bear the heaviest burden of shame: Christ's place . . . 'is among the beggars, especially among the blind, people made as pure as sun through their patience and distress'" (*Saving Shame*, 41). Corpse meditation comparably insists that "repulsiveness" is "a matter of the mind itself" and discounts the notion that "the source of the abject is ultimately located in the matter of the body,"[22] thus liberating meditators to associate lovingly, without judgment, in the muddied milieu of life.

Whether the iconic grotesque "Suffering Servant" or "Man of Sorrows" of Isaiah 53, the appearance of which can be tracked in art history to thirteenth-century northern Europe, comparably catalyzed the mendicant movements or expressionistically represented their energy has been historically difficult to track.[23] What can be noted is that the social effects of the new money economy in the newly urbanized regions of medieval Europe pressed significant numbers of persons into new devotional articulation and life styles. As Dorothee Soelle puts it in *Suffering*, "Mystical theology"—the breeding grounds for which were the heretical lay movements of the Beguines, Beghards, and Free Spirits—"arose under the monstrous weight of suffering in the late Middle Ages and mirrors the helplessness of people in their woes and their protests against them" (95–96). Amidst this rapid urbanization, combined with the setting aside of the gift economy for the first waves of capitalism, lay religious or "secular" (non-enclosed) orders developed a "a mental climate around 1200 that was increasingly sensitive to social differentiation, the pernicious influence of credit and business on social relationships, the rising divide between rich and poor, and the marginalization of the weaker elements in society, like lepers, the elderly, and the urban poor."[24] Like modern hippies, asserts historian Robert Lerner, many persons, especially any number of aristocratic women, "rejected their parents' profession and wealth because their businesses were tainted by speculative gain."[25] As these persons saw it, "voluntary poverty enabled them to redress the injustices created by the search for greater wealth." And "liberated from such social obligations of property, they could devote their life to the care of the indigent."[26] Far from being rural, the Free Spirit "heresy . . . was found in urban centers—Strasburg, Mainz, Cologne, Erfurt, Brussels—and middle-sized towns. . . . with most beguines of at least urban patriciate and/or landed aristocracy."[27] At least within the community represented in the first biblical letter of Peter, identification with the suffering servant of Isaiah 53 led persons "dislocated" or "alienat[ed] from at-homeness in the world . . . by conversion" to a practice of endurance amidst "local public hostility" and its stigmatizing and criminalizing labeling of Christians.[28]

While a direct link between the icon of the suffering servant and these movements has not been established, one does wonder about the transformative power of the icon to move one through aversion and so enable love to remake persons, especially here any number of urban aristocratic women, who became "seculars"—that is, religious persons living outside the monasteries or cloisters and working in relation to the displaced urban poor. To learn to love a God become corpse, become political torture victim, thus grotesque: Is this not always already a training of the affective intelligence? While vicarious or substitutionary atonement—the view that God sent his son, Jesus, to die as a substitute for the death mandated of sinners themselves—when defined as blood sacrifice, horrifies any number of us, could the core of it not be the expansive, affective willingness to carry the abject weight of another's life? In the mystical orders, suffering named not just the disposition of an abject other, but a devotional way of becoming loving, serene, and free for the other by taking leave of narcissistic hope.[29]

As such insights have rubbed against the bones of Christian liturgical ritual and texts, I began to wonder if a parallel to corpse meditation, maybe even some kind of redress of the grotesque or monstrous by way of training toward equanimity in the face of disgust, might not have been inherent within Christian narrative iconography related, most particularly, to Jesus crucified. Or if it has not been inherent, might we not improvise from this locus toward a practice that would enable "the let-down of repulsiveness"?

In an article entitled "Ascetic Theology before Asceticism? Jewish Narratives and the Decentering of the Self," biblical scholar Lawrence M. Wills invites a reading of biblical narrative as figurative novels within which one might find a narrativized pattern for meditative, ascetic practice, for example, kenosis or ego displacement, begging, fasting, and so on. Ascetic practice, Wills explains, might be described as a means of discipline for remaking the self or for "decentering of the self," a self shaped by cultural values not congruent with one's religious orientation. Rather than deprivation of the body aimed at wholesale rejection of life in the world, and far from a religious aberration, ascetic disciplines—a form of cultural resistance—rescale bodies so as swerve culture and its ideology of everyday life ("Ascetic Theology," 903, 904). With asceticism now widely recognized as a positive cultural reconstructive innovation of the late antique period, Wills reconsiders Qumran, pre-Christian Jewish, and novelistic texts, for example Daniel, Judith, and Esther, as narrativizations of ascetic rituals, with the hero/ine at the center of the narrative exemplifying "a certain enactment of ascetic discipline" (ibid., 902, 910, 911). In other words, narratives were assumed to act as something like textual icons, as instructive practices. Under colonial occupation, asceticism—the renunciation of the culturally engendered self so as to generate a self more congruent with religious values—may not have been confined to desert communities of practice, but may have been as close to the world of urban Jews and Christians as the epic was to them and the novel is to us. Wills adds that asceticism thus "may exist in a purely idealized, fictional context" (ibid., 920). That is, one merely needed to know how to lift the figure and ritual from the fictional context so as to use it as a rule of life, as a discipline, an affect practice.

In chapter 1, I have shown how Isaiah 53 (and Isaiah 54, Van Gogh would surely add) can function in this way. Here is another example. When Paul invited readers in the kenotic hymn of Philippians 2 to "have this mind among yourselves," he may have merely made an overt allusion to what readers had expected of the text: a model of what we would describe today as mindfulness practice.[30] If narratives of ascetic practice were as broadly distributed w:thin that era's urban milieu as novels are today, then the narrative Jesus likely yielded a pattern of behavior distinct from and over against that of the ideal citizen of Rome. If gospels were something like urban novels, cosmopolitan members of the Jesus movements were potentially being invited into an ascesis from culture, invited to consider an alternative horizon of value—invited to circulate their own lives sacrificially. This might well have involved carrying the pain of one another, even the pain of those lives marked as the economic and social waste of imperialism, even to "laying down their lives for their friends" (John 15:13). Ellen Bradshaw-Aitken's *Jesus' Death in Early Christian Memory: The Poetics of the Passion* comes close to articulating just such an understanding, though by insisting upon the liturgical nature of these texts: "The memory of Jesus' suffering and death developed in relation to the cultic practice of various early Christian communities," the accounts inherently formed by "the dimension of ritual practice" and forming in turn the community's everyday practice of "endurance and solidarity in suffering," including bearing up under reproach (20, 16, 160).[31]

Yet the tendency toward iconic suppression of the humiliated and suffering body, this specular repression, quite surprisingly has been no different within centuries and regions of formal Christian theological discourse, despite the argument that could be made for asserting that "the Christian body is grotesque body."[32] Even as Isaianic thought appears to be one of the most consistent intertextual interpretative frames for Christian thought—see Matt. 8:17 and 26:63a; Mk. 15:28; Lk. 22:37; John 12:38; Acts 8:32–33; Romans 10:16; 1 Peter 2:22–25, 1 Cor. 11:24 and 15.3[33]—Christian theology has been quick and consistent in dismissing and/or transposing this disfigurement, making it nothing more than an auspicious sign of metaphysical power (a trajectory discussed in my *Spirit and the Politics of Disablement*) or commuting it from ugly to beautiful, an aesthetic convention stretching from the second century to the present. New Testament scholar Stephen Moore, writing in his *God's Beauty Parlor*, explains:

> The assertion that Jesus was ugly only made theological sense within the framework of a preexistence Christology, a framework whose central strut was the Fourth Gospel. Before this framework was firmly in place, Christian authors seem not have known what to do with Isaiah 53:2–3. . . . But by the end of the second century . . . Isaiah 53:2–3 was being whipped out fearlessly and

repeatedly by the apologists and other Christian authors, confident that
the "before" snapshot of Jesus that it represents merely serves to accentuate
the "after" snapshots that are readily available now that he has undergone the
miraculous makeover of crucifixion with resurrection. (127)

Such a trajectory of Christological thought as flagged by Moore, which
seems surely to have been picked up by Warner Sallman in his famous
twentieth-century images of the softly feminized Jesus with flowing
brown locks, as in *The Lord Is My Shepherd* (1943) and *Portrait of Jesus*
(1966), assumes "the age-old inclination to equate looks with worth, which
in antiquity, crystallized in the physiognomic handbooks of the second to
fourth centuries c.e.," yet "finds its quintessential expression in our own
time in the U.S.-led entertainment industry" (Moore, *God's Beauty Parlor*,
127–28). Grotesque iconography—the "narrative iconography" of the servant songs of Isaiah 53 and 54, taken into the theology of the Jesus movement, as well as visual art relating the grotesque Christ, the Christ on the
cross (as available in stained glass cathedral windows as in kitsch art)—has
been intimately available to Christian liturgical worship as well as meditative practice. But Christians, when presented a grotesque at the heart of
our figurative iconography, have been, for the most part, unwilling to live
with it.

By contrast, queer theologian Marcella Althaus-Reid associates Mary,
Jesus, and God with urban scavengers and untouchables so as to disrupt the
moral, sexual, and economic laws of the global city (for her, Buenos Aires),
as well as theological ideology. As Althaus-Reid explains, moral and economic laws—inherently also laws of tact, of touch—always already map
disgust. In her essay "*El Tocado*," Althaus-Reid describes Jesus as born not
of one we revere as *theotokos* or "God-bearer," brightly haloed and backlit,
but as born of an untouchable woman: "Mary is the woman who could neither be touched by men nor by God" (396). Jesus, she asserts, must then be
a contaminated Messiah: "Jesus brings together extreme touchability ('The
Word becomes a human being') and extreme untouchability by bringing
contamination and contagion into Divine revelation" (396).[34] Rather than
seeing Mary as model of modest humility, this approach remembers Mary
as herself one of the humiliated ones—hardly clothed in heavenly, beatific
blue. Think of her now as the war rape victim, mutilated by machete. You

fill in the region: Central America, Sierra Leone, Bosnia, the refugee camps of Haiti, the crip on the city street.

For Althaus-Reid, we embrace such a contaminated God at our own risk—at the risk of contamination, that is, which yields an alternative law of tact in the city: The divine economy proves itself an alternative to the path of industry, of production, of cultural comeliness, an alternative to the laws of sexual and class propriety ("*El Tocado*," 396). "A graffiti Jesus," she writes (referring to a political cartoon capturing the figural imposition of a scavenger on a cathedral wall, circumstantially and ironically under the banner "Jesus is reborn"), "may show us the presence of a moving Scripture" (399).

While Christian theology has managed the grotesque either by metaphysical transmutation or by sheer repression, I simply suggest the possibility of other, subaltern readings of Jesus as figurative grotesque, possibly historical, but more relevant to us as iconography (whether narrative or figural) for meditative practice. Read in this way, the iconography of Jesus on the cross is an example of what Mikhail Bahktin called "grotesque realism."[35] "Grotesque realism shows the body without clear boundaries, focusing on the apertures, convexities, and offshoots. There is an emphasis on activities in which the body exceeds its limits, such as copulation, pregnancy, childbirth, agony, eating, drinking, and defecation"—also wounds, blood, and pain.[36] Given the power of images, of iconography, used by Rome for advancement of its own imperial economy,[37] what might the ramifications have been of deploying, among the early Jesus movements, this grotesque Christ? Or inasmuch as historical realism proves not so much the point, what could be its effects—through liturgical and meditative practice—among us still? On the laws of tact or touch in the city? What could be the effects if we were to set aside historical Jesus realism, set aside "action-figure" Jesus, and assume the Christic imaginary—including Mary and Van Gogh's Lady Sorrow—as iconography for remaking our own affective intelligence so as to learn to breathe through disgust, to still a retching gut, to calm impulses to strike out? Christianity has at various junctures situated the emotional intelligence of a God who feels, if by groaning, at the pivotal center of the urban street ballet so as to generate a geography of resistance by expansive, fleshy generosity.

Yet the institutionally held and canonical images, such as Jesus as Man of Sorrows or Suffering Servant, are neither summary nor prescriptive.

Our iconographic repertoire may include contemporary film, art, and literature, because our work will be to learn to engage empathically and with equanimity bodies that we construe as marked by affliction, disgust, disfigurement, and/or revulsion within our own locale;[38] for "how we look, and look at each other . . . determines in large part how we make our way through the world and how we treat one another."[39] After all, "a misfit occurs when world fails flesh in the environment one encounters."[40]

The images to which canonical Christianity returns again and again—to Christ as corpse or on the cross—suggest both a way of meditatively employing the images of the scorned, disfigured, abused, imperial torture victim, and a way to break through transcendentalist metaphysics. Religious images are but icons for redirecting our aversions so that we might more mindfully engage those bouts of aesthetic nervousness, unique to each of us, that grip us on the streets of our mongrel cities.

The narrative icon of Animal from Indra Sinha's fictional account of the Bhopal disaster, *Animal's People*, does precisely this: offers an image for ethical cross-examination, for calling into question our ways of knowing and organizing the world, for challenging our moral numbness. Novels can of course be used as fabulating machines for the affective intellect—to "move" us, that is; even Sinha's Animal agrees and tells us his story for that sole reason: "Books should change things" (*Animal's People*, 10). Living with Animal as pivotal grotesque requires us to engage self-recognition, then anger at ourselves and one another, and, when the heart grows wide, forbearance toward one another and ourselves. To find a place of equanimity, of deep love and insight about the world, humanity, and our situation, to love *this* world, then, might be a training of the affections in relation to Animal. Animal becomes the meditative grotesque through whom we are invited to cross so as to love our future.

The Ruins of God: Toward a Crip/istemology

But to suggest this focus on the iconography of Christ as corpse or on the cross is to do no more than to admit what we already know in our minds and guts today: God has been positively ruined—that is, ruined, but positively so—both inside of and outside of formal theological channels. Within theology, Althaus-Reid, for example, insists that "God becomes exemplarily irregular in God's own translation in Jesus, a touching God outside the hegemonic affective and economic structures of production" ("*El Tocado*," 403). And then she wonders aloud with us, "Was the departure from God-self in the incarnation of Jesus somehow an act [within which] deep dissatisfaction with Godself . . . made of God *El Tocado*, that is, an untouchable, contaminated and transgressive God," but a God, as I have argued here, whose narrative enables "an affectionate knowledge or 'amatory know how' for crossing borders of tact?" (ibid.). Such theism has already worked through the aversive, because "love is not an otherworldy, intruding . . . power—and to meditate on the cross" or on a contaminated, untouchable Godhood, including Mary and Jesus, "can mean to take leave of that dream" (Soelle, *Suffering*, 148). This has been in no small way the conclusion of the 1960s "death of God" theologians, including Dorothee Soelle and any number of us who write in their wake.

Burrus, too, reminds us that the vision of a wholly contaminated, ruined, and "disgusting" God is no recent Christian theological insight. Flesh, the dynamic if ever-leaky fluid physics of embodiment that always escapes the transcendentalist metaphysical containment or idealized whole of "the body," affectively enabled by relationship to the God whose life has traversed the abjection of the flesh, became in Christianity "the site of a deliberately offensive, explicitly countercultural faith," Burrus suggests (*Saving Shame*, 52). Icons of a body disfigured have held this God in ruins before our eyes, a God who has assumed the position of the abject, not as an invitation to a moribund ridding of our own flesh, as might have been imagined of the grotesque within the horizon of cultural idealism, but rather so that we can live flesh, mortality, finitude, transience, even our own disgust with ourselves, with "a defiant shamelessness . . . that retrieves dignity without aspiring to honor" (ibid., 8). With this God, life has traversed disgust and shame and so also the death of the ego in order to live ever more flush with the flesh. Thus our theological father Tertullian assumed that God "will love the flesh which is, so very closely and in so many ways, [God's] neighbor—although infirm . . . although disordered . . . although not honorable . . . although ruined, although sinful . . . although condemned.'"[41] The religious path draws us intimately toward the flesh, its scintillation—the sacred now but a thin, breathy sheath, easily ruptured in our breathless rush, sheltering flesh against injurability.

Consequently, the figure of Christ as grotesque—or the theology of the cross—actually can signal the intent to navigate disgust differently. The figure of Christ, as interpolated through Isaiah 53, would not be "the vital, pure and busy Jesus" of Adolph von Harnack and modern theology—Jesus the healer, who is not touched by illness himself.[42] Christian theology, rather, ventured a God who was cast in the pall of the abject, a Roman torture victim, one who likely repulsed Roman cultural aesthetics that valorized the rational mind-soul exerting control over a body. Up against the symmetry and order of that Roman mind-self, Christian movements brought a different practice of presence to life: the figuration of a grotesque, of vulnerable flesh still passionate about life.[43] What has grown in Christianity among its practical emphases, in this theism of the ruins of transcendence, is a commitment to navigate disgust by incorporating abjection into the sense of and responsibility of the self to be in solidarity with flesh, so as to valorize material existence itself.[44]

This path of navigating disgust differently becomes as important to post-theists as to theists, since any of us might one day come suddenly to wear the infamous thyroid cancer necklace, just as we must also live knowing the guilt of environmental noncomprehension and the consequent ethical offloading of the risks of our own behavior. In this, the subsistence farmer, killing weeds with 2-4-D to reclaim another furrow in the garden, may have been culpable along with global corporations, though I would argue that the farmer's level of ethical responsibility was not equal to that of the global corporation, nor did he or she have an equal ability to flee responsibility geographically and fiscally. Given the slow violence of environmental toxins, we may all come to swallow ourselves in abjection as we come face-to-face with our mutating selves or the abject faces of the ones we blame and resent. We live within mutational reach of the figural image of Professor David Lurie in J. M. Coetzee's novel *Disgrace*, caught in waves of sexual and racial shifts of power in post-apartheid South Africa, complexly culpable and brutally disfigured, if transformed. The cross-examination worked through Isaiah 53 becomes, within Christianity, conflated with the grotesque on the cross; and might not this way—in which persons train themselves to overcome the judgment or abjection of the socially despised, of being just ugly and stupid, by identification with a love that doesn't flee the flesh—be equally important today? To learn to carry Christ, the despised one, within (2 Cor. 4:10, Gal. 6:17)—as also Mary, the humiliated one, and Lady Sorrow, the sociosexually marginalized one—can enable persons, by way of transference, to navigate the riptides of despair so as to hold the heart wide open still.

But for many in the West, God has not been quite so "positively" ruined, given the history of colonialism and racism, patriarchy, sexism, and heterosexism, along with extremist Christian actions—like that of Norwegian anti-Islamist Anders Breivik, the religiously motivated suspected assassin of seventy youths in a progressive political summer camp on July 22, 2011. Of at least equal, if not greater, concern is the political trend to tie Christianity to ideological absolutes, such as those of Tea Party politics in the United States. The postmodern deconstruction of metaphysics has hardly been as widely broadcast as intellectual and ideological aversion to and quiet cultural dismissal of all things religious. "Protest atheism," as theologian Elizabeth Johnson terms it, arose several decades ago in response to a perceived impasse between science and religion, as well as in protest to inexplicable suffering and cultural change. "Atheism arises out of human suffering," observed Soelle, "when the one who causes suffering and takes it away [or not] is proclaimed as God" (*Suffering*, 143). That practical theologian Gretta Vospers attempts to move the suppressed dissent public, urging us toward commitment to one another "with or without God," is today but one symptom of an even more emphatic revulsion in our time, sometimes simply marked as revulsion against transcendence or belief itself.[45]

To be sure, theologians such as Richard Kearney, among others of us, share some of the sentiment that theism can get in the way of the visceral physics of love, of what Kearney, in his *Anatheism: Returning to God after God*, calls "flesh and blood immanence" (20).[46] In such proposals, God becomes flesh, emptied, some nothing-something, so that we are face-to-face with one another, with the sensual flush of sentience and its precarious vulnerability, its injurability. But even more to the point, some feel compelled to admit, now stepping beyond cultural acknowledgment of religious pluralism, that religions are of the human imagination, are a poetics and aesthetics of world inhabitation.[47] For some of us, humility regarding the

religious path and our own egoic separation from "idolatrous fusion with
the totality of Being" (Kearney, *Anatheism*, 62) seem as necessary to the
practice of the religious path as to the becoming of human community today. Kearney consequently insists that "after the terrors of Verdun, after
the traumas of the Holocaust, Hiroshima, and the gulags, to speak of God
is an insult unless we speak in a new way" (ibid., xvi). As Kearney puts it
along the way to what he comes to call the "anatheistic" location, "Mindful
of the inherent art of religion, we are more likely to resist the temptations
of fetishism and idolatry—that is, avoid taking the divine literally, as something we could presume to contain or possess" (ibid., 14).

In *Anatheism*, Kearney advances along a religious path between the
world nihilism of "dogmatic theism" and the abjection of religious discourse via militant atheism or, less vociferously, the atheism that slumps or
slouches into a resolute moral melancholy, into cynicism. Hoping for a
third option, anatheism—that is, what can be said of "*ana-theos*, God after
God"— attempts, like a fox looking for a nest in grasses into which it has
never before ventured, "another way of seeking and sounding the things we
consider sacred but can never fully fathom or prove" (3).[48] Kearney's venture begins not unlike mine—in moments of engaging "an uninvited visitor" (as did Abraham under the Mamre tree, Mary with Gabriel, and
Muhammad in his cave), while I try for the street ballet and especially the
psychic pirouette of turning a street corner. Kearney, too, locates the religious as response to the "advent of alterity in the midst of the human" (4).
"Anatheism," he goes on to explain, "is about the option of retrieved belief," because it is "an invitation to revisit what might be termed a primary
scene of religion: the encounter with a radical Stranger" who is always already "associated with the name of God" (7, 21). In other words, anatheism
"resists absolutist positions either for or against the divine" by directing us
rather toward generating of ourselves a faithful portal for alterity: "The
divine, as exile, is in each human other who asks to be received into our
midst" (16, 20). Where I have mapped out the traversal of disgust or abjection, Kearney positions "the decision for hospitality over hostility" which
must be made ever again in a day (19).

Having myself attempted to lift to consciousness the psychic inhibition
become metaphysical exclusion surrounding "disability," I hardly disagree
with Kearney. But I do worry that redressing the xenophobia of difference

as Kearney proposes, a work with which Western culture has been engaged over the last several decades of humanist revisions by way of feminism and other civil rights movements, does not quite deal with the postapocalyptic scenarios into which we appear to be tumbling. I worry that Kearney's view of the alterity of the stranger, of difference, remains within the scope of humanism, retaining its "cruel optimism"[49] and its vortex of well-rounded, if still wounded, identities,[50] rather than addressing "the visibility of 'indecent' pain."[51] As theologian Cleo McNelly Kearns puts it, "To witness abjection," that touchstone of primitive terror, "is . . . often to become oneself abject and ethically disenabled, reduced to the babble of inarticulate repulsion," swallowed up in "disgrace" or, in a last-gasp effort to escape it, propelled into horrific acts of cleansing. But, she continues, "it is only in confronting this horror and enduring its ordeals that any speaker can achieve both the power and the pathos needed to make that address" to suffering "effective."[52] But disability, this keystone of modernity, which keeps us from bringing suffering into speech, into view, has not been dislodged: The suffering body remains a hidden, grotesque, and forbidden image in the West.

Disabilities theorist Lennard J. Davis, writing in an essay for *The Chronicle of Higher Education* of the humanities and their aversion to disability in the academy, notes how, despite the years of work on the integration of difference, disability remains unseen, unspoken:

> It's not that disability is simply excluded from visual and narrative representations of diversity in college materials; it is rarely even integrated into courses devoted to diversity. Anthologies in all fields now include theoretical perspectives devoted to race, gender, and sometimes social class, but disability is almost never included. Indeed, in my field, literary theory and cultural studies, *The Norton Anthology of Theory and Criticism* had only one essay on disability in its thousands of pages, and that was removed in the second edition.[53]

Indeed such exclusions, assuming disability studies to be merely peripheral, of minor concern and consequently a dissolution of critical humanities discourse, rather than the keystone of modernism that it is, have been recently rather forthrightly asserted. In an August 17, 2011 article for the *Los Angeles Times* titled "Take Back the Liberal Arts," Andrew Hacker and Claudia Dreifus hold up as exemplary of what is distracting students from "a broader and deeper understanding of the world" a Yale-based course on how disabilities are depicted in fiction. "Classes like these suggest that professors are using the curriculum as their personal playgrounds," conclude Hacker and Dreifus.[54] From a disabilities studies angle, such views merely leave in place the main character-development strut of modern realism, wherein disabled characters, always marginal, dependent, or of questionable morals, have been used as foils of character development for the able bodied—to display a character's sympathy, compassion, heroics, goodness of character, and so on.[55] That such emplotment comes to inform the cultural character of readers and film viewers, as well as medical and cultural politics more broadly, does not apparently occur to Hacker or Dreifus.

So it would appear that "disabled," "the one identity one cannot and presumably should not choose," has been excluded from whatever we have meant by difference. Variously, difference may apply to one's ethnicity, but apparently not to one's biological, morphological, and therefore medical characteristics. Leonard Davis concludes that "disability isn't just missing from a diversity consciousness . . . disability is antithetical to diversity as it now stands." While "diversity nicely suits neoliberal capitalism" inasmuch as it "conceals financial inequality" and does not challenge "neoliberal belief in the free and autonomous subject," it can be prized "only as long as we discount physical, cognitive, and affective impairments," the "collective *memento mori* of human frailty." Consequently, Davis arrives at a hardly surprising conclusion: "That peculiar sameness of difference in diversity has as its binary opposite the abject, the abnormal, and the extremely marginal."[56] So it would seem to me that Kearney's anatheistic passage must, in fact, dig below the neoliberal notions of subjectivity, including its celebration of difference.

That is why I have proceded directly to the affective intellect—that is, to the gut, or more precisely, to disgust, "the gatekeeper emotion,"[57] by developing or extending religious practices, these arts of the self.[58] The problem lies not in "the other," but with idealist fantasy or existential dread that bunkers down in cynicism and moral melancholy, both of which suggest entrenched positions of resentment against life. While not accusing Kearney of such, let me nonetheless suggest how radically different the account of Mary might be should we traverse the path of our aversions.

Kearney reads Mary as the epitome of hospitality to the stranger and the strangeness of Gabriel. "She chooses to say yes, carnally, courageously," he writes, later adding the amendment, "she volunteers" (*Anatheism*, 24–25). But let's think Mary with Althaus-Reid's queer, postcolonial hermeneutic as "contaminated" and with Jane Schaberg as a probable rape victim.[59] Given the narrative's location within an imperially militarized zone, this would hardly be a surprising turn of events, as Muslim women raped by Serbs during the recent Bosnian war would surely testify. While Kearney recognizes the internal negotiation that Mary undergoes to admit this strange ethereal presence, that is, Gabriel, might we not rather imagine, given the relentless violation of women in war zones, something more compromised than "volunteeristic" agency? Could (not) her "Yes!" have been as difficult as navigating the riptides of personal revulsion the violation of one's body can loose, then learning again to find equanimity, learning again to trust, to take up life from within this locus of ruin? As theologian Alyda Faber concludes in regard to Professor Lurie in J. M. Coetzee's *Disgrace*, so I would suggest equally of Mary, even as these two figures represent distinctly different scales of culpability: "There is only this exposure, which requires all the attention and love that we can give it, and even that is not enough."[60]

I would argue that *ressentiment* against life has been held in the location marked *disability*, and that this concept of disability has far more to do with the roiling unconscious, resenting the terms of life and becoming, than it has been honestly about persons living with impairments (as "disabilities"). This existential ridge we must now negotiate without claim to the simple innocence of a world of becoming, but rather admit its complicated circuit with and through human nature. To cultivate devotion to this world—a world in which agency belongs among a multiplicity of orders of being, a world striated by diverse forces acting over different scales of time, a world in which humans nonetheless must accept and become ethically accountable for the fact that we are apparently now the dominant drivers of planetary evolution—will require that we learn to catch ourselves in all of the various and diverse fits of indignation and patterns of disgust that we spew against life, remembering, as Nietzsche would remind us, that the most hidden form of *ressentiment* remains idealism, which cannot help but be easily buttressed today by melancholy.[61]

Emerging into the Anthropocene epoch, loving "human nature" and humans—already referenced in so much anticipatory and reflective literature, as "Wreckers" (Moira Young's term, in her young adult dystopic novel *Blood Red Road*, for a civilization that has wasted the landscape), "Animals" (in Sinha's sense), or the "disgraced" (in Coetzee's sense)—will be, as I've already noted, among our most difficult human social challenges. Flesh will not be loved if not through the extension of forbearance—accepting flaws, frailties, faults, and mortal entanglements.

Forbearance suggests a way of negotiating tectonic shifts, the susceptibility of life to swerves and chaos, with equanimity. Forbearance names the soulfulness of being able to forestall the ways in which we strike out against life, God, or ourselves for the vulnerabilities of the flesh, pain, and our limited capacity to know, and for how easily culpability settles unwittingly upon us. Forbearance refuses to allow us to foreclose on one another, insists instead that we stay open to the human discourse: "We are obligated to respond to our environment and other people in ways that open up rather than close off the possibility of response," Kelly Oliver writes, putting this sensibility into something of a Golden Rule, a wisdom teaching.[62] Forbearance serves, in this way, as an immanent practice of keeping faith with life.

Crossing through the mucky, muddy ground of affective disgust or disability disqualification provides us with a new way of seeing the world, with a crip/istemology, if you will.[63] A crip/istemology refuses judgment, expecting that in a world of becoming, among multiple agencies, things happen. This cannot be held against "God," or the world, or, where disability has previously occasioned the judgment "in/valid," against one another. Alyda Faber has written, "We are social creatures exposed to others in susceptibility to harm, aggression, or love. . . . [A] re-orientation towards truth does not come through 'labyrinthine processes of self-examination but in illumination from outside.'" Yet if "we are undone and transformed only through responsiveness to others,"[64] that undoing and transformation takes the civic form of corporeal generosity woven through with patience—or, more forthrightly, the form of forbearance.

Forbearance and Corporeal Generosity

Within the field of fleshy relations and affects, forbearance—as distinct from human rights, which patrol the body as enclosed territory—becomes so very important. Let's assume the community aquatic center as a micro-cosm of the city for the purpose of practicing forbearance. Hillcrest Aquatic Center was repurposed from a 2010 Olympic skate training site. As such, it is a beautiful new facility nestled among diverse ethnic communities.

Our Zen koan for the day will be, "What's slower than a one-legged woman on a kickboard?" When the "Slow" lap lane is collapsed into the "Leisure Lanes" at 6:30 a.m. on a Wednesday morning, "diversity" gets in-teresting. Thrasher's shoulders seem permanently locked, such that, when she does a back float, persons two lanes away complain about the threaten-ing environment of a morning swim. Sonic somehow imitates a whale for the entire hour of his swim; the feel of a sound wave underwater is, admit-tedly, curious. Pods of two, three, or five persons chatter in Mandarin, Urdu, Punjabi, and chopped English as they do their aerobic routines, rid-ing swimming noodles as if they were seahorses. Now add me into that mix: Trying a side stroke, I wobble here and there as I seek to build up enough trunk control even to stay in a lane. But on the kickboard, I am posi-tively slow (I can already feel your frustration breathing down my neck, firing your deltoids and flipper kick: breathe; relax into forbearance), and either the pool jets or the wake of a water-aerobics pod can cause a fishtail-ing of my trunk that pulls me out of "my" lane. Traffic infractions are multiple and sometimes proximally intimate. Stir also into this mix a pho-bia, among some ethnic Chinese, about death and disease contamination, which has literally struck out at me several times, landing blows on my right arm.

Forbearance is not a refusal to claim justice, but a restraint in the face of provocation, an inner reset that lands us back on the buoy of equanimity so that we constrain our own worst impulses in the face of anger, hurt, or fear. One might hope that the work on the self then can proceed in both directions—that he will be working through encultured disgust and quea-siness, as I will be staying present to him, insisting that he work on his own impulse control while I restrain my own hostility.

When Thrasher strikes and one swallows a snort of chlorinated water, it would be easy to run to the guard and demand one's rights, just as some of the senior water-aerobics gang will demand their rights in regard to the slow swimmer interfering with their free-form aerobics and swimming through their gossip pods. Forbearance demands, I think, a more grassroots approach. Over the weeks of our being thrown into the pool together, the Sikh mother and daughter have made moves to open a "swimming lane" between them when I'm around. And the Mandarin-speaking grandmother and I learn to bob our heads at each other, like pecking chickens: Somehow we know that this means we wish each other a good morning and, later, upon parting, a good day. Slowly we build solidarity and familiarity that provides a measure of care and respect for the other. Traffic infractions produce mutters that we each take to be "Sorry." As an exercise in forbearance, this work on the self in the midst of the aquatic agora—well, it can equal in difficulty the challenge of learning, at fifty-five years of age and with one leg, to swim. One must at times qualify one's own work on speed, technique, and endurance so as to learn to countenance the other. That becomes an equally important part of each swim session.

Forbearance might be seen as a specific form of love related to disgust; and love, writes William I. Miller, is "that state in which various disgust rules are relaxed or suspended." It includes a "tolerance for bodies and a willingness to excuse their foibles as well as to indulge their dangerous and polluting qualities." There is not necessarily any reward promised in forbearance: "The confrontation with disgust"—as proximate as a death-riddled body or a smoker's breath, or a homeless person's accumulated body odor, or an ethnic other's cooking smells, seeping from sweaty pores or locked into clothing fiber—"unlocks no special pleasures lurking within the disgusting." Rather, forbearance, assuming we are in a world of becoming and also mutually immanent one to another, simply overcomes disgust in favor of caring and concern.[65] As much as we might chase grand architectural and technological utopias, learning to control disgust, this "gatekeeper emotion," can be the key to the effective city, the utopian city—to cosmopolis.

Forbearance is a breath, a roominess, a receptivity, a style of flesh punctuated by mercy that we bring to the entanglements, political and fleshy, of a messy metropolis. The biopolitical responsibilization of the self to be as healthy as you can be, enacted through workplaces and insurance companies, including Medicaid, though most pervasively enacted informally, through a cultural moralization of bodies, has come increasingly to patrol and sort bodies,[66] deciding who should have claim to collective, common resources. Forbearance, however, assumes providing hospice, shelter, toward alterity, thus enfolding one another in social flesh.[67] By suspending all judgments, representations, or assumptions, one opens out a sheltering presence to encounters that may be jarringly disjunct, different, disgusting. Forbearance thus is an observation of the First Commandment—a refusal of idolatry or representation when encountering the divine within and among the human community.

Forbearance becomes politically significant when one realizes that persons declared homeless are, in the majority of cases, also deemed disabled. Having trained the self to love, one can break free of self-obsession and walk across the rolling waves of nausea. In a political world locked into cynical retreat (a self-protective measure against what seems a politically and media-manipulated public) or, contrarily, vengefully demanding a regulatory metaphysics (whether among militant theists or atheists), forbearance opens up a path of patience and good will. It steps aside from "a command morality" to counsel "'agonistic respect' and 'critical responsiveness' as the civic virtues appropriate to the contemporary world of multidimensional pluralism," knowing that such can be cultivated and held only by working on ourselves and our dispositions toward others.[68]

Forbearance, then, enjoins us to receive and hold the world, even as its tectonic plates shift, without putting our adrenals on red alert. "Christianity demands that one accept suffering with courage as an element of finitude and affirm finitude in spite of the suffering that accompanies it," Paul Tillich insisted (quoted in Soelle, *Suffering*, 107).[69] Soelle comments, "This affirmation is only part of the great love for life as a whole that Christians express with the word 'believe.' To be able to believe means to say yes to life, to this finitude" (ibid.). Such surely implies forbearance in our relation to life itself—releasing expectations about the way the world "should be" and should work; forgiving life and now "human nature" for not being ideal, promising happy endings, or offering us prominence or recognition. Forbearance—this form of generosity, a soulful transcendence by way of stretching of the heart—can deal with suffering and mutual wounding as a given, thus moving beyond the era of rights, the anger at being victimized. To be sure, the sense of "a world of becoming" has—with the advance of humanity as the strongest evolutionary force affecting the planet—become far less innocent than Tillich's stoic resolve could have recognized. Modernity's dream of time-saving and labor-saving miracles, its hope for the remediation of time's troubles, have had unintended consequences. Our bodies soak in toxins as well as sizzle under the burning rays of the sun, while corporations have not only denied, but escaped responsibility through legal and financial buy-outs and bankruptcies. Never denying the need for people's movements for human rights and justice, forbearance—this form of forgiveness by way of giving up our narcissism—must also be brought to soften the hard, resentful, cynical edges we have cultivated toward one another. Forbearance knows that "all flesh is grass," that any of us can at any time be caught in personal or social delusions—without any Archimedean point for discernment. This does not resolve into mere tolerance of all things, but it gives passional roominess for the ethical negotiation of our entangled nature—a form of neighbor love that does not collapse even amidst the necessary defense of justice, even justice for oneself. Love, theologian Alyda Faber reminds us, "means the desire to stay near another person in their disorientation in the world, their wretchedness, their unloveability—the symptomatic excess of always unfinished efforts at social legitimation."[70]

At this point, disability experience, as Jean Baudrillard suspected, becomes an experiential authority for navigating somatically, ethically, spiritually the ruins of globalization's superstructure. That, too, is part of crip/tography. Help yourself imagine how to love life through it all. You might be surprised that there's much joy and good laughter. We laugh at ourselves and with one another; we're not surprised by flesh.

Here's a small initial practice for training the urban soul in forbearance: Let some dandelions grow, if not as a free-for-all human dietary tonic, then on behalf of another necessary species. While dandelions have been greeted as some form of urban plague,[71] these blooms—among the first blooms of spring—have been found necessary to the survival of bees as they wake and stir, looking for food. The practice of tolerating dandelions will also surely rile up neighbors whose aesthetic sensibilities prefer a grassy monoculture: more practice in forbearance. Perhaps there is also a time dimension to forbearance such that we allow our pace to be interrupted by the different agencies of place. Such environmental notions of forbearance might well have been practiced within the Israelite Jubilee and Sabbath cycle, which allowed for a year or two (in the fiftieth year) when weeds and domestic plants intermingled.

Christianity has at various junctures situated the emotional intelligence of a God who feels at the pivotal center of the urban street ballet so as to (re)generate a geography of generosity and justice. While the original "death of God" theologies from the 1960s aborted transcendentalist metaphysics in the face of the genocides and holocausts of the mid-twentieth century but may have gotten intellectually stuck on resistance or maybe even resentment, disability now forces yet again the question of metaphysics. Jean-Luc Nancy suggests that the cultural death of "the body" (of God) traverses in its own way the question of "ontotheology." God risks

> exposing himself *dead* like *the world of bodies*. On the one hand, the divine body rotting, putrefied, petrified, the face of Medusa and Death—and on the other, *as the other side of the same death of God*, the divine body exposed, the first material extension of a world of bodies, God infinitely modified. In other words: no God, not even gods, just *places*. Places: these are divine *because rid* of God's Body, and of Death in Person. Places divine through an opening whereby the whole "divine" collapses . . . , places of *limon terrae*.
>
> This is the way God's glory is shared: Death, the World. Rotting as Mystery, mud as the manner and *ductus* of places. All ontotheology is traversed and worked through by this ambivalence about the truth of the body as a *glorious body*. A single gesture . . . erects God as the Body of Death: *and* delivers space to the multiplication of bodies.[72] (emphases in original)

The practice of forbearance within our urban communities of multi-ethnically informed flesh obviously has its challenges.[73] Christian Parenti, writing in *Tropic of Chaos: Climate Change and the New Geography of Violence* about "the catastrophic convergence of poverty, violence, and climate change"—occasioning the probability of 700 million climate refugees by 2050 as well as pogroms and social breakdown—tracks the resolve of governments in the face of failed states and, as in Rio de Janeiro, zones of cities turned neofeudal (5, 7, 10). In the "new Dark Ages" (*Tropic of Chaos*, 15), plagued with conflicts over such basic resources as food and water, scoured by economic damage to coastal cities, particularly to Third World megacities, and the real probability of new tribalisms, military forces, such as those of the United States, train now as "Urban Warriors." "After [Somalia]," Parenti writes, "the Pentagon began to think more seriously about how to fight irregulars in cities and failed states" (ibid., 18, 22, 35). The strategy of "small wars, limited war, low-intensity conflict" more suited to the mazelike conditions of Third World megacities or Third World–like aspects of megacities elsewhere has been known as "counterinsurgency." Whereas "conventional warfare seeks to control territory and destroy the opposing military . . . counterinsurgency seeks to control society" and does so by rupturing and tearing "the intimate social relations among people, their ability to cooperate and the lived texture of solidarity." Or simply call it "social mutilation" (ibid., 23, 26). "The social wreckage of counterinsurgency," already obvious in Mexico, among other states, "will be evident in the form of crime, smuggling, civilian militias, death squads, regions glutted with light arms and routine use of detention and torture" (ibid., 36). Yet this undeclared militarization of cities in the name of protecting a global elite settles, here in North America, upon an inherited form of democracy riddled with contempt: "The mutuality of contempt is much of what pluralistic democracy is all about. What democracy has done is arm the lower [class] with some of the contempts that only the high had available to them before."[74] To hold the sacred in relation to sociality, to flesh, amidst planetary urbanization is to challenge the strategy of counterinsurgency and its elite-state mentality.

Flesh can be lived otherwise, or so I've discovered. Chuck is among the quite healthy-looking homeless men who encamp at Jericho Beach—he, near the bathhouse. He's a "binner," operating a bicycle that pulls an unbelievably long carriage of garbage canisters into which he sorts what he finds. He's never one to tell his story, but will greet you with exuberance and the banalities of social care. ("How are you? Great weather.") It's somewhere after 5:15 a.m., my start time for bike rides, and my eighty-pound dog, Lyra, is running beside me. In the process of my hopping (literally!) off the bike to dispose of her waste, the bike goes completely out of gear. I'm stranded: My bike does not carry crutches to compensate for my one leg, and I'm five kilometers from home. No cell phone. My partner is out of town anyway this morning and won't even know I'm not back. And I have a large dog, off leash, illegally so. It's barely dawn. And I can see no way to fix the bike. I begin to make the most immediate and necessary decisions, grabbing my dog's collar to keep her close. Chuck slides up behind me like a shadow. "Don't worry," he utters, trying to calm what must be waves and waves of anxiety rolling off my back. "Don't worry. We'll take care of you. We know where you live, and we'll get you home."

In that second, I'm simultaneously horrified (these guys know where I live???!!!) and relieved. His soothing reassurances as he settles on his knees beside my bike are soon interrupted by the Parks and Recreation garbage truck coming over the hill. Chuck, as much a shadow as when he arrived, slides back into the cover of trees. The following spring, I'm making some of my first rides of the season—late, because spring has been cold and wet. "Where were you?" calls a voice, registering some level of irritation. "Don't you know we've been worried about you?" "Sorry, Chuck," I call, and then mutter inanely, "I didn't know how to check in." Flesh can stretch, can take new shapes of surprisingly compassionate and nonjudgmental care.

Flesh can also play across the near-anonymity of the city. The intimacy of the hug, reaching around me from behind, threatening the balance of my pirouette on crutches, shocks me: It's been so long since this has happened! Most people never even dare imagine how they might hug a woman on crutches. Who could this be? Whose arms have wrapped around me, crutches and all, as I stand before the fish counter? Now she lays her head into the crook of my neck, close enough that I can just catch a whiff of her; her long, dark, black, curly hair brushes against my ear and flicks briefly before my eye. Yes, definitely "her." And then the voice—it's Spanglish articulation, and I know it—Martha, one of the counter staff. She's always got the most incredible smile for me; and while it took us some months to develop facility in a shared English, that inviting face makes me feel like I will always have a friend in the world. Somehow, I must be, in the midst of this city, the same for her—at least, transitionally so. It's rather a thin economy of relation—the flash of smile, the poke in the ribs, and the hug from around the back. But I'm telling you, it has been a long time since anyone has dared to hug me like that.

One day she makes quite a production of our relationship. (You must understand, we've never sat down to talk; it transpires only within the gaps she opens in her workday.) I need help getting my coffee to the table, and she loudly volunteers from behind the serving counter of the deli. There's a waiting line at "Place Orders Here." It doesn't seem to stress her, as it does me. Without any obvious register of that press of bodies demanding her, she grabs a towel, wipes down a table, gathers a napkin, a pat of butter, knife and teaspoon, and sets the table. Oh, also a glass of water. Then comes what I had actually ordered—just a coffee and muffin, in a "to go" bag, which she opens and sets on a plate with the pat of butter. Tears slip out of the corners of my eyes at her act of gracious nurture. I wonder when the disciplines of Western culture will correct her, or whether we'll continue to get away with this workaday friendship, its levels of touch, of tact. It keeps both of us alive, but remains suspect in the city of rights, this simple human form of love.

The nascent becoming of flesh seems likewise the work of Occupy Wall Street, the movement of "the 99 percent"—suggesting a coincidence of interests between generations and working classes, emerging during fall 2011 to counter growing Western economic inequality, set in motion by neoliberal economics, as well as the corporate stranglehold on democracy. "I thought of Aristotle, of all people, while I watched the Zuccotti Park demonstrators hold one of their 'general assemblies' the other day," writes critic Michael Kimmelman in an October 16, 2011 *New York Times* news analysis essay, "The Power of Place in Protest." "We tend to underestimate the political power of physical places," he goes on to note, pondering the import regarding sociality I've been addressing here: "In his 'Politics,'" Aristotle argued that the size of an ideal polis extended to the limits of a herald's cry. He believed that the human voice was directly linked to civic order. A healthy citizenry in a proper city required face-to-face conversation" (SR1). In Zuccotti Park, protestors were giving birth to a new "architecture of consciousness" (ibid., SR6), to a new style of flesh that incorporates mutual care (over against the primacy of self-interest), social and planetary responsibility (as over against mere individual responsibility), and a renewed vision of the public and of the commons (as distinct from a moral hierarchy of who is deserving): social flesh.[75]

FIVE

The Ballet of the Good City Sidewalk: Releasing the Optics of Disability into Social Flesh

> Each urban encounter is a theatre of promise in a play of power.
>
> —ASH AMIN AND NIGEL THRIFT, *Cities: Reimagining the Urban*

> Obligation is a relation of flesh to flesh, a transubstantiation in which the flesh of the Other transforms my body into flesh.
>
> —JOHN CAPUTO, *Against Ethics*

"The Winter Market," a short story by Vancouver-based cyberpunk author William Gibson, does not create the image of Vancouver that sells either tourism or real estate. Published initially in the October 1985 issue of *Vancouver Magazine*,[1] Gibson's science fiction short story imagines the now-popular public market of Granville Island (an artificial island created by dredging and dumping), tucked under the steel spans of the Granville Street Bridge, as a postapocalyptic urban industrial wasteland. As Nickianne Moody notes in "Untapped Potential: The Representation of Disability/Special Ability in the Cyberpunk Workforce," far from suggesting biblical and now green hopes for a city within which all infants and elders lives out full lifetimes, eating the fruits of their own urban subsistence gardens (Isaiah 65:18–25), speculative literature assumes the aesthetics of urban decay and cross-examines social life under the struts of postindustrial corporate capitalism (91).

Cyberpunk—and Gibson is credited with initiating this genre of speculative literature, with "The Winter Market" among his early forays—plays in the dystopian register, exploring our anxieties about the collapse or deflation of capitalist economics, about life built on the platform of an oil-based infrastructure, about the failure of work (the only form of social cohesion systemically built up by modernity), about the social anarchy potentially occasioned in the wake of such losses. It explores—imaginatively, speculatively—the potencies already sleeping under our bridges, bodies not soothed or sustained by the communal life of corporate belonging. But in cyberpunk, "the ruins of modern architecture often provide the building materials and habitats for the next generation."[2] "While cyberpunk dramatizes special abilities and exciting youth cultures, it also maintains a dark future of inequality [and] insecurity" (Moody, "Untapped Potential," 103). Now furthered in literature categorized as postapocalyptic, speculative, or dystopic, it is a genre that at the end of the first decade of the third millennium has gone off the charts, especially within the spectrum of young adult literature. And in common with this genre in general, Gibson's early postapocalyptic story brings together the ecological and industrial ruin of the city, human and sociocultural transition, technological detritus (often creatively detourned), and, finally getting a starring role (is that what it is?), disabled bodies: "Cyberpunk visualizes a future of common disability . . . In this fictional future the dialectic between impairment and disabling is resolved; . . . the social environment of the future disables everyone, if not equally" (ibid., 90, 91).

The setting of cyberpunk literature seems now—after the first decade of the twenty-first century—not all that speculative, as we've begun to feel the ravages of weird weather, the pinch of oil scarcity on food prices, the decline of American political sway over the world, and the apparent decline of a way of life. Postapocalyptic anxieties seem to be entering into personal and political life of the twenty-first century without conflagration (at least so far in North America), by slow drip—as evidenced in the economic downturn, demoralizing workers and those aspiring to dreams of house and home, felt as a generational betrayal between the boomers and their children. As much as persons ply cities for work, for dreams of a better way of life, for getting out of poverty (for which urbanism has served well, according to journalist Doug Saunders[3]), some making incredibly perilous journeys, there's an anxiety under the pace and gleam even of global cities—an anxiety that our children, all children, will receive but the inheritance of loss.[4] Even here in "the most livable city on earth," as Vancouver has been named for years running, that dread—as Gibson's literary invention evidences—crawls out from under bridges and pounds against the floor-boards of our hearts in the deep of night.

That cyberpunk—with its lifting from the unconscious into waking anxiety urban ruins, technological detritus, and the commonality of human fleshy fragility—should be born under the bridges of the emerald city of Vancouver seems all too ironic. Yet the 2011 spring-time trilogy of Fukushima's earthquake-tsunami-nuclear meltdown has on the West Coast intimately etched the postapocalyptic into waking consciousness. For the ruins of Fukushima serve not merely as a morality tale about the late humanist and technological hubris of another city sitting on a tectonic faultline waiting for "the big one," but are even biomutationally predictive of bodies' futures across the width of the Pacific. Undoubtedly more of us will be wearing, at the least, the infamous necklace scar of thyroid cancer.[5] Can the presence of disability within the postapocalyptic genre be more than a scare tactic, a sign of ultimate catastrophe?

But disabled bodies seem to do more in postapocalyptic literature than merely remark upon existential anxiety—if also undeniably they do that. They seem not only to sport a resilient strength, but to serve as experiential authority for navigating—somatically, ethically, spiritually—the ruins of globalization's superstructure. Jean Baudrillard made just such a claim: "By the force of circumstance the disabled person is a potential expert in the motor or sensorial domain. It is not by chance that the social is aligning itself more and more with the handicapped, and their operational advancement: they can become wonderful instruments because of their handicap. They may precede us on the path towards mutation and dehumanization."[6] As with many strains of speculative literature, Baudrilliard's comment—when read in full—seems, admittedly, to be under the sway of a certain enthrallment with the technological prostheticization of the body.[7] Yet postapocalyptic or speculative literature, this literary imaginal for "trying on of fleshly style," this way of conceiving ourselves among a diversity of physicalities—don't we borrow disability in this way to test the waters of a world outside the encryptment of idealism, the waters of a world outside "the global resonance machine,"[8] to see if such a world is livable, lovable? If we can grow attached to it? Today that's a ripe question, since our future may sport more of this "ruined," wabi-sabi texture.[9]

The Future Breaks with Normality: From Disability to Social Flesh

With the aestheticization of fear, disgust shapes the active and moral imaginal of the city, both sculpting the geography of global cities and choreographing behavior there. It props up the social and built architecture of "high culture" and "civilization" even as it also maps where the waste goes, who deals with it, where those bodies live who deal with it, how much they get paid, and the squelching of our taste or desire for such persons.[10]

Disability, as I've suggested, is itself iconic in this regard. Inasmuch as this label marks out bodies that we choose not to think about and, in some ways, wish not to live, it occludes passages of thought—metaphysical, ethical, spiritual, even urban planning. Here I deal more broadly with its position at the crux of a cosmopolitan philosophy, of a possible life practice or spirituality, for the city—with disability as/and life.

In the last two chapters, I suggested practices that promote the embrace of social flesh and foster forbearance. The result of such practices, bringing nonjudgment into a cultivated appreciation for a "world of becoming," prepares one for "the studied exposure of our mutual vulnerability"[11]—for love of the flesh. *Flesh* names, not so much corpuscles and goose bumps at the skin line of a body, as a kind of social commons and sacred horizon in respect of this shared, if sentient, tissue: "a kind of social flesh, a flesh that is not a body, a flesh that is common, living substance . . . an elemental power," like the force of the wind or the sea, from the potential of which we may form a new society.[12] But flesh, as Richard Kearney points out, reading Merleau-Ponty, who worked beyond the mind-body dualism, also names the "kenotic emptying out of transcendence into the heart of the world's becoming"—of God becoming flesh of our flesh, and nothing more (or less): "The Christian God wants nothing to do with a vertical relation of subordination" (*Anatheism*, 94, 91). Speaking of this not so much as a God "hidden in immanence" as a "sacramental acoustic of natural existence," Kearney—applying the phenomenological suspension of assumptions—

simply speaks appreciatively of "the holy *thisness* of our flesh-and-blood existence" (ibid., 94).

Given the repulsion from dirt and disease, from matters of flesh and the passages of life, at the core of urban culture, North American urbanization first went reeling, sprawling into suburban tendrils, only now to reverse that flow by forming castlelike urban cores, protected with an aesthetic surveillance system regarding bodies that matter. As scholar-activist Mike Davis puts it regarding urbanism in general, "We live in 'fortress cities' brutally divided between 'fortified cells' of affluent society and 'places of terror' where the police battle the criminalized poor. . . . 'Security' has less to do with personal safety than with the degree of personal insulation, in residential, work, consumption and travel environments, from 'unsavory' groups and individuals, even crowds in general."[13] But such repulsion, dug into a "naturalized" resentment and paranoia of contamination and legitimized as an aesthetic of the city, leads to defensive individualism in the city, to paranoia about encountering one another. It prevents us from talking through differences, from conspiring, from breathing together.

Disability, when encountered hysterically as "monstrosity," threatens the clenched order imposed by fear. "The existence of monsters," wrote philosopher and physician Georges Canguilhem, "calls into question life in its capacity to teach us order. . . . All that is needed is one loss of this confidence, one morphological lapse, one specific appearance of equivocation, and a radical fear seizes us."[14] Stated from the perspective of one so labeled, "to be perceived as invalid" or "monstrous" is "to be seen [as] anomalous or contrary to order."[15]

There's even something more to the fear of monstrosity than there is to the fear of death, transience, and spoilation: The fear of monstrosity fuels the urge to euthanize disability, the sentiment of "I'd rather be dead than live like that," the "quality of life" debates—debates that typically do not include persons living with disability. Canguilhem first parsed this distinction between the fear of disease and death and the fear of the presumed abnormal, fear of the living menace: "The fear of death, affecting all life, does call humanity into question and, more narrowly, my identity"; but "this fear," Canguilhem notes, "does not cast doubt on me as an individual and normal human being."[16] Monstrosity, on the other hand (if there is one, she chuckles), "is the accidental and conditional menace of incompleteness or of distortion in shaping the form, it is . . . the negation of the living by the nonviable,"[17] and it casts doubt on our individual or cultural ontological and social sense of order.[18]

If *monstrosity* names "a difference that generates a dark terror," as Henri-Jacques Striker writes in *History of Disability* (6), *disability* nonetheless serves as the corporeal rubric of our hopes for cosmopolis and the best hope for urbanism. *Disability* names the material in situ of the postmodern challenge—"love of difference or passion for similarity" (ibid., 11). Life in our cities is pinned to loving acceptance of the flesh in its capacity to differ, openly, without ever rounding anything back to "one," to wholeness. But the fear of "disability" is in our love of order and control, such that the fear unsurprisingly rears its head when our beloved sense of life is usurped, undermined—when "growth economies" stop growing; when progress stops progressing; when the presumed order of our worlds is thrown askew, ruined; when the rich use the law to pull away from the middle class and poor; when it feels as if government has abandoned us; when one's religious convictions are used to support unthinkable ideological goals; when the neighbor next door isn't like us.

When there appears before the eyes of the beholders a "catastrophe" to which we did not know reality could give birth, then that sight must be allowed to work itself affectively into our guts, to be held there meditatively. If monstrosity "lies in the conditions and the figurations in which we receive what is born and appears" (Stiker, *History of Disability*, 12), we will meditatively arrive at the realization that how we have understood the law of life has been, at the very least, narrow, if not in error; that we have found in ourselves a refusal, buried in metaphysics or cosmology, to love life as a series of mutations (ibid., 6, 120).

After all, as Derrida put it, "The future . . . is that which breaks absolutely with constituted normality and can only be proclaimed, *presented*, as a sort of monstrosity."[19] And the neo-Marxist philosophers Michael Hardt and Antonio Negri agree. In a subsection of their volume *Multitude* entitled "The Monstrosity of the Flesh," they note that "postmodern society is characterized by the dissolution of traditional bodies," but that the experience of the "living social flesh that is not a body," the experience of our embodied interdependence, "can easily appear monstrous. . . . The unformed and the unordered are horrifying."[20] In other words, the passage through postmodernity and postapocalyptic urbanism requires—lest we nostalgically turn back, potentially aggravating forms of social exclusion—some art of the self attuned to navigating an aversion that is not as easy to capitalize upon as has been the registrar of difference, liberally conceived. Such a sense of social flesh can be gained only if we relax into a "highly democratized, decentralized, free-flowing and adaptive" connectivity and collective effort.[21] In other words, we must come to tolerate a much messier, even, yes, sometimes riskier sense of the metropolis. That looser weave, that "organic flexibility," has—as something of a surprise for those of us who love order and taking charge—everything to do with urban livability, and is, yes, simultaneously its biggest potential flaw.[22]

This is not simply to suggest that persons living with disability might finally be liberated and so enter the amended catalog of modern humanism. Rather, I wish to address disability as it functions in its broadest cultural sense, as an unresolved psychic sediment of Western cultural idealism. "Disability" is, as mentioned in the last chapter, a residual cultural symptom, not a somatic problem of a particular set of bodies. A culture that categorically keeps a set of bodies in reserve and labels them *in/valid* is a culture that not only clings to its normative ideals,[23] but one that cultivates an entrenched resentment against life. Categorically designating a reserve of bodies as "disabled" is a sign that we're still clinging to a "law of life," whether by means of theism, ecospirituality, or secular rationalism—anything that would promise surety and transcendental security. At the least, a culture that *sees* "disability" clings to developmental immaturity—more precisely, the immaturity of the "mirror stage" of early childhood, wherein we're cathected to what disabilities theorist Lennard Davis, based on insights of Jacques Lacan, has called "the hallucination of wholeness."[24] Twenty-first-century cultural conditions suggest that instead, we need a spirituality of resilience that knows how to negotiate the shoals of idealism, turbocapitalist surrealism, and melancholy, that final gasp of idealism, so as to love the world and our place in it (within cities, that is) in this epochal turning.

We need, in short, to become cognizant of our social flesh and of the responsibilities that such an awareness brings with it. When disability resolves into variation within a world of becoming, a becoming flesh of my flesh, which will include that form of generosity known as forbearance, then we might have the resilience to withstand the inheritance of loss. And yet, that requires growing out of resentment against life itself.

Disability and Aversion: The Denial of Social Flesh

Jeremy Stolow, a scholar working on the interface between media and religion, insists that the Western notion of free speech, especially as it relates to an economy of visibility, remains limned with its own iconic suppression. "The so-called secular world also depends on its own system of forbidden images," Stolow notes. Having engaged as an example of the media/ted interface between religion and globalization "the Danish cartoon affair," the publication of cartoon images of the Prophet Muhammad printed September 30, 2005, in the Danish newspaper *Jyllands-Posten* and reprinted in multiple papers throughout northern Europe and Canada, generating cascading circuits of public protests, "including the images of protestors against images," Stolow concludes: "Rather than assuming as self-evident that . . . no reasonable person would take offense at a mere cartoon . . . we might wish to explore the origins of the Western secular aversion of images of the humiliated and suffering body."[25]

In the opening chapters here, I have explored some of the elements of the aestheticization of fear in cosmopolis. With regard to disabilities, to the "dis-ing" of "disability," disability in fact "serves in the modern period as 'the master trope of human disqualification,'" as disabilities theorist Tobin Siebers has argued.[26] The "aesthetics of disqualification" transpire "when we turn a corner and find ourselves face to face with another body," as Siebers notes. Yet "the presence of disability affects not only emotional response, but also aesthetic judgment. . . . Having aesthetic judgment, sometimes called 'taste,' indicates superiority."[27] So as we turn a street corner, the violence of disability disqualification can take place in a split second—the disavowal of our shared and common humanity legitimated by the refreshing flush of assurance, the superiority of cultured taste.

Modernity, given its assumption of the neutrality of vision, "has a particularly pervasive capacity to produce . . . people . . . who disturb its fragile 'cognitive, moral and aesthetic boundaries and challenge its rather overbearing sense of order,'" disabilities theorist Bill Hughes reminds us

("Constitution of Impairment," 157, 156). And indeed, as we saw in chapter 3, Richard Sennett, the sociologist of urban space, traces the development of this hostility toward the iconic intrusion of bodies deemed somatically averse to the Protestant Reformation and thus to the development of a modernist anthropology within which the human carries the essence of self and God within (that is, internally), while libidinally neutralizing the body along the skin line.[28] By extension, this anthropology produces a sterile cityscape: Western cities as much as human souls have been landscaped to avoid or exorcise, in various ways, images of suffering bodies, bodies in pain.[29]

But it is not enough to insist that disabilities disqualification happens *aesthetically.* We need to begin to dig into the guts of the intellect, to delve into the affects or bodily feelings upon which ideation and other cultivated tastes have been established. "The plain view of reality" presumed by modernity, modernity's presumption that seeing is believing, precludes an awareness of the phenomenology of perception and the multiplicity of brain functions that generate our knowledge practice (Hughes, "Constitution of Impairment," 160).[30] We have assumed, notes Siebers, that "gut feelings" are merely innate and natural: "Nature supposedly announces in our feelings the truth about the body before us, causing us to reject harmful bodies and to embrace benevolent ones."[31] However, he insists, "This is why the study of oppression requires an understanding of aesthetics," that is, "the sensations that some bodies feel in the presence of other bodies"; "Oppression uses aesthetic judgments for its violence."[32] The aestheticization of fear in the presence of "disability" involves a conjunction of ideation and the gut impulses upon which this "naturalist fallacy" has been built.

Persons living with disabilities—disability culturally imagined as a humiliation of bodily life—might well relate to Stolow's and to Sennett's diagnoses of aversion within Western culture's urban, specular, and subjective economies. As the disabled enter the scenes of public life, refusing to stay in/valid, guts churn, waves of fear threaten to swamp us all. Having been something of an extreme extrovert prior to the onset of my disability, I have had to learn to navigate more gingerly in view of the riptides of fear my body looses in public spaces—to navigate hostile encounters without throwing proverbial fuel on the fire, as, for example, when the bicyclist plays chicken with my crutches-enabled body on the city sidewalk.[33]

"Disability" has to do with the psychological disposition of the beholder and his or her sense of the constitution of the world. It emerges from the point where affect and metaphysics meet. Disability marks encounters or experiences in which one's projection of "the law of life," whether in the form of a sovereign God or a presumed law of nature, fails; and so, as Canguilhem concludes, for such a person, for the beholder, "that which diverges from the preferable" will not be "the repulsive," but more exactly, "the repulsed."[34]

Following Nietzsche's assessment of persons attracted to the "winter doctrines" of stasis and essence, who "express persistent resentment against the flesh, pain, limited capacity to know, vulnerability to disorganization and susceptibility to death that mark the human condition" and whose "existential resentment infiltrates into stingy moral ideals, conceptions of truth, practices of identity, judgments of normality, and systems of punishment,"[35] political theorist William Connolly identifies that psychological disposition as *ressentiment*. *Ressentiment* shows itself as a refusal of "the most general terms of human existence . . . of mortality, suffering, grief and the irreversibility of time."[36] *Ressentiment* is born of resentment, as "disappointed drives . . . cross over into the terrain of entrenched dispositions towards revenge"; the refusal to believe in world time, in becoming, can build, burrow, and bunker down into *ressentiment*, and vice versa. As Connolly notes, "The time we inhabit . . . exacerbates strains of existential resentment always simmering as a possibility in mortals who must come to terms with the issues of mortality, economic inequality, suffering, sickness, exploitation, and fundamental misfortune."[37] These everyday resentments interact with one another, then fold over and into a deep ridge of existential *ressentiment* that itself shapes political, economic, and religious ideologies: "The existential dimension" of *ressentiment* "may even be accentuated today," Connolly surmises, "in part because of the minoritization of the world taking place before our eyes at an accelerated pace." And for persons who "unconsciously resent the world for not coming equipped with assurance of salvation," such *ressentiment*, Connolly observes, can and often will be projected against "those constituencies . . . who have . . . opened a wound in your creed."[38]

It thus is not hard to arrive at the conclusion that disability names one location where *ressentiment* comes into sociocultural formation. *Ressenti-*

ment counterproduces the cultural hallucination *ableism*—the belief in wholeness, integrity, the fit and perfect body, and a sense of ontological order, just as, Julia Kristeva argues, the "powers of horror" (or "the abject") "counterproduce the sublime," serving as a reminder yet again that idealism (the yen for normalcy, for comfortable, categorical analyses) hides, as Nietzsche insisted, both disgust for and deepest despair of the world. Disability, when encountered as "monstrosity," thus rends the creed of the beholder.

Conversely, when religions seize the power of purity and when cultures seize the power of the "normal," the whole, the civilized, and the "able," inside each of these constructs may be found the power of horror, the disgust reflex, which is often associated with such properties as sliminess, filth, smell, decay, disease, foulness, stickiness, and dirt. By their means religions and cultures create a power of resentment by which to prop themselves up. Disgust, explains philosopher Martha Nussbaum in her *Hiding from Humanity: Disgust, Shame, and the Law*, "hooks us on an unrealizable romantic fantasy of social purity" (106). To be a civilized, liberal, wholly secular society is just one such fantasy, a fantasy that the disgusting does and should happen outside of our view, if at all; such a view ironically assumes "civilization" to be above the workings of disgust.

This *ressentiment* has in the West taken two primary forms: Christian scales of transcendence, which presume Edenic origins and heavenly horizons without mutation and/or pain, and evolutionary views of natural order, which see "beautiful mutants" as "gross, retarded, animalistic, early primate type individuals"[39] to be extinguished in the fight that awards survival to the fittest. Both of these have been ways of judging the world wherein a presumed order has been asserted by refusing or destroying variation. A social insistence on natural order motivates the desire to cull out "disabled bodies" for the sake of the constructive pleasure of (class) superiority and the orderliness, as distinct from the vital energetics, of materialism. So "disability" incites existential *ressentiment* that has been rationalized and/or theologized.[40] Categories of disability oddly, punitively, remark upon the mere—if apparently intolerable—fact that human becoming remains mutable, vulnerable, that our sociality, policies, urban design, biological and ecological considerations of technology must all take this into account. In other words, to speak of persons as "disabled" constitutes a judgment against life that must be resolved if we are today to believe in the world as becoming and to embrace social flesh.

Disgust thus suggests a formation of sentient consciousness always already caught on the cusp of offering up judgment about fleshy matters and therefore easily co-opted by the generative power of cultural normativity.[41] Nussbaum has noted that on the other side of the trap door of disgust and its diverse social formations is the fantasy of a pure, ideal, or sublime state (*Hiding from Humanity*, 107). Disgust, ideationally speaking, always obversely makes a claim to a magical state of being—a state of being pure, even of pure thinking and pure doing, thus removed from life concourses (ibid., 122).[42] Given the events in Norway of July 22, 2011, when children of liberal political party leaders were shot to death by a lone gunman longing for a racially "pure" nation and resenting Norway's multicultural immigration policy, an event that echoed the shooting of U.S. Congresswoman Gabrielle Giffords in Arizona in January 2011, we see how quickly this disgust reflex can today be aggravated, and with what cataclysmic results. Espying a "flawed other," those who merely valorize gut instinct do not consciously think through and ethically act within a world of becoming. The aesthetics of cosmopolitanism have assumed self-mastery of the body, with such "neutralization" along the skin line only then supporting the practice of tolerance. There is within such cosmopolitan ideation no soulful depth, no practice of stretching the heart that might encourage one to breathe through the inevitable stimulus of the disgusting.

To be sure, Christian theology and culture has had a shorthand existential declaration for speaking about disability that sees itself as accepting the variations, even the pain, of nature ever differing with itself—namely, "brokenness." Numbers of persons living with disability have suffered the presumptive whitewashing of our difference in this proposal for world inclusion: "We are all broken anyway." While the cultural confession that "we are all broken" (or more simply, in liturgical and cultural rhetoric, we speak of our "brokenness") acknowledges fragmenting within world becoming, it also problematizes it. (Persons disabled, I would venture, identify our bodies as neither "broken" nor "wounded," nor do we worry these into an existential problem.) Lamenting brokenness, assuming that one is thereby siding with the marginalized of modernity, insidiously and inherently reasserts a God's-eye view and thus also a creedal belief in some order and integrity from which we've presumably deviated. In this vein, Hughes instructs us: "The multiple constitutive power of the ocular is . . . at its most telling and negative in the annals of the Judeo-Christian religions in which the gaze of God—in testaments old and new—gives testimony to the monstrosity and sinfulness of impairment. . . . From the moment that the complexity and chaos of the visible are reduced to order, the bad and the ugly enter the domain of the known" ("Constitution of Impairment," 163).

Yes, humans can miss the point of human existence and so live unskillfully, exacerbating suffering—which is how I would define Christianity's teaching of original sin. But to miss the point of existence cannot fairly be summed up in the confession of brokenness rhetorically exchanged in our culture. In fact, this kind of pathologization of the body so culturally pervasive in the West actually contributes to what the ancient and Reformation fathers identified as sin, the tendency to be "curved in upon the self," to make the self the project of a lifetime, even if here in the name of cures, health, transformation. The rhetorical naming of our self in the world as broken, given our Oprah-philic wound culture of sofa confessionals, can lock us into the egoic project of governance of "the body," rather than living the self as social flesh with the neighbor, toward the good of all. The rhetoric of brokenness refuses to accept life as a chaotic stew, continuing to hide from self-consciousness its existential *ressentiment*. As such, amidst the collision of bodies, it locates the centrality of the right to power, the right to define, with the powerful and in the eyes of the dominant (Hughes, "Constitution of Impairment," 163). And frankly, such a way of naming our residence within the world actually misses the sense of humor of persons living with disabilities, misses the irony in "queering" ourselves as crips who have already slipped away from that way of seeing the world. What allows us to self-identify as "dis/abled" is the queering snigger that all of humanity always also lives precariously on the virgule of life.

"Life and biology have their share of risks," notes Henri-Jacques Stiker (*History of Disability*, 12). Or to put it another way, "Where things are mobile at bottom, Being, as stable essence, never arrives."[43] And yet social systems have been more or less murderous in protecting their notions of order—whether metaphysics, the order of creation, social normalcy, or cultured taste. (From a disabilities studies angle, systemic integration and rehabilitation can be felt as efforts at some level to make our difference disappear, rather than to see it as integral within a world of becoming.) Categorically establishing "disability" prevents us as humans from recognizing, honoring, and living into a world of becoming. It justifies a metaphysics of control and mastery, rather than building solidarity around inescapable vulnerability: "The very *primordial* function that the disabled fill" is "proof of the inadequacy of what we would like to see established as references and norm. They are the tear in our being that reveals its open-endedness, its incompleteness, its precariousness. . . . They are the thorn in the side of the social group that prevents the folly of certainty and of identification with a single model" (Stiker, *History of Disability*, 10). No human culture has been to date ready to accept nature as a generator of differences (ibid.).[44] Yet cosmopolis, this best hope for cities, remains—despite our technological prowess—dependent upon our human capacity to accept nature, therefore human flesh, as social flesh, as unfolding difference.

Given that a sense of contamination sits at the core of the disgust reflex, repression and, more convulsively, purging are not unusual psychic responses to what is deemed disgusting. Yet it is "social teachings regarding animality, mortality, and related aspects of gender and sexuality" that "all factor into shaping the form that disgust takes" (Nussbaum, *Hiding from Humanity*, 106, 96). Consequently, despite how tempting it is to theologize our gut instincts (whether as religious observant, as "spiritual, but not religious," or as secular rationalist), disgust, whether in the seemingly most innocuous encounter on the city street or even within more decisive moral decision making, is, to say the least, "an unreliable guide to public practice" (ibid., 13).[45] When the affect of disgust seeks its own authoritative legitimation and becomes yoked with a majority power of law and/or cultural normativity, disgust becomes particularly dangerous. What Stolow and Sennett, along with disability theorists, have helped us recognize is that the disgusting within Western culture will repressively collude around specular images of "the humiliated and suffering body."

This emotional and affective upset at images presumed aversive within bodily life suggests something that is actually not particular to "suffering bodies," which disabled bodies generally are assumed to be, but rather indicates a hiccup or hitch within the physics of love. "Contending with love," theologian Alyda Faber asserts, "means confronting the extremity of human affliction" and requires "a kind of attention . . . to 'the cruel radiance of what is.'"[46] Here in the Western reaches, where cultural Christianity might at the least be coincident with a philosophy of love, love does not know how to negotiate disgust with equanimity.

"One must learn to love." It was thus that Nietzsche explained the process of passing through aversion, disgust, and resentment. Learning to love— what I have called the character of forbearance—is something like learning to listen to a musical style not of one's preferred modality:

> This is what happens to us in music: First one has to *learn to hear* a figure and melody at all, to detect and distinguish it, to isolate it and delimit it as a separate life. Then it requires some exertion and good will to *tolerate* it in spite of its strangeness, to be patient with its appearance and expression, and kindhearted about its oddity. Finally there comes a moment when we are *used* to it, when we wait for it, when we sense that we should miss it if it were missing; and now it continues to compel and enchant us relentlessly until we have become its humble and enraptured lovers who desire nothing better from the world than it and only it.
> . . . That is how we have *learned to love* all things that we now love. In the end, we are always rewarded for our good will, our patience, fair-mindedness and gentleness with what is strange: gradually it sheds its veil and turns out to be a new and indescribable beauty. That is its *thanks* for our hospitality.[47] (emphases in original)

Cities, musically speaking, are a concatenation of rhythms—an improvisational measure of jazz, layered on a heavy metal bass line, "a kind of force-field of passions that associate and pulse bodies in particular ways."[48] Forbearance names a way of entering into that pulsing, passional process of urbanism, its immanent force, by loosening our rigid reluctance, paranoia, and self-protectiveness. "Being in the city is not," write geographers Ash Amin and Nigel Thrift, "about visiting rights . . . about claiming abstract rights . . . about an imagined or perfect ideal state," but is rather "about the right to citizenship for all, the right to shape and influence."[49] Forbearance not only desires and seeks to protect the urban right to citizenship (a not insignificant right, given that global cities are flooded by persons often not holding voting rights or national privilege), but enables the virtuous extension of the self toward the reconstituting of a public, a social commons.

Just one thing, in the end, determines the quality of life in the city—sociability, or what Edward W. Soja calls "synekism."[50] Synekism, at its most elementary, simply means that we humans like to live together in urban agglomerations. As Soja sees it, such urbanism has been the ethos of human history for the last ten thousand years.[51] The opportunity for sociality draws most people to the city and holds them there as much as the promise of technological proficiency and financial gain and despite the loss of dreams, of wealth, of health that transpires for any number of urban migrants. What makes cities livable, including in terms of safety and social cohesion, has to do, as Jane Jacobs already recognized in *The Death and Life of Great American Cities*, with corner gossips, the street ballet, and "the rich mix of activities" generated among persons. It has to do with the folds—the enfolding and unfolding—of social flesh.[52]

Bodies and Social Flesh

I have argued that *ressentiment* emerges from the point where affect and metaphysics meet. Where "disability" rends the creed of the onlooker—that is, the presumed natural law or theological sense of divine order—we also encounter existential *ressentiment*. And given this conjunction of intellect and affect, as Jean-Luc Nancy surmised, the metaphysics that legitimates world *ressentiment* has been held in place by commodifying "the body." Feminists recuperated the term *body* and its material terrain from the underside of an earlier cultural, dualistic management strategy that has valued the masculine spirit or mind more than the feminine body or physicality. Feminist theology contrarily argued appreciatively for human embodiment with and through an immanence of Spirit. Yet feminism's recuperation of the undervalued body has not necessarily impeded either disability abjection or the ways in which cultural ideologies today capitalize upon the body. Given the cultural command performances expected of the body's ability, health, beauty, and productivity, it appears that just as "Nature" has proven to be "a transcendental term in a material mask,"[53] the valorization of the body, even loosed from any conscious religious scaling, likewise can hide a transcendental demeanor in a corporeal overcoat.

Whereas the term *body* thus can invite the hallucinatory delusion of wholeness and thus the temptation to believe in agential mastery and control, *flesh*, I would propose, admits our exposure, our vulnerability one to another, if also to *bios*, to social flesh. Flesh, the dynamic and fluid physics of embodiment, cannot as easily as the body submit to transcendentalist metaphysics.[54] Flesh suggests that the capaciousness of a life resembles a teacup crackled with ten thousand veins. Consequently, "flesh," philosopher John Caputo chuckles in *Against Ethics*, "fills metaphysics with anxiety" (200), which is what I've been claiming here about that fleshly becoming named *disability*.

Thinking "flesh" challenges the naturalization or normalization of the body and thereby the sociocultural and economic value of ability. Whereas the concept of the body has already been submitted to a cultural, scopic regime of wholeness by way of hallucinatory imagistic totalization, as even Jacques Lacan insisted, the corporeality of flesh differs with itself daily. Flesh is a locus of flux; insomuch as flesh differs with itself day to day, flesh situates difference as preceding identity. Flesh, in other words, makes alterity central and might also, therefore, allow us to talk about what metaphysics has often hidden from the sociocultural agenda, what we know to be true of lives—pain difficulty, disease, transience, aging, error, fear, and corporeal limit, if even also the epiphanies and critical insights that come with illness, as Virginia Woolf insisted in *On Being Ill*. Flesh, John Caputo reminds us, "can never achieve . . . absolute invulnerability" (*Against Ethics*, 201). This openness, this porosity to influence, which scares every one of us, we've held against persons with disability.

The reversible fold of flesh might even be described as presenting us with "a primary vulnerability to others, one that we cannot will away without ceasing to be human." Flesh leaves us always uncomfortably inside-out or, simply, "outside ourselves," as Judith Butler puts it.[55] Not only does the religiophilosophical practice of nonviolence begin at this level of flesh, she continues, but "our political situation consists in part in learning how best to handle—and to honor—this constant and necessary exposure."[56]

John Caputo conceives this obligation as itself eucharistic and the scene of an unlikely transubstantiation: "In the economy of obligation, the I is always structurally an agent body while the other . . . is . . . always structurally liable to be reduced to flesh. . . . Structurally, the I always poses a threat to the flesh of the other" (*Against Ethics*, 213). True, "there are always 'relations of power' wherever there is flesh, and we are accordingly always awash in a sea of power," as Foucault well knew. But, insists Caputo, Foucault did not notice "the battery of signals" sent up from flesh, the radiating power "that issues a command against violence" (ibid., 214). Even as we want most to hurt each other by striking out and landing our anger in the flesh of the other, making them hurt, flesh calls us to our obligations to each other: "Obligation happens in and with the steady pulsating of the pulse of flesh, with the irrepressible powers that emanate from it." "I," when responsive to this call of flesh, am transubstantiated from the defensive control locus of "the body" to the mutuality of flesh (ibid., 216).[57]

Philosopher Jean-Luc Nancy, especially in the essays in *Corpus*—many written between 1990 and 1992, and including "The Intruder," written ten years later, following upon his heart transplant, and about living with someone else's heart—is one of those who has attempted to think the body as ever differing even with itself, as informed by a sense of indeterminacy, thus as "disintegrated."[58] We "neither have nor are" body, Nancy insists; rather, *body* names the location, like an artist's stretched canvas, "where being is exscribed"—where existence is "addressed to an out-side" (*Corpus*, 19). "Body" thus is the site of our extensive "exposure to the world."[59] "Bodies," Nancy continues, "are open space . . . more properly spacious than spatial, what could also be called a place." But if "bodies are places of existence," and if *body* is a term for "the world as stretched out here" (ibid., 15, 33), as Nancy puts it, then bodies bear greater resemblance to the city street scene than, as humanism has conceived, to vessels or defensible property or, therefore, to proper, wholesome subjects.

As the failure of his heart disrupts Nancy's comfortable familiarity with himself, in "The Intruder" he reflects upon, perhaps surprisingly, the spiritual virtue of hospitality, even in relation to one's body during a time of illness: "The intruder"—and we assume Nancy implies as much his failed biological heart ("My heart became my stranger") as the transplanted heart—"introduces himself forcefully, by surprise or by ruse. . . . To welcome a stranger . . . is necessarily to experience his intrusion." "From the very outset," Nancy concludes, "my survival is inscribed in a complex process interwoven with strangers and strangenesses" (*Corpus*, 163, 161, 164).

The disaggregated and exscribed body suggests that ever and again we will be, most intimately, as also most politically, "strangers to ourselves," as Kristeva puts it.[60] If body is the location where being is "extensively, spaciously opened," and if this open sensory membrane might also be recognizable as the architectonic possibility of love (Nancy, *Corpus*, 29), then discovering practices of hospice becomes as intimate a demand as it becomes politically and civically necessary. Further, refusing to recognize that we are strangers to ourselves aggravates the "power of horror" that we then attribute, by projection, to the essence of the other—hence, among other things, again the "dis-ing" of disability.

Nancy's first philosophical reflections on body, in *Corpus*, appear to be written as meditations on the eucharistic pronouncement "This is my body" in the wake of the "death of God"—a sensibility that situates the sacred as always already respecting life as exposed and given into the world, without reserve or transcendental remainder. (Nancy also speaks of this elsewhere as the conviction of "transimmanence."[61]). "'God is dead' means: God no longer has a body" (*Corpus*, 59). Yet the death of God means here nothing more—or less—than an invitation to "the world of bodies" (*corpus*) by way of a suspension of a discourse on "the body" (*le corps*) itself.[62] Insomuch as "to *be* that body and *be nothing but that*, forms the principle of Western (un)reason," an economy of the "the body proper," Nancy suggests, has led to a capitalist banalization of life, including of the neighbor: "'The body' . . . is our old culture's latest, most worked over, sifted, refined, dismantled, and reconstructed product" (*Corpus*, 7). A discourse banking on "the body proper" commits Western culture, he concludes, to "an irreversible coma" (ibid., 7, 91). Hence, the "death of God" (also known as the "death of metaphysics") means nothing more than the failure of an epochal pattern of sense, of a particular economy of life—as particularly anchored, as Nancy sees it, in "*the* body of God."

In this failed pattern of sense, in which the body is "totally parasitical upon the incorporeality of sense," an externalized saturation of the body to the point that "it volatizes it," working out our own salvation has amounted to "saving bodies through health, sports . . . pleasure" and, I would add, mystification of Spirit, instead of living bodies as "masses offered" (Nancy, *Corpus*, 23, 7, 85).[63] Nancy suggests that precisely what is lost to us within the economics of the culture of "the body," especially where it is spiritualized to the point that it "denies and renders catatonic its extendedness and its spacing" (ibid., 23), is meaning and mattering, which have been identified as among the problematics specific to urbanism. Conversely, "meaning begins where presence is not pure presence, but where presence comes apart [*se disjoint*]."[64] Such disjointedness (can I ignore disability as an analog thereof?) refuses the vertical scaling of the body to significatory ideals, to essence, and instead cultivates the contiguity of ever "being with."[65] "Meaning, in Nancy's view, thus is not created by the intention of a subject but through a context or network—of contacts and touches. To begin to make sense of something is to come into contact with it, to touch it,"[66] such architectonics of sense being unavailable, because occluded, to the "discarnate."[67]

Nancy writes, again in eucharistic mimesis, "I am, every time I am, the flexion of place, a fold or motion through which it prof-fers (itself)" (*Corpus*, 7). Today, the "death of God," whether what is now passing through Western culture under the banner headlines proclaiming religion's near extinction[68] signals our cultural absorption of the disruptive insights of the 1960s or a second generation thereof,[69] suggests also the cultural possibility that "meaning and mattering" might otherwise emerge by thinking the body as a "mass" proffered the neighbor, as "making room for existence" (ibid., 15), a being with and for others.

Nancy's sense of body as "spacious place," as place that admits even the intrusion of strangeness, is one way to understand how bodies in the cosmopolis participate in the social flesh of great cities. Nancy insists: "What is coming to us is a dense and serious world . . . with nothing to oversee it or sustain it, no Subject for its destiny, taking place only as a prodigious press of bodies. . . . What is coming to us is . . . a world-wide world, one that doesn't refer to another world, or to an other-world, that is no longer 'international' but already something else, and that is no longer a world of appearances or aspirations." But, he concludes, "it's still a world, a proper place . . . for the spacing of our bodies . . . for the sharing of their resistances" (*Corpus*, 41).

Social flesh, the dynamic and fluid physics of embodiment, cannot as easily as "the body" submit to transcendentalist metaphysics.[70] Flesh, more than a unitary body, is a plane on which bodies encounter one another and become involved, entangled. The rawness of flesh admits our exposure, our vulnerability to one another, and is unable to hide the wounds, tears, disfigurements, and desires that a more abstract language of embodiment often can. And yet to write of social flesh does not relieve us of the sacred (Nancy, *Corpus*, 47).[71] Rather than thinking of God as the death or devaluation of the world of bodies, Nancy insists that the death of God opens out "*here*, the world of bodies, the worldliness of bodies, and *there*, a cut off, incorporeal discourse" (ibid., 61). Emptying the ontic discourse related to "God" opens out now upon the horizon of social flesh.

So to be rid of "*the* body of God" does not necessarily evacuate theological discourse. "This is the way God's glory is shared," Nancy writes, explaining how, "*rid* of God's body," we are opened to/as places, "Places divine through an opening whereby the whole 'divine' collapses and withdraws, leaving the world of our bodies bare" (*Corpus*, 63). The withdrawal of God, as Nancy writes it, leaves its shimmering or shattering wake, its "spaciousness," its hallowed-out space. Intriguingly enough, although Nancy does not recognize it, this sense of Spirit or God as "wide space" or "broad, open space for living" recalls a secret name of the holy within Jewish Kabbalistic tradition, *Makom*.[72] Saint Basil in the fourth century insisted that Spirit names in Christian tradition such a sense of place. If "this world of bodies . . . properly offers us our chance and our history," Nancy continues, rather we might now speak of God as the open, extensive, spacious hospitality of place—not, as Nancy qualifies, that the open is substantive. This "spacious openness" that is neither nothing nor something serves nonetheless as the architectonics of love. Or rather, "love is the touch of the open" (*Corpus*, 79, 29).

"The irreducibility of flesh, of the signals it sends forth," is of the essence of that "jewgreek poetics" or "jewgreek kinesis" we call Christianity, John Caputo writes (*Against Ethics*, 215, 216, 218). If Christianity might but witness to social flesh, this spacious hallow, learning to welcome strangeness without colonizing it, a cosmopolitan, wishing to live an examined life, could learn from this thin theology of flesh an affective practice that supports the dream of a "street ballet" not so prone to the judgments of gut instincts. As feminist philosopher Diane Perpich acknowledges in regard to Nancy's writing in *Corpus*, including "The Intruder," "Nancy's thought does something very well: it takes account of those bodies usually considered borderline"—the intersexed, surrogate, and pregnant bodies, punk

bodies, cyborgs and androids as well as composite bodies like Nancy himself, after his heart transplant—"without having to position them at the
outer limits (or, for that matter, at the center)."[73]

To create an urban ethos, I'm imagining embodied spiritual practice of
the examined life—of crip/tography—as the choreography of bodies moving through a certain environment at a certain tempo, a choreography that
makes the space of the global city a living, lively place. This dynamic energy, the event of the place ballet, is what draws people to take up residence; the place ballet generates a sense of belonging and even then
responsibility and generosity. A good city is one that proliferates these
places where, "more than a place of common access and encounter," the
city can become again "a place of becoming," a locus for "the fulfillment of
social potential, of democratic experimentation through the efforts of citizens themselves, as free and socialized agents."[74] The vitality of social flesh
enlivens personal choreographies (how we tend to move along a certain
geography in our daily lives) in which, amidst density and diversity, we
tumble and bumble over one another, such that we want to hang out in or
pass through these "places" again and again, because we might catch a certain pitch of excitement or encounter or possibility. Spiritual practice—
insomuch as it informs how we artistically or aesthetically engage the place
ballet—becomes then something of a theater of social change, where "attention to the lived intricacies of embodiment offer alternatives to normalization efforts aimed at homogenizing social outsiders" so as also to "provide
opportunities for unique combinations of social becoming."[75]

Of Cosmopolis and Its Carnivalesque Inversions: What if the Opposite of "Good" Is "Real"?

In *Poser: My Life in Twenty-Three Yoga Poses*, Claire Dederer confesses that
she "started going to yoga because I wanted other people to admire my
goodness." Obsessed with pushing just the right stroller, choosing the most
ecologically conscious diaper, and appropriately performing attachment
parenting, Dederer's portrait of her core values suggests the just intentions
of many North American liberals. And yet as yoga poses work their way
through various energy locks on her body, it is just this well-intentioned

goodness of a "judging mind" that comes into question. "What if the opposite of good . . . was real?" she asks herself one day (*Poser*, 271), realizing that the "goodness" she had been cultivating had more to do with hypervigilance (thus with fear, self-consciousness, and insecurity) than with honestly engaging, through sweat and struggle, the reality at hand. The judging mind—cathected to goodness, hyperextended to "the perfect"—covered over the feeling body, the way of deep listening and, thus, acting with the world. In the end and in spite of what William Gibson might call her "discarnate" or pretentious beginnings, yoga, Dederer concludes, "helped to reverse the goodness-to-reality ratio in my life" (303).

In other words, yoga helped Dederer "to have done with judgment," as philosopher Gilles Deleuze puts it[76]—helped her to step away from mastering the craft of a perfect, ideal world so as to take up instead the "martial arts" or "yoga" of social and soulful wisdom in a shared world. If the judging mind covers over the possibility of and preference for an enspirited, feeling, and malleable body, comparably, when disability falls back from the specular (and deficient, imperfect and "in/valid") into somatic variation, then the judging mind will have found its way back into an efficacious way of living into an open democratic cosmopolitanism.

Dismodernism, as disabilities theorist Lennard Davis names such a view, may thus hold promise, even as it occasions leave-taking from our bourgeois norms for "gracious living." In dismodernism, we assume we are all nonstandard, refuse rigid breaks with the animal body, and a sort of carnivalesque inversion of culture's somatic and social hierarchy transpires: We live free of the ontological views that frame human perception, free of the false seriousness of petty preoccupations,[77] whether of sweat, flatulence, or dribbling food on the chin, or the somatic class markers of working muscle, callused hands, and worn clothing. To be sure, dismodernism shares this with the rules presumed on the floor of any good yoga studio, which teaches just that—the nonjudgment of bodies.[78]

If persons might still be aesthetically disgusted with disability, perhaps there's also, contrarily, given the current "culture of the mind" in postindustrial America,[79] a certain envy of the soulful encounter with flesh among persons disabled. With disability, life—as over against the facades and simulacra of civility and forced sincerity and over against the unanchored labor of mentality or the spin of virtuality—knows what it is up against:

We feel our world, its gravity, its intelligence. Crips sound out our way, living with an awareness of agencies other than our own.[80] In this lived experience, we find gravity and psychic ground (perhaps also "authenticity"), a quite rare experience when so many things today are subject to "spin." The world before us is particular in shape, requiring our calculated and truly singular experiential discernment, delimited in scale, and definitively not subject to our delusions of omnipotence. Isn't disability, with its honesty about embodiment, the permission to assume a different scale of life—a recognition that we cannot be, none of us can be, the "im/possible naturalization" that has informed humanist notions of ability?[81]

Disability tends to weight the mind back toward evolving with the body in ways not unlike that technique of putting rocks in her pocket used by my adopted daughter to keep herself in place. The "terrible grace" of techno-enabled bodies, as novelist William Gibson names it, might be preferable to the loosing of mind's virtual infinity, to its endless projections, fears, and anticipations: A limiting bump against the carbon exoskeletal prosthesis forces us to be "here," to feel the "runner's wall" that self-consciousness must finally hit (Gibson, "Winter Market," in *Burning Chrome*, 129).[82] "The claiming of disability, thus, may be read perhaps . . . as passion, as being claimed by the im/possible performativity . . . performativity without . . . a dominance of subjectivity over and against the world."[83] In other words, disability may today be read as an enviable way of being with the world in its own quirks of becoming. Becoming crip allows one to resign from the terrible task of mastering the world, of mastering even our own private worlds. Such resignation interrupts the Western projects of psychological and spiritual self-cultivation, both of which have been in the West given over to narcissism (yes, even in some of the current "spiritual, but not religious" forms). "'Virtue,'" as Iris Murdoch asserted, "is the attempt to pierce the veil of selfish consciousness and join the world as it really is."[84] Disability, in the way it today forces one to become cognizant with the world "as it really is," suggestively points toward a path of spiritual resilience and forbearance. Crip/tography, in that way, tracks the haunts of Spirit in social flesh.

"Take My Yoga Upon You" (Matt 11:29): A Spirit/ual *Pli* for the Global City

> What would it mean to live
> in a city whose people were changing
> each other's despair into hope?
>
> —ADRIENNE RICH, "Dreams Before Waking"

Cities appear on the human horizon as enticing as a hive for honeybees—as places where the intermixture of human energies, especially ideational and aesthetic, might tumble, bumble, entangle, and synergistically catch. "Each urban moment can spark performative improvisations which are unforeseen and unforeseeable. . . . Each urban encounter is a theatre of promise."[1] This creative, bustling stew allows us to spark ideas one off the other, makes spontaneous relationships, creativity, entertainment and education possible.

Urbanism thus also suggests a human disposition toward a preferred loose weave of social relations. Cities, after all, inherently open us to relations beyond "kith and kin"—to the neighbor, to the friend, to the incidental encounter, to relations of choice. Philosophers such as Gilles Deleuze and Gianni Vattimo would argue that the postcolonial conditions of urbanism today make possible and make preferable these less Oedipally determined or otherwise encoded relations. While the Greeks recognized the affiliative significance of friendship amidst urbanism, the effect of "the creation of philosophy" was, Deleuze surmises, nonetheless to deterritorialize human relationships, abstracting them from place and person in such a way as to "violently force the friend into a relationship that is no longer a relationship with an other but one with an Entity, an Objectality, an Essence."[2] Summarizing Deleuze's thought, Todd May writes that consequently for Deleuze, today within these zones of deterritorialization, friends must think together "how to mobilize the deterritorialization . . . in the service of new ways of living together."[3] In the face of the flood of former colonial subjects from the African continent into Europe and from the presupposition of reconceiving Christianity after metaphysics, Italian philosopher and political activist Gianni Vattimo likewise argues for the theological value of friendship: "The death of the moral God marks the impossibility of preferring truth to friendship." In other words, "the consummation of objective truth" culminates "in different manifestations of friendship."[4] And so for humans, whether predisposed toward urbanism, as theorist Edward Soja surmises—"Human beings . . . are essentially urban by nature"[5]—or because "globalization spells urbanization,"[6] we now need ways to deal with global cities in which urbanism appears as an open and unobligated relational milieu.

Yet if cities promise unprescribed relations, the conditions of postmetropolis, a chaotic urbanism without a center and admitting uneven development, challenge us anew.[7] Cities today are characterized "by hitherto unimagined fragmentation; by immense distances between [their] citizens, literal, economic, cultural, social and political," writes Canadian geographer and urban planner Engin Isin.[8] This loose weave of urban relations leaves us vulnerable to the apartheid of wealth and poverty, to psychic loneliness, to the compulsory, individualist task of human identity formation, and the potential political ineffectiveness of that singularly crafted identity.[9]

In the 1990s, urban poverty already was becoming "'the most significant and politically explosive problem'" of the twenty-first century, the World Bank warned.[10] Yet the growing urban divide factors neither into contemporary economic reason (this version of capitalism gone global without a safety net) nor into the human rights agenda (with Western philosophy exiling need and necessity, such as access to food and water, clothing and shelter, outside the realm of neoclassical liberal thought). In *Planet of Slums*, urban theorist Mike Davis argues that today's "urbanization with deindustrialization" nonetheless will make "urbanization and favelization synonymous" (14, 17). In stark contrast to the promising narrative offered by neo-Marxist philosophers Michael Hardt and Antonio Negri in *Multitude: War and Democracy in the Age of Empire* (for which Davis himself might secretly hope), Davis warns that today's urbanism—this face of globalization resulting from "labor made redundant"—makes possible and likely rhizomatic connections such as gangs, piracy, and criminal syndicates. This is made more likely by governmental agencies that abdicate urban reform as neoliberal economics abandons welfare nets and citizens shutter themselves against mutuality (ibid., 7).

Complicating citizen responsiveness to this scenario of interurban as well as intraurban apartheid is the fact that during modernity, dominant power has been exercised as mobility, itself conflated with the spiritual, psychosocial, and political promise of freedom. If the rivers of humanity loosed on the planet during modernity have been of two orders—the flow of migrant and now redundant labor and the flow of the cosmopolitans, among whom must be counted any of us who have been brought through the Western academy—this newly fluid mass of humanity could have been set in motion only by assuming "the mobile personality."[11] Theologian Mark C. Taylor traces this modern personality back to the Reformation and insists that we recognize it as precisely "the good" that is now being globalized.[12] Modernity, following a certain Christianity-infused transcendentalism of the self, "neither Jew nor Greek . . . male nor female" (Galatians 3:28), insists on the shedding of tradition, ethnocultural identities, and rituals.[13] It has worked assiduously to release bodies from obligation and obedience, from all ligatures, including that of religion. If that makes possible the urban spirit of friendship, it has also unwittingly induced psychosocial disintegration.[14]

It is for these reasons that I work to loose Spirit within cosmopolis, that I utter a plea, or more aptly, a *pli*—a pleat, a fold, a manifest—of Spirit over cosmopolis. As if in echo of the dislocated cosmopolitans of the ancient world, Spirit—despite how tempting it could be, given Hegel's history of immanent, world Spirit, to link this back nostalgically to the siren call of Being, of History, or of Reason—has evocatively emerged yet again. In theology, in addition to its appearance in ecotheology and some science-theology conversations,[15] Spirit has emerged as a placeholder of the sacred within the work of conceiving religion after metaphysics. It has emerged specifically, in the critique of ontotheology and in theologies informed by an immanentalist Deleuzean ontology, as in the work of Catherine Keller, all of whose major works end by evoking pneumatology.[16] As Santiago Zabala puts it, summarizing his reading of Gianni Vattimo: "Learning to live without anxiety or neurosis in a world lacking fixed, guaranteed structure depends on our transferring the real as we now experience it to the level of spirit."[17]

John Caputo has consequently resorted to a "Derridean hauntology"[18] to work desire across the frigid skins of moral melancholics trying to wake to life in the ruin of God. Nietzsche earlier surmised—and contemporary pneumatological evocations pick this up—that modernity suffers an erotic problem. In the wake of the accomplishments of modern reason, including science and technology, moderns suffer a failure of desire—itself notable in modernity's lament of losses innumerable. But as philosopher Robert Pippin argues, Nietzsche suspected that this mood itself might be symptomatic of a narcissistic grandiosity and/or melancholia, a failure to release the losses being grieved—including the God of metaphysics.[19] Consequently, melancholy, a moralizing self-critique that freezes love of life, has settled over liberal Western culture. Spirit, as Caputo supposes, might be but a theopoetic whisper of desire, a haunt that does not profess doxic certainty, but nevertheless offers a locus, a passional vortex, that yields yet again the practice of faithfulness to life.[20]

Here, working within a diversely "spiritual, but not religious" scene, I explore how we might think constructively with the manifold or *pli* of Spirit. In a cosmopolitan world in which many "cannot escape the feeling that something fundamental is missing from their lives of affluence, longevity and independence,"[21] in which, for the globally mobile personality, everything is possible but nothing matters, in which the loss of social consciousness and therefore of generosity stems from a person's felt social and political irrelevance,[22] mere "pluralism is not enough," as Keller argues.[23] Consequently, I suggest that what I will call, in a Deleuzean sense, the *pli* of Spirit, Spirit conceived of as the pleat or fertile "fold" of difference within immanence itself, that "many-one," not "an essence," but "an operative function," "a correspondence and even a communication" within difference,[24] offers hope for the utopian dream of "a city/region in which there is genuine connection with, and respect and space for, the cultural other and the possibility of working together on matters of common destiny, a recognition of intertwined fates."[25] The *pli* or fold of multi*pli*city does not so much then signal plurality in opposition to unity, as it looks to the actualization of plural space, of the many-enfolded—thus, of the active and energetic manifold.

The work of religions within this scene, the work of anatheism, even then the work of secular reverence for life, is that of growing corporeal generosity into a social flesh. As theologian Felix Wilfred has likewise argued in "Christianity and Religious Cosmopolitanism," "Cosmopolitanism needs to be sustained by solidarity" (117). Asserting that "all religions belong to the entire human race and no religion is in possession of the immediate community of its believers" (113), he imagines that religious wisdom can be garnered so as to weave the ligatures of urban solidarity:

> [T]he contributions of the religions to the future of humanity and its destiny will depend on the extent to which they are able to instill, promote and sustain moral *obligations*. Bereft of solidarity, cosmopolitanism will turn out to be contemplative pluralism that marvels at the plurality of cultures, ethnicity and so on, but with little of enriching interaction. In cosmopolitanism imbued with the spirit of solidarity, there is a sense of mutual obligation which is not found in contemplative pluralism or in indiscriminate syncretism and hybridism. (117; emphasis added)

Consequently this chapter develops the spiritual prosthesis of the practiced vow—the *yoke* or *yoga*—of corporeal generosity to creature need within the interreligious milieu of today's postcolonial cities.

The *pli* of Spirit, as Vattimo surmised, has historically been congruent with proffered relations of friendship. Although terms such as *friendship*, *neighbor*, and *Spirit adoption* might well have been borrowed from the ancient philosophical repertoire into urban Christian experience amidst the diasporas induced by ancient empires, these relational ligatures—or at least their correlation with urbanism—have slipped from our theological awareness. Then again, the human urban disposition and resultant urbanism itself appear to be a strange secret that Western Christian theology has kept from itself. Paradoxically, during the nineteenth and twentieth centuries, as North America was aggressively entering into its own urban articulation, pastoralism infused our literature and theology, from our reading of the Christian gospels as presenting Jesus as noble savage, to American Transcendentalism (Thoreau, Whitman, Emerson), to recent ecological spiritualities.

Today, however, a dense urban postcolonial manifold, which I will argue can be remembered in and through the *pli* of Spirit, must cross-check our theological tendency to repress the urban disposition of the human animal. Because nature, too, can serve as a transcendental term while hiding in "a material mask,"[26] and reason, as Jean-Francois Lyotard alerts us, carries its own totalizing impulses, situating Spirit in nature invites not only nature's but also secular rationalism's disclosure of their mutual tendency toward "a single, authoritative basis of public reason and/or public ethics."[27] If Spirit and nature can be neither wholly identified nor neatly distinguished, holding these distinctive perspectives simultaneously, agonistically, acknowledges that there is no longer "a transcending God whose dictates we must follow or whose substance we must seek in our lives to resemble . . . no longer a transcending Other that can lay claim upon our faith or our behavior."[28] If Spirit thus marks our release from a tired theism, it nonetheless also names the movement of what philosopher Jean-Luc Nancy calls "dis-enclosure . . . inscribed at the heart of the Christian tradition." Proposing an alternative history of Christianity, seen otherwise than as willing the totalizing closure of and self-serving management of the world, in *Dis-Enclosure: The Deconstruction of Christianity* Nancy explains that "Christianity designates nothing other, essentially . . . than the demand to open in this world an alterity" (11, 10).

Spirit and Urban Diasporas

A theology of the manifold loosed in this stew of urbanism cannot help but be influenced, as I have been here, by the resident polyphony of world religions—set swirling by capitalism, liberalism, educational encouragement toward multiple religious valuing, and the postcolonial flow of bodies to diverse global cities. As theologies fold through and as theological communities serve as folds within cosmopolis, inasmuch as today's megacities differ considerably from the ethnic and/or nationalist determinations of

Christianity in northern Europe and North America during the modern, colonial passage, Christianity, when loosed from its relation to the nation-state and into the postmetropolis, necessarily will be changing shape.[29] But Christianity may recognize itself anew, when living in intimate relation-ship with an evangelical Tibetan Buddhism[30] or with the yoga of Vedic thought and practice, as I have suggested in previous chapters. Especially where Christianity must find some new way to become operational, it may sound itself out amidst the religious polyphony of the city. In this way, as I have elsewhere argued, Christianity can remember itself as a practice.[31]

Considering the northern band of the Western Hemisphere, that is, northern Europe (to which I would add Canada as well as the northeastern and northwestern coastal corners of the United States), where others have argued that Christianity is growing irrelevant, in "The Myth of the Twen-tieth Century: The Rise and Fall of 'Secularization'" (1999) Harvey Cox wondered whether Christianity might rather be acquiring "more Asian sensibilities": "Could Christianity . . . be moving away from an institution-ally positioned model and toward a culturally diffuse pattern, more like the religions of many Asian countries, and therefore more difficult to measure by such standard means as church attendance and baptism statistics?"(Cox, "Myth," 139). Ten years later, in his 2009 text, *The Future of Faith*, Cox moved to the declarative, announcing "a "tectonic shift in Christianity," a shift into "The Age of the Spirit" in which the religious returns as "a way of life rather than a doctrinal structure," as the experiential practice of "faith and love," as distinct from belief (Cox, *Future*, 3, 8, 10, 13, 21). So as the theology of the manifold goes on location within the global city, we may find that the persons with whom we think about this theology share not so much a common religious heritage as a commitment to practiced paths of faithfulness to life.

Where "Christianity as belief" traveled well through the modern passages, a new regionalism saturates the sensibilities of practitioners. In Cascadia, for example, this Pacific Northwest cathedral of nature whose mountains, forests, and oceans cradle the cosmopolitan, emerald cities of Vancouver, Seattle, and Portland, "*Spirit*" designates a place-holder, an im-manental religious sensibility. Owing to postcolonial flows, our trinity is as likely to include the parlor dance of the Buddhist goddess of compassion Kuan Yin, the Buddha, and the Christ as the triuning fold of classic

Christian theism.[32] Spirit plays well in this locale, because Spirit, as theologian Jay McDaniel reminds us, "is not reducible to Christianity," and Spirit honors those who would be "spiritual, but not religious" or "theistic."[33]

Spirit operates as a locus of multiplicity that does not always necessitate a distinctive name of belonging and refuses the theist/nontheist divide. Then again, the *pli*, or manifold,[34] of Spirit might well have developed within just such a multicultural, diasporic basin of ancient empire. In ancient venues then, as one hopes also here and now, Spirit, as a theopoetic concept, counters the sheared relations and dis-integrated psyches of diasporas inasmuch as it is practiced as neighborliness and adoptionism. That said, Christianity admittedly remains for this theologian the strongest shaper of entrustment to life and of political ethics. But if, as Karl Jaspers suggests, axial religions developed transcendence as an elite fear of the masses and hence as elite avoidance of urban multiplicities,[35] the concept of Spirit, first constructively formulated among dislocated persons in the imperial stew, multireligious milieu of the ancient Roman world, then triangulated into repression for fifteen hundred years within that transcendentalist phase of Christian theology, returns here as the fold or *pli* of postcolonial cosmopolitan religious multiplicity, as a decidedly affective locus weighted towards corporeal generosity.

So I conspire with Spirit in its ongoing constructive hybridization toward its own new becomings. If religions have been and can ever again be used toward violent ends, religions may also, as Felix Wilfred points out, provide diverse wisdoms for lived solidarities. Within the postmetropolis, Spirit, if we refuse to let it escape into idealist fantasies and pay attention to the explicitly spatial politics of the city, can provide that necessary third space between differences, a combinatory interval or fold that refuses oppositionalism. Spirit has shown itself before as a strange attractor that loves and so refuses to shatter amidst heterogeneous mixing. So Spirit might here "provide the occasion for new and varied forms of bonding," writes womanist philosopher bell hooks. The spatial ruptures of postmetropolis will be those places where the critical, organic intellect will need to come into play.[36] In cities threatened by "no-go" zones and gated communities, Spirit walks through enclosures and exclusions, seeps under gates, partitions, and the fortresses of human aversions. Spirit offers itself as a dynamic fold across territorial and psychic separations.

The Yoga of Neighbor Love

In the vacuum of meaning and starvation by dislocation occasioned among the multitude by the British Raj, Gandhi countered with a *"religare"* or "rebinding" of relations—the renovation of the vowed life centered in the Satyagraha Ashram. Vows, Gandhi wrote, work to heal "that hurting indifference which keeps one human being from another." As relations were diffused and dispersed owing to colonialism, Gandhi advocated the yoga of neighbor love: A person's "first duty" is to his or her "neighbor."[37] Given the limitless extension of life opened out in the wake of colonialism, an extension that simultaneously wreaked local havoc, Gandhi made "sacrifice," the hindrance or yoke of neighborly immediacy, an aspect of the practice of neighbor love, for example, wearing only cloth spun within the community.[38] Neighbor love, a spiritual practice, worked against the colonial energies to become boundless.

The yoga of neighbor love, one might imagine, countered the way in which persons' dreams and aspirations could be pulled into the circulation of colonialism, a propagandistic sense of "the good life" that was not then materially available to locals. One could likewise imagine, owing to the ways in which colonialism—and now globalization—scatters communities of belonging at great distance, that neighbor love can encourage a certain adoption of place, a grounding of life in place, so as not to get caught in the backwash of nostalgia. Inasmuch as "neighborhood" today, given the sociological effects of modernity, has become a "zombie institution,"[39] making the localization of neighbor love into a religiospiritual practice can begin to generate the physics of meaning and mattering. Further, thinking now from an ecological perspective, the practices of neighbor love may help us learn to live the limits of mortality and the boundaries of ecological respect rather than their overcoming, as the idealist metaphysics of modernity incites.

Gandhi's particular reconstruction of sacred obligations swelled up from the *pli* or fold where "some of the recessive elements of Christianity," for example, the Sermon on the Mount, found resonance with "congruent . . . elements of Hindu and Buddhist world views."[40] Setting out from two convictions—that our birth, itself of a sacrificial nature, makes us debtors all our lives, and that "the one who serves his [or her] neighbor serves all the world,"[41] Gandhi constructively invented the yoga of nonviolence in order to liberate Indians and likewise to liberate the British from their "panicky, self-imposed captivity," "from the. . . . psychology of British colonialism."[42] An existential loss of bearings was here countered by religious obligation. The yoke brings life out of isolation—a not insignificant gift, if we can in anyway analogically compare the pain owing to the vacuum of meaning in global cities to that of Indians relationally dispersed, dislocated, and economically ill-disposed by earlier stages of colonialism.

THE YOGA OF THE CHRISTIAN GOSPELS

Huston Smith situates the birth of Western philosophy in a comparable scenario. He argues that the Pythagorean and Epicurean schools of philosophy of the ancient world arose during a period of skepticism: "The ancestral order had dissolved and men and women were looking for an alternative way to get their bearings." Finding the "rootlessness, rudderlessness" of skepticism intolerable, they reached for philosophy—not merely to titillate the mind, but as "a way of life and death," as salvation, as a *practice* to free them from anxiety.[43] If ancient and contemporary imperially dislocated and relationally truncated bodies were redressed by religious vows, by assuming the "yoke" or yoga of philosophical practice, the Christian gospels, too, might be read not for "belief," but as themselves acts of the creation of ligatures (the etymological base of both the word *religion* and the word *obligation*) amidst the vacuum occasioned by the Roman Empire's destruction and reconstruction of life worlds.

For readers of Matthew's gospel, "Jesus' call" (Matt. 11:28 n30), "Take my yoke upon you . . . for my yoke is ['merciful']," Jesus—whom Ravi Ravinda has called "Christ the Yogi"[44]—offers the Beatitudes as a locus of reverence, as a yoke or harness of desire amidst the shearing of psychophysical trauma and social dislocation. Matthew's intended audience, biblical scholar Warren Carter surmises in *Matthew and Empire*, resided in or lived near Antioch in Syria (36). Not only had Cicero declared that "Jews and Syrians were born to be slaves," the urban milieu of Antioch was for the majority of inhabitants, "who existed to provide services," hardly conducive to well-being. With a population density exceeding that of contemporary Mumbai and Calcutta (Antioch was the third elite city in the Roman

Empire), amidst xenophobia and filth, laborers could not expect the univer-
salism of the Empire to provide them with a social identity or integrate
them into its civic religion. Rome "could not solve the issues of social identity; it failed to penetrate the everyday life of the mass of the people," even
as it sheared them of prior meaning worlds (Carter, *Matthew and Empire*,
48–50). With labor so intricately woven into the imperial system, and given
that with it came not only exhaustion, but "loss of heart," "Take my yoke
upon you . . . for my yoke is ['merciful']" was, Carter asserts, "addressed to
all those who labor desperately to keep themselves in the economically op-
pressive and destructive system of Roman imperialism" (115, 116).[45] It was
an invitation to take up a set of positive obligations to one another in place
of the destructive yoke imposed by the Empire.

The fact that *yoke*—as the term has been translated into English—and
yoga share the same etymological base in Sanskrit might begin to help us
break through the simplistic way Christians have thought Christianity as
mere belief, have thought "yoke" as mere metaphor. "No teaching worth its
salt can be understood only by the mind, for the simple reason that a *teaching*, a *yoga*, is not simply a set of propositions for the mind to assent to or to
argue over," explains Vedic scholar Ravi Ravindra. He concludes: "Above
all, what a teaching demands is that one engage in practice" (*Christ the
Yogi*, 91).

If the Beatitudes (Matthew 5, Luke 6) might spell out for Christians the
"most basic rules of life," as theologian Bonnie Thurston insists, the Beatitudes thus constitute a yoga of resocialization into "indiscriminate love"
lived in new models of kinship, of civic relations without respect to status,
and of nonviolence (Carter, *Matthew and Empire*, 127–28), a practice of generous availability to one another amidst a lot of good reasons to be afraid.
While a yoga or yoke implies submission, here one might read "submission
as opening oneself outward—in this case, toward a covenant of trust with
the neighbor. "The real point of obedience," Thurston insists, "is not to do
someone else's will," but to cultivate "'an emptiness' . . . a 'space'"—an
openness not already subjected to self-will, to one's own purposes.[46] To be
sure, "the progressive liberation from . . . one's own little ego is the purpose of any transformational teaching or spiritual path," as Ravindra instructs us (*Christ the Yogi*, 107). But for Christianity, that freedom arrives
through entrustment, by binding one's self to the neighbor. As Paul Knitter

wrote in a more consciously theistic vein, "to be loyal to Christ, one must be vulnerable to others."[47]

The concept of Spirit, first constructively formulated among persons in diaspora, owing to a multireligious, multicultural milieu, signaled, I would suggest, a similar yoga among readers of the Gospel of John. The Johannine gospel situates Spirit as the "sanctuary" of new life (John 3:1–15). Persons dislocated—as likely to be educated cosmopolitans as migrant laborers, perhaps as ethnoculturally or socioeconomically distinct as today's Pentecostals are from today's "spiritual, but not religious"—worked the yoga of Spirit so as "to prepare a place" (John 14:2) for themselves where the tentacles of empire had flung them.

For bodies strewn at the whim of empire, whether because of the mobility of mercantilism or because of empire's policy of deportation, of razing and rebuilding cities with foreign persons (thereby undermining powers of resistance), ancient place-based religions—tied, for example, to Mount Gerizim, the Samaritan well, or tied by ancestral pilgrimage patterns to the city of Jerusalem (see John 4: 20)—could no longer offer meaning. In "To Prepare a Place," biblical scholar Tod Swanson writes, "In times of catastrophic dislocation, such as the Judean exile to Babylon," as also during the later military and economic reconstruction of Palestine owing to the Roman Empire, "traditional rituals lost their power" (242). Owing to such diasporic conditions, Spirit—a theological concept developed when Hebraic convictions were folded with Hellenistic and Stoic philosophies—denoted the sheer immanence, if cosmic in scope, of the divine.[48] Spirit—the Gospel of John expressly ties this concept back to a Genesis account of the cosmos (Genesis 1:1–2)—was seen as conceptually broad and spacious enough to gather in those scattered and fragmented by empire, to absolve and then obligate one to another beyond ethnic and territorial separation (Swanson, "To Prepare a Place," 244–45, 251).

If this constructive *pli* of Spirit suggests the potential sacrality of all places (Swanson, "To Prepare a Place," 242),[49] folded implicitly therein is the Hebraic sense that *ruach* (Hebrew, "spirit" as "breath") names the experience of the divine as breathing room, as "the space of freedom in which the living being can unfold."[50] Tracing the history of Spirit as a religiously viable concept, Mircea Eliade found, digging into the texts of Hebrew prophets and priests (Genesis, Ezekiel, Isaiah), that Spirit was developed as a sacred metaphor during times of catastrophic dislocation, when religious persons were disarticulated from their sacred lands. If with exile "space threatened to become permanently emptied of meaning," Hebrew prophets suggestively constructed "Spirit" as the placeholder spelling "the potential sacrality of all spaces," even "the decentralized spaces of . . . exile" (Swanson, "To Prepare a Place," 242). For ancient persons who had lost their religiocultural maps of meaning and mattering and whose lives were constricted by ethnocultural xenophobia, Spirit named "broad, open space for living" again.[51]

While this new way of valuing space in terms of Spirit may have eventuated in Christianity's "delegitimizing [of] all territorially based religions" and its own ignorance of place, as Swanson argues ("To Prepare a Place," 257), one might—holding well-founded suspicions of campaigns against indigenous space in abeyance for a moment—also recognize the constructive relief occasioned by the concept of Spirit among diasporic bodies. As religious identity was deterritorialized, Spirit named a mobile, nonterritorially specific, but nonetheless religiously meaningful locus. From it, through it, one could practice a certain "courage to be with" others. Swanson suggests as much when he notes that "the Johannine map" was "a plan of action" and that, like crip/tography, Christian love was expected to re-map bodies into a quickening hold of obligations (ibid., 258).[52]

Obligation and the "Great Open"

Obligation in a postmodern register cannot mean "answering the call of Being, or of the History of Being, or of the History of Spirit, or of the Voice of God," as philosophical theologian John D. Caputo says in *Against Ethics.* He continues, in a humorous if confessional vein, speaking for many of us, "I have . . . lost all communications from On High" (5). Caputo expresses the unmooring of obligation from any transcendental other or elsewhere, given the intellectual rigor of deconstructive postmodernism and its dispelling of our social, ontotheological delusion: "I have for some time now entertained certain opinions that I have been reluctant to make public. But . . . the time has come. . . . I am against ethics." He declares, "Here I stand," mimicking Luther's famous declaration at Wittenberg; "I cannot do otherwise" (1). Wanting to keep metaphysics to a minimum (93), Caputo releases us into a chaotic world of events. Metaphysical "minimalism means having been cut off from a guiding star and a Meta-event, a point outside of what happens that explains, legitimates, or gives meaning to what happens. . . . Events give joy or they do not. . . . But they do not as a whole have a meaning (*sens*, direction)." In fact, he concludes, "the History of Spirit . . . is a dangerous invention" (233, 235). Yet if Caputo stands "against ethics" for presumptively arriving with a prescriptive fix in hand, he does not cancel out "obligation. Ethics provide false safety in a deconstructive milieu, but if "the oldest and most honorable work of ethics has been to defend and honor obligation" (4, 5), then whence the call of obligation, which, Caputo makes quite clear, happens to us from the outside?

Caputo explains: "I have in mind a very earthbound signal, a superficial-horizontal communication between one human being and another, a certain line of force that runs along the surface upon which you and I stand: the obligation I have to you . . . and the both of 'us' to . . . other living things generally" (*Against Ethics*, 5). The mechanics of obligation locate us in a gravitational field of sensible passion; it is "a 'materialist' operation," he underlines. "At least as old as Being or Truth or the Spirit or the Will to Power," this corporeal field force (obligation being felt as significantly "more like a pathos"), Caputo insists, might be "transcendence itself." A transcendental force—within immanence, let us recall—and corporeally sunk, obligation can be evoked only poetically, he argues, through paradigmatic stories, and can be interrogated "by imagining its effect on the receiving end." Consequently, he concludes, "The decision to obey it or disobey it is a choice about the effects," which are "always in the sphere of facticity and feeling," and "not an adjudication of the *arche* from which it proceeds" (26–27). In this way, Caputo underscores his point that obligations "forge the links of 'you' and 'I' and 'we' . . . forming little links that spread tenuously across the surface of the little star [the earth], weaving a thin tissue of tender, fragile bonds and multiple microcommunities." "Obligations," he continues, "form a delicate gossamer surface across the face of the little star" and in this way might be seen as "acts of defiance" (249, 19).

Although appreciative of Caputo's confessional stance and the clarifications and cosmology it assumes, nonetheless I want to examine critically his poetic phenomenology of obligation. As William Connolly summarizes his position, Caputo wants to pull us away from metaphysics and systematics by "bind[ing] suffering to flesh and flesh to obligation," since flesh and hence obligation are what "we are all made of."[53] Caputo himself puts it this way: "Obligation consorts with disasters, with what Levinas likes to call 'the widow, the orphan, the stranger'" (Ex. 22:21) (*Against Ethics*, 28). He suggests that obligation names "the feeling that comes over us when others need our help." It is "a feeling that grows in strength directly in proportion to the desperateness of the situation of the other," he concludes. (5).

In other words, the flesh he presumes to help has a paradigmatic, constitutive pattern—an assumed template of "neediness," or the abject shape of "walking disasters." To be sure, Caputo intends to allow his felt obligation to be helpfully interpolated by a Hebraic biblical tradition, the tradition of the *anawim*, the "little ones," the economically marginalized or exposed. While I too want obligation to move through the intelligence of the gut, to fill the mouth of the hungry, to warm the chilling indifference of the global city, this approach to binding suffering to flesh and flesh to obligation needs some renovation. As I have been arguing throughout, it needs a broader, more inclusive conception of social flesh as mapped out by the cartography and choreography of crip/tography in the global city.

Not only does the pathologization of bodies in need inherently presume to know which bodies are needy and what they need, thereby threatening to scale bodies to sociocultural patterns of normalcy when carrying toward them, even in the name of generosity, a diagnostic fix, it occludes and so endows with sovereignty another set of bodies.[54] Such an exchange between a self and an/other presumed needy has already implicit in it "the asymmetrical forgetting of generosity" through which some "bodies have accrued value, identity and recognition" at the expense of others, as philosopher Roslyn Diprose counsels in *Corporeal Generosity* (8). In such a skewed relationship, generosity appears as the practice of a sovereign, virtuous self toward one needing remediation. And doesn't that then still retain the choreography of a body relying upon a transcendental elsewhere?[55] Further, doesn't Caputo's presumption subtly rest on a corporeal economy we've already put to the test? To be sure, Caputo and I might both agree with Theodore Jennings's definition of theological thinking as "above all . . . a thinking of the conditions of generosity and solidarity, of a non-allergic being with one another."[56] So how else might we think obligation within metaphysical minimalism?

THE GRAVITY OF OBLIGATION

In the fifteenth year of my life reborn after trauma, I find myself amidst something of a psychological turmoil. I feel, I mutter to a friend, as if I am being unfaithful to what happened to me—to the occasion when my life lay intimately close to death, I mean, the occasion that left me mobility challenged. But how precisely—and to what—could trauma have obligated me? Why does it feel as if I have—through trauma, no less—taken on the yoke of religious commitment? How do I explain to myself this sense of obligation, this "feeling . . . of being bound," of "being taken hold of from without" by a "dislocating force" that "knocks me out of orbit?" (Caputo, *Against Ethics*, 7, 8). From whence this gravity of obligation, given that *I* am a "walking disaster"?

Thirteen years old when involved in an auto accident that meant he would proceed through life as a paraplegic, Matthew Sanford writes in *Waking: A Memoir of Trauma and Transcendence* of what I might call, at the point of interpolation between disability experiences and the work of Jean-Luc Nancy, an obligation to the "great open."[57] Refusing the Western script of "willfully overcoming adversity," Sanford writes:

> Something had happened to me—not just the accident, not just the loss of my father and sister or my ensuing paralysis—something else had happened too. I felt like I had been left with a secret. . . . I could not articulate what it was, but I did have a nagging sense of what it was not. It was not to simply live a relatively normal life. I felt far too weighty, too heavy, like there's a purpose to what I have experienced. (145)

But dredging for the source of that obligation, he can speak only of "the 'openness' left by trauma," of cultivating the "silence" as "itself . . . the insight I was sensing," a silence that, like the silence described by apophatic theologians or "the greater consciousness" of Buddhist practitioners, sheared through all one presumes to know about "how the world worked and what it needed" (Sanford, *Waking*, 150, 146, 148).

Reminding us that the body, not just the mind, is conscious, Sanford explains, by analogy to standing at the edge of the Grand Canyon, the gift wrestled from the intensity of his trauma experience: "The act of 'opening' consciousness makes us feel both uncertainty and the onrush of silence that comes with it. . . . It is both awesome and unsettling—one knows not to stand too close to the edge. The feeling of openness and a confrontation with silence are deeply related" (*Waking*, 184). The great open had wrestled with him, and he with it. If we might acknowledge this as but an occasion of religious response to mystery, to the sublimity of life beyond our grasp, suffering may be a perhaps surprising spiritual rite of passage. For Sanford it was—literally—his initiation into the practice and teaching of yoga.

Mark Matousek—a journalist living with HIV—has heard multiple outpourings of pain, illness, disease, and trauma. In *When You're Falling, Dive* he has tracked the ways in which such suffering has served as "rite of initiation." A spiritual seeker in the face of his own diagnosis, Matousek writes so as to understand what his body already knows—that "HIV had actually saved my life" (7). A reporter of tales of "savage grace," of those occasions when "terror can be a door to enlightenment," an opening to a life baptized in awe and not constrained by fear or its bipolarities (good/evil, pleasure/pain, success/failure), Matousek sets out—first taking leave of a high-status job (with Andy Warhol)—"determined not to lose track of what [he'd] learned in the mortal zone or to forget the miraculousness of things" (8).[58]

Matousek's personal story, told in *Sex, Death, Enlightenment* as well as in *When You're Falling, Dive*, a collection of similar tales, cuts through modernity's dismissal of pain so as to let pain's paradoxical blessing out of the bag, to "put it to its natural use" (*When You're Falling*, 7). "There's vitality in facing life's extremes," he insists, naming this energy *viriditas*, a term used by medieval theologian Hildegard von Bingen to speak of Spirit's immanent humor, of how nature enfolded with Spirit courses with "greening power." He explains: "Though we're immersed in this power at every moment, survivors realize how profoundly quality of life is determined by how skillfully . . . we harness ourselves to that evergreen force at the heart of things." Oddly, what we've grown to call the tragic and a sense of holy mystery—yielding generosity, courage, egolessness, and "the fraternity of the *anawim*"—are not mutually exclusive. "Epiphanies happen where life and death meet," Matousek asserts, given that "the very walls we construct to protect our lives hide the full glory of those lives from us" (ibid., 10, 11, 13). This locus, this point of reverence, this flash of satori, and the discipline of walking with its hindrances, I mark as Spirit.

The opening of consciousness, prolonged in my case through an extended recovery, allows for a critical, constructive dissociation—which in the case of trauma and disability is not always self-chosen—from social geographies of meaning and value, from normalcy, from life as it is. Yet I, caught in awe, take my vows to the great open—this sheltering nowhere. I awake inveterately in love with the world. (I am not ignorant of the fact that this "naturalism" comes to me from Christian theism, from its impetus to love the world as God has loved it. God, too, said Lutheran theologian Joseph Sittler, is "an undeviating materialist."[59]) But the intrigue for me—reflecting on my own experience, and also Matousek's and Sanford's—is the poignancy and power of living with something like religious vows . . . without "belief," even if or when traumatically induced. If suffering opens us, "the open"—or Spirit, if you will—somehow also sets its demands on us, "binds" or folds us back. To be alive is to be obligated—harnessed, yoked, devoted.

"THE CUT THAT BINDS"

In his essay entitled "The Cut that Binds: Time, Memory, and the Ascetic Impulse," Elliot Wolfson, Jewish scholar of Kabbalah, addresses circumcision, the fleshy seal of Jewish males' covenant with God. Wolfson sets out to read Kabbalists, specifically Nahman ben Simhah of Bratslav (1772–1810), by employing the hermeneutical lens of David Levin's phenomenalogical psychology. Levin's studies concluded that "'the very essence of circumcision—the heart of the matter, as it were—lies in the fact that the incision *opens*'" (emphasis added). Wolfson, picking up from Levin, explicates Nahman's teaching to suggest that "the path opened by circumcision" is that of spiritual memory—the memory of a path beyond the spiritual amnesia induced by realism—specifically, the recollection of the greater mind or Godlike consciousness of the everything-nothing of the universe (Wolfson, "Cut that Binds," 103). In Nahman's cosmology, Wolfson explains, "temporal consciousness is really a lack of consciousness and supratemporal consciousness is perfected consciousness." Since "the very nature of circumcision is . . . that it negates the natural instincts that are time-bound," circumcision "connects the individual with the spiritual root in a dimension above time." Circumcision thus makes possible the path of true knowledge, which for Nahman was "the perspective of being beyond time, a seemingly impossible state of mind for consciousness to comprehend in its temporal deportment" (ibid., 120, 111). Nahman used disability experience, specifically the Hasidic story of "The Seven Beggars," to link "the cut that binds" with the disarticulation of disablement, the beggars all being disabled, the seventh—the one without feet—being the consummate dancer, the Messiah, encouraging persons to perceive the world in a less limited way than realism imposes.[60]

To be sure, Nahman in a pietistic vein connected perfect knowledge—"openness to time beyond time" and its reversal of values—with the transcendence of the phenomenal world and somatic desires, "when one becomes fully aware of that which is beyond time, beyond the limitations of eros" (Wolfson, "Cut that Binds," 123). But as Jean-Luc Nancy has said in *Dis-Enclosure*, "the 'other world' . . . never was a second world, or even a world-behind-the-worlds" (10), and the "cut that binds" binds back, in a de-essentializing move, upon a promissory open, a consciousness attuned to becoming without the imposition of an organizing judgment. Nahman's sense of memory as a "recollection that transcends the linearity of time by gathering together past, present, and future in the circular resumption of what has never been, a calling to mind that allows one 'to see old things with a newer, farther look'" (Wolfson, "Cut that Binds," 104), finds a resonance with philosopher Gilles Deleuze's embrace of substance as folded, of past, present, and future as co-im/*pli*/cated, thus posing the possibility of "anomalous becoming."[61]

Deleuze assumed Henri Bergson's dense sense of "duration"—of the enfolding of the "'totality of the past'" into the thickness of the present, "a thickness that the linear conception of time cannot recognize." The present, infrasensibly saturated, is in Bergson's sense "suffused by a realm of difference that lies coiled within it, offering the possibility of disrupting any given identity."[62] Thus, if from distinct somatic loci, both Deleuze and Nahman have attempted to "think beyond the human condition."[63] But if "the function of the sign of circumcision" has been to guard one against the temporal simplicity that results "in spiritual amnesia," with this eventuating in Nahman's "mandate . . . to begin each day anew, to see oneself reborn in every moment" (Wolfson, "Cut that Binds," 127, 109), then pain and/or suffering likewise fold back upon a similar promissory zone: Deleuze's body without organs, the deterritorializing space within becoming from which thought opens out. In other words, might I understand the obligation of my own trauma—the flaying of my mortality, the folding of the edges of my mortality in upon my life, the harness of limitation—as something analogically like the mark of circumcision?

THE *PLI* OF INTERCORPOREAL GENEROSITY

Being a patient of life (a "becoming" that is other than managed by the will to be in control, to overcome) can be the subjective locus to which pain initiates one. Pain introduces one to a certain "submission" or "patience" with life. (As F. Scott Fitzgerald was asked to contemplate, is it even "my" pain, "my" trauma, or am I feeling with, in sympathy with, nature folding and tearing through me?[64]) Suffering allows our rigid, defensive selves to move through an unmarked door of disorganization and reorganization, to recognize the nominal looseness and, equally, the permissiveness of existence. But as William Connolly somewhat inadvertently suggests in *Why I Am Not a Secularist*, there's something phenomenologically analogous— at least amidst the late effects of modern humanism—between suffering, which "resides in the underside of agency, mastery," and an "ethos of generosity," which "moves us beyond mastery, will to control" (47, 16).[65]

The religious sense of obligation lived out of a relation with pain, enacted as a sense of generosity toward the world, might strike modern Western persons as paradoxical, perplexing (as it has befuddled me for quite some time). Yet this coincidence between suffering and generosity, this coincidence within "visceral intersubjectivity" (Connolly, *Why I Am Not a Secularist*, 3), appears, theologically speaking, hardly unique. As the Buddha knew, to touch such a cut, an opening, was flush with the form of generosity known as compassion; where Buddhism situates the open, it carries a heart quality—a generosity. "Gratitude for life," Connolly explains, re-marking in a Nietzschean-Deleuzean mode, "draws an ethics of generosity partly from those energies and attachments that exceed established conventions"—those that sneak through even suffering's disorganizing whirl (ibid., 65).

Contrary to Caputo's scene in which obligation swells in relation to "walking disasters," generosity, Roslyn Diprose insists, is "not reducible to an economy of exchange between sovereign individuals." Indeed, "Generosity is not one virtue among others but the primordial condition of personal, interpersonal and communal existence." She explains:

> Primordially, generosity is not the expenditure of one's possessions but the dispossession of oneself, the being-given to others that undercuts any self-contained ego, that undercuts self-possession. Generosity . . . happens at a prereflective level, at the level of corporeality and sensibility, and so eschews the calculation characteristic of an economy of exchange. Generosity is being given to others without deliberation in a field of intercorporeality, a being given that constitutes the self as affective and being affected, that constitutes social relations and that which is given in relation. (*Corporeal Generosity*, 4–5)

While Caputo would commendably have us practice social availability to the other, generosity, Diprose insists, underlining several times the "nonvolitional" nature of it, implies openness prior to identity (ibid., 68, 69, 9). In other words, the practice of corporeal generosity begins for Diprose within the milieu of intersubjective relations (in fact, generosity names this intersubjective milieu), and not at the level of property, status, identity, and value. A demonstrative example might well be in order: During my first training unit in the use of a wheelchair at G. F. Strong Rehabilitation Centre, I met David and Jonathan, two adolescent males, both of whom—in separate accidents reflective of the extremes of mountain biking —became lifelong wheelchair users. Born of their situation was a friendship of visceral depth. Both had quickly learned to practice the bawdy body humor that belongs among the disabled. And both retained in their wheelchair training some of the love of risk that brings any number of persons through the doors of a rehab hospital. Yet both were also typical young, straight males—not wanting to show too much feeling, covering their own pain in humor and antics.

Then came the day we were to practice picking ourselves up from a fall by first intentionally flipping ourselves so as to occasion a spill out of our chairs. (Disability is not for the faint of heart!) Jonathan dared to go first, but owing to the chaotic—and not yet habituated—firing of nerves in his still newbie quadriplegic body, he convulsed as he spilled over. All of us felt our stomachs drop in that moment, but David's compassion betrayed his adolescent cool. His feelings for his friend literally pulled him likewise into a gut-coiling spasm of compassion that took him slithering out of his own chair and onto the ground. It was one of the most moving, intimate moments in which I have ever been privileged to participate.

This zone of interdependent feeling—below volition and in an openness that is "carnal and affective" (Diprose, *Corporeal Generosity*, 9)—seems to me to be of the nature of that generosity to which Diprose points us. If obligation calls from within the deeps of intercorporeal tissue, then effulgence or plenitude—corporeal generosity itself, in other words—is what obligates, as distinct from a notion of generosity imposed as a duty where scarcity prevails. To locate one's self with and in the open of corporeal generosity also leads one to renounce any superior sense of the self arising from access to wealth or wholeness, and also to release the resentful envy thereof. Corporeal generosity catches us up in an affective effulgence; the intensity of affect felt between bodies draws us into an exuberant, energetic carnival. When one assumes the practice of a spiritual path, setting out from the locus of this great open, in this zone of corporeal generosity, one might experience both the beggar and the CEO, like pain, as one's spiritual teacher—as an opening to the practice of generosity, of sympathy with the cellular. The yoga or obligation of neighbor love, it seems to me, is born of this, develops this as the choreography of bodies in the cosmopolis.

Responsiveness to the obligation felt within corporeal generosity challenges the humanist self. Corporeal generosity suggests that the self can practice "the open" in a way beyond its mastered and patrolled defensive lines (property, identity). Setting out from the locus of the great open, this intercorporeal field, corporeal generosity does not presume to relate to another as a "classification, but simply as a creation of God."[66] A spiritual practice of the open calls us from below mastery, from below sovereign selfhood, where the phenomenology of suffering links up with generosity. As Caputo himself has observed, "Obligation is the sphere of what I did not constitute. . . . It comes to me . . . in a curved space which lays me low, producing a kind of disequilibrium in me" (*Against Ethics*, 26–27). That curve, given culturally prescribed lives of linear progress, is telling.

TOWARD AN URBAN NATURALIST COSMOLOGY

"I don't know what purpose we have as humans other than to be one another's servants," muttered one who might well epitomize Cascadia's "spiritual, but not religious" population—a therapeutic massage therapist with an array of healing practices including ayurvedic therapy and aromatherapy (rosemary and orange, for me), color therapy (green for improving liver function), Chinese herbal and acupuncture therapy, and tribal South African and Amazonian Indian therapy. Yet as we traded conversation about what it might mean to think about obligation to each other in a city like Vancouver (and after she had balked at the word *obligation* as soon as I uttered it, thinking that it somehow related her to a set of duties to an externality, such as God, not as something felt in the heart, her declared authoritative center), the words tumbled out of her mouth as a somewhat surprising confession, even to herself. "Servant. I know it's kind of a funny, old word," she began apologetically. And yet as she spun her own thought, she heard herself saying, "Why, even the rest of the natural world—like trees, like ants, like bacteria—have a servant role." Indeed: The turning of our soft tissues one to another, this submission or entrustment of the soft tissue and heart of ourselves so as to be folded through one another's lives, constitutes some aspect of neighbor love. The theological reformer Martin Luther might be pleased to hear the yoke of servanthood interpreted as a naturalist cosmology for twenty-first-century urban dwellers.

Luther's "summary of the Christian life," his treatise *The Freedom of a Christian* (1520), which, concisely stated, reads "the Christian is 'lord of all,'"—"subject to none"—and a "servant, completely attentive to the needs of all,"[67] was drafted in mind of a humanity "prone to find security in earthly 'addictions,'"[68] not unlike our own contemporary urban humanity. In light of the foregoing, Luther's insights might also be traceable to the phenomenological intercorporeal fold, the nonmastered relation with life that suffering and generosity might share (for example, his terror, when cut loose from parental blessing, in the midst of thunderstorm). Luther set sight on a vast permissible open—a "boundless open," not unlike Buddhist *sunyata*,[69] which he then theologically explicated. While Luther cathected the open as Christ-identified, as a relational locus of "being loved by" God,[70] out of which one "knows nothing except this sense of spontaneous joy" (Luther, *Freedom of a Christian*, 83),[71] that relational yoke was transferred by Luther to the needs of the neighbor and the world.[72] In the great open, informed for Luther by the character of God's prodigal love, humans can turn our soft, vulnerable flesh toward one another. "For Luther faith [as] trust . . . was the fundamental perspective for all of life." It involved "an orientation of the whole self"—not just the intellect as "belief."[73] Perhaps it might yet be read even as a nature cosmology, a cosmology of life, inherently relational, turned servantlike one toward another.

Luther writes: "We freely and willingly spend ourselves and all that we have. . . . This is just as our Father does, who gives all things to all people richly and freely, making 'his sun to rise on the evil and on the good' (Matt. 5:45)." This great permissiveness, of experiencing the heart as "free . . . from all [guilt], laws and commands" (Luther, *Freedom of a Christian*, 83, 89), might well today be expressed in the postmodern life without even the siren call of Being, World Spirit, or God. As Buddhist Masao Abe puts it, "In Christianity . . . the kenosis of God is fully realized," and as God "completely empties God-self, the dynamic relationship of mutual domination-subordination or mutual immanence and mutual transcendence between human beings and God, and human beings and nature, can be fully realized. This is possible only by overcoming," as the deconstruction of Christianity has overcome, "the theocentrism innate in Christianity."[74] That overcoming, as we've found, has opened nonetheless upon the vista named *"corporeal generosity."*

Spirit as Prosthesis

The Kabbalist Nahman, like the reformer Luther and the contemporary philosopher Gilles Deleuze, each push us toward a locus of consciousness that exceeds—by offering an alternative to—the map of consciousness drawn by Descartes, the "supreme will to power" that "imposes upon becoming the character of being."[75]

"Hegel, Schelling, and Hölderlin were the first to have understood, following Kant's lead, that to make room for a rational faith it was necessary to open rationality to the dimension appropriate to the absolute, or again to a 'higher reason,'" Jean-Luc Nancy notes. However, "The lesson of the last two centuries is that neither philosophy nor poetry sufficed to assure this, whereas science, for its part, resolutely turned away once and for all from that which seemed apt to sketch out in it . . . the same elevation of reason" (Nancy, *Dis-Enclosure*, 2–3). For the same reason, William Connolly—without marking himself a theist—insists he is not then "a secularist" (*Why I Am Not a Secularist*). The "cut that binds," the opening that obligates, unfolds the great vastness—in a Deleuzean sense, the dense virtuality of what might yet be. Elsewhere I have marked this verdant open as Spirit—as did Hegel. But if Spirit might prevent the rationalist foreclosure of the intercorporeal fold, the foreclosure of generosity, how can we employ the term "Spirit" without reverting to strong theology, to the metaphysics of presence?

THINKING RELIGIOUSLY IN THE RUIN OF GOD

"It is not our concern to save religion, even less to return to it," writes Nancy (*Dis-Enclosure*, 1). He is not averse to faith, although clearly distinguishing it from belief. Warning of terrorism as "the conjunction of despair and a unifying will" and of the bankruptcy of reason and humanism, which appears simultaneously with "the possibility of a . . . hyperreligious upheaval or surrection" (ibid., 147, 41, 2–3), Nancy nonetheless insists that ours is not a question of bringing Christianity up to date. (To acknowledge that Christianity "has ceased giving life" to many would be finally to admit the obvious, the elephant in the room [ibid., 141].) Looking at the detraditionalizing effects of modernity, Nancy reminds us to think this as the unfolding of Christianity, not its deviation: "Christianity has delivered Western society" to this point, the point of its own dissolution. And because this is so, he argues, "the essence of Christianity" is itself "dis-enclosure"—or, simply, "opening" (ibid., 143–44, 145).

Nancy's "dis-enclosure" of Christianity disrupts a certain Enlightenment myth we have used to colonize Christianity as well as our Western past: "The West was born not from the liquidation of a dark world of beliefs, dissolved by the light of a new sun. . . . There was no reduction of the unknown, but rather an aggravation of the incommensurable. . . . Christianity designates nothing other, essentially . . . than the demand to open in this world an alterity or an unconditional alienation." (*Dis-Enclosure*, 8, 10). Nancy finds something of this same demand in the kenotic impulse, an impulse that resembles Laurel Schneider's sense of the ruined distinction between God and world, a resolutely dirty conception of God (ibid., 36).[76] In a world threatened by foreclosures of reason and of religion, Christianity, the "'religion of the egress/departure from religion'" (ibid., 5–6, 146, 142), the religion daring to think religiously "after God," is inheritor of an obligation to the open, under obligation of the "dis-enclosure . . . inscribed at the heart of the Christian tradition" (ibid., 11).

Noting that "faith always comes down to adherence to the infinity of sense," Nancy concludes his "dis-enclosure" of Christianity: "We are becoming a culture of pure faithfulness: the faithful assured not only to be obliged, but to want to be faithful. . . . Faithful to no other thing than to the very gesture of faithfulness" (*Dis-Enclosure*, 154). I hear Nancy to resonate with H. Richard Niebuhr's own swerving of the question of faith—amidst the Cold War of the 1950s and McCarthyism—into the question of felicity, of keeping faith with one another.[77] As Nancy himself puts it, "Christianity is . . . not . . . the obvious. . . . critical negation or despair of sense." Rather, Christianity can be lived—beyond itself—as the demand of "opening," as faithfulness beyond "discernible community . . . to the infinity of sense" (ibid., 147, 145, 154). Working with Nancy, Christianity might at the least serve as a way of becoming religious "after God," of becoming affectively related, obligated.

A God who is emptied into this world—the locus from which both Nancy and Vattimo set out—suggests a way of thinking within which God empties God's self of transcendence, God yields sovereignty so as to become with the world. Spirit folds back upon nature, God implicating God's self in such a way that it may be as possible to declare "spirit to be the character of nature"[78] as to invoke nature. God, according to Nancy, submits God's self—God turns God's self—to the world without reserve, such that Nancy essentially empties Luther's sense of the "hidden God": "The site to which [God] has withdrawn has neither depths nor hiding places." God "is a god whose absence in itself creates divinity, or a god whose void-of-divinity is the truth, properly speaking" (*Dis-Enclosure*, 36). If God has been "ruined" or "dirtied" in such a way that neither nature/spirit nor God/ world can be clearly, cleanly distinguished,[79] Spirit suggests a conceptual commitment to "opening," to "the open."

Spirit, one might say, prompts attention to irreducible multiples within immanence. While Nancy's sense of "the open" does not necessarily announce that it presumes to look upon the field of multiples, the disenclosure of all totalizing worlds must set us on such a vista. "How do we recognize 'the ungraspability of being'?" Nancy asks, already alerting us to Spirit's sheer relevance to multiplicity. "How do we touch, or let ourselves be touched by, the opening of the world/to the world? How, if not by a gesture . . . that passes outside of knowledge without unreason?" Nancy goes on to suggest the relationship between this gesture and what he marks as faith in faithfulness itself: "This gesture or act, which measures neither knowledge nor certainty, an act neither objectifying nor subjectifying, the necessary accomplice of a writing (of a song, of a tone, of a touch), could we not, must we not call it 'faith'? A faith that would stand up unflinchingly to the atheism without reserve in which it would be nothing other than the 'courage' invoked to say the 'strange'" (*Dis-Enclosure*, 73). While Nancy hopes to preclude any false illusion about or Romanticization of the open, he nonetheless insists on keeping faith with it—a posture not unlike Luther's relation to the hidden God, at least on this point.

Yet the "great open" (Nancy is using here the poetics of Hölderlin; *Dis-Enclosure*, 157) does not so much "exist" as "it . . . defines and mobilizes existence: the opening of the world to inaccessible alterity (and consequently a paradoxical access to it)" (ibid., 10). Such a "thin" notion of Spirit is surely to be distinguished from a Wisdom or Logos theology within which Spirit's polyvalent and polyocular omnipresence overwhelms world complexes. Nancy rather evokes or obligates us to a "poverty of spirit"[80]—to Spirit that is not, except perhaps in our gesture of openness, except perhaps in our lived choreography thereof. And yet in that gesture, corporeality becomes generous.

AS PROSTHESIS, SPIRIT CAPACITATES BECOMING

Within a philosophy of becoming that has moved through the deconstruction of ontotheology, we perhaps would not so much say that Spirit "is" per se, but that it capacitates being. J. Edgar Bruns, in *The Christian Buddhism of St. John*, hypothesized that John may have been "the earliest Christian writer to manifest a knowledge of Indian, specifically Buddhist, teaching" and that "the key to Johannine thought lies in an understanding of Buddhist concepts" (28). Consequently, Bruns reads 1 John 4:16 through what he identifies as a *prajna paramita* hermeneutic: "There is no difference between loving and being one with God, because God is simply another name for love, and without love there is no present God. . . . God does not do something. God is the doing of something, which is why John calls [God] spirit, light and love. . . . Consequently God does not generate love in us, but rather, our loving generates God" (30–31). If so, "Spirit," given this now "religionless religion," this religion without belief, does not so much name some existent something as serve as a conceptional locus. Spirit is not an essence, but capacitates a practice.

We can think of Spirit, then, as something of a prosthesis,[81] as what can augment or capacitate "belief in the world" or, as per Nancy, sheer "faithfulness"—something like a cane or a crutch upon which one does not bear weight, but which nonetheless capacitates movement, enables agility. Precisely because the self is open to "'wounding, outrage, and pain,'" prosthesis, borrowing upon its somatic model, can, ethically speaking, refer to a necessary "transfer into otherness." In other words, it supplements the self, enabling it to reach out to the other.[82] "Prosthesis is semiosis, the making of meanings and bodies," Donna Haraway notes, concluding by qualifying her thought—"not for transcendence, but for power-charged communication."[83] Analogous to Foucault's concept of "queer" not as a substance or positivity, but as a positionality,[84] Spirit as prosthesis allows us to improvise a distinct art of the self—openness to the intercorporeal field, toward social flesh, weighted toward corporeal generosity.

Admittedly leaning upon a certain Christian interpretation of the world, an understanding of Spirit as prosthesis capacitates "this impious, nontheistic reverence for life" (Connolly, *Why I Am Not a Secularist*, 54) that may not be wholly severable, in Nietzsche's case or mine, from the Lutheran cradle. Luther insisted—and both Vattimo and Nancy sound as if in echo of this point—that "the justice of God . . . is the free gift of God surrendering God's self to us,"[85] of God submitting God's self to the world. This insight was later summarized in Lutheran teaching by F. C. Oetinger in the statement, "Corporeality is the end of God's path."[86] Spirit as prosthesis capacitates our corporeal becoming with the world. As a prosthesis capacitates the body, Spirit capacitates our "belief in the world," enables the mutual submission—or entrustment—of flesh one to another.

Donning the prosthesis, the shuffle begins:

> Shifting from one to the other as though there could be some sort of even transfer or equal distribution, as though beyond it all there was perfect or at least functionally satisfactory balance between the two, and failing to find it, failing to find an end to the discomfort of one and the other position, the one too ready to give way under prolonged exertion, the other too rigidly secure in its own uprightness, and in the interstice no easy middle, no ground for rest or resolution.[87]

So David Wells observes of his father, slipping on his prosthetic leg. Donning the conceptual prosthesis of Spirit situates us similarly—agonistically—between two economies: what is culturally available (rationalism or "secularism") and the "divine economy," the fold of corporeal generosity.

In an amenable Nietzschean vein, Tyler Roberts describes Spirit as a locus of difference disrupting reason's totality, thereby reorienting—not repressing—desire. Spirit might be described, Roberts surmises from Nietzsche's work, "as life cutting into life, as an instrument used by life in its efforts to enhance itself."[88] Far from occasioning serenity, Spirit suggests a way of forming the self around fundamental alterity. Inasmuch as Spirit "open[s] the self to the undomesticated power of life," honing Spirit, he suggests, can allow us to live "body in a different key."[89] In other words, the spiritual life feels a bit more like Jacob wrestling the angel than like serene, contemplative placidity. Embracing the social flesh of corporeal generosity takes some practice, a redistribution of weight, never finally resolved.

Crip/tography and Spirit: A Theology for Seculars

To don Spirit as prosthesis is to adopt a new way to choreograph the relations of bodies for cosmopolis, a new map of the global city—the choreography and geography of crip/tography. Spirituality, as theologian Philip Sheldrake puts it, is not so much a personal intimacy of the self with an imagined beyond as a practice of our availability within the particularity of a place—more precisely, "the practice of everyday living in the heart of the world of human places."[90] For Sheldrake, as for me, the place that concerns us is the city, which "both represents and creates a climate of values that defines how humans understand themselves . . . and also shapes their sensibilities and ways of seeing the world."[91] The disciplined practice of corporeal generosity, the embrace of social flesh (that is, responsiveness to this "curve" thrown up from below ego), is here being invoked as an alternative to what fragments the city between those with economic access and those without access to the commons of life, leaving many on both sides shivering in their self-protective loneliness and cynicism.

Assuming the prosthesis of Spirit, the locus of opening and the harness of corporeal generosity, implies practicing through the "vacuum of meaning"—here, specifically, as ways of "being with" one another in the city. In the global city, idealization shears off difference, leaving us without the humbling, bumbling ballet of "the good sidewalk," without need to negotiate interactions, and, as a result, we remain resolutely cool in our indifference, our detachment, our neutralization of one another. For life in postcolonial cosmopolis, we need ligatures of friendship amidst the rampant dislocation—not that we imagine a great communitarianism, but rather that through friendship we might live an alternative to the existentialist individualism, which this "spiritual, but not religious" ethos can engender—a theology for seculars.

While speaking most specifically of gay relations, Foucault emphasized friendship as "a mode of life . . . that our sanitized society can't allow a place for without fearing the formation of new alliances and the tying together of unforeseen lines of force." Where order, law, professional status, and class are expected to manage difference, friendship can "yield intense relations not resembling those that are institutionalized . . . as well as yield a culture and an ethics."[92] Friendship—breaching the enclosure aggravated by modern humanist individualism (the guarantees of a money economy and the self-protective paranoia of dislocation) without collapsing the ethical autonomy of persons developed during modernity—can provide enough affiliative sheltering so as to allow us slowly to submit or entrust our vul-

nerable flesh one to another. Loving, after all, does involve softening and
yielding our flesh one to another. There is no civic being, no friendship, no
neighbor, no public, no commons, without a mutual yielding of our tissues
and the shared embrace of social flesh, of intercorporeal generosity.

MENDICANTS OF THE FREE SPIRIT

Noting that Deleuze and Guattari consider the urban flow to be one of
the apparently irresolvable difficulties of the capitalist axiomatic, Todd
May invites us to think towards "an urbanism that is Deleuzian" by
"jostl[ing] the reins of the majority identity in order to investigate . . . new
ways of becoming," "to live in accordance with a difference that is always
there, always subsisting within the world that is presented to us" (*Gilles
Deleuze*, 146; 167, 150, 170). Deleuze's "becoming minor" includes microso-
ciological practices—perhaps something, then, of the order of loosing a
secular mendicant order of the Free Spirits wielding friendship. If religion's
power has too frequently been used to generate a transcendent elsewhere
masking sovereign power and generating thereby subjected peoples rather
than "free radicals," Spirit here invites dis-enclosure of identity, invites us
to break with the wealth insulation and isolation of those identity formations so amenable to free market capitalism.[93]

I might suggest this mendicant order of Free Spirits begin by practicing
the yoga of "becoming whale." Whales—the pet of the sacred, in the words
of the ancient poet (Psalm 104:26)—have become, in the last several centuries, vulnerable to the human species. Whales—creatures in relation to the
sea what humans are to the land, that is, "a kind of parallel 'us'"—are a
complex, socially structured species, each pod having something like its
own unique culture and dialect. Like humans, they sing, they leap in joy,
they are curious, they grieve, they wail in distress. Their vulnerability as a
species arises, most obviously, from the advances in technology enabling
their being hunted by humans, and human ocean-going traffic, inducing
accidental animal deaths along shipping lanes. But seismic testing and the
use of high-tech sonar, especially in military operations, have also become silent banes of whale existence. Yet as reporter Charles Siebert
writes in "Watching Whales Watching Us," among whale researchers,
one of the more intriguing whale-human interactions remains whales'

cavorting with, and their curious soliciting of affection from, humans (26–35, 44–45).

Dubbed by researchers "the friendlies," the forty-foot-long, many-ton mastadons make their approach towards humans, slide their hidden hulls up close to the research crafts, then lift only their slow-blinking eyes up out of the water—as if in something like a provocative wink. "The baby gray glided up to the boat's edge," writes Siebert, "and then the whole of his long, hornbill-shaped head was rising up out of the water directly beside me, a huge ovoid eye slowly opening to take me in." He concludes in a note of awe, "I'd never felt so beheld in my life," he concludes in a note of awe ("Watching Whales," 32). Mother grays, often the first to initiate human contact, once will, having established relations will then retrieve their calves, showing them off—as if in their own version of a stroll to the park. After taking the baby home, the whales return for a final hug, which implies, it seems, mutual massaging: The whale glides up close, inviting humans to scratch its tongue or rub its back; then returning touch, the whale bumps or lifts—on its back—the underside of the boat. Despite the impact of human life upon the species, they seem nonetheless to remain intrigued with communicating with their land-based peers; they seem to have found it in themselves to forgive us our "transgressions" and "to trust us again" (ibid., 31). Despite human betrayal, the ovoid eye acknowledges us, holds us. "A fellow mammal breaking the boundary of its domain for a long look at you is beguiling in and of itself," Siebert notes. But, he concludes, "such behavior becomes downright otherworldly . . . when you consider the . . . history of human-whale interactions" (ibid., 32).

With the concept "becoming-animal," Deleuze invites persons into a process of metamorphosing, into a process of undoing codes and of deterritorializing learned, habituated coordinates.[94] By "becoming whale" I would invite us, within the coordinates of cosmopolis, to "desanctify elements of ourselves" (Connolly), to offer ourselves as "friendlies"—to offer one another the beholding gaze. "Basic trust in mutuality is that original 'optimism,' that assumption that 'somebody is there,' without which we cannot live," wrote psychologist Erik Erikson in *Young Man Luther*. After detailing children's failure to thrive, their vulnerability to intellectual and emotional shut-down, in an environment void of basic trust—a scene which we might relate to life in cosmopolis—Erickson concludes by noting that the "meeting with the perceiving subject" becomes "the anchor-point" for "all the developments which culminate . . . in the establishment of psychosocial identity" (118). More than a "civil religion" or as a yoga thereof, we need the loving eye.

Intriguingly, Erikson wrote this within his analysis of Luther's cathection to a providential God—that is, the one "whose face shines upon us" (Numbers 6:25, and also Psalms 4, 31, 80, 119), this refrain serving as Luther's psychological, stabilizing chant. This "ideological formula," Erickson suggests, provides the anchor, "provides nutriment for the soul as well as the stomach, and the screen for the environment so that vigorous growth may meet what it can manage." "Of all the ideological systems," Erikson then concludes, without any arrogant disdain, "only religion restores the earliest sense of appeal to a Provider, a Providence"—whether in benediction ("The Lord's face shine on you"), or as icon (e.g., the Madonna, Jesus the friend, Kuan Yin, or Buddha), or through prayer and meditation. "One basic task of all religions is to reaffirm that first relationship," Erickson instructs us, "for we have in us deep down a lifelong mistrustful remembrance of that truly metaphysical anxiety." Erikson seems to refer to a deep anxiety of our being supplemental or extraneous to the universe as also, more immediately, the simple anxiety as to whether or not we will be recognized (*Young Man Luther*, 118–19). That anxiety, I would maintain, can become reactivated amidst cultural dislocation, especially when, as within global cities, the scene may not provide means for psychosocial integration. In that vein, Erickson's prescriptive diagnostic is intriguing: "One basic form of heroic asceticism, therefore, . . . is to retrace the steps of the development of the I, to . . . step down and back to the borderline where the I emerged from its matrix" (ibid., 119)—to shine our faces one upon another, to double-bind ourselves in this way.

In his essay entitled "On a Divine Wink," Nancy writes, "there is no wink of god, but . . . god is the wink" (in *Dis-Enclosure*, 119). If Spirit transpires in the wink of an eye, might we secular mendicants, we urban Free Spirits, simply begin to home life in the city, to loose the flow of generosity and trust, by assuming the yoga practice of "becoming whale?" Urban mendicancy—the roving of a band of Free Spirits—might attend to persons' inchoate suffering, but also to provide "ports of trust" for the socially dislocated, those of us needing a solid psychological base from which we might then engender a generous public. In the wink of an ovoid eye, we might let loose love of a world in which God has been positively ruined.

NOTES

INTRODUCTION

1. Statistics as reported by Asian Development Bank and McKinsey Global Institute. See Lawrence Bartlett, "7-Billionth Person Expected this Fall."

2. Christopher Flavin, "Preface," in Worldwatch Institute, *State of the World 2007: Our Urban Future*, xxiii.

3. Harvey Cox, "*The Secular City* Twenty-Five Years Later," 1029.

4. Gordon Lynch, *After Religion? 'Generation X' and the Search for Meaning*, 3, 120.

5. Catherine Keller, "Pluralism Is Not Enough" (home page), Polydoxy: Theologies of the Manifold (web site).

6. Doug Saunders, *Arrival City: The Final Migration and Our Next World*, 23.

7. Edward Glaeser, *Triumph of the City: How Our Greatest Invention Makes Us Richer, Smarter, Greener, Healthier, and Happier*; David Owen, *Green Metropolis: Why Living Smaller, Living Closer, and Driving Less Are the Keys to Sustainability*.

8. David Owen, "Manhattan is the Greenest City in North America."

9. Mike Davis, *Planet of Slums*, 7. For a thick—experiential, subjective—description of life in the "undercity," see Katherine Boo, *Behind the Beautiful Forevers: Life, Death, and Hope in a Mumbai Undercity*.

10. Davis, *Planet of Slums*, 16–17.

11. Charles Bowden, *Murder City: Ciudad Juarez and the Global Economy's New Killing Fields*.

12. Donna Haraway, *Modest_Witness@Second_Millennium. FemaleMan© _Meets_OncoMouse*, 3.

13. Flavin, "Preface," xxiv.

14. Leonie Sandercock, *Cosmopolis II: Mongrel Cities of the Twenty-First Century*, 4.

15. Flavin, "Preface," xxiv.

16. Gayatri Chakravorty Spivak, *Death of a Discipline*, 72–73.

17. Sandercock, *Cosmopolis II*, 2, 47.

18. Jane M. Jacobs, *Edge of Empire: Postcolonialism and the City*, 4.

19. Saunders, *Arrival City*, 1.

20. Harvey Cox, in *The Secular City*, did, of course, draw attention to just such a conjunction of the rise of urbanization and a massive shift in the nature of traditional religion. "Secularization," he explained, "marks a change in the way [humans] grasp and understand their life together, and it occurred only when the cosmopolitan confrontations of city living exposed the relativity of the myths and traditions [humans] once thought were unquestionable" (1). As he points out in an essay revisiting his thesis twenty-five years later, "secularization"—which he distinguished from secularism, its "calcification into an ideology"—"is not everywhere and always an evil. It prevents powerful religions from acting on their theocratic pretensions. It allows people to choose among a wider range of worldviews" (*"The Secular City* Twenty-Five Years Later," 1025). Despite the much-vaunted thesis of the resurgence of religions worldwide, as forwarded for example by Philip Jenkins, *The Next Christendom: The Coming of Global Christianity*, the cosmopolitan zones of global cities, at least across the coastal and northern swathes of North America and Europe, seem to be consistent still with Cox's earlier surmise. To be sure, religion operates differently within arrival cities than in cosmopolitan centers of global cities.

21. Lester K. Little, *Religious Poverty and the Profit Economy in Medieval Europe*, 19; xi.

22. In this I am in essential agreement with Alain de Botton, who argues in *Religion for Atheists: A Non-believer's Guide to the Uses of Religion* that religions have been "repositories of a myriad ingenious concepts with which we can try to assuage a few of the most persistent and unattended ills of secular life" (13).

23. Philip Sheldrake, *Spaces for the Sacred: Place, Memory, and Identity*, 147.

24. John D. Caputo, *Against Ethics: Contributions to a Poetics of Obligation with Constant Reference to Deconstruction*, 5.

25. Jean-Luc Nancy, *Corpus*, 81.

26. Paul Knitter, *Introducing Theologies of Religions*, 209.

27. Chris Beasley and Carol Bacchi, "Envisaging a New Politics for an Ethical Future: Beyond Trust, Care, and Generosity, Towards an Ethic of 'Social Flesh,'" 280. Cited in text hereafter.

28. Isabell Lorey, "Becoming Common: Precarization as Political Constituting."

29. Sarah Seltzer, "Elizabeth Warren Puts the Kibosh on GOP's 'Class Warfare': Nobody in this Country Got Rich on His Own."

30. The Occupy [Wall Street] movement that has settled into public spaces in major North American cities—as also its international parallels of 2011 (e.g., Tarir Square)—constructively works at just such an ethos of creating social

flesh as I've set as the concern of this text: life is, beginning with and extending outward from birth, interdependent, which also means that life is shareable. Stepping out of cynicism and its sequestration, Occupiers, many of the generation just arriving at the threshold of a world of work made exceedingly precarious (and joined by any number of already homeless persons), demand a livable life, a livable future, demand to be released from being treated as disposable. By being for one another (often at the basic level of eating, sleeping, learning, and medical care), by rebuilding the muscles of mutual accountability, by practicing grassroots democracy, Occupiers regenerate social flesh. They tend the precarious, if productive, interval of relation. In that, Occupiers performatively exemplify how we each might learn to take responsibility for place (so seriously negated by modern humanism and our current economic structure), grow human resilience, and beget, as urbanism often demands of us, forms of attachment beyond kin and kind.

31. Judith Butler, "New Thoughts on Solidarity."

32. In addition, Butler explains: "Precarity designates that politically induced condition in which certain populations suffer from failing social and economic networks of support and become exposed to injury, violence and death. Such populations are at heightened risk of disease, poverty, starvation, displacement, and of exposure to violence without protection" ("Performativity, Precarity and Sexual Politics," ii). Neoliberal economics leverages and metes out degrees of precariousness attendant to life, especially access to basic needs, thus producing social insecurity and anxiety (Butler, "New Thoughts on Solidarity"). In fact, "precarization has become a governmental instrument of normalization" (Lorey, "Becoming Common"). Precarization "functions to make life contingent on capital and its constant movements and shifting demands." Manual labor, for example, has been left, to a significant degree, to a migrant workforce, often without citizen rights, and work, more broadly, has become insecure—the condition of freelancers and casual, seasonal workers. Such workers remain anxiously, constantly, "on stand-by," subordinate—because of their need for money to access the economy—to another's time frame. While "neoliberals," including urbanist Richard Florida, "tend to celebrate a certain type of freelance, educated precarian as the 'creative class' of the 'New Economy' . . . in practice, neoliberalism benefits from the denial of social rights to precarious workers." Equally, it benefits from the migrant flows of skills and trades on the tendrils of globalization, keeping noncitizen workers anxious, fearful, and politically quiescent (Andrew Robinson, "Precaritans of All Countries, Unite!"). *Precarity,* in other words, names the fragmentation of social flesh in such a way as to assume for itself financial and material surplus while off-loading existential risk, most specifically, the insecurity of access to basic needs, the volatility of financial markets, and environmental risk.

33. Judith Butler, *Frames of War: When Is Life Grievable?* 23.

34. With her analytic intervention, Butler segues from ontological to ethicopolitical precarity, insinuating the need for persistent ethical reflection on ontology, but also already thereby emphasizing "the uneven distribution of this basic human fragility," as Brett Neilson and Ned Rossiter put it in "From Precarity to Precariousness and Back Again: Labour, Life and Unstable Networks." Butler, with reference to Achille Mbembe, explains that precarity "is at once a material and a perceptual issue, since those whose lives are not 'regarded' as potentially grievable, and hence valuable, are made to bear the burden of starvation, underemployment, legal disenfranchisement, and differential exposure to violence and death" (*Frames of War*, 25).

35. A culture's fear of pain, its lack of wisdom for how to navigate pain, becomes—projected here as a dominant representation—a marginalization of persons placed outside of the reach of justice. Such "unreformed bodies" pose in their own way a "security threat," the threat of "mutual influence"—not just that the abject other might need me, but that I might be "touched" by this abject other, that pain should touch me. Contact aggravates the riptide of abjection and awakens consciousness to "a disavowed vulnerability," vulnerability to pain and to proximal ethical reflection, to ethical responsibility (Margrit Shildrick, "Unreformed Bodies: Normative Anxiety and the Denial of Pleasure," 328–29). Razing such a dominant representation implies differently negotiating the feeling-ful sentient web that culture has rejected when sealing off pain. The anesthetization of pain does not relate simply then to certain bodies, but has become an inadmissible moral knowledge culture wide: "Cognition depends upon our biochemical lives"—our feeling states, that is—"capturing the interactions with the environment to stay linked to practical agency and reality. . . . By making present our connectedness with the world and our fellow beings, feeling states help us find our way" (Linda Holler, *Erotic Morality: The Role of Touch in Moral Agency*, 78). To mind the earth, given the effects of global climate change, as to mind the neighbor, given the swell of urbanization, requires learning again to think through pain as an aspect of our moral and political agency. Retraining ourselves so as to traverse aversion, anxiety, and fear with ethical presence of mind will best be remediated, advises philosopher Franz Rosenzweig, through ritual, if also including art. See Robert Gibbs, "Unjustifiable Suffering," 30–31.

36. Tertullian, *On the Resurrection of the Flesh*, 9. Cited in Virginia Burrus, *Saving Shame*, 56–57.

37. Burrus, *Saving Shame*, 52.

38. Gianni Vattimo, "Pain and Metaphysics," 72.

39. Charles Edgley, "Health Nazis and the Cult of the Perfect Body: Some Polemical Observations," 257–79.

40. Kathleen M. Sands, *Escape from Paradise: Evil and Tragedy in Feminist Theology*, 10.

41. On refusing the ideological absolutism of rationalism, see William E. Connolly, *Why I Am Not a Secularist.*

42. William E. Connolly, *World of Becoming,* 5.

43. William James, *A Pluralistic Universe,* 162. Quoted in Finlayson, ed., *Democracy and Pluralism: The Political Thought of William E. Connolly,* 16; 231.

44. In that vein, I wish to complicate the argument of Philip Goldberg's *American Veda: From Emerson and the Beatles to Yoga and Meditation: How Indian Spirituality Changed the West*—its cosmopolitan genus of the "spiritual, but not religious" as well as "Cascadian spirituality" more specifically. Goldberg points out that interreligious conversation with Vedic thought has been shaping North American thought and practice since the nineteenth century, occasioning certain undeniable and appreciable accents—the patterns of humans stepping outside of religious institutions, of seeking direct or unmediated experience, of pragmatic and empirical emphases brought to bear on the practice of religion.

45. Analytically speaking, nature does not have a sovereign power; ecospiritualities will need to deal with that as Christianity has needed to deal with the "death of God." But see for recent developments on this point Sallie McFague, "Where We Live: Urban Ecotheology," 121–42.

46. So, for example, Vancouver's proud bearing of its first-place ranking on the "livability" index ignores the colonial haunting and racial crosscurrents of this place. This "City of Glass"—and Vancouver does resemble in its urban architectural profile a resplendent crystal cathedral, shimmering off the waters and mirroring the mountains—forgets the subtle racial innuendos laced through arguments set in motion when the Wall Centre, completed in 2001, was being outfitted to its heights with dark glass glazing. "Public interest" was to be served rather when the glass tower stood forth as "a shining pinnacle of light," as "clear and light and transparent." See Frances Bula, "Up Against the Wall," 15–17. During the early to mid-twentieth century, racial tensions did periodically erupt in Vancouver: a shipload of East Indians, all British subjects, aboard the Komagata Maru tried to immigrate in 1914 and were turned away; a Chinese encampment in Coal Harbour was burned in 1887 and Chinatown was mobbed in 1907; Japanese Canadians were put in internment camps in 1942. Given that history, how shall one read the arguments surrounding the glass curtaining of the Wall Centre?

Similarly, amidst the intense migration from Hong Kong (as China reasserted sovereignty over its city-state of Hong Kong), Vancouver chose in 1992 to design its library in the shape of the Roman Coliseum. Recalling that the ancient Roman arena was, as historian Alison Futrell puts it, a harsh public space that replicated "the brutality of empire in a controlled environment" (*Blood in the Arena: The Spectacle of Roman Power,* 4), what should one make of this? The simulation, suggests Clint Burnham in "Late Empire," "tapped into Vancouver's shallow Eurocentrism" and might be seen as "representative of both the triumph of global capital and the last exercise of power held by white Vancouver." In a Pacific Rim city, "with its own history of aboriginal settlement and Asian demographics, . . . the Colosseum returns," concludes Burnham, "like Freud's repressed, to impose on Vancouver's centre of learning the very 'grisly and ironic reversal' of its civilized intent" ("Late Empire," 36, 37). Cities, as these examples suggest, shape disgust into symbol, build it into an architectural statement, and so route human sociality through its bowels.

47. That said, Vedic thought—like Christian theology—has until recently also been stricken by a kind of practical, if not philosophical, dualism aimed at transcending the body. With the introduction of tantric philosophy, as in anusara yoga, a more flesh-respecting form of thought and practice has been developing. See Karen Gram, "Philosophy: The Evolution of Movement: Yoga is Deeply Engrained in the West Coast Lifestyle." A reminder to any number of us smitten—in a kind of Orientalist mood—with Eastern philosophies: Hinduism, too, has been charged with patriarchalism, caste hierarchy, abuse within its teaching tradition, and so on, such that it, too, is involved in reconstructive thought, for example, "Open Source Hinduism."

48. Jean-Luc Nancy, *Dis/Enclosure: The Deconstruction of Christianity*.

49. John B. Cobb, Jr., *Spiritual Bankruptcy: A Prophetic Call to Action*, 176.

50. John McClure, *Partial Faiths: Postsecular Fiction in the Age of Pynchon and Morrison*.

51. Henri-Jacques Stiker, *A History of Disability*, 15.

52. Rosemarie Garland-Thomson, *Freakery: Cultural Spectacles of the Extraordinary Body*, 12.

53. Jay Black, "Hiding the Homeless: A History of Olympic Street-Sweep Laws."

54. Rob Kitchin, "'Out of Place,' 'Knowing One's Place': Space, Power and the Exclusion of Disabled People," 343.

55. David Batstone, Edourdo Mendietta, Lynne Lorentzen, and Dwight D. Hopkins, eds., *Liberation Theologies, Postmodernity and the Americas*, 6.

56. John Panteleimon Manoussakis, *God after Metaphysics: A Theological Aesthetic*, 2.

57. Tobin Siebers, "Aesthetics and the Disqualification of Disability," page 2 of presentation.

58. Jane Jacobs, *The Death and Life of Great American Cities*, 50.

59. One catches what I mean by the inimical nature of "disability theology" in Scott DeShong's essay "The Nightmare of Health: Metaphysics and Ethics in the Signification of Disability," where he challenges the metaphysics of health, goodness, and wholeness as itself hallucinatory or a projection that symbolically overscripts by totalizing and that ignores irredeemable

tearing, wounding, fragmented becoming. Then he comments that "my references to the divine are subject to . . . definitional reversal," such that "saying 'God is good' may be read as saying that goodness is what 'God' means" (282–83 n. 19).

60. Petra Kuppers, "Toward a Rhizomatic Model of Disability: Poetry, Performance and Touch," 228, 233; 228, 233.

61. The phrase *death of God theologies* names the release of the supernatural, omnicompetent God above the world—the *deus ex machina* God. These theologies, privileging the sacred in the midst of the world, without ineffable reserve, also revisit the question of pain and suffering as "within" the sacred. Such theologies are not necessarily equivalent to secular rational dismissal of religion, although the discourses may share a sense that Christianity, as it has been known in the West, "no longer functions" and a desire to value the only world we know. See also Mary-Jane Rubenstein, *Strange Wonder: The Closure of Metaphysics and the Opening of Awe*, 222 n. 101.

62. Nancy Eiesland, *The Disabled God*, 89; 102, 89. This image has proven to be one of the most profound gifts Eiesland has offered the Christian community, hitting up against a theology that thought itself as already endorsing incarnation and therefore embodiment at a deeply primal level.

63. Rebecca Chopp, "Introduction," in Eiesland, *Disabled God*, 11.

64. Dietrich Bonhoeffer, *Letters and Papers from Prison*, 134.

65. "Weak theology"—theology loosely said to be developing in the wake of the 1960s "death of God" theologies and as proposed, for example, by John D. Caputo, Jean-Luc Nancy, and Gianni Vattimo—admits the deconstruction of the metaphysics of presence, the loss of foundations, and the loosening of truth claims and hence assumes an immanentalist, historicist, and more tenderly humbled frame. See for example Vattimo, *After Christianity*; Caputo, *The Weakness of God: A Theology of the Event*; and Nancy, *Dis-Enclosure*. The notion of "weak" tends to bother feminists as well as disability theologians and might more constructively be mitigated by the turn toward theologies of flesh. See Sharon V. Betcher, "Becoming Flesh of My Flesh."

66. Indra Sinha, as summarized by Rob Nixon, *Slow Violence and the Environmentalism of the Poor*, 56.

67. Gil Anidjar, "Secularism," 52–77, argues that "secularism is . . . Christian imperialism" (66) and that it might be said to be, citing the words of Edward Said, a "'naturalized, modernized, and laicized substitute for (or version of) *Christian supernaturalism*'" (68).

68. Connolly, a political theorist, subtly insinuates that Christianity, especially in some of its earlier monastic forms, developed valuable wisdom, or "arts of the self," that might appropriately and effectively be deployed in redeveloping the democratic public: "Ecclesiastical practices of ritual are translated by

Nietzsche and Foucault into experimental arts of the self and by Deleuze into an experimental micropolitics of intersubjectivity. Each tries to shift ethical practices that impinge on the visceral register from their uses, say, in the Augustinian confessional . . . but each also strives to make investments in this domain that exceed the scope of secular self-representations. Such strategies . . . are important to thinking and theory because such work on oneself can sometimes untie knots in one's thinking; they are important to politics because such work can pave the way for new movement in the politics of becoming; and they are pertinent to the ethos of a pluralist culture because such work can help to install generosity and forbearance into ethical sensibilities in a world of multidimensional plurality. To change an intersubjective ethos significantly is to modify the instinctive subjectivities and intersubjectivities in which it is set" *(Why I Am Not a Secularist*, 28). In a later work, he insinuates his political borrowing of the ecclesiastical arts of the self as an invitation: "You might even become attracted to *experimental tactics to deepen visceral attachment to the complexity of human existence itself during a time when the automatic sense of belonging to this world is often stretched and disrupted*" (Connolly, *World of Becoming*, 57; emphasis added). Along with Connolly, I would hope that cosmopolitans broadly, Christians, theists or not, as well as persons thinking of themselves as "spiritual, but not religious," might recuperate the "experimental arts of the self"—the ancient ascetic disciplines as well as the practice/able aspects of ritual—as a wisdom to be lent to this new cosmopolitan, if increasingly planetary, ethos.

   North American Christianity's "new monasticism" makes sense in this regard. Consider the popularity of Kathleen Norris's works, for example, *The Cloister Walk* and *Acedia and Me: A Marriage, Monks, and a Writer's Life*. Also see John McClure's focus on this in literature, in, for example, *Partial Faiths*, and Jason Byassee, "The New Monastics," 38–47. The relational arts of the self "involve the selective desanctification of elements in one's identity, e.g., vengefulness, anxiety, stinginess" (Connolly, *Why I Am Not a Secularist*, 146) and the generation of humility, gentleness, equanimity, commensality. As Connolly has argued, "The cultivation of an ethical sensibility" is "as important to a generous public ethos as commitment to the practice of justice" (ibid., 11, 9). I follow Connolly's lead by redeveloping such practices—in interreligious dialog—in order consequently to cultivate world attachment, to cull out "reactive attachment disorder," to grow "soul-fulness" without transcendence as we bleed out idealism.

   69. That this disaffected rationalism, still so much the mood of scientific laboratories, has its genesis within the spiritual meditations of Descartes explains their shared disposition, but this shared origin might well shock the secular world, which assumes to have left religion behind.

   70. Dorothee Soelle, *The Silent Cry: Mysticism and Resistance*, 18.

71. Process theology, developed from the philosophical framework of Alfred North Whitehead during the twentieth century, proves something of an exception. Whitehead presumes that all sentient beings are feeling beings who live by prehending our interdependent relations. (Thus Whitehead levels the unique presumption to consciousness among humans.) Further, process theology presumes aesthetics as an everyday creative modality of integrating our prehensions. Consequently, in process theology, God is spoken of as the Heart of the Universe or as Empathy at the heart of the Universe. Even God affectively, empathically, feels God's way with and so creatively weaves the compossibility of a world. Theism in the process perspective has more to do with what motivates us to love, to have passion for life, to live with entrustment or attachment to the universe. By contrast, most theist/atheist arguments have taken place, I would dare to say, within rationalist philosophical terms.

72. Manoussakis, in *God after Metaphysics*, connects this affective, aesthetic disposition of theology to a thoroughly incarnational approach. "What is at stake" in thinking God after metaphysics "is an effort to disengage God from His [sic] metaphysical commitment to the sphere of transcendence by learning to recognize the ways [God] touches our immanence—an Incarnational approach through and through" (5).

73. Nixon, *Slow Violence*, 57.

74. Luce Irigaray, *I Love to You: Sketch of a Possible Felicity in History*.

75. Petra Kuppers, "Journey to the Holocaust Museum in Berlin, 2011."

76. Darren O'Donnell, *Social Acupuncture: A Guide to Suicide, Performance and Utopia*, 38–39.

77. Michel de Certeau famously developed the practice of walking the city as a way to enter into the psychogeographies of intimacy—and as distinct from the macro view of urbanism. See his "Walking in the City," chapter 7 of *The Practice of Everyday Life*, excerpted in Bridge and Watson, eds., *The Blackwell City Reader*, 383–92. Such a practice has an intimate relationship with religious walking meditations—for example, that of Thich Nhat Hanh. Or see Kosuke Koyama, *Three Mile an Hour God*. Crip/tography leans upon these insight practices while attempting more explicitly and disruptively to connect affectively with other cosmopolitans and urban politics.

78. Siebers, *Disability Aesthetics*, 24.

79. Sharon L. Snyder and David T. Mitchell, *Narrative Prosthesis: Disability and the Dependence of Discourse*, 24.

80. Siebers, "Aesthetics and the Disqualification of Disability," 12.

81. Jean-Luc Nancy, *The Creation of the World, or Globalization*, 23.

82. Paul Delany, "'Hardly the Center of the World': Vancouver in William Gibson's 'The Winter Market,'" 186.

83. McClure, *Partial Faiths*, 20.

84. McClure, *Partial Faiths*, 53–62.

1. CRIP/TOGRAPHY

1. Global cities are to be distinguished from *arrival cities* (Saunders) and *undercities* (Boo). The term *global city* or *world city* refers to that urban formation which has tended, by virtue of sociological and especially economic processes, to supersede any sense of territorial locale. Such cities tend to be referenced then on a "first name" basis, e.g., London, New York, Mumbai. While most global cities sport a population exceeding 20 million, other dynamics also occasion identification as a global city. These dynamics may include extremely high immigration and therefore the generation of intense multiethnic basins—as is true for Vancouver. Global cities tend, economically speaking, to be "postindustrial" and sell themselves moreover as a "cultural" experience; indeed, culture becomes their business. Because of this relation between economics and culture shaping global cities, occasioning something of a landing pad for the economic elite, not all cities with populations exceeding 20 million are grouped into the category of world or global cities. Most world cities have large research universities, but the research is notably focused toward fields such as biotechnology, physics, etc., not the humanities. Further, even as the elite of such cities prove extremely mobile (moving among the global cities themselves), no global city lives without a migrant underclass; even in or especially in the wealthiest of communities within these cities, the nurturant activities, from those of nannies to nurses to cleaning services, will be maintained by a migrant populus.

2. Raymond J. Bakke, "Urbanization and Evangelism: A Global View," 225.

3. Gayatri Chakravorty Spivak, "Globalicities: Terror and Its Consequences," 74.

4. Mark Kingwell, *Concrete Reveries: Consciousness and the City*, 11.

5. Spivak, "Globalicities," 77.

6. Spivak, "Righting Wrongs," 545.

7. Spivak, "Globalicities," 77.

8. Michel Foucault, "Faire vivre et laisser mourir: La naissance du racisme," 60. Also cited by Rey Chow, *The Protestant Ethnic and the Spirit of Capitalism*, 11.

9. My argument here is parallel to that made by such theorists as Laura Levitt, who assert that "liberalism and colonialism are in fact two sides of the same coin." See her "Letting Go of Liberalism," 162.

10. Warren Magnusson and Karena Shaw, eds., *A Political Space: Reading the Global through Clayoquot Sound*, 2. True to most axial religions, Christian theology has assumed the categories of time—hence, eschatology and kairos—as the realm of freedom. But, warns Jane M. Jacobs: "[H]istory that speaks only of time on the deactivated 'stage' of space (space as an 'empty interval, a natural given') is imperial history." Christian theologies turning towards postcolonial

conscientization will want to cultivate Jacobs's insight that "to activate space, to produce a spatial history, is fundamental to [the] project of taking history beyond imperialism" (*Edge of Empire: Postcolonialism and the City*, 22). Such, for example, is the work carried out by Susan Stanford Friedman under the rubric of a "locational approach to feminism" in *Mappings: Feminism and the Cultural Geographies of Encounter*, 3–4.

11. Don Mitchell, "The Annihilation of Space by Law: Anti-Homeless Laws and the Shrinking Landscape of Rights."

12. Sharon Zukin, *The Culture of Cities*, 38–39.

13. Michael Hardt and Antonio Negri, *Empire*, xii, 142–46.

14. Robert Young, *Colonial Desire: Hybridity in Theory, Culture and Race*, 180.

15. Don Mitchell, "The Illusion and Necessity of Order: Toward a Just City," 227.

16. David D. Yuan, "Disfigurement and Reconstruction in Oliver Wendell Holmes's 'The Human Wheel, Its Spokes and Felloes.'"

17. Brendan Gleeson, "A Place on Earth: Technology, Space and Disability," 96, 90–91.

18. Rob Imrie, *Disability and the City: International Perspectives*, as cited by Rob Kitchin, "'Out of Place,' 'Knowing One's Place': Space, Power and the Exclusion of Disabled People," 346.

19. Harlan Hahn, "Advertising the Acceptably Employable Image," 178–79.

20. Mitchell, "The Annihilation of Space by Law," 163–64, 190.

21. Zukin, *Culture of Cities*, 2.

22. "The public geography of a city is civility institutionalized." Richard Sennett, *Fall of Public Man*, 264.

23. See Wendy Brown's parallel analysis of tolerance, *Regulating Aversion: Tolerance in the Age of Identity and Empire*.

24. Jacobs, *Edge of Empire*, 4.

25. Leonie Sandercock, *Cosmopolis II: Mongrel Cities in the Twenty-First Century*, 1.

26. David M. Halperin, *Saint Foucault: Towards a Gay Hagiography*, 62, 66; 54.

27. As David Harvey's integration of "body talk" with "globalization talk" suggests, postcolonial practice must address the construction and choreography of bodies in order "to redefine in a more subtle way the terms and spaces of political struggle open to us in these extraordinary times" (*Spaces of Hope*, 15, 18). Jacobs concurs: "The geographical articulations of imperialism are not simply laid out across the landscape," but "exist in the 'opaque' intersections between representational practices, the built form and a range of other axes of power which . . . includes the uneven geography of capital investment, legal and judicial regulatory regimes as well as the various territorialisations and

deterritorialisations of space which occur through protest, violence, ironic art-istry, or simple dwelling in place" (*Edge of Empire*, 10).

28. See Seth Mydans, "What Makes a Monk Mad: Karma Power." Mydans explains that in Myanmar, which has as many monks as soldiers, "the military rules by force, but the monks retain ultimate moral authority. The lowliest soldier depends on them for spiritual approval" (1), not incidentally because "these young monks remain closer to the lives and concerns of the people whose alms they receive" (14). When the monks inverted their begging bowls as they led antigovernment protests, thus refusing daily donations, they also deprived the soldiers of moral authority and karmic well-being; they rejected the military junta . . . and that rejection brought with it terror and crucifixion.

29. Donna Haraway, "Ecce Homo, Ain't (Ar'n't) I a Woman, and Inappropriate/d Others: The Human in a Post-Humanist Landscape," 87; 87, 91. Haraway borrows the term "inappropriate/d others" from Trinh T. Minh-ha, "She, the Inappropriate/d Other."

30. Yvonne Sherwood, "Passion-Binding-Passion," 183; 188. Sherwood's conclusion evolves from her reading of the *Akedah*, the story of the binding of Isaac (Genesis 22), as but "simply the most famous of a series of tableaux" (178). Reading this as a series of tableaux, beginning with the night wrestler left "crip" hero, Jacob, and the "limping nation" bearing his name, allows also for the possibility that the cripped iconography at the heart of Christianity might interpolate us into a different location on the streets of today's mongrel cities. On "limping nation," see Holmes Rolston III, "Does Nature Need to Be Redeemed?" 220.

31. Adolf von Harnack, *The Mission and Expansion of Christianity in the First Three Centuries*, 1:109.

32. Gayatri Chakravorty Spivak, *Human Rights, Human Wrongs: The Oxford Amnesty Lectures 2001*, 169.

33. Spivak, *Human Rights*, 169.

34. Zygmunt Bauman, *Liquid Modernity*, 95.

35. Sennett, *Fall of Public Man*, 264.

36. James Perkinson, "Theology and the City: Learning to Cry, Struggling to See," 95–114.

37. Janet Jakobsen, "Can Homosexuals End Western Civilization as We Know It? Family Values in a Global Economy," 59.

38. Kelly Oliver, *Witnessing: Beyond Recognition*, 15.

39. Marcella Althaus-Reid, *Indecent Theology: Theological Perversions in Sex, Gender, and Politics*, 1, 9.

40. Where civility offloads responsibility, civility cedes its interests to im-perialism, avoids the encounter with strangeness, refuses to engage and there-fore to live with difference by putting difference—as in Guiliani's "Project

Civil City"—in geographic set aside. "Production-consumption values inevitably place a central priority upon utility, upon reward for people who can perform useful tasks," explains biblical scholar Walter Brueggemann. And, I would add, at this point in the globalization of consumer capitalism, it places priority upon appearance. "Such values," Brueggemann continues, "tend to discard people without utility. And Jesus, the center of land-history, announced and embodied the conviction that in the new land (the kingdom) the issue of utility as a means of entry was not pertinent (cf. Luke 14:12–14, 21–24)." Walter Brueggemann as cited by Andrew Davey, *Urban Christianity and Global Order: Theological Resources for an Urban Future*, 73.

41. Kathryn Tanner, *Theories of Culture: A New Agenda for Theology*, 113. Tanner argues against thinking Christianity as a culture onto itself. Rather, Christian practice, she asserts, has to do with ways of making meaning of the cultural artifacts we find around us.

42. Steve Pile, "Introduction: Opposition, Political Identities, and Spaces of Resistance," 2–3.

43. Bauman, *Liquid Modernity*. Philosopher Martha Nussbaum puts this wisdom about humanity's shared incompleteness, its vulnerability, at the heart of the social contract, as a needed correction to "the psychological foundations of liberalism." See her *Hiding from Humanity*, 16.

44. Douglas John Hall, *The Cross in Our Context: Jesus and the Suffering World*, 175.

45. James Perkinson explains that "In the first centuries of the church's life . . . , to become a believer . . . meant to enlist. In the Roman imperial order, a *sacramentum* was an oath of loyalty taken by a soldier to Caesar. For Christians living under the imperial regime, celebrating 'sacraments' like the eucharist was a practice of political resistance in a struggle that engaged war-making as its nonviolent, but combative opposite" ("Theology and the City," 98).

46. Fustel de Coulanges, *The Ancient City: A Study on the Religion, Laws and Institutions of Greece and Rome*, 193, 205.

47. Davey, *Urban Christianity and Global Order*, 72.

48. Sennett, *Fall of Public Man*, 326.

49. Sennett, *Fall of Public Man*, 333–36.

50. Despite the emphatic teachings of the fathers, Christian theology has lived quite comfortably within Roman sensibilities of ownership of property, of the commons, since the fourth century: "The Roman law theory-and-practice of ownership, which the fathers attacked and sought to replace, has retained the ascendancy all through the Christian centuries that have elapsed since their thundering critical voices fell silent." Charles Avila, *Ownership: Early Christian Teaching*, 11.

51. Mitchell, "Annihilation of Space by Law," 166–67.

52. Spivak's notion of "collectivity" ironically mimics the ways in which liberalism marks off "primitive" or "less developed" cultures. Her intent seems to be that liberal education needs to assume a cultural axiomatic of being responsible to the other, to assume "that it is natural to be angled toward the other" ("Righting Wrongs," 537).

53. Ward, *Cities of God*, 118; referencing John D. Zizoulas, *Being in Communion: Studies in Personhood and the Church*.

54. See also Graham Ward, "Bodies: The Displaced Body of Jesus" and "Suffering and Incarnation."

55. Marcella Althaus-Reid, "'A Saint and a Church for Twenty Dollars': Sending Radical Orthodoxy to Ayacucho," 110.

56. Ward, "Bodies," 169.

57. Wendy Brown, *States of Injury: Power and Freedom in Late Modernity*, 61. To put it another way, whereas one might hear in Peter Brown's narration of early Christianity's move to identify with the poor, to posit its inheritance among the poor, something on the order of being called by the other, Ward's theology, by contrast, remains a way to avoid being challenged by the subaltern. His methodology turns on the concept of "an analogical relationship" between the City of God and human cities, "re-inscribing the urban symbolic production and exchange . . . within a Christian theology of signification"—a relationship that "establishes true difference with respect to various similarities" (Ward, *Cities of God*, 233). But Ward thus avoids subjecting the self to "a fractured relation to subjectivity"; instead, he seeks to "yoke the emotions to belief, which then is led to/by reason," as Spivak characterizes the project of modernity ("Righting Wrongs," 567 n. 16). Although fashioned as an anti-metaphysics (and Ward, as a good poststructuralist, recognizes changing cultural *epistemes*), his method is a way to reassemble a version of absolute transcendence—albeit more tenuously called "analogical." While Ward recognizes "how the body . . . disseminates itself through a myriad of other bodies" and how "ghettoisations and the segregations" of structural violence "injure me" (*Cities of God*, 92), the analogical worldview takes into account neither the call of the other, nor, when it comes to the practice of responsibility, the willingness to let the subaltern teach us. "In opening myself to be 'othered' by the subaltern," Spivak explains, "it is this broader more mysterious arena of the subject that the self hopes to enter." Without a working engagement with subalterns, "without this effortful task of 'doing' in the mode of 'to come' . . . 'thinking' [remains] in the mode of 'my way is the best,'" as Spivak notes ("Righting Wrongs," 568 n. 16).

58. De Coulanges, *Ancient City*, 193, 205. Ward cited this passage from de Coulanges in a public lecture on theology and global cities at Vancouver School of Theology, Vancouver, B.C., on September 26, 2007.

59. To be sure, Ward does not hand us yet again the modern Jesus—the Healer and Savior of the degenerate—or a figural map for the politics of rescue. If we read cripped bodies from within Ward's proposal, Ward would insist, I think, on a soulful, supplemental value not encoded by culture—something like Richard Kearney's *prosopon*, a relational sense of the irreducible alterity of the other, which does prevent the wholesale devaluation of bodies. Richard Kearney, *The God Who May Be: A Hermeneutics of Religion*, 18–19. And yet, eucharistic participation—as evidenced perhaps by the ways in which even liturgical ritual can foreclose upon disabled bodies—may not reach across today's worldwide apartheid. Disability, I am assuming, might be indicative of that apartheid's dividing of the subaltern—"those removed from lines of social mobility" (Spivak, "Righting Wrongs," 531)—from the cultured. Disability may then be indicative of "outlier groups," since this difference—as distinct from race and gender—can never aspire to the subjective idealization at the heart of liberal humanism, nor to the "translocationality" of the body in today's globalizing capitalism. See Ward, "Bodies," 168.

60. Anita Silvers and Leslie Pickering Francis, "Justice through Trust: Disability and the 'Outlier Problem' in Social Contract Theory," 42.

61. Silvers and Francis, "Justice through Trust," 41, 62.

62. Spivak gives an intriguing illustration of a noncontractural "nationality" based in responsibility in her essay "Globalicities" (78–80). This leads to her concept of "a 'para-individual structural responsibility'" (79).

63. What happens to humanity's capacity for trust as humans shift that trust toward modern institutions that require trust in abstract systems is at the heart of Anthony Giddens, *The Consequences of Modernity*.

64. Ward, "Bodies," 168.

65. An analogy may help: When I started practicing Pilates, my instructors would name a muscle that I was then to try to locate and mobilize. Being well trained in Augustinian prayer practice, I would shut my eyes to locate what I construed as inward or "internal." The zen slap, palm on palm, of my instructor would not too patiently remind me that muscles are exercised in relation to a lived world, that closing my eyes shut off 90 percent of my relational interface with the world. By referring us outside of social context, Ward's analogical method avoids encountering the necessity of discerning among immanental intelligibilities, of risking commitment to the possible good—not some idealized good. Kathleen Sands, *Escape from Paradise: Evil and Tragedy in Feminist Theology*, 63. Conversely, invoking Spirit—that intriguing biblical concept accompanying bodies colonized and cripped, that theological concept scaled to negotiate the political and not so much the universal—might itself avoid the dualism of transcendence/immanence into which Ward's methodology might otherwise return us. As Paul Newman explains, "Prophecy"—connected with

Spirit and in contrast to Wisdom—"is not a discernment of perennial and universal truths about the human condition; rather prophecy is a passionate, concerned insight or action in *particular* crises and situations that call for judgment or action in light of the promises of God" (*Spirit Christology*, 118).

66. Martin O'Kane, "Picturing 'The Man of Sorrows': The Passion-Filled Afterlives of a Biblical Icon," 64.

67. New English Bible, Isaiah 53:2. A. S. Herbert, *The Book of the Prophet Isaiah: Chapters 40–66*, 106–07; Isaiah 53:3 in Joseph Blenkinsopp, *The Anchor Bible, Isaiah 40–55*, vol. 19a, 34–35. In the NRSV, Isaiah 53:2–3 reads: "He had no form or majesty that we should look at him, nothing in his appearance that we should desire him. He was despised and rejected by others; a man of suffering and acquainted with infirmity; and as one from whom others hide their faces he was despised, and we held him of no account."

68. David J. A. Clines, *I, He, We, and They: A Literary Approach to Isaiah 53*, 17.

69. Isaiah 54, "The Song of Lady Sorrow," has been overlooked precisely because of the overcoding of Jesus with Isaiah 53.

70. Clines, *I, He, We, and They*, 61.

71. O'Kane, "Picturing 'The Man of Sorrows,'" 67.

72. O'Kane, "Picturing 'The Man of Sorrows,'" 89.

73. As happens in a teaching environment, one's thoughts may be picked up, worked over, and submitted back—now having the quality of a pearl as distinct from one's initial mutterings. I'm grateful to my student Jessica Schaap for rethinking with me a Christology opened off the Suffering Servant songs. Jessica Schaap, "Notes towards a Eucharistic Prayer," paper given at Vancouver School of Theology, Vancouver, B.C., April 18, 2007.

74. Barbara Ehrenreich, in public speech related to the publication of *Nickel and Dimed: On (Not) Getting By in America* (2001). Quoted in Michael Funke, "Ehrenreich Urges Economic Justice Movement."

75. Warren Carter, "Proclaiming (in/against) Empire Then and Now," 154.

76. Neil Elliott, "The Anti-Imperial Message of the Cross," 167–83.

77. Rowan Williams, *Resurrection: Interpreting the Easter Gospel*, 21.

78. The subheading above is modeled on a passage from the novel: "Every relationship worth keeping sustains, at the very least, splintered glazes, hairline fractures, cracks. And aren't these flaws the prerequisites of intimacy?" (Kallos, *Broken for You*, 295).

79. Gilles Barbedette, "The Social Triumph of the Sexual Will: A Conversation with Michel Foucault," 38. Also cited in Halperin, *Saint Foucault*, 82.

80. Adoption is not unusual within spirit traditions, including Judaism and Christianity; in fact, across many cultures, "spiritual kinship" has been honored as stronger than blood, more enduring than biological filiation. Jesus' question in response to the news that his mother and brothers were looking for him—"Who is my mother? Who are my brothers?" (Matthew 12:48ff.)—

would appear to evolve from such a presumption. Even the Annunciation story in Luke, in which God's "holy" name will be given to the illegitimate "son of Mary," could be read as an adoption story—not unlike Paul's sensibilities about the adoption of the humiliated into an alternative "history" to that of Rome (Romans 8).

81. Decolonizing theorist Ashis Nandy has identified the psychopathologies of the West as "the ideologies of progress [cloaking "the ancient forces of greed and violence"], normality and hyper-masculinity." See his *The Intimate Enemy: Loss and Recovery of Self under Colonialism*, 30, x.

82. Avner Offer, *The Challenge of Affluence: Self-Control and Well-Being in the United States and Britain since 1950*, 347.

83. Harvey, *Spaces of Hope*, 16.

84. Scott DeShong, manuscript in possession of the author. See his "The Nightmare of Health: Metaphysics and Ethics in the Signification of Disability," 81.

85. Ward, "Suffering and Incarnation," 194.

86. Gilles Deleuze and Felix Guattari, *Anti-Oedipus: Capitalism and Schizophrenia*, 362.

87. Gordon Lynch, *After Religion? "Generation X" and the Search for Meaning*, 3, 120.

88. Spivak, *A Critique of Postcolonial Reason: Toward a History of the Vanishing Present*, 355 n. 59.

89. Mark Lewis Taylor, "Spirit and Liberation: Achieving Postcolonial Theology in the United States," in *Divinity and Empire: Postcolonial Theologies*, 40.

90. Mircea Eliade, *Cosmos and History: The Myth of the Eternal Return*, 141–62. Also cited in Tod D. Swanson, "To Prepare a Place: Johannine Christianity and the Collapse of Ethnic Territory," 242.

91. Paula Cooey, *Willing the Good: Jesus, Dissent, and Desire*, 144.

92. To speak of Spirit as "prosthesis"—as an assumed conviction in relation to the world—is a concept that developed in dialog with my student, Beatrice Marovich, within her directed readings in Theologies of Becoming, Vancouver School of Theology, July 2008. But also see Bernard Stiegler, "Derrida and Technology: Fidelity at the Limits of Deconstruction and the Prosthesis of Faith."

93. Sandercock, *Cosmopolis II*, 4.

2. "FEARFUL SYMMETRY": BETWEEN THEOLOGICAL AESTHETICS AND GLOBAL ECONOMICS

1. Saskia Sassen, "From *Globalization and Its Discontents*," 161–70.

2. "Vancouverism: Architecture Builds the City" was the title of an exhibit curated and produced by Trevor Boddy that ran from January 16 to March 27,

2010, held at Woodwards Atrium in downtown Vancouver. Also see Serena Kataoka, "Vancouverism: Actualizing the Livable City Paradox," 42–56.

3. Douglas Coupland, *City of Glass: Douglas Coupland's Vancouver* .

4. Sassen, "From *Globalization and Its Discontents*," 162.

5. Peter Stallybrass and Allon White, "The City: The Sewer, the Gaze and the Contaminating Touch," 133–34.

6. James Perkinson also makes this point in his "Theology and the City: Learning to Cry, Struggling to See."

7. Alan Hollinghurst's novel *Line of Beauty* (2005) mocks art as make-believe for the rich. See also Charles Bock's *Beautiful Children* (2008); Sarah Strohmeyer, *The Sleeping Beauty Proposal* (2008); Cecilia Samartin, *Tarnished Beauty* (2008); and Dinaw Mengestu, *The Beautiful Things that Heaven Bears* (2007). In literary theory, see Elaine Scarry, *On Beauty and Being Just* (1999) and Roger Scruton, *Beauty* (2009). Theologically, I have in mind the resurgence of research on Hans Urs von Balthazar, including David Hart's *The Beauty of the Infinite: The Aesthetics of Christian Truth* (2003); the appeal to aesthetics within the radical orthodoxy movement, e.g., *Theological Perspectives on God and Beauty* (2003); the resort to beauty within liberation theologies, e.g., Alejandro Garcia-Rivera's *The Community of the Beautiful: A Theological Aesthetics* (1999) as well as Ivone Gebara's "Yearning for Beauty"; the flirtation with beauty that rides covertly through theologies of eros, e.g., Virginia Burrus and Catherine Keller, eds., *Toward a Theology of Eros* (2006), and also the longer-standing development of theology as aesthetic practice and God as "tragic beauty" within Whiteheadian process philosophy and theology.

8. Tobin Siebers, "Kant and the Politics of Beauty," 43–45.

9. Siebers, "Kant and the Politics of Beauty," 42–43.

10. Fyodor Dostoevsky, *The Idiot*, 402. While Dostoevsky is commonly cited as the author of the concept that "beauty will save the world," in *On Beauty and Being Just* Elaine Scarry suggests a more expansive genealogy for this notion, tracing it back to Homer and Augustine (24).

11. Gary Bridge and Sophie Watson, "Introduction to Part II: Reading Urban Economics," 113–14.

12. Susan S. Fainstein, Lily M. Hoffman, and Dennis R. Judd, "Introduction," 5.

13. William Blake, "The Tyger":

Tyger Tyger, burning bright,
In the forests of the night;
What immortal hand or eye,
Could frame thy fearful symmetry?
. . . .

In what distant deeps or skies
Burnt the fire of thine eyes?
On what wings dare he aspire?
What the hand, dare seize the fire?

In *The Complete Poetry and Prose of William Blake*, 24.

14. Mike Davis, "From *City of Quartz: Excavating the Future in Los Angeles*," 323. Cited in text hereafter.

15. Zygmunt Bauman, *Liquid Fear*, 4.

16. Bauman, *Liquid Fear*, 111.

17. Cited in Ion Beseliu and Kees Doevendans, "Planning, Design and the Post-Modernity of Cities," 234.

18. Cited in Barbara Hooper, "The Poem of Male Desires: Female Bodies, Modernity, and 'Paris: Capital of the Nineteenth Century,'" 24. Thanks to my research assistant Clara King for bringing this to my attention.

19. Stallybrass and White, "The City," 139; 144–45.

20. Tim Cresswell, *Place: A Short Introduction*, 102–03.

21. Brendan Gleeson, "A Place on Earth: Technology, Space and Disability," 90, 94.

22. Rob Kitchin, "'Out of Place,' 'Knowing One's Place': Space, Power and the Exclusion of Disabled People," 349.

23. Mike Davis suggests the formation of a more insidious, if glamourous version of such a panoptican: the privileged may, he writes in his *City of Quartz*, enjoy such a panoptically protected fortress in the downtown core itself, where architectural and geographical densification occasion more elite on the streets at all hours, generating greater, if more subtle (because now citizen deployed or private security employed) surveillance of which bodies may acceptably inhabit the streets. In other words, the assemblage of bodies controls who may appear in public ("From *City of Quartz*," 323).

24. Paul Zanker, *The Power of Images in the Age of Augustus*, 115, 112.

25. Bridge and Watson, "Introduction to Part II," 109.

26. Sharon L. Snyder and David T. Mitchell, *Cultural Locations of Disability*, x.

27. "And What about Beauty? It's Biologic, Baby!" reads the subsection headline in the chapter "What's Up with the Arts?" in Michael Gazzaniga, *Human: The Science Behind What Makes Us Unique*, 226–27.

28. Snyder and Mitchell, *Cultural Locations of Disability*, x.

29. Richard Spencer, "Beijing Olympics: Faking Scandal over Girl who 'Sang' in Opening Ceremony," *The Telegraph*, August 12, 2008. Also see Richard Spencer, "Beijing Olympics: 'Ethnic' Children Revealed as Fakes in Opening Ceremony," *The Telegraph*, August 15, 2008.

30. Jim Byers, "Vancouver Makes No Promises for Its Show," *Toronto Star*, August 13, 2008, News, A21.

31. Richard M. Millard, "Whitehead's Aesthetic Perspective," 262.

32. Jane Jacobs, *The Death and Life of Great American Cities*, 50.

33. David Harvey, "The Urban Process under Capitalism: A Framework for Analysis," 113.

34. Sharon Zukin, "From *Landscapes of Power: From Detroit to Disney World*," 200.

35. Ecologically speaking, this representational economy results in a stylized and eventually ecologically unsustainable notion of beauty. Civil codes assume an aesthetics that makes actual urban agricultural production a "guerrilla activity" or even, in a *reductio ad absurdum*, outlaws "ugly food." ("'Straight' bananas must be 'free from malformation or abnormal curvature'" according to European Union regulations.) See Chris Turner, "Guerrilla Barley Growers Go Against the Grain," and Bruno Waterfield, "Ugly Food Tastes as Good as Pretty Food, So EU Ends Ban on the Bent and Knobbly." While regulations that control the sale of "misshapen" fruits and vegetables, occasioning "an estimated 20 percent of the British harvest [being] thrown away," will be revoked for twenty-six types of fruits and vegetables, they will remain in place for apples, strawberries, tomatoes, and bananas, among other things. Stylistically disposed order determines valorizations that have ramifications from socioeconomics to biology. See M. Christine Boyer, "From *Dreaming the Rational City*," 39.

36. Ivone Gebara, *Longing for Running Water: Ecofeminism and Liberation*, vii. Gebara can, on this point, be heard to echo womanist Audre Lorde's insistence that "poetry is not a luxury" as well as Simone Weil's sense that "workers need poetry more than bread" (180).

37. Siebers, "Kant and the Politics of Beauty," 44–45.

38. Charles Jencks, *The Language of Post-Modern Architecture*, 9. Also see Charles Jencks, ed., *The Post-Modern Reader*, 24.

39. Harlan Hahn, "Can Disability Be Beautiful?" 26. Hahn, who works between urban studies and disabilities studies, has raised the question of whether disability can be beautiful, noting the reluctance of disabilities studies to engage aesthetic categories despite the persistence of defining disability by visible bodily traits.

40. Scarry does not suggest that beauty instantaneously leads to justice; she registers herself as not concerned about the time lapse, given her assurance that "the equality of beauty enters the world before justice and stays longer," as well as her confidence "in its generously being present, widely present" (*On Beauty*, 108).

41. Snyder and Mitchell, *Cultural Locations of Disability*, 12.

42. Garcia-Rivera, *Community of the Beautiful*, 60.

43. Siebers, "Kant and the Politics of Beauty," 48, 35, 44.

44. Tobin Siebers, "Disability Aesthetics," 63–72. See especially his claim that "disability is integral to aesthetic conceptions of the beautiful and that the influence of disability on art has grown, not dwindled, over the course of time" (67).

45. Edgar Allan Poe, "Ligeia," 112. Also cited in Siebers, "Disability Aesthetics," 63, 65.

46. Siebers understands Kant's remark that "beauty is disinterested" in this way: "Kant . . . disallows individual *reasons* for embracing the work of art as beautiful: 'no interest, whether of sense or reason, extorts approval' of the object of taste. . . . The otherness of the art object . . . remains consistently in view, both refusing to be externalized and asking us to contemplate it as a necessary part of our world" ("Kant and the Politics of Beauty," 43–44).

47. Henri Lefebrve, *The Production of Space*, 190. Also cited in Kitchin, "Out of Place,'" 352.

48. Immanuel Kant, *Critique of Judgment*, 91–95. Cited in Stephen O'Connell, "Aesthetics: A Place I've Never Seen," 479.

49. Felix Guattari, *Chaosmosis: An Ethico-Aesthetic Paradigm*, 131.

50. O'Connell, "Aesthetics," 480.

51. John Inge, *A Christian Theology of Place: Explorations in Practical, Pastoral and Empirical Theology*, gives a philosophically complex analysis of the loss of the place axis in Western culture. See especially chapter 1, "Place in Western Thought and Practice." Both deep ecological and feminist thought, Susan Brooks Thistlethwaite confesses (her constructive work, like mine, having been worked through both veins of theory), have tended likewise to enforce this history and so to divert transcendence from "second nature," from the city. See Thistlethwaite, "Why Are Our Cities Dying?" 20.

52. Thistlethwaite, "Why Are Our Cities Dying?" 25.

53. Karl Jaspers, cited in Thistlethwaite, "Why Are Our Cities Dying?" 19 n. 2. "Axial Age" refers to the period 800–200 B.C.E., which saw the rise of Platonism (which was to greatly influence Christianity), Jainism, Buddhism, Confucianism, and Zorastianism. See also Schmuel N. Eisenstadt, "The Axial Age: The Emergence of Transcendental Visions and the Rise of Clerics," 294–314. It is well worth considering whether the opening six chapters of Genesis, narrating the Fall or expulsion from Eden, might suggest an account of humanity's arrival into the urban scene, such that the Christian bible then sets us immediately into the issues of urbanization (Eisenstadt, "Axial Age," 21). Bruce Lerro arrives at similar conclusions, as did Jaspers regarding the elite posture of transcendence: "Just as God becomes a transcendental beyond the power of human influence, so the upper castes seem to occupy the same unapproachable position relative to the lower classes" (Lerro, *From Earth Spirits to Sky Gods*, 303).

54. Gilles Deleuze, "Nietzsche and Saint Paul, Lawrence and John of Patmos," 46.

55. Edward Soja, *Postmetropolis: Critical Studies of Cities and Regions*, xv, 3.

56. Thistlethwaite, "Why Are Our Cities Dying?" 20.

57. "Beautyway" is the name of a Navaho healing chant. Each ritual is "a complex symphony of the arts, designed to harmonize relationships of individuals or groups with the orderly continuum of interrelated events that constitutes the Navaho universe." The beauty way rituals intend not to entertain but to "literally re-mind us" of, especially to affectively restore us to a sense of place, given the importance of land in Navaho cosmology (Leland C. Wyman, ed., *Beautyway: A Navaho Ceremonial*, 3).

58. Carolyn Steel, *Hungry City: How Food Shapes Our Lives*.

59. Warren Magnusson, "Politicizing the Global City," 296.

60. Robert Sacks, *A Geographical Guide to the Real and the Good*, 16–17; 6. "Autarky, tyranny, and chaos," Sacks goes on to say, "are morally objectionable uses of place" (26).

61. Sacks, *Geographical Guide*, 26, 31, 253.

62. Siebers, "Kant and the Politics of Beauty," 36, 39–40, 46.

63. Gebara, "Yearning for Beauty," 24.

64. Augustine, *City of God*, trans. Henry Bettenson, 1062; cited by Virginia Burrus, Response to Sharon V. Betcher. For further elaboration on Burrus's point, see her "Augustine, Rosenzweig, and the Possibility of Experiencing Miracle" and Burrus, Jordan, and MacKendrick, eds., *Seducing Augustine: Bodies, Desires, Confessions*, 105–12.

65. Burrus, Response to Betcher; commentary on Augustine, *City of God* 22.29.

66. Burrus, Response to Betcher, incorporating quotation from Augustine, *City of God* 22.30.

67. Norman Pittenger, "Beauty in a World in Process," 247.

68. Alfred North Whitehead, *Adventure of Ideas*, 296. Chris Dierckes has asserted that "Whitehead's definition of religion as contemplation of the beauty of holiness [derives] from his Anglican practice," specifically from the liturgy of the *Book of Common Prayer* within which Psalm 96 was a favorite: "O, worship the Lord in the beauty of holiness; let the whole earth stand before him in awe" (Chris Dierckes, final paper for Process Theologies, October 27, 2008, Vancouver School of Theology). In other words, process theologians would be well advised to accept responsibility for the fact that "beauty" is a hermeneutical or interpretive stance.

69. Roland Faber, "De-Ontologizing God: Levinas, Deleuze and Whitehead," 215.

70. Catherine Keller, *Face of the Deep: A Theology of Becoming*, 7.

71. T. Carmi, "The Gate," in *At the Stone of Losses*, 71. The closing service of Yom Kippur is called *ne'ilah*, which means "closing" or "locking." Thanks to colleague Rabbi Dr. Robert Daum for bringing this poem to my attention.

72. Charles Darwin, *On the Origin of Species*, 396. Also cited in Alejandro Garcia-Rivera, "Endless Forms Most Beautiful," 125.

73. In urban carnivals of the Middle Ages, "'Carnival masks, costumes, and grotesque distortions of the body served to destabilize fixed identities and role differentiations.' The prominence of physical differences or disabilities at festivals . . . posed a threat that the established order of bodily images might be over-thrown by unleashing repressed instincts that could exceed the repressive capacities of civil or religious leaders" (Hahn, "Can Disability Be Beautiful?" 28).

3. BREATHING THROUGH THE PAIN: ENGAGING THE CROSS AS *TONGLEN*, TAKING TO THE STREETS AS MENDICANTS

1. Iain Chambers, *Popular Culture: The Metropolitan Experience*, 183.

2. "Disability" has no place within Western cities. In fact, not only are bodies so designated seen as an intrusion on public space, despite the poor having nowhere else to be, but recently some states and cities have resorted to drug tests and electronic fingerprinting to assure themselves of the legitimacy of a person's need. See "Punishing Poverty," *New York Times*, November 1, 2011, Opinion, A26.

3. Marx made disability a trope for the effects of capitalism, particularly the division of labor: Industrial manufacturing "converts the worker into a crippled monstrosity" (Nicholas Brown, "Marxism and Disability: Review of *Aesthetic Nervousness*," 187–92). Zygmunt Bauman, among others, locates this divide between a mobile elite and "wasted" lives. See his *Wasted Lives: Modernity and Its Outcasts*.

4. Susan Schweik, "Begging the Question: Disability, Mendicancy, Speech and the Law," 58.

5. Roslyn Diprose, *Corporeal Generosity: On Giving with Nietzsche, Merleau-Ponty, and Levinas*, 9.

6. See Nate Berg, "The Big Fix: Vancouver Aims to 'End' Homelessness."

7. Chris Hedges, "City of Ruins."

8. Clearly the statistics also need to consider that in Canada today, 65 percent of all indigenous persons are now urban; modernity grouped "primitive" persons as "degenerate," thus as "disabled." In other words, there are several crosscuts of modernity's analytic scaling of bodies that still effectively sort bodies even within contemporary urbanism.

Disability has, of course, been indexed to nothing so much in the Western aesthetic as the lack of symmetry (see chapter 2, "'Fearful Symmetry'"). This has resulted not only in employment discrimination and foreclosure from social circuits, but in what came to be called "ugly laws"—municipal laws that, merging pain aversion with aesthetic and economic norms, moved disabled bodies out of view. The last of the "ugly laws"—initially brought into being with the public networking of urban areas by rail during the late nineteenth century so as to allow for "crackdowns on mendicancy"—were only recently repealed. But citizens have not necessarily moved beyond such spectral relations to disabled persons. Indeed, as Susan Schweik goes on to note, "The most powerful examples of recent resistance to the legacy of the unsightly beggar ordinances reflect profound engagement at that very meeting ground of poverty, urban marginalization (or annihilation) and disability where ugly law culture first began to germinate" ("Begging the Question," 59, 67).

The end of welfare capitalism, the pursuit of neoliberal economics, and our recent economic downturn are today eviscerating the middle class, splitting the populus in two. The "vox pop" has, amidst fear and stress, turned—as a recent *New York Times* editorial noted—crude, dismissive, self-protective. See "Compassion Deficit," *New York Times*, October 23, 2009. That "civil city legislation" increasingly removes from sight bodies that fall under the demarcation *disabled* suggests that our "civil" impulses carry habituated aversions to pain, disarticulations in the circuit of sympathy.

9. Karmen MacKendrick, *Counterpleasures*, 10.

10. Antonio Damasio, *Descartes' Error: Emotion, Reason, and the Human Brain*, 264; 264, 267.

11. Consequent interpolations of Jesus as imperial torture victim, for example, Grunewald's body of Christ pocked with the black plague, or even Van Gogh's daring Christological statement *Sorrow*, surely insinuate that Christian thought has understood in various subjugated strands that to love will include suffering with the other.

12. Richard Sennett, *The Conscience of the Eye: The Design and Social Life of Cities*, 45–46.

13. David B. Morris, *The Culture of Pain*, 242. Also cited in Linda Holler, *Erotic Morality: The Role of Touch in Moral Agency*, 127.

14. Pema Chodron, *Start Where You Are*, 38.

15. To think of Jesus as a grotesque I'm setting aside "historical Jesus realism" for a kind of iconography.

16. Stephen R. Munzer, "Beggars of God: The Christian Ideal of Mendicancy," 327–28, 309. An "attitude of mendicancy," explains Munzer, is composed of "humility, a disposition to acknowledge dependence on God and interdependence with others, gratitude for the good things in life, acceptance of the bad things that befall one," and, as able, "renunciation of one's self and its will and desires" (327–28). Through poverty, whether life-induced or ritu-

ally sanctioned, the mendicant learns "complete trust in divine providence" (309). Let me be clear that I intend to invoke mendicancy not as a viable location for "the disabled." Indeed, "precisely because the history of begging and the history of disability have so long been practically synonymous . . . the twentieth-century disability rights movement formed itself to a significant extent by developing narrative alternatives to and repudiations of the dynamics of mendicancy" (Schweik, "Begging the Question," 58). Rather "the attitude of mendicancy" applies to Christians, citizens, cosmopolitans, bourgeois bodies of Western culture, seculars, and, again, suggests a willingness, as of social flesh, to mutually carry the pain of being.

17. Philip Sheldrake, *Spaces for the Sacred: Place, Memory, and Identity*, 147.

18. Philip Sheldrake, "Spirituality and Social Change: Rebuilding the Human City," public lecture, p. 1 of manuscript.

19. *Mendicant* etymologically derives from either the Latin root *menda*, meaning "fault," or *mendum*, "physical defect," or possibly from the Sanskrit *minda*, also meaning "physical defect." In antiquity, we can find nearly "equivalent expressions in almost all cultures." See Hokusai09, "Mendicant—The One Who Gave Up Crown, Queen and Child."

20. Munzer, "Beggars of God," 319.

21. Jane Naomi Iwamura argues in *Virtual Orientalism: Asian Religions and American Popular Culture* that the Asian monk has become something of an iconic placeholder for a liberal audience's alliance with subaltern peoples or for persons forced to live in America's shadow, even as baby-boomer hippies could not finally break with their inherited privileges (142).

22. Patricia O'Connell Killen, "Memory, Novelty and Possibility in This Place," 83. In Cascadia, "religious life followed and still follows economic life and individual aspiration. . . . From the time of early Euro-American settlement this has made it difficult for religious institutions that understand part of their community's role as care for the common good to advance projects of caring for the wider community as part of religious/moral obligation" (ibid., 78).

23. Margrit Shildrick, "Unreformed Bodies: Normative Anxiety and the Denial of Pleasure," 329. Urbanization, especially where the off-loading of environmental risk affects populations (whether in certain regions of the city, e.g., near waste incineration facilities, or among world cities, e.g., wherein certain world cities become sites of polluting industries), aggravates conditions labeled as disability. See, for example, Eric Jaffe, "City Smog Linked to Cognitive Deficits in Children." And globalization as urbanization, with its rupturing of social structure and social networks, has been linked with increased risks of mental illness. "The types of rapid urbanization that are a consequence of globalization . . . decrease social capital"—that is, "the levels of civic participation, social networks and trust," Kwame McKenzie notes in "Urbanization,

Social Capital, and Mental Health," 364. This can be compounded if persons were displaced to the city via immigration, thus facing the difficulties of new settlement, including the unfamiliarity of a host culture, the navigation of its institutional infrastructure, the narrowing of affiliative networks. Because all of the various dimensions of displacement as well as the rupture of social networks and trust diminishes persons' psychological well-being, "the social environment" will be at least as important to urbanites' well-being, if not more so, than access to urban infrastructure (water, sanitation, etc.), McKenzie insists (361). Studies in Sweden have indicated that incidences of "psychoses and depression rose with increasing levels of population density" (ibid.), and urban densification over the next century will be rampant, both by design (Vancouver, as a model city, has urged urban densification in order to stave off encroachment on our agricultural reserve) and by "happenstance" (that is, as rural economies collapse and as human population swells and multiplies). Further, "Social fragmentation," when "defined as a composite measure of mobility in the previous year [and various forms of] single person households," has "predicted the strongest association with psychosis, increasing the risk twelvefold, compared to a five-fold link to deprivation" (363). If social fragmentation constitutes one of the primary and broad terrains of pain within urbanism today, meanwhile, the popular imagination "reels" with fears of mutant viruses and diseases veritably reinforcing tendencies toward isolation, as expressed, for example, by such films as *Contagion* (2011), *Carriers* (2009), *The Happening* (2008), *Pontypool* (2008), *The Crazies* (2010), etc. Hardly restorative of the social environment, these films—unless they can be used iconographically, as mirrors of ourselves—leave us rather adrenally hyped, with a slightly paranoid eye turned upon one another, especially toward any exhibition of disease.

24. Shildrick, "Unreformed Bodies," 328; 329.

25. Judith Butler, *Precarious Life: The Powers of Mourning and Violence*, 32.

26. The film *The Visitor* (2007), although it deals not with fear of disease but with the loss of social capital (not just among immigrants, but also among the seemingly well-established), may suggest an alternative and helpful interruption of this trajectory toward fearful dispersion and self-alienation.

27. Glucklich expressly disagrees with Elaine Scarry's surmise in her *The Body of Pain* that pain inevitably isolates by collapsing all communicative capacity.

28. David B. Morris, *The Culture of Pain*, 1–2; 5, 1, 3.

29. When trying to get one's bearings on Sennett's assessment regarding the blandness or neutrality of Western urbanism, think about how North America was reputedly encountered by Protestant colonists as "empty," as "wilderness." Sennett suggests that a kind of energy vacuum, which has to do with Protestant cultural projection, still obtains in our culture, now affecting the vitality of cities themselves.

30. Gianni Vattimo, "Pain and Metaphysics," 72; 72–73.

31. Vattimo, "Pain and Metaphysics," 77.

32. Chris Beasley and Carol Bacchi, "Envisaging a New Politics for an Ethical Future," 279–98.

33. Roland Faber, "De-Onto-ogizing God: Levinas, Deleuze and White-head," 217–19.

34. John Caputo, *Against Ethics*, 200. I've worked with disability studies theory to deconstruct and reconstruct the concept of Spirit in my *Spirit and the Politics of Disablement* (2007).

35. According to Max Weber, "The question of *theodicy* becomes particularly keen with the emergence of the 'salvation religions,'" which he simultaneously links to "furthering the *rationalization of religious belief*." Quoted in John F. Sitton, *Habermas and Contemporary Society*, 5. Marcella Althaus-Reid makes the same point in *Indecent Theology: Theological Perversions in Sex, Gender and Politics*: "theology is a surplus value of human suffering" (27).

36. Wendy Brown, *States of Injury: Power and Freedom in Late Modernity*, 75.

37. Tyler T. Roberts, *Contesting Spirit: Nietzsche, Affirmation, Religion*, 55, 63.

38. Benjamin D. Crowe, "Nietzsche, the Cross, and the Nature of God," 245.

39. "Men go to God when he is sore bested, / Find him poor and scorned, without shelter or bread, / Whelmed under weight of the wicked, the weak, the dead; / Christians stand by God in his hour of grieving." See Dietrich Bonhoeffer, *Letters and Papers from Prison*, 131.

40. Emmanuel Levinas, "Useless Suffering," 116. Also cited in Gibbs, "Unjustifiable Suffering," 24.

41. Amy Hollywood, "Performativity, Citationality, Ritualization," 93–115.

42. Franz Rosenzweig, *The Star of Redemption*, 5. Also cited in Gibbs, "Unjustifiable Suffering," 17.

43. Ian Buchanan, "The Problem of the Body in Deleuze and Guattari, Or, What Can a Body Do?" 88.

44. Buchanan, "Problem of the Body," 82.

45. Levinas, "Useless Suffering," 116. Also cited in Gibbs, "Unjustifiable Suffering," 24.

46. Emmanuel Levinas, *Difficult Freedom: Essays on Judaism*, 89. Also cited in Judith Butler, *Giving an Account of Oneself*, 91.

47. Hermann Cohen, *Religion of Reason Out of the Sources of Judaism*, 157–58, 135–36. Also cited in Gibbs, "Unjustifiable Suffering," 21.

48. Gibbs, "Unjustifiable Suffering," 20–21.

49. Cohen, *Religion of Reason*, 157–58. Also cited in Gibbs, "Unjustifiable Suffering," 20.

50. Cohen, *Religion of Reason*, 135–36. Also cited in Gibbs, "Unjustifiable Suffering," 21.

51. Any number of people find the fumbling bewilderment represented by Larry Gopnik, the central character of Joel and Ethan Coen's movie *A Serious Man* (2009), set in 1960s suburban Minneapolis, a less-than-compelling unraveling, more merely trivial and laughable than Job-ian (for example, he ponders whether his religion requires him to pay burial expenses of his wife's extramarital lover), especially when compared, say, with the depth of suffering represented by Alan Paton's novel reflecting the same general era, *Cry, the Beloved Country*. (First published in 1948, Paton's novel deals with the pains of decolonization and racial apartheid in South Africa.) But if one might be permitted to take a peek into social psychology through the retrospective lens of these filmmakers, might we not spy the suburban somnambulance we've inherited from these earlier cultural decades? As much as monocultural lawns, picket fences, and suburban privacy became the canvas of life, the dreamscape behind the 1950s, 1960s, and 1970s in North America was a haunting—an awareness of human-generated atrocity for which one seemed both responsible and irrelevant, and there seemed an easy exit from ever having to cope with it—somnambulance, a kind of walking, waking ignorance by aspiring into middle class or more cosmopolitan culture. After all, if we were mindful, how could we bear ourselves?

52. Richard Bauckham, "'Only the Suffering God Can Help': Divine Passibility in Modern Theology," 6. Similar shifts can be tracked during this period across theological and philosophical spectrums of thought. Simultaneously, "the Spanish philosopher Miguel de Unamuno developed a doctrine of the infinite sorrow of God" (ibid.), the Japanese Lutheran theologian Kazoh Kitamori published his famous *Theology of the Pain of God* (1946), and the radical "death of God theologians" announced precisely what their name suggested. This radical movement included Jewish as well as Christian theologians. Commitment to the "pain of God" was consequently also taken up in process theology, which characterizes God as fellow sufferer (ibid.).

53. Julia Kristeva, *New Maladies of the Soul*.

54. Blaise Pascal, "Prière pour demander a dieu le bon usage des maladies," in *Oeuvres complètes*, 363. Also quoted in Morris, *Culture of Pain*, 44.

55. Mary Daly and Jane Caputi define the "presence of absence" as the glut of mental and spiritual bloat, including ideologies, that makes person sensorally absent to their worlds. See *Websters' First New Intergalactic Wickedary of the English Language*, 89. Others have spoken of Christians in Germany during the Holocaust as "the presence of absence."

56. Concerned biblical theologians and social activists today continue to produce and project Jesus portraits—not just Marcus J. Borg, in, for example, *Meeting Jesus Again for the First Time* (1994) and John Dominic Cross, in *Jesus, A Revolutionary Biography* (1994), but also Deepak Chopra, *The Third Jesus: The Christ We Cannot Ignore* (2009) and Rex Weyler (founder of Greenpeace, a

movement born in my Kits neighborhood of Vancouver), *The Jesus Sayings: The Quest for His Authentic Message* (2009). But if metaphysics has a tendency to anesthetize pain, thus leaving us to deal with pain from a location outside of sentient relation, outside of social flesh, therefore only assuming a dominant representation thereof, the historical Jesus also may not be quite the answer to addressing pain in such a way as to maintain solidarity among humanity. Such projections do not help much in navigating the fear, aversion, and other affective swamps of our relation with pain. While I would not deny that these scholars and activists might be motivated by the same waking hope—that is, to make a difference in the world—I worry that to think analogically through Jesus inures persons to our enfo_dment in social flesh, given the way in which the West engenders subjectivity.

57. Marcella Althaus-Reid, "*El Tocado (Le Toucher)*: Sexual Irregularities in the Translation of God (The Word) in Jesus," 396; 399.

58. Althaus-Reid, "*El Tocado*," 396.

59. "Enlightenment means rising above thought," Tolle insists, and links thought—what I would call "rationalization"—to "the pain-body." See *The Power of Now*, 21. Also see his *A New Earth: Awakening to Your Life's Purpose*.

60. Tolle further insists that his teaching, this wisdom, "is not derived from external sources, but from the one true Source within, so it contains no theory or speculation." Rather, he claims, "I speak from inner experience" (*Power of Now*, 10). Certainly, this presumed separation of inner and outer, bolstered by a claim to unmediated spiritual authority and authenticity, grates on the conscience of any poststructuralist. That said, he appeals to persons wishing for institutional freedom to craft their own spiritualities, to reclaim a relationship with the world—as over against a felt abstractness of modern knowledge as well as "belief" among the established religions.

61. Robert Price, "Practicing the Present (Eckhart Tolle, *The Power of Now: A Guide to Spiritual Enlightenment*)," 108. Price provides a philosophically relative and sympathetic, if not uncritical, reading of *The Power of Now*.

62. William Connolly, *Why I Am Not a Secularist*, 49.

63. Simone Weil, "Meaning of the Universe," in *Gravity and Grace*, 127. Also see *The Notebooks of Simone Weil*, 1:19.

64. On this point, see Henri-Jacques Stiker, *A History of Disability*. As Stiker reads Francis of Assisi, St. Francis insisted on an immanentalist—rather than a transcendentalist—passage through pain: "Francis did not change the course of economic history, but he did effect a change of mentality with regard to those who were both rejected and aided. . . . To merge with God, almost all mystics recommend that one detach oneself from the world; when one has thus escaped from the world, one is ready for the mystical union. Francis of Assisi proposed a journey not from animate creation but in and through it" (81). Stiker explains, "The poor individual was no longer one to whom you gave

alms but one in whom you recognized God, one who became like a living sacrament, like the sacred itself. There is no longer any sacrality outside the fraternal bond. And the fraternal relationship finds its highest expression in the relationship with the poor"—the poor being archetypically configured as the leper (ibid.). Stiker concludes by suggesting that "Francis' poverty of life with the poor and like the poor constitutes a substantial revolution, since the monastic poverty earlier practiced in Christian communities expressed itself in quite different forms. It was cultivated poverty . . . almost disinfected." Francis of Assisi, contrarily, "lived among beggars, and borrowed their clothing" (82). In fact, "the city of Assisi castigated him for becoming a beggar and for associating himself with those who enjoyed no status in the hierarchy" (83).

65. Tolle also published an audio book entitled *Living the Liberated Life and Dealing with the Pain Body* in 2001.

66. Price, "Practicing the Present," 113.

67. Given Tolle's covert deployment of the Vedic teaching that "atman [self] is Brahman" and his description of the path of liberating knowledge, his philosophy, at its core, appears to be predominantly sourced from Vedantic philosophy, though he has idiosyncratically reconstructed that philosophy. Anantanand Rambachan, scholar of Advaita Vedanta, explains, "In the view of the Upaniṣads, it is the attainment or gain of the Infinite"—which resembles Tolle's "Presence"—"that truly resolves the human problem" (*The Advaita Worldview: God, World, and Humanity*, 32). Tolle comparably explains that "Enlightenment . . . is simply your natural state of felt oneness with Being" (*Power of Now*, 12). The path of liberation also proceeds comparably—Rambachan pointing toward "the introspective technique of distinguishing between the 'knower' and the 'known'" (*Advaita Worldview*, 33), while Tolle stresses the distinction between "thinking and consciousness," as also between "thinking and knowing" (*New Earth*, 28, 55, 8).

Tolle's work, at its best, may offer Western persons who have become emotionally locked in psychic pain, owing to a substantialist materialist cosmology and individualism, a roominess, a soulfulness, beyond this formation he calls "the pain-body"—the acute suffering linked to egoic compulsions to identify with an object world (*New Earth*, 34–35).

68. Moses P. P. Penumaka, "Luther and Shankara: Two Ways of Salvation in the Indian Context," 252.

69. Rambachan himself warns Westerners about our tendency to reassert our habitual dualisms at this point—thus, reading *bliss* as having become free from pain—when that would not be consistent with Vedic thought: "Does the bliss of the *atman* then manifest itself only when sorrowful mental states give way to conditions of happiness? The obvious difficulty with such an understanding is that it represents the *atman* as limited by time since it implies that

there is a mental state (viz., sorrow) when the *atman* is absent. This would con-
tradict the Upanishadic teaching that the *atman* is timeless and present in all
states and mental conditions" (*Advaita Worldview*, 40–41).

To be sure, Tolle acknowledges that "[i]llness is part of your life situation,"
then points—as an Advaitan would—in the direction of Brahman: "Underneath the various conditions that make up your life situation, which exists in
time, there is something deeper, more essential: your Life, your very Being in
the timeless Now" (*Power of Now*, 217). Nonetheless, the warning about succumbing to dualistic scales of bliss versus negativity needs to be much emphasized here, where Tolle's teachings are appropriated for self-crafted philosophies
which become as puritanically avoidant of "negativities"—other humans, the
daily news—as, in another time, a Baptist might have stayed away from alcohol
or dance. Given that New Thoughters suspect that "negative attitudes inside
one's head bring about negative external conditions to match them" (*Power of
Now*, 110), the whole enterprise can shut down critical thinking, which is often
misconstrued as negativity. Deutsch comparably explains that for Advaita Vedanta, the saving knowledge that "atman is Brahman" does "enable the knower
to overcome all pain, misery, ignorance, and bondage" (*Advaita Vedānta*, 47).
However, this does not eviscerate the "reality" of experience of pain, fear,
worry; "atman is Brahman" informs such experience, allows one to approach
and honor the other as herself or himself a spiritual being.

70. Again, this will not come far from Soelle's claim to see the world, reality, even suffering then, through love. Not unlike Soelle, Tolle contends that
pain can be "use[d] . . . for enlightenment," that "suffering has a noble
purpose"—namely, as he puts it, "the evolution of consciousness and the burning up of the ego" (*Power of Now*, 217, 102). After all, pain, because it is not
willed, "weakens the most basic level of the body-self as the agent who 'owns'
every experience" (Glucklich, *Sacred Pain*, 60). But Tolle seems, perhaps unwittingly, to promise a bliss path—contrary to Soelle, who openly acknowledges
that detachment from ego opens itself upon experience after experience of renunciation, thus of suffering, and who speaks consequently of the path as itself
a passion. Tolle can be overheard as urging something of a narcissistic ego
drive "that wants everything without detour," that wants to settle down in the
immutable, the eternal, as if to inure one against life. "To meditate on the
cross," Soelle would surely inform Tolle, "means to say good-bye to the narcissistic hope of being free of sickness, deformity and death," so that "all the energies wasted on such hopes" can be freed for affectively engaging the world in
its travail of becoming (Soelle, *Suffering*, 131). Identifying with "atman as
Brahman" does not offer one a giant eraser for pain, but a portal through
which one enters into love of the world itself—a passion in a double sense, both
of desire and the labor of working that desire (that is, suffering). In Luther's

language, Tolle's path appears to be "cheap grace," for "to live conscious of our oneness with the whole of life"—which is how I understand "atman is Brahman," as I also understand "God is love"—implies learning to suffer in a way that loves life unrelentingly, without judgment. What it does not do is foreclose pain and passion itself (Soelle, *Suffering*, 141).

71. Weil, *Gravity and Grace*, 128–29.

72. Ann Pirruccello, "Making the World My Body: Simone Weil and Somatic Practice," 479.

73. Pirruccello, "Making the World My Body," 481, 482.

74. Peter Winch, explicating Weil in *Simone Weil: "The Just Balance,"* 134, 136.

75. Pirruccello, "Making the World My Body," 483.

76. David Cockburn, "Self, World and God in Spinoza and Weil," 182.

77. Simone Weil, "The Love of God and Affliction," 79.

78. Anne Carson, *Decreation: Poetry, Essays, Opera*, 179.

79. Simone Weil, quoted in Carson, *Decreation*.

80. Carson, *Decreation*, 235.

81. Cockburn, "Self, World and God in Spinoza and Weil," 178. My reading of Weil, especially on this point, has been shaped by Beatrice Marovich, "Consent To Be Creature: The Politics of Creatureliness in Simone Weil's Theological Cosmology."

82. Cockburn, "Self, World and God," 174.

83. Alyda Faber, "*Dancer in the Dark*: Affliction and the Aesthetic of Attention," 97.

84. Cockburn, "Self, World and God," 180.

85. Thich Nhat Hanh, *The Miracle of Mindfulness*, 49.

86. Shildrick, "Unreformed Bodies," 328–29.

87. Holler, *Erotic Morality*, 78.

88. Faber, "*Dancer in the Dark*," 85.

89. William E. Connolly, *Why I Am Not a Secularist*, 57.

90. Gibbs, *Suffering Religion*, 30–31.

91. "The politics of becoming occurs," explains William Connolly, "when a culturally marked constituency, suffering under its negative constitution in an established institutional matrix, strives to reconfigure itself by moving the cultural constellation of identity/difference then in place." "Under these circumstances," he advises us, "it takes a militant, experimental and persistent political movement to open up a new line of flight from culturally induced suffering." "Such a movement, to succeed, must extend from those who initiate cultural experiments to others who respond sensitively to those experiments, even when the experiments disturb their own sense of identity" (*Why I Am Not a Secularist*, 51). And yet Christians might be, above all, those informed by our dramaturgies—often iconically centered on the body in pain—to tend this zone

of creative justice and so work to move "a mode of suffering . . . from below the reach of justice to a place within its purview" (ibid., 63).

92. Rosenzweig, *Star of Redemption*, 5. See Gibbs, *Suffering Religion*, 17.

93. Roberts, *Contesting Spirit,* 92, 28, 178–81.

94. Anna Mercedes, "*Effluit Nobis*: Luther and Melanchthon on the Benefits of the Cross," 89–90.

95. Mercedes, "*Effluit Nobis*," 90.

96. Roberts, *Contesting Spirit*, 180–81.

97. Pema Chodron, *When Things Fall Apart*, 93.

98. Philosopher Luce Irigaray has noted Western Christianity's tendency to hold its breath—"as if the less we breathe, the nearer we come to correct thinking," she laughs sarcastically. When you enter our religious places, she observes, you notice that despite invocations of Spirit as breath, "scant attention is paid to the need for ventilation" (*I Love to You: Sketch of a Possible Felicity in History*, 121–22). Irigaray commends interpolating religions with breath so as to "spiritualize bodies without removing them from their flesh," so as to become religious subjects of the earth, "the places we inhabit" (ibid., 127, 15). Breath, Thich Nhat Hanh helpfully adds, yokes "life to consciousness . . . body to thoughts." By means of the breath, one can "take hold of the mind" (Hanh, *The Miracle of Mindfulness*, 15).

99. *Epistle to Diognetus* 9:206, circa 130 C.E.

100. Penumaka, "Luther and Shankara," 253.

101. Sogyal Rinpoche, *The Tibetan Book of Living and Dying*, 197–98.

102. Martin Luther, *Luther's Works*, 26:284. Also cited in Arland Hultgren, "Luther on Galatians," 236.

103. To be sure, Anselm's notion of God's honor had to do with the integrity of the creation, not simply with a psychic disposition.

104. Kathryn Tanner, "Incarnation, Cross, and Sacrifice: A Feminist-Inspired Reappraisal," 36.

105. Brian A. Gerrish, "Atonement and 'Saving Faith,'" 183.

106. Rudolf Otto, *The Idea of the Holy*, 100–2.

107. Tanner further insists that "the saving effects of the incarnation on this classical model are felt throughout Christ's life but no more so than on the cross, where those life-giving powers of the divine nature of Christ are so much needed" ("Incarnation, Cross, and Sacrifice," 41). On this view, as noted above, "God saves by assuming the life of suffering and death" (43), which in her view still requires that "Jesus must be obedient unto death"—not carrying any penal load for us, but so that humanity's existence, even its awful extremities of experience, becomes thoroughly saturated with and, if you will, by the Word (44, 46). The "saving force" of the Word entering into human experience carries Jesus from birth through the conclusion of his mission, his execution being here but a brutal political realism—not a necessity.

108. Developed by Indian Buddhist teacher Atisha Dipankara Shrijnana, born in 982 C.E., then written down by Kadampa master Langri Tangpa (1054–1123), the practice became more widely known when Geshe Chekawa Yeshe Dorje (1101–1175) summarized the points in his *Seven Points of Training the Mind* (see Wikipedia s.v. "tonglen").

109. Pema Chodron resides at Gampo Abbey, Cape Breton, Nova Scotia, the first Tibetan Buddhist monastery for Westerners.

110. Pema Chodron, *The Places that Scare You: A Guide to Fearlessness in Difficult Times*, 55.

111. Rinpoche, *Tibetan Book of Living and Dying*, points out that modernity has tended to treat pain as meaningless, pointless. Not only does tonglen use one's own pain as training ground, it suggests dedicating one's own breathing through pain to the alleviation of the suffering of others (224–25).

112. Hanh, *Miracle of Mindfulness*, 49.

113. Holler, *Erotic Morality*, 133.

114. Chodron, *Start Where You Are*, 115, 74.

115. Daphne Hampson, "Luther on the Self: A Feminist Critique," 336.

116. Chodron, *When Things Fall Apart*, ix.

117. Otto, *Idea of the Holy*, 104. Gerrish, too, objects to the emphasis on a rationalist objectivity that makes of even "substitutionary atonement" a mere juridical action.

118. Gerrish, "Atonement and 'Saving Faith,'" 183.

119. Chodron, *When Things Fall Apart*, 34.

120. Martin Luther, *Luther's Works*, 17:223. Cited in Randall C. Zachman, *The Assurance of Faith*, 55.

121. Chodron, *Places that Scare You*, 58.

122. Christine Longaker, *Facing Death and Finding Hope: A Guide to the Emotional and Spiritual Care of the Dying*, 72.

123. Gerrish, "Atonement and 'Saving Faith,'" 56–57.

124. Marit Trelstad, "The Way of Salvation in Luther's Theology: A Feminist Evaluation," 239–41; 237.

125. Trelstad, "Way of Salvation," 241.

126. Martin Luther, *Luther's Works*, 27:281. See Hultgren, "Luther on Galatians," 237.

127. Martin Luther, *Luther's Works*, 54:154.

128. Levinas, *Difficult Freedom*, 89; see also Butler, *Giving an Account of Oneself*, 91.

129. Friedrich Schleiermacher, *The Christian Faith*, 456. See Ray, *Deceiving the Devil*, 147 n. 30.

130. Darby Ray, *Deceiving the Devil*, 17.

131. John Makransky, *Awakening through Love*, 179.

132. See Bauman, *Wasted Lives*.

133. Thanks to my student Ann Turner for bringing this novel to my attention.

134. Vattimo, "Pain and Metaphysics," 76–77.

135. Sheldrake, "Spirituality and Social Change," 14.

136. Joel Kotkin, *The City: A Global* History, xvi. Thanks to Philip Sheldrake for introducing me to this text.

137. Kotkin, *The City*, 119–2c.

138. Sheldrake, "Spirituality and Social Change," 14.

4. IN THE RUIN OF GOD

1. Tobin Siebers, "In the Name of Pain," 183.

2. Shelly Tremain, *Foucault and the Government of Disability*, xvi.

3. Alan Klima, "The Telegraphic Abject: Buddhist Meditation and the Redemption of Mechanical Reproduction," 568; Julia Kristeva, *Powers of Horror: An Essay on Abjection*.

4. Klima, "Telegraphic Abject," 553–54.

5. Alyda Faber, "The Post-Secular Poetics and Ethics of Exposure in J. M. Coetzee's *Disgrace*," 309.

6. Kristeva, *Powers of Horror*, 3, 9.

7. See also Ato Quayson, *Aesthetic Nervousness: Disability and the Crisis of Representation*, 17.

8. William Connolly, *Why I Am Not a Secularist*, 161.

9. That the cross did not become the major icon of Christianity until after the fourth century, maybe as late as the tenth century, has been recently argued by feminists Rita Nakashima Brock and Rebecca Ann Parker in *Saving Paradise: How Christianity Traded Love of This World for Crucifixion and Empire* (2008). Karen Armstrong draws upon their scholarship and asserts the same in her *The Case for God* (2010). Brock and Parker clearly intend to promote a more pleasure-focused or life-focused—rather than otherworldly—Christianity. Atonement theories of the second millennium have, contrarily, storied a God who sent his son to die as guilt payment, a focus that simultaneously associated the guilt of material existence with women and directed human attention toward an afterlife. I disagree with them on neither point. However, the early Jesus movements surely knew suffering; their sense of paradise could not have been unrelated to the phenomenon of living amidst empire—unless our modern lens, splitting pain and pleasure, is to intrude here, which I fear it may be. Brock and Parker hesitate to acknowledge any constructive function for suffering and struggle amidst imperial resistance. Yet even Brock in her earlier *Journeys by Heart: A Christology of Erotic Power* (1992) asserts that "our very survival depends upon how we come to terms with our pain" (1). Even if we do not have cruciform icons from the early centuries, we do have at the least, as I've

noted, narrative iconography of the Passion, which may have informed popular consciousness through liturgical drama. Colin Eisler, in "The Athlete of Virtue: The Iconography of Asceticism," argues that "the events of the Passion, the Agony in the Garden, the Stripping, the Flagellation, and the Crowning with Thorns, in the later life of Christ, all suggest a curious inversion of the Graeco-Roman program of the triumphant athlete" (83), an inversion that Eisler hypothesizes served to inform the athletic prowess of the Christian martyr (94). It's this inversion to which I advert—even if political torture did not result in something we categorize as grotesque. The figural images of the Passion could have been intended to suggest, via meditation, strength through suffering (90).

10. Julia Kristeva, "Stabat Mater," in *The Kristeva Reader*, 179. Cited in Virginia Burrus, *Saving Shame: Martyrs, Saints and Other Abject Subjects*, 55.

11. Quayson, *Aesthetic Nervousness*, 3.

12. Salman Rushdie, *Midnight's Children*. But then of course those who know Christian tradition will also hear a hymnic refrain about another child of midnight, i.e., "It Came upon a Midnight Clear."

13. Rob Nixon, in *Slow Violence and the Environmentalism of the Poor*, defines *slow violence* as taking aggressive economic advantage of off-loading technological and ecological risk into "the different timelines of mutation—international, intranational, intergenerational, bureaucratic, and somatic" (209).

14. Heather Snell, "Assessing the Limitations of Laughter in Indra Sinha's *Animal's People*," 1.

15. Nixon, *Slow Violence*, 54.

16. See Adam Frank, "The Anthropocene: Can Humans Survive a Human Age?" The term *Anthropocene* was developed by Nobel Prize–winning atmospheric chemist Paul Crutzen to name the increasingly massive impact of humans on the evolution of the planet. See Nixon, *Slow Violence*, 12.

17. Simone Weil, *Gravity and Grace*, 179. In her phenomenological attention to affliction, Weil notes two phenomena that we've incidentally happened upon, in a manner that might, in her philosophical practice, be termed "unskillful"—the tendency to allow disgust to deflect our attention, to carry us on its waves away from the source of aversion, and the contrary tendency to want to eradicate the disgusting. In *Waiting for God* she writes that humanity "has the same carnal nature as animals. If a hen is hurt, the others rush upon it, attacking it with their beaks. . . . Our senses attach all the scorn, all the revulsion, all the hatred that our reason attaches to crime, to affliction" (71). She concludes this phenomenological observation with a quick reference to the alternate possibility of having worked spiritually with disgust: "Except for those whose whole soul is inhabited by Christ, everybody despises the afflicted to some extent, although practically no one is conscious of it" (71). This, in fact, seems to constitute the epitome of Christology in her philosophical vision: to

lovingly span the chasm toward what has been made accursed by affliction, to break the "law of gravitation" by which humans attack that which might revulse them (*Waiting for God*, 72, 75).

18. Ann Pirruccello, "Making the World My Body: Simone Weil and Somatic Practice," 479. Pirruccello makes the interesting point that Weil's thought was contemporary with the phenomenology of Maurice Merleau-Ponty, but that Weil worked that phenomenology through a philosophical spiritual practice so as "to 'read' the world differently" (480). Pirrucello notes that "she believed a great deal in the power of body-centered practices" (485). "The crucial requirement for going beyond a mediocre life," Pirruccello explains of Weil's thought world, "is to undergo a shift in the everyday interpretive mode, for that manner of reading is plagued by various degrees of egocentrism" (482). This shift would be engaged through philosophical practice, especially in relation to suffering, since "somatic knowledge requires suffering" (486).

19. Klima, "Telegraphic Abject," 565.

20. George D. Bond, "Theravada Buddhism's Meditations on Death and the Symbolism of Initiatory Death," 238.

21. Desiderius Erasmus, *Preparing for Death* (*De Praeparatione ad mortem*; 1534), in *Spiritualia and Pastoralia*, 412 (vol. 70 of *The Collected Works*, Toronto edition). Location of this statement in other editions: LB V, 1302A (*Desiderii Erasmi Roterodami opera omnia*, ed. J. Leclerc [Leiden, 1703–06; rpt. Heldesheim: G. Olms, 1961–62]); ASD V-1, 358 (*Opera Omnia Desiderii Erasmi Roterodami* [Amsterdam: North-Holland Publishing, 1969–]).

22. Klima, "Telegraphic Abject," 567, 570.

23. Ellen M. Ross's *The Grief of God: Images of the Suffering Jesus in Late Medieval England* does examine the growing volume of art depicting the suffering Jesus between the twelfth and fourteenth centuries and the consequent devotional life, but across the sea—in medieval England. Her study suggests that rather than presenting us with "a gospel of gore," this artwork was pivotal in conveying the breadth and extent of divine mercy as well as inspiring the transformation of humans in this direction: "The polymorphous evocation of the divine compassion manifested in the suffering Christ goes beyond a demonstration of God's love. . . . The flooding of viewers' senses with extravagant depictions of pain and anguish . . . evoke[s] the believer's compassionate response. . . . Empathetic reflection was a cornerstone of medieval religious life. . . . The believers' alliance of compassion with Jesus enabled them to perceive Jesus in other humans" (6–7). "The figure of the suffering Christ," Ross goes on to suggest, "does function to empower individuals"—especially religious women—"to stand over and against society" (7–8).

24. Walter Simons, *Cities of Ladies: Beguine Communities in the Medieval Low Countries, 1200–1565*, 62.

25. Robert E. Lerner, *The Heresy of the Free Spirit in the Later Middle Ages*, 240.

26. Simons, *Cities of Ladies*, 65.

27. Lerner, *Heresy of the Free Spirit*, 231.

28. David Horrell, "Between Conformity and Resistance: Beyond the Balch-Elliott Debate towards a Postcolonial Reading of 1 Peter," 138, 140, 131, 127, 139.

29. Soelle, *Suffering*, 96–100, 147.

30. The kenotic hymn of Philippians, Karl-Joseph Kuschel insists, proposes a model for the attitudes that should govern the life of the Christian community. See Karl-Joseph Kuschel, *Born Before All Time? The Dispute over Christ's Origin*, 242–66, especially 261 and 264–66.

31. To be clear, Aitken is claiming that contrary to scholarship that locates the passion of Jesus in either historical remembrance or scribal traditions, the texts can be read as shaped by and shaping the ritual life of various communities: "To tell a story about Jesus' death was . . . to tell a story about the identity of the community," including "things done" by the community—"the cultic actions in which Jesus' death was remembered" (*Jesus' Death*, 26, 16). For a helpful review of Aitken's text, see Erik M. Heen, Review of *Jesus' Death in Early Christian Memory*.

32. Ola Sigurdson, "The Christian Body as a Grotesque Body," 244.

33. Scholars debate the influence of Isaiah 53 on the Christian testament. Helmut Koester argues for "very close linguistic parallels" between Isaiah 53 and 1 Corinthians 11:23 and 15:3. See his "The Memory of Jesus' Death and the Worship of the Risen Lord," 347. Julian Morgenstern argues that the songs of the suffering servant (Isaiah 40–56) constituted a festival drama, then concludes that "probably no section of the entire Old Testament is quoted in the New Testament more frequently and at greater length than is our drama and . . . not merely Isaiah 53, but practically the entire drama." See his "The Suffering Servant—A New Solution." Martin Hengel, in *The Atonement: The Origins of the Doctrine in the New Testament*, argues that "neither the formula of the 'surrender' of Jesus nor that of his representative dying 'for many' or 'for us' would have come into being without the background of this mysterious prophecy" (59). Also, in an essay entitled "The Effective History of Isaiah 53 in the Pre-Christian Period," Hengel documents the role of Isaiah 53 "in a wide variety of pre-Christian Jewish writings," suggesting its broad provenance and the currency of vicarious suffering in Palestinian Judaism, and notes that "the earliest Church *could* have known and appealed to them" (76). Ellen Bradshaw Aitken, referring to Isaiah 53 as "one of the hymns or psalms of the suffering righteous," likewise asserts that "Isaiah 53 . . . the portrayal of the servant, was already central to the process of reenacting the cult legend of Moses and the Israelites in the wilderness" in Second Temple Judaism, "and thus became a

key element in the reenactment of that legend in terms of Jesus" (*Jesus' Death*, 32, 73).

Other scholars suggest that there is little evidence of the use of the suffering servant motif in early Christianity, except for 1 Peter 2:22–21. In this vein, consider the summary of recent scholarship offered by Daniel G. Powers in *Salvation through Participation: An Examination of the Notion of the Believers' Corporate Unity with Christ in Early Christian Soteriology*: "The greatest stumbling block against accepting the influence of the Fourth Servant Song upon early Christian ideas of atonement is the fact that there is so little solid evidence that it was actually employed by the earliest writers in reference to or in support of any type of notion of reconciliatory death" (25). Powers based his work on studies by scholars such as biblical commentator C. K. Barrett, plus Morna Hooker, *Jesus and the Servant: The Influence of the Servant Concept of Deutero-Isaiah in the New Testament*, and Marinus de Jonge, *God's Final Envoy: Early Christology and Jesus' Own View of His Mission*. Indeed, such scholars suggest that there's almost a complete absence of the Isaiah 53 motif before 165 C.E., except for 1 Peter and Acts 8, which they claim may have been a mid-second-century insertion.

A second question follows from this line of thinking: With Isaiah 53, to what extent would persons of the early common centuries have seen a grotesque as distinct from an instance of "verism"—the wrinkled face, worried brow, and angular features of one with requisite experience for the mantle of authority? On verism, see Jeremy Tanner, "Portraits, Power and Patronage in the Late Roman Republic," 18–50. Tanner does intriguingly argue that verism, with its stress on such physiognomic features as "facial asymmetry . . . signs of aging from sunken and hollow cheeks to crow's feet and bags under the eyes" (19), was a distinctive development of second-century Roman culture, in contradistinction from previous Hellenistic portraiture. But equally intriguing is the connection of verism with "salvic potency" and patronal protectiveness (45).

More recently, David Horrell's postcolonial reading of 1 Peter, one of the most definitive carryovers of Isaiah 53 into the Christian testament, appears to argue for a more dramatic, liturgical lineage. In "Between Conformity and Resistance: Beyond the Balch-Elliott Debate towards a Postcolonial Reading of 1 Peter," he maintains that persons of the community represented in 1 Peter, displaced to provinces of Asia Minor, lived in "conscious resistance to imperial demands" (137) and may have anticipated suffering, but "the suffering is depicted as sharing in the sufferings of Christ" (138). Horrell argues that 1 Peter constitutes "the earliest attempt to turn the stigmatizing label" of *Christian* "into one which, for insiders at least, is a badge of honour" (140).

I am persuaded by and so follow the trajectory of scholarship suggesting that Isaiah 53, including its predecessor text of Psalm 44, was already prominent within the rituals, liturgical drama, and life of Second Temple Judaism. That is not to say that I dismiss the strength that comes through the iconicity of the grotesque; indeed, sometimes that is precisely the nature of the grotesque for an onlooker—the particular coincidence of strength and suffering or, comparably, of intellect and disability.

34. See also David Tombs, "Crucifixion, State Terror, and Sexual Abuse," 89–119. Tombs, recalling "how recent Latin American regimes used terror," especially "sexual humiliation and violence," so as "to create fear and promote fatalism," suggests that "the Gospel accounts indicate a striking level of public sexual humiliation in the treatment of Jesus" to which we have, through metaphysical myth and belief, closed our eyes (89–90). But if "crucifixion was intended . . . to reduce the victim to something less than human in the eyes of society" (101), then the befriending of this grotesque icon speaks of an amazing faith in God become flesh, an insistent love of life even in the face of this.

35. See Mikhail Bahktin, *Rabelais and His World*.

36. Istvan Czachesz, "Metamorphosis and Mind: Cognitive Explorations of the Grotesque in Early Christian Literature," 207.

37. See Christopher A. Frilingos, *Spectacles of Empires: Monsters, Martyrs, and the Book of Revelation*. "Spectacle was a particularly effective mode for the production of authoritative knowledge about other and self under the Roman Empire," observes Frilingos (11). "Rome's was," he continues, "a public society in which everything, everyone was at all times on display. . . . Under Roman rule, imperial shrines and spectacles—the gladiatorial combats, beast-hunts, and public executions of the amphitheater—pervaded the cities of Asia Minor" (16). In the Book of Revelation, the counterspectacle is, of course, "the monstrous Lamb" (114), if equally the bodies of Christian martyrs; such spectacles were meant to put pressure on the passions (115), but in such a way that Christians identified with the martyrs' heroism (118).

38. For example, Alyda Faber discusses the film *Dancer in the Dark* as an elaboration of Simone Weil's attention to affliction; see Faber's "*Dancer in the Dark*," 85–106. She writes, "The film *Dancer in the Dark* when engaged with empathic living attention can enlarge our capacity for responsiveness to deep suffering" (85).

39. Rosemarie Garland-Thomson, "Misfits: A Feminist Materialist Disability Concept," 596, here summarizing the argument of Linda Martin Alcoff.

40. Garland-Thomson, "Misfits," 600.

41. Tertullian, *On the Resurrection of the Flesh*, 9. Cited in Virginia Burrus, *Saving Shame*, 56–57.

42. Adolph von Harnack, *The Mission and Expansion of Christianity in the First Three Centuries*, 1:101–09.

43. Soelle incidentally mentions just such a proposal: "One needs to compare the artistic portrayals in Roman portraits with those out of the autumn of

the Middle Ages in order to see the difference between stoic self-restricting tranquility and the 'sweetness' of mystical suffering" (*Suffering*, 99).

44. Cleo McNelly Kearns, "Suffering in Theory,"67–68.

45. See Gretta Vospers, *With or Without God: Why the Way We Live Is More Important than What We Believe*. Canadian United Church pastor Vospers follows upon the work of Bishop John Shelby Spong, arguing that religious persons must work on "visceral commitment" more than ideational belief (11), even as she claims "the radical simplicity that lies at the core of Christianity—an abiding trust in the way of love"—as an energy that could occasion the world's survival and thriving (4).

46. Kearney and I share a sense of wrestling with "God" to the point of inducing a psychic full stop within theistic trajectories. He writes in this vein that anatheism requires "critical and iconoclastic atheism" to expose "the murderous potential of religion," without which we cannot welcome the stranger in his/her difference (*Anatheism*, 39).

47. See, among others, Charles E. Winquist, *Desiring Theology*, and John D. Caputo, *The Weakness of God: A Theology of the Event*, as well as Kearney, *Anatheism*.

48. Later in the book Kearney defines *anatheism* as "a form of post-theism that allows us to revisit the sacred in the midst of the secular" (*Anatheism*, 57).

49. See Lauren Berlant, "Cruel Optimism," 20–36. Berlant defines cruel optimism as "the condition of maintaining an attachment to a problematic object," an object of desire representing "a cluster of promises" (20–21). Further, "cruel optimism . . . grows from a perception about the reasons people . . . choose to ride the wave of the system of attachment that they are used to" (23), whether that is, as for Berlant, the economic "life-building modalities that can no longer be said to be doing their work" (23) or, as I'm suggesting, the promises surrounding the humanist subject.

50. See Wendy Brown, the chapter titled "Wounded Attachments: Late Modern Oppositional Political Formations" in her *States of Injury: Power and Freedom in Late Modernity*. Brown suggests that the civil movements of the late twentieth century have been built around "the white masculine middle-class ideal," such that these new identities then always also carry a depressive wound in relation to this ideal that absorbs the subject in self- and civic transformation: "Politicized identities generated out of liberal, disciplinary societies, insofar are they are premised on exclusion from a universal ideal, require that ideal, as well as their exclusion from it, for their own continuing existence as identities" (65). Further and more seriously, in Brown's opinion, the white masculine middle-class ideal forecloses serious critique of capitalism, which hides itself within the aspirational ideal (61).

51. Alyda Faber, "'The Shock of Love' and the Visibility of 'Indecent' Pain: Reading the Woolf-Raverat Correspondence," 58–64. Faber reads the 1920s

correspondence between Virginia Woolf and Jacques and Gwen Raverat "when [Jacques] Raverat was dying of disseminated (multiple) sclerosis," concluding that "love . . . means the desire to stay near another person in their disorientation in the world, their wretchedness, their unloveability—the symptomatic excess of always unfinished efforts at social legitimation" (58). After Jacques' death, Gwen (who had been her husband's scribe in the Raverat-Woolf correspondence and who had tended Jacques during the excruciating passage of his disablement and death) "interprets loves as the possibility of exposing indecent pain"—referring in an exemplary way to the dying cry of Christ from Psalm 22: "My God, my God, why have you forsaken me?" and also to Goya etchings and parts of Shakespeare.

52. Kearns, "Suffering in Theory," 63.

53. Lennard J. Davis, "Why Is Disability Missing from the Discourse on Diversity?"

54. Also see Andrew Hacker and Claudia Dreifus, *Higher Education? How Colleges Are Wasting Our Money and Failing Our Kids—And What We Can Do About It*, 84.

55. David Mitchell and Sharon Snyder, *Narrative Prosthesis: Disability and the Dependence of Discourse*.

56. Davis, "Why Is Disability Missing?"

57. See Susan B. Miller, *Disgust: The Gatekeeper Emotion*.

58. Kearney likely does not so much disagree with this, given his assertion that "hermeneutics . . . begins in our nerve endings, organs and sensations," as simply address it by assertion (*Anatheism*, 46).

59. Jane Schaberg, *The Illegitimacy of Jesus: A Feminist Theological Interpretation of the Infancy Narratives*, 1.

60. Faber, "Post-Secular Poetics," 314.

61. Melancholia, according to Freud, has to do with a way of intellectually recognizing loss but refusing to give up the lost object—thus, it arises from an inability to integrate difference, new identities, change. Melancholy has to do with transcendent illusions, which we know not to be true but can't release— such that these assumptive illusions are now shaded with despair. Melancholy will go so far as craving a "deserved" punishment or destruction (for our "ambition" or "growth economics," for example); but even this craving continues the longing for the lost object, for that assures us of promised cosmological order and purpose. See Robert Pippin, "Nietzsche and the Melancholy of Modernity," 496.

62. Kelly Oliver, *Witnessing: Beyond Recognition*, 15.

63. The term *cripistemologies* is credited to Merri Lisa Johnson and has been taken up by disabilities-queer theorist Robert McRuer, who speaks of cripistemologies as "seriously twisted ways of knowing in the current global

order" among "subjects [who] are treated as refuse and refused basic services, protections, and dignities, but [who] themselves also generate a series of interconnected refusals—of privatized identities, national borders, diagnoses, compulsory forms of pleasure and consumption." From his lecture "Cripping Sex; or Globalizing Otherness," University of British Columbia, March 7, 2011.

64. Faber, "Post-Secular Poetics," 309.

65. William I. Miller, *The Anatomy of Disgust*, 136.

66. For example, workplaces can preclude hiring smokers without legal infringement of antidiscrimination laws in the United States, and insurance companies have charged obesity penalties. See Tom Baker, "Health Insurance as Governance: Wellness Programs and the New Responsibility to Be as Healthy as You Can."

67. Dorothee Soelle insists that Christianity precludes "distinguish[ing] between right and wrong suffering, between proletarian and middle class suffering" (*Suffering*, 106).

68. Mark Wenman, "William E. Connolly: Pluralism without Transcendence," 163.

69. See also Paul Tillich, *Systematic Theology*, 2:70.

70. Faber, "'The Shock of Love,'" 58.

71. Richard Mabey, *Weeds: In Defense of Nature's Most Unloved Plants*.

72. Jean-Luc Nancy, *Corpus*, 51, 63.

73. Urban studies theorists are not an optimistic bunch. Mike Davis recently delivered a presentation in Vancouver titled "The Battle of Rio and the Future of the Slum." Davis laid out the struggles of Rio de Janeiro, a city that will be home to the 2016 Summer Olympics, a city in one of what today constitute our shining, triumphant economic states—Brazil. Davis described the scene of some thousand-plus *favelas* (slums, shantytowns)—most of them subject to landslides ("slums begin with bad geology"), tightly packed into zones with no public space, verticalized (with buildings four to six stories high) and thus with extreme human density—no longer under state authority, but enduring a new feudalism of gangs and drug lords. Slum clearance in Rio, owing to increasing land value, has been going on since the 1970s—long before the beautification process that inevitably sets in with the hosting of the Olympics. See also Mike Davis, *Planet of Slums*, 122, 93, 99, 102, 108, 157.

James Howard Kunstler presented at the same Simon Fraser University–sponsored urban lecture series several years ago. He described—his vision assuming urbanization after peak oil—the veritable demise of strip malls and the slum-ification of suburbia, its sprawling ribbons of car-dependent infrastructure choking access to work, to livelihood. Suburbs, he predicts, will be our new slums—home of the poor, forced to live in the decrepit hulks of a past era, forced to spend precious dollars on long commutes. He wondered aloud with us as well about the food supply of our growing megacities, given that contemporary agriculture has been fingered as one of the biggest users of petroleum. See James Howard Kunstler, *The Long Emergency: Surviving the End of Oil, Climate Change, and Other Converging Catastrophes of the Twenty-First Century.*

These are grim pictures. Can we grow attached to a world outside the encryptment of idealism, outside "the global resonance machine"? Can we find it livable, lovable? Recalling the vilification of Christians during the calamities (earthquakes, famines, epidemics, and military disasters) of the early centuries of the Common Era, in *Forbearance and Compulsion: The Rhetoric of Religious Tolerance and Intolerance in Late Antiquity*, Maijastina Kahlos warns, "The forbearance of a community is particularly tested in times of crisis" (136).

74. Miller, *Anatomy of Disgust*, 234.

75. See George Lakoff, "How Occupy Wall Street's Moral Vision Can Beat the Disastrous Conservative Worldview."

5. THE BALLET OF THE GOOD CITY SIDEWALK: RELEASING THE OPTICS OF DISABILITY INTO SOCIAL FLESH

1. "The Winter Market" was republished in *Burning Chrome* (1986), a collection of Gibson's early short stories.

2. Sabine Heuser, *Virtual Geographies: Cyberpunk at the Intersection of the Postmodern and Science Fiction*, 55.

3. Doug Saunders, *Arrival City: The Final Migration and Our Next World*, 20. See * at bottom of page.

4. Kiran Desai's recent postcolonial novel *The Inheritance of Loss* (2006) gave a conceptual name to this dread. For sociological analysis of the humiliation experienced by immigrants, treated fictionally by Desai, see Suzanne Daley, "Chasing Riches from Africa to Europe and Finding Only Squalor," *New York Times*, May 25, 2011, A1. Colonialism creates a desire for and faith in the dream that a better life awaits in the metropolitan center.

5. A 35 percent increase in pregnancy losses on the West Coast of North America was registered in the mere weeks after the spectacle of Fukushima's meltdown; containment of nuclear contamination had not yet wholly been achieved as of Fall 2011. See Janette D. Sherman, M.D., and Joseph Mangano, "Is the Dramatic Increase in Baby Deaths in the U.S. a Result of Fukushima Fallout?" Also see Alex Roslin, "Fukushima Brings Big Radition Spikes to B.C.," 13, 15.

6. Jean Baudrillard, *The Ecstasy of Communication*, 52. See my chapter in *Spirit and the Politics of Disablement* on Haraway and wholeness as a basic as-

sumption toward which cyborg incarnations are directed, i.e, "Putting My Foot . . . Down."

7. Disabled bodies and our technological supplementation, i.e., prostheses, are often borrowed by transhumanist discourse; but as Fiona Kumari Campbell suggests in *Contours of Ableism: The Production of Disability and Abledness*, "the transhuman project" appears to any number of us "as founded on an unbridled form of ableism combined with an 'obsessive technological compulsion.'" Consequently, transhumanism "involves a meager shuffling of deckchairs," as it "reasserts systems of ranking bodies" and simply discounts the desirable fleshly virtues of sympathy for suffering, joy in pleasure, and awareness of death (73). See also James Overboe, "'Difference in Itself': Validating Disabled People's Lived Experience."

8. William E. Connolly, *A World of Becoming*, 135–42. The "global resonance machine," is, first of all, in a Deleuzean sense, "an abstract machine"— that is, "a cluster of energized elements of multiple types that enter into loose, re-enforcing conjugations as the whole complex both consolidates and continues to morph" (135). Connolly consequently uses the phrase *global resonance machine* to describe the concatenation of englobing neoliberal economics that have taken shape since the close of the Cold War. "The elements from which it was formed include loose energies of resistance released by the close of the Cold War, a world divided roughly into regionally based religions with significant internal minorities, uneven economic exchange between regions that correlate approximately with a distribution of religious differences, extreme dependence by hegemonic states upon foreign oil supplies, the rise of a world derivatives system that places the fate of numerous states in its hand while increasing the difficulty of identifying accountable agents responsible for that fate, the accentuated role of mass media in most regions, the hubris of many capitalist elites and dominant states about their ability to control the world, and simmering resentments felt by many on different sites in this machine about the place of morality and time in the human condition" (138).

9. Gibson's recent remarks (if the narrator within another short story can be taken to stand in for Gibson's authorial voice) on his "dystopian" trajectory might suggest that he himself imagines a spiritual, philosophical "silver lining" to this stream of thought. In his only other short story written specifically about Vancouver (this one about his own neighborhood and mine, namely, Kitsilano, known as "Kits"), a story entitled "Dougal Discarnate" (in *Darwin's Bastards*, 231–41), Gibson insinuates that Kits—a community constituted in the 1960s of ex-pat, United States–born hippies, conscientious objectors to the Vietnam War, and Greenpeace activists, and now by yoga aficianados become urban farmers—has a kind of irreality and anonymity that gives him what he had called, in "The Winter Market," "a kind of low-grade chill" (in *Burning Chrome*, 145). Vancouver author Douglas Coupland registers a similar sentiment: "Kits is

so perky that it almost begs the question, 'Does it have a dark side to it?' The answer may well be, no, which is, in itself, a kind of darkness" (*City of Glass: Douglas Coupland's Vancouver*, 82). Considering this, Gibson gives the former hippie neighborhood, where residents have indeed followed their bliss but not remembered their hippie, antimaterialist mantras, a dusting down via dystopian storytelling. Further, he explains, "One person's raging dystopia is another's hot immigration opportunity" (Gibson, quoted by Zsuzsi Gartner in "A Few Hundred Words from the Editor," *Darwin's Bastards*, 5). Gibson goes on—again in what seems a semi-autobiographical narrative voice—to suggest how he carried this dystopian impulse home with him from New York City before its' "regooding"—before the mayoral administration of Rudolf Guilliani and his "clean city" strategy, I presume. Gibson then explains the trajectory of desire within cyberpunk: "It was about wanting something else badly enough, the secret semi-utopian flipside, *the freedom of a splendidly broken metropolis . . . A lawlessness, and the absolute need to abide by the real, the unwritten rules" ("Dougal Discarnate," 238; italics added).

Having confessed to intentionally loosing this disorientation of values and loss of rules upon "discarnate" Kits, a neighborhood replete with white Sufis, multiple yoga centers, and the headquarters of Lulu Lemon Athletica, Gibson seems to be challenging the virtual epicenter of the "spiritual, but not religious"— incidentally headquartered at or at least resourced by Kit's now forty-year-old storefront, Banyen Books. Gibson says he is disappointed to learn his literature is called "dystopic" ("Dougal Discarnate," 237–38)—just as any number of us cosmological variants (or shall we call ourselves, borrowing comparable terminology, "Darwin's bastards"?) are disappointed to be reduced to our appearance, to "the disabled."

10. A proposed hospice at the University of British Columbia, located on what is now some of the most highly priced land in the city of Vancouver, encountered local fears of both "death/suffering contamination" and loss of property values when proposed in 2010–2011. And wars on poverty or homelessness can be more about fears of filth and contamination than about compassion for other humans. Even as Vancouver's tourist sublime sells the city and tries to create a sense of home by way of transcendentalization, cosmopolitanism can here also be riddled with a moral melancholy that is afraid to leave behind the shackles of restrictive humanism. Robert B. Pippin, in "Nietzsche and the Melancholy of Modernity," argues that Nietzsche's "death of God" should be read as flagging a cultural symptom—namely, melancholy, a "depressive attachment to a loss that has not been worked through" such that desire collapses, rather than as itself an ideational problem per se (501–2, 496).

11. Alyda Faber, "The Post-Secular Poetics and Ethics of Exposure in J. M. Coetzee's *Disgrace*," 309.

12. Michael Hardt and Antonio Negri, *Multitude: War and Democracy in the Age of Empire*, 192–93.

13. Mike Davis, "From *City of Quartz: Excavating the Future in Los Angeles*," 324.

14. Georges Canguilhem, "La monstruosité et le monstrueux," 28. Cited in Henri-Jacques Stiker, *A History of Disability*, 6–7.

15. Bill Hughes, "The Constitution of Impairment," 157.

16. Canguilhem, "La monstruosité et le monstrueux," 31. Quoted in Stiker, *History of Disability*, 8.

17. Canguilhem, "La monstruosité et le monstrueux," 31. Cited in Stiker, *History of Disability*, 207 n. 7.

18. Consequently, monstrosity, disability theorist Henri-Jacques Stiker insists, is tied to difference in a way that the fear of death is not. Stiker follows Canguilhem in warning of the murderous impulse that arises in response: "The peculiarity represented by malformation or deformation . . . provokes a kind of panic both internal and public. . . . In embryonic form the desire to kill, to see dead, is extended to all those who are stricken" (*History of Disability*, 9, 8). The temptation to murder has been implicit with the presumed breach of order; our historically quickest resolve toward that which shatters our expectations has been the desire to do injury thereto. Given the relative coincidence of attitudes toward disability with aspects of racism and colonialism—in fact "the history of colonialism—and its post/neocolonial aftermath—is indeed a history of mass disablement," encounters on streets can be riven not just with dread, but with this more radical fear. See Clare Barker and Stuart Murray, "Disabling Postcolonialism: Global Disability Cultures and Democratic Criticism," 230.

19. Jacques Derrida, *Of Grammmatology*, 5.

20. Hardt and Negri, *Multitude*, 190, 192.

21. Carlo Ratti and Anthony Townsend, "The Social Nexus," 45.

22. Ratti and Townsend, "Social Nexus," 48. This messier, riskier sense of the metropolis may be what cyberpunk novelist William Gibson has in mind, as he tries to communicate his conviction that a messy metropolis is far more livable. As much as cyberpunk has been taken to be dystopian, Gibson reminds us *au contraire* that "cities can be at their experiential richest during periods of relative disjunction. . . . Relative ruin, relative desertion, is a common stage of complex and necessary urban growth. Successful . . . cities are built up in a lacquering of countless layers: of lives, of choices encountered and made." He then offers his urban wisdom: "The city you want," especially "as a young creative person, is partially ruined, marked by areas of semimoribund in real estate values. Low rents, minimal policing, casual welding allowed on sidewalks" (Gibson, "Life in the Meta City," 89). If "ruin" is in this way an index of urban livability, then we must speak of forbearance. Forbearance, this form of love,

"means that your fastidiousness, your own purity of being, must be subordinated" to some public or generational sense of well-being (William I. Miller, *The Anatomy of Disgust*, 134).

23. Wendy Brown explains that "politicized identities generated out of liberal, disciplinary societies, insofar as they are premised on exclusion from a universal ideal, require that ideal" ("Wounded Attachments: Late Modern Oppositional Political Formations," 65).

24. Lennard Davis, "Nude Venuses, Medusa's Body, and Phantom Limbs: Disability and Visuality," 54. While working in ecological spirituality, Duane Elgin asks and responds to a similar question: "How grown up do you think humanity is?" In *Promise Ahead: A Vision of Hope and Action for Humanity's Future*, he gathers evidence to suggest that humanity has developed only to adolescence—fixated on appearance, reckless and oblivious of consequences. Now that we have entered into the Anthropocene, an epoch when humanity has become the evolutionary edge of Planet Earth, the soulful maturity of humanity becomes exceedingly imperative.

25. Jeremy Stolow, "Religion, Globalization and Visibility: Some Problems of Definition." Stolow has in mind the repression of images of dead soldiers, of children, of tortured bodies.

26. Tobin Siebers, *Disability Aesthetics*, 24, citing Sharon Snyder and David Mitchell. While the category of disability has presumed to include only the naturally obvious—a medical or biological pathology, an individual defect or symptom of disease, located within an obviously impaired body (hence, the judgment of inferiority and the "dis-ing" of disability), Siebers suggests that we trace this process of human disqualification through the symbols and stigmas attached to disability identity and back to the sociological and intercorporeal substrata—to how bodies feel in the presence of one another. He notes, "Bodily feelings are the substrata on which aesthetic responses"—that basis of intellectual ideation—"are based" ("Aesthetics and the Disqualification of Disability," 2).

Richard Sennett notices such aversion informing life on the city streets of North America, even shaping, then, expectations regarding public space itself: "[H]ostility marks now the way the homeless and mentally disturbed are seen on the streets; they are resented because they, who are obviously needy, are visible. The very sight of their need is an intrusion upon the self" (*The Conscience of the Eye: The Design and Social Life of Cities*, 45–46).

27. Siebers, "Aesthetics and the Disqualification of Disability," 2, 10.

28. Sennet, *Conscience of the Eye*, 45–46.

29. Hughes has critiqued the modernist assumption of the neutrality of vision, as has Sennett, but Hughes then twists this slightly differently, in a way that equally needs to be heard: "The sociological fascination with strangers, outsiders, pariahs, those existing on the margins of society is deeply rooted in

the voyeuristic tradition of symbolic interactionism—a species of theory and method that translates the Anglo-American, Liberal love of the underdog into a sociology of the misunderstood" who are to be remade—through the patronage of the system—in the image of normality ("Constitution of Impairment," 158).

30. Thinking across the disciplines from philosophy into neurobiology, William Connolly explains: "Affect, in its most elementary human mode, is an electrical-chemical charge that jolts or nudges you toward positive or negative action before it reaches the threshold of feeling or awareness" (*World of Becoming*, 150). "Thinking," he elsewhere explains, "operates on several registers of being" (*Why I Am Not a Secularist*, 148). Then citing scientist Joseph LeDoux, *The Emotional Brain*, Connolly details the body's multiple centers of intelligence—its multiple "brains," including the gut, the amygdala, the cerebellum, and the limbic brain (*Why I Am Not a Secularist*, 29). Stylings of the self, whether called "arts of the self" or "ascetic practices" (including those of Christian monasticism), Connolly suggests, have worked especially well on the interface between the gut, where disgust churns, and the lightning-fast responses of the brain region called the amygdala (ibid., 29, 36, 176). Current city living has, perhaps not surprisingly, been correlated through neuroepidemiological studies with increased activity in the amygdala, especially when persons' felt sense of personal space is invaded. See Alla Katsnelson, "The Stress of Crowds," 18.

31. Siebers, "Aesthetics and the Disqualification of Disability," 11.

32. Siebers, *Disability Aesthetics*, 26. Siebers gives his preliminary definition of aesthetics, based on the work of Alexander Baumgartner, on page 1 of the book.

33. And yet, can I really talk about the aesthetic repression of the suffering body in a city such as Vancouver, which hosted the 2010 Winter Olympics and its sideshow, the 2010 Winter Paralympic Games? Further to the point, when Sam Sullivan, then the mayor of Vancouver, received the passing of the Olympic flag from its 2006 Winter Olympic host city of Turin, his wheelchair had to be fitted with a holster enabling him to bear that flag. Yet with its games and goals still geared to the grid of ablism (and the Olympic goals of "stronger, higher, faster") and given that most Paralympians—let's be honest—are "able-disabled" and/or will burn out their bodies in feats that imitate the able, this outside, "Para"-Olympic afterthought simply proves the norm of the fit and able. P. David Howe notes that "the able-disabled," like wheelchair racer Chantel Petitclerc, have become "a part of contemporary sporting culture. However, it is only this very able disabled image that is recognized. For those whose bodies are more impaired the stigma remains." See his "The Tail is Wagging the Dog: Body Culture, Classification and the Paralympic Movement," 514.

As Sharon Snyder and David Mitchell explain, "[T]reating people with disabilities as an exception valorizes able-bodied norms of inclusion as the naturalized qualification of citizenship. . . . Ablenationalism results in the modern formation of disability as a discrete, sociological minority." Consequently, "nations assure themselves that a handful of exceptional cases entail an embrace of all" ("Introduction: Ablenationalism and the Geo-Politics of Disability," 122). This form of inclusion does not empty out the expectation of ablism and may rather continue but to inflate a script of "overcoming" tragedy, itself a "sacred myth" among many North American viewers. (The myth and media script of the supercrip are not without their boomerang repercussions upon bodies differing.) In fact, the Paralympian motto, "empower, inspire, and achieve," presumes just such a role.

Further, if sporting events might offer, in a postsecular environment, one of those shining, sacred moments of communal belonging "when something so overpowering happens that it wells up before you as a palpable presence and carries you along as on a powerful wave," as philosophers Hubert Dreyfus and Sean Dorrance Kelly argue, such events remain tied to the classical body—as these philosophers note, but do not critically trouble (*All Things Shining: Reading the Western Classics to Find Meaning in a Secular Age*, 194, 201). Mikhail Bakhtin distinguishes the classical body from the grotesque body in *Rabelais and His World*. The classical body is an "entirely finished, completed, strictly limited body, which is shown from the outside as something individual"; with its "valleys" covered over and its protuberances smoothed out, it also appears impenetrable (320). The grotesque body, on the other hand, "is never finished, never completed," and is perceived as persistently, whether generatively or spoilatively, "transgressing" its own limits (317). The advertising slogan for the Vancouver 2010 Winter Olympics was "Do You Believe?" to which the implied answer was, "Yes, I believe," in obvious imitation of an ecclesial call-and-response liturgy. So Dreyfus and Kelly's point is not inconsequential. But in the end, in Vancouver, Paralympic events, despite the equal billing in advertisements, were poorly attended and were not broadcast. People did not seem to expect that these games might offer the same kind of sacred moment. In a global city that toned itself even more toward the idealization in which it was already held, first in the process of vying for the Olympic bid, and then in readying itself for the event, the Paralympics seemed but to suffocate integral difference in a presumed, if obviously secondary, performance of inclusion. Thus, for example, the city banished the homeless from the streets and expanded its infrastructure, including housing, a portion of which was to be social housing units. Yet the balconies there could not accommodate wheelchair athletes. And the city could not afford, in the end, to turn these units over to social purposes. In his foreword to Stiker's *A History of Disability*, David Mitchell, summarizing Stiker's argument, writes, "The 'success' of integration" relies upon "a disturbing ideology . . . the social ideal of erasure' (xi). He explains, "A professed will to integration characterizes most epochs' treatment of people with disabilities, yet none to this point in history has committed themselves to a belief in the 'naturalness' of physical and cognitive differences" (ibid.). Mitchell concludes, "To elide our engagement with the reality of difference by promoting ambiguous language of civil(ized) homogeneity becomes tantamount to denying disability the uniqueness of its demands upon the individual and sociality alike" (ibid., xii). In other words, through policies of inclusion, "forbidden images" can be hidden in plain view.

34. Georges Canguilhem, *The Normal and the Pathological*, 240. Cited in Hughes, "Constitution of Impairment," 157.

35. William Connolly, "Suffering, Justice and the Politics of Becoming," in *Why I Am Not a Secularist*, 259–60.

36. Connolly, *World of Becoming*, 14; Connolly, "A World of Becoming," in *Democracy and Pluralism*, 228. Leon Wurmser, in "The Superego as Herald of Resentment," provides a psychoanalytic overview of resentment, reminding us that "resentment is the main motivational force in all phenomena of fanaticism" (388).

37. Connolly, *World of Becoming*, 6, 228, 61.

38. Connolly, "World of Becoming," 229–30, 228.

39. Adam Pottle, *Beautiful Mutants*, 23. Evolutionary realism hides a motivating cosmology, an assumed law of nature. Moreover, as Frans de Waal's work on primates suggests, our early evolutionary scenarios also refuse the evolutionary development of empathy.

40. To be sure, because disability is also often informed by background assumptions of karma, sin, or other moral contentions, its presence is also often riven with moral panic as well. I see this as a second-stage projection of reaction formation.

41. Sharon V. Betcher, "Becoming Flesh of My Flesh: Feminist and Disability Theologies on the Edge of Posthumanist Discourse," 112. What I'm discussing is distinguished from contemporary "wound culture"—as, for example, that of Oprah Winfrey's therapeutic confessional. A wound culture or confessional assumes the pivotal superiority of cultural normalcy and has converted the person into the central judge against himself or herself. Not to be denied is a certain pleasure or power found both in the process of reaching ever deeper into the body, biological and social, multiplying thereby the list of dysfunctions and the social exposure of "confessional" thereof. "Wound culture" contributes to making persons governable, "making them identify themselves in order to make them governable." See Shelly Tremain, *Foucault and the Government of Disability*, 6.

42. R. Chris Hassel, Jr., in "Hamlet's 'Too, Too Solid Flesh,'" reads Shakespeare's *Hamlet* in relation to the Lutheran theology current at Shakespeare's time and makes the point that Hamlet is uneasy with human frailty and so is paralyzed by his desire for perfect knowing and doing. Hassel quotes T. S. Eliot to suggest that "disgust . . . remains to poison life and obstruct action" (609). I hear that to be a fitting conclusion for many of us raised within the regime of modern reason. Nietzsche speaks likewise of "the will to truth"—to unconditionality and verifiability—"all out of a hatred for the contingency and suffering unavoidable in life" as leaden with *ressentiment*. See Pippin, "Nietzsche and the Melancholy of Modernity," 507.

43. Connolly, "Suffering, Justice and the Politics of Becoming," 264.

44. Stiker, *History of Disability*, 10.

45. William Connolly, linking disgust with various political discussions, including, for example, queer rights, likewise warns us that while "indispensable to life and ethical judgment," disgust "sometimes breeds ethical thoughtlessness" (*Why I Am Not a Secularist*, 163).

46. Alyda Faber, "*Dancer in the Dark*: Affliction and the Aesthetic of Attention," 86.

47. Friedrich Nietzsche, *The Gay Science*, 262. Also cited in Ellen K. Feder, "Tilting the Ethical Lens: Shame, Disgust and the Body in Question," 644–45.

48. Ash Amin and Nigel Thrift, *Cities: Reimagining the Urban*, 84.

49. Amin and Thrift, *Cities*, 143, 142.

50. Edward W. Soja, *Postmetropolis: Critical Studies of Cities and Regions*, 12–14.

51. Soja develops the notion of *synekism* from Aristotle's term *synoikismos*, meaning "the condition arising from dwelling together in one house," via insights accrued from also reading Henri Lefebvre (*Postmetropolis*, 12, 19). As Soja himself explains, "By reducing the friction of distance in everyday life while increasing population densities, human interaction and sociality were creatively intensified. More time and opportunity were opened for leisure, for arts and crafts, for religious ceremonies, for expanding the exchange of goods and services beyond the family unit, clan, or band, for adding new kinds of productive work, and for . . . *phronesis*, the practical and political reason involved in creating, managing, and sustaining a territorially defined community, a synekistic metropolis" (46). Further, economics and human spatial presence on the earth cannot be conceptually separated from this socially desirous energy.

52. As journalists Carlo Ratti and Anthony Townsend put it, speaking in relation to a wired city, "It turns out that sociability, not efficiency, is the true killer app for cities" ("The Social Nexus," 45). Or yet again, this time in the words of economist Edward Glaeser: "Cities bring opportunities for . . . the

creative inspiration that can result only from face-to-face contact with others. . . . Cities deliver the random exchanges of insight that generate new ideas for solving the most intransigent problems" ("Engines of Innovation," 50, 54). While any number of us bemoan human nature today, Gleason finds hope in precisely this social dimension: "Humankind continues to confront enormous challenges. . . . I have enormous confidence in the ability of *homo sapiens* to work miracles when people cooperate. Our greatest gift is our ability to learn from one another, to work together, to solve problems by leveraging our collective intelligence" (ibid., 55). But if so, then I suspect forbearance must become one of our civic virtues.

53. Timothy Morton, *Ecology without Nature: Rethinking Environmental Aesthetics*, 14.

54. For theological critique of a tehomaphobic, or chaos-aversive, scaling of transcendence, see Catherine Keller, *Face of the Deep: A Theology of Becoming*.

55. Judith Butler, *Precarious Life: The Powers of Mourning and Violence*, xiv, 27.

56. Judith Butler, *Giving an Account of Oneself*, 31–32. Butler is here summarizing the work of Adriana Cavarero, but in such a way, as I understand it, that it becomes the basis of her own exposition. Like Butler, John Caputo studies this intercorporeal zone commending not security measures, like purity practices or transcendence (which fortresses the body against life), but vigilance regarding the wasting and the cruelty of excessively carnivorous practices, given that the truth of flesh is its edibility—summarily, flesh feasts on flesh. In Caputo's words, "To become flesh is to become consumable"—as, for example, "to be eaten away by disease," to suffer "consumption" in its many forms, the most dreaded being the passage of a life, he wittily if wisely observes (Caputo, *Against Ethics*, 198–99). (On the other hand, "heart attacks"—he only half-jokes with us—"seem cleaner, crisper, more Greco-German deaths," since these tend to be brought on by working our agential selves to death; ibid., 199.) Such a practice of vigilance as he urges and which he sees as the core teachings of "the lyrical philosophical discourses" of Judeo-Christianity becomes nominally in Caputo's writing "the economy of obligation," of encountering flesh as flesh—unseating one from the locus of the masterful cogito into ethical, affective flesh of my flesh (ibid., 217).

57. Theologian Rebecca Parker, recognizing in a scene of personal terror this thin, yet persistent power of flesh's pulse to interrupt violence, arrives at a similar conclusion: "To live is to be haunted by presence, presence that will not let us rest easy with violence, presence that will not let us become numb to pain. . . . Nothing erases violence. . . . There is no universal strategy by which the deeds of evil are resisted and life has a chance of being restored. . . . But, sometimes, the power of presence gets us through, literally saves us to live on, to heal, to work for justice" (Rita Nakashima Brock and Rebecca Ann Parker,

Proverbs of Ashes: Violence, Redemptive Suffering, and the Search for What Saves Us, 211, 213). What we hold sacred—or rather, how we hold life sacred—transpires here, in our responsivity to flesh. "The point, after all," Caputo concludes, referring to the economy of obligation, "is to minimize the disasters and to multiply the several possibilities of joy," to loose "a joyful anarchy that celebrates the multiple forms which flesh can take, its heteromorphic possibilities for pleasure, affirmation, and joy" (*Against Ethics*, 212).

58. Diane Perpich, "*Corpus Meum*: Disintegrating Bodies and the Ideal of Integrity."

59. Perpich, "*Corpus Meum*," 79.

60. Julis Kristeva, *Strangers to Ourselves*.

61. Jean-Luc Nancy, *The Muses*, 35.

62. Mary-Jane Rubenstein, in *Strange Wonder: The Closure of Metaphysics and the Opening of Awe*, comments in this regard that "the end of . . . metaphysics says nothing more and nothing less than the senselessness of existing with an exhausted set of concepts; a configuration of sense comes undone, a philosophical, political or spiritual order decays" (117).

63. Nancy, as my comment suggests, is wary of the new spiritualities, which may actually participate in and even extend the kind of transcendentalist judgment of the Christian body, as he remains equally wary of nostalgic ontotheologies.

64. Jean-Luc Nancy, *Being Singular Plural*, 2.

65. Nancy, *Being Singular Plural*, xvi. See also Perpich, "*Corpus Meum*," 77, and Rubenstein, *Strange Wonder*, 112, 115.

66. Perpich, "*Corpus Meum*," 85.

67. Gibson, in "Dougal Discarnate," insinuates that the projects of health and ecological righteousness, these goodness projects, can occasion disconnection from the affective interface, that the project of the body—via yoga and being "spiritual, but not religious"—can lift away or freeze the lines of desire, veritably disarticulating one from the flesh of the real.

68. Frank Appleyard, "Religion Faces Extinction in Canada: Social Pressure Contributing to Rise in Non-Affiliation in Several Western Countries," *Vancouver Sun*, March 23, 2011, B4.

69. As Rubenstein emphasizes, Nancy's point, however, is to expose the exhaustion in the *cultural* discourse, in the capitalist banalization of bodies (*Strange Wonder*, 119). "The death of God" today occasions both a "loss of sense," inasmuch as we have organized ourselves on the logic of incorporeal sense in/forming "the body," and "a sense of . . . loss," which is anguish (Nancy, *Corpus*, 81).

70. *Flesh*, of course, has a considerable theological history that needs to be distinguished from this proposal for "social flesh." For Luther, reading the Pauline letters, *flesh* named an orientation toward the world based on human

reason, prudence, even practiced righteousness. Quoting Luther's phrases, R. Chris Hassel has written, "Luther's 'eight great traps' of the flesh included: 'external goods' like 'power, honors, parents, friends, family, relatives'; 'physical goods' like 'health, strength, beauty'; 'spiritual goods' like 'talent, memory, intellect, prudence'; 'knowledge and skills,' 'bodily and mental'; 'physical, that is human, wisdom,' as in 'liberal arts, philosophy, etc.'; 'intellectual wisdom'; 'heartfelt grace in righteousness, devotion, gifts of the Holy Spirit, etc., in meditations'; and finally 'God as He is revealed to us in His divine properties'" ("Hamlet's 'Too, Too Solid Flesh,'" 616). All of this was suspect because, as Luther saw it, humans are naturally egocentric, a condition that fouls reason, even our will to do good, even how we come to link up "properties" with God that we can then pretend to defend. Whereas "the prudence of flesh" seeks to know and to do perfectly, "the wisdom of spirit" or "the prudence of spirit knows that it must fail, but is cheerful in the companion knowledge of God's mercy" (613). On social flesh as a contemporary ethicopolitical ideal, see Chris Beasley and Carol Bacchi, "Envisaging a New Politics for an Ethical Future: Beyond Trust, Care and Generosity towards an Ethic of 'Social Flesh.'"

71. Nancy, as I read him, might worry that "incarnation" still assumes spirit as disembodied, coming into so as to signify flesh, or that flesh always already assumes meaning only as raised to the exponential of spirit (*Corpus*, 69, 75–76). His philosophy insists upon precisely the inverse thereof (87), which I take to be a spiritualizing of flesh, a way of living body as "mass"—without any transcendental outside. "The world of bodies has neither a transcendent nor an immanent sense. If we wanted to keep these words," he writes, "we'd have to say that one takes place within the other, but without being dialecticized—that one takes place *as* the other, and that such a taking-place is what *places* are. Places, places for the existence of being . . . *are* the exposition of bodies." In this account, "the neighbor would be what comes, what takes place in an approach" (89, 91). To be sure, Nancy fears that any theological evocation threatens to generate significance outside the transpiration of flesh, that "theology" actually thereby closes off the senses. "God, Death, Flesh: the three-fold name of the entire body of onto-theology," Nancy writes, suggesting how a whole system can be carried in a concept or a trinity thereof (75). Yet as I'll explicate more fully shortly, he does not appear to close off the use of philosophical or spiritual technologies.

72. Jurgen Moltmann, *The Spirit of Life: A Universal Affirmation*, 43.
73. Perpich, "*Corpus Meum*," 87.
74. Amin and Thrift, *Cities*, 143.
75. Snyder and Mitchell, "Introduction: Ablenationalism," 113.
76. Gilles Deleuze, "To Have Done with Judgment," 126–35.
77. Lennard Davis, *Bending over Backwards: Disability, Dismodernism, and other Difficult Positions*, 32.

78. Even political theorist William Connolly, in *A World of Becoming*, re-calls the blind seer, Tiresias, in Sophocles' *Antigone* augering the vagaries of the ancient city so as to challenge cultural presumptions. More precisely, Connolly borrows from this ancient tradition of conceiving persons living with disability as more affectively aware so as to enable today a certain spiri-tual art of the self. Connolly first explains the role of affect in intelligence: "Affect consists of relatively mobile energies with powers that flow into con-scious, cultural feeling and emotion. . . . The human being thus absorbs pressures from the world that both help to compose its subjectivity and ex-ceed it."

Then he explains what he considers to be Tiresias's relationship to affect, a relationship differently developed and more distinctly than would be the case in those typically consumed with a sense of personal agency: "Seers make more of such a network of inter-involvements than most of us do" (151). More decisively, "a seer sees how crucial shifts in the pace of events and the timing of responses are to the world, while heroes and rulers invested with the hubris of consummate agency often fail to appreciate how they can be-come pawns of time" (ibid., 153). This latter phenomenon likely has to do with the ways in which normalcy "reaches into the very soul" so as to hold the body hostage, as disabilities theorist Fiona Kumari Campbell asserts (*Contours of Ableism*, 6).

For Connolly, what this affective sense, narratively lodged in disability, makes possible is an ascetic technology—an attunement to durational time, to the "concatenation of contingent events, hubris, and timing" that can be at-tentively and wisely traversed, as distinct from the sociocultural and political pace, itself incessantly informed by ontotheology, whether in the form of fate, secular progress, or God (*World of Becoming*, 152). Hidden away in disability as in a cleft, this affective knowledge can be practiced by all: "The seer does read omens . . . in a way that has affinities with how sensitive thinkers strive to read natural and cultural signs during fateful moments in modern life, when a new disequilibrium is emerging and established modes of knowledge and moral judgment may be insufficient." In other words, "disability"—the seer/ing wis-dom of blind Tiresias—marks "this disposition toward exquisite sensitivity" to a universe without overarching providence (ibid., 156, 159). However, the seer was commonly kept at a distance, consulted only in ominous times—he or she was as marginalized as "the disabled" today remain. Might not such existential resentment as keeps disability marginal thus preclude the very wisdom practice Connolly urges on us?

79. Kathryn Marie Dudley, *The End of the Line: Lost Jobs, New Lives in Postindustrial America*, 60.

80. Alfred North Whitehead, the father of process philosophy, might have described this as the difference between an orientation toward "causal effi-

cacy" and an orientation toward "presentational immediacy," a felt embeddedness within which one discerns action, rather than a relationship to a distantiated horizon of thought.

81. Scott DeShong, "The Nightmare of Health: Metaphysics and Ethics in the Signification of Disability," 275.

82. Matthew B. Crawford, *Shop Class as Soulcraft: An Inquiry into the Value of Work*, suggests that the creation of a culture of "knowledge workers," the form of idealism that takes leave of material reality, likewise "leads persons to feel useless" and "occasions a feeling of being dispirited" (3, 5).

83. DeShong, "Nightmare of Health," 271.

84. Iris Murdoch, *The Sovereignty of Good*, 91.

6. "TAKE MY YOGA UPON YOU" (MATT 11:29): A SPIRIT/UAL *PLI* FOR THE GLOBAL CITY

A version of this chapter was published in *Polydoxy: Theology of Multiplicity and Relation*, edited by Catherine Keller and Laurel Schneider (London and New York: Routledge, 2010) (ISEN 978-0-415-78136-7).

1. Ash Amin and Nigel Thrift, *Cities: Reimagining the Urban*, 4.
2. Gilles Deleuze and Felix Guattari, *What is Philosophy?* 3.
3. Todd May, *Gilles Deleuze: An Introduction*, 148.
4. Gianni Vattimo, *After Christianity*, 104, 105–6.
5. Edward W. Soja, "Seeing Nature Spatially," 184.
6. Gayatri Chakravorty Spivak, "Globalicities: Terror and Its Consequences," 74.
7. Edward W. Soja, *Postmetropolis:Critical Studies of Cities and Regions*, 148.
8. Engin Isin, "Metropolis Unbound: Legislators and Interpreters of Urban Form," 123; citing Robin Bloch, "The Metropolis Inverted: The Rise and Shift to the Periphery and the Remaking of the Contemporary City," 225. Also quoted in Soja, *Postmetropolis*, 231.
9. Zygmunt Bauman, *Liquid Modernity*, 31–39.
10. Mike Davis, *Planet of Slums*, 20.
11. Talal Asad, *Genealogies of Religion: Discipline and Reasons of Power in Christianity and Islam*, 11.
12. Mark C. Taylor, *After God*, xvi, 3, 44, 55, 64.
13. Anthony Giddens, *Runaway World: How Globalization Is Reshaping Our Lives*, ch. 3, "Tradition." Giddens notes the proliferation of addictions worldwide in the face of detraditionalization. He also insists that "fundamentalism is a child of globalization," owing to context dislocation (49). Even as Giddens critiques fundamentalism for its rejection of ambiguity and multiplicity of any kind, such as interpretation (49), he challenges cosmopolitans to think through the concern he believes to be raised by fundamentalism: "Can we live in a world where nothing is sacred?"—a question he himself answers in the negative,

leaving us to contemplate how we rouse the passions of cosmopolitans (50). See also Bauman, *Liquid Modernity*, 3–4.

14. Bruce Alexander, *The Globalization of Addiction: A Study in Poverty of Spirit*, 61. This failure of meaning and mattering, which Alexander labels a "poverty of spirit," affects those living a well-resourced life and the resource-excluded equally: "The destruction of psychosocial integration is shockingly obvious in the homeless, the physically violated and the destitute, but . . . it affects the protected, safe and wealthy with a similar force" (ibid.). Dislocation exacerbates the self-enclosure of the mobile, individualistic personality, which can itself be reinforced by hard technology—iPods, the internet, private domestic habitats. Humans wither under the loss of "'the protective covering of cultural institutions,'" even when those seem to have been willingly shed (ibid., 91, quoting Karl Polanyi). Without obligations, ties, loyalties, customs, rituals, or kin folds, the psyche may be thrown into a vacuum of meaning. Given that "free market society exploits human cultures in the same relentless way that it exploits the earth's minerals . . . even the people who benefit the most from free-market society," Alexander insists, "cannot escape the feeling that something fundamental is missing from their lives of affluence, longevity and independence." For the now globally mobile personality, everything is possible, nothing matters. The loss of "social consciousness" and therefore of generosity, Alexander concludes, stems from people's felt social and political irrelevance (ibid., 105, 93).

15. Mark I. Wallace writes: "The critical analysis of the God of philosophical theism paves the way for a countermetaphysical, biblically-rooted, and earth-centered reenvisioning of the Spirit as the 'green face' of God in a world under siege" ("God Is Underfoot: Pneumatology after Derrida," 197). See also sources as diverse as Laurel Kearns and Catherine Keller, eds., *EcoSpirit*, and Wolfhart Pannenberg, *Toward a Theology of Nature: Essays on Science and Faith*.

16. See, for example, Gianni Vattimo, *After Christianity*; John D. Caputo and Gianni Vattimo, *After the Death of God*; and Catherine Keller, *Apocalypse Now and Then*, ch. 7, "Spirit: Counter-Apocalyptic In/Conclusion"; *Face of the Deep: A Theology of Becoming*, ch. 14, "Pneumatic Foam"; and *On the Mystery: Discerning God in Process*, ch. 8, "Open Ending: Spirit in Process."

17. Santiago Zabala, "Christianity and the Death of God," 37, 35–36.

18. John D. Caputo, "The Power of the Powerless," 145.

19. Robert B. Pippin, "Nietzsche and the Melancholy of Modernity," 495–520.

20. John D. Caputo, *The Weakness of God: A Theology of the Event*.

21. Alexander, *Globalization of Addiction*, 105.

22. Alexander, *Globalization of Addiction*, 93.

23. Catherine Keller, "Pluralism Is Not Enough."

24. Gilles Deleuze, *The Fold: Leibniz and the Baroque*.

25. Leonie Sandercock, *Towards Cosmopolis*, 125.

26. Timothy Morton, *Ecology without Nature: Rethinking Environmental Aesthetics*, 14.

27. William Connolly, *Why I Am Not a Secularist*, 5. It is for this reason that William Connolly argues against being identified as a "secularist."

28. May, *Gilles Deleuze*, 35.

29. So, for example, during modernity Christianity was cathected to high-culture media and was operationalized as "truth speech," as preaching and teaching producing "belief."

30. Tibetan Buddhism may see itself as threatened with extinction, given its expulsion from Tibet. While some religious communities so threatened choose to pull inward to preserve their language, their practices, and their culture, Tibetan Buddhism has chosen to give itself away—to give away, that is, its perspective on the world: compassion.

31. Sharon V. Betcher, "Christianity as Path and Practice," 19.

32. See *Eve and the Firehorse* (2005), a Vancouver-based movie directed by Julia Kwan about growing up religious and ethnically Chinese. At one point, Eve experiences a somewhat dreamlike dance taking place at night in her living room; the dancers are the crucified Jesus, Kuan Yin, and Buddha. The movie presents an interesting study of the continuum of religious hybridities. Whereas Eve's mother creates a nonintegral syncretism of practices, and whereas Eve's sister finds life in belonging within the singularity of conversion to Catholicism, Eve herself hybridizes the Chinese belief about children born in the year of the firehorse (best wisdom: drown them) with Christian baptism, acting as her own priest in a bathtub ritual to reimagine the horizon of her life.

33. Jay McDaniel, *Living from the Center: Spirituality in an Age of Consumerism*, 5, 28.

34. The notion or sense of the sacred as "manifold" has been developed in relation to the logic of multiplicity—as distinct from a theology of "the One"—in Catherine Keller and Laurel C. Schneider, eds., *Polydoxy: Theology of Multiplicity and Relation*. In his essay in the collection, theologian Roland Faber explains, citing Gilles Deleuze, "Multiplicity is . . . an 'irruption of incompossibilities on the same stage' . . . without pre-established unity. . . . Instead of a divine Law that establishes a harmony of *exclusion* of the incompossible from a world of divine consistency (Leibniz), poly-harmonic multiplicity consists of any number of multiplicities of *reciprocal and reciprocally incomplete* series of events or reinventions of harmonic becoming" ("The Sense of Peace: A Para-Doxology of Divine Multiplicity," 41). Keller and Schneider explain in their introduction, "If multiplicity addresses the diversity unfolding as a cosmos, and relationality addresses the interconnections that enfold creatures one in another, . . . the fold, the *pli*, . . . distinguishes multiplicity from mere plurality." And, they note, "That enfolded and unfolding relationality"—or "manifold"—"suggests not a relation

between many separate ones but between singularities, events of becoming folded together, intersecting, entangled as multiples" (*Polydoxy*, 7). Explicating the fierce thought of Anne Conway, Keller (in her essay in *Polydoxy*, "Be a Multiplicity") thinks with Conway to suggest that Spirit, like a "manifold"—the "lines of force or flight" that riddle the crease of the fold in being—"yields a force of cohesion," distinctly in and through the pressures of multiplicity, even as incompossibities (88).

35. Karl Jaspers, cited in Susan Brooks Thistlethwaite, "Why Are Our Cities Dying?" 19–21. A similar claim is made by Bruce Lerro, *From Earth Spirits to Sky Gods*: "Just as God becomes a transcendental power beyond the power of human influence, so the upper castes seem to occupy the same unapproachable position relative to the lower classes."(303). Cited by Laurel C. Schneider in *Beyond Monotheism: A Theology of Multiplicity* (188).

36. bell hooks, *Yearning: Race, Gender, and Cultural Politics*, 31. Cited in Soja, *Postmetropolis*, 281.

37. Mohandas K. Gandhi, *Vows and Observances*, 159, 155. Neighbor love is the essence of the observance Gandhi called "swadeshi."

38. Gandhi, *Vows and Observances*, 155.

39. Bauman, *Liquid Modernity*.

40. Ashis Nandy, *Intimate Enemy: Loss and Recovery of Self under Colonialism*, 49.

41. Gandhi, *Vows and Observances*, 149–50, 90.

42. Nandy, *Intimate Enemy*, 51.

43. Huston Smith, "Western Philosophy as a Great Religion," 217.

44. Ravi Ravindra, *Christ the Yogi: A Hindu Reflection on the Gospel of John*.

45. Carter insists that the NRSV's "God's yoke is easy'" is a poor translation; here I follow his suggestion that the opposition between Roman power and "infinite mercy" sets up the contrast of opposing yokes (126).

46. Bonnie Thurston, *Religious Vows, the Sermon on the Mount, and Christian Living*, 90.

47. Paul Knitter, *Introducing Theologies of Religions*, 209.

48. Marie E. Isaacs, *The Concept of Spirit: A Study of Pneuma in Hellenistic Judaism and Its Bearing on the New Testament*.

49. See also Mircea Eliade, *The Sacred and the Profane: The Nature of Religion*, 137.

50. Jurgen Moltmann, *The Spirit of Life: A Universal Affirmation*, 43.

51. Moltmann, *Spirit of Life*, 43.

52. Swanson argues for "the non-transferable quality of sacred places": graves, memorials, pilgrimage sites, and indigenous territories. I do not disagree with his respect for these places, but we must keep in mind that any number of our bodies have had to make sense of unknown spaces, have had to use religious obligations to weave something of "the space of freedom in which

the living being can unfold" (Moltmann, *Spirit of Life*, 43). But the space of ultimate freedom always comes nonetheless by way of a yoke, e.g., neighbor love—as Gandhi also surmised.

53. Connolly, *Why I Am Not a Secularist*, 49.

54. To be sure, Caputo writes, "obligations come over us from the other whose transcendence shocks our freedom and autonomy" (*Against Ethics*, 27). But Caputo links this transcendence with an inherent "neediness." Contrarily, Gandhi, observing the British occupying forces in India, knew that oppressors' lives were equally skewed by colonialism. He also felt obligated in relation to them. Cosmopolitans suffer a vacuum of meaning: this obligates me. If we are all flesh, if flesh is life, if flesh means exposure, if flesh names a certain vulnerability (ibid., 158), has Caputo not introduced a shortcut to obligation that preserves the superiority or "humanism" of the economically well-situated?

55. Diprose herself insists that humanism retains superiority over "the needy" when she notes that individual sovereignty is tied to a certain metaphysics of presence (*Corporeal Generosity*, 8).

56. Theodore W. Jennings, "A God without Sovereignty."

57. The movie *Fearless* (1993), starring Jeff Bridges, also provides some phenomenological sense of this passage.

58. See also Matousek, "Savage Grace: The Spirituality of Illness," 104–11.

59. Joseph Sittler, "A Theology for Earth," 373.

60. For Nahman, as for other Kabbalists, what accrues in our world as disability might rather be owed to "the superlative distinction of the perfection of their level and stature." In other words, the culturally supposed deformities of the seven beggars—blindness, hunched back, stuttering, deafness, amputation— turn out to be but concealing cloaks of their virtue. In a parallel to the act of circumcision that binds Jewish males to spiritual memory, the teaching tales of "The Seven Beggars" suggest that "'the world of reality we live in is really an illusion'" (Wolfson, "Cut that Binds," 121).

61. Keith Ansell Pearson, *Germinal Life: The Difference and Repetition of Deleuze*, 3.

62. May, *Gilles Deleuze*, 47, 55.

63. Pearson, *Germinal Life*, 3.

64. F. Scott Fitzgerald, *The Crack-Up*, 74.

65. Connolly, *Why I Am Not a Secularist*, 47, 16.

66. Pramila Jayapal, "India's Silent but Singing Revolution."

67. Martin Luther, *The Freedom of a Christian*, 24, 50.

68. Mark D. Tranvik, "Translator's Introduction: Martin Luther's Road to Freedom," 28.

69. Masao Abe, "Kenotic God and Dynamic Sunyata," 30. Abe suggests two distinctions between Buddhist *sunyata* and Luther's sense of Christian freedom: First of all, Luther maintained a religious anthropocentrism such

that the human could not be read as servant of nature, which I've here amended. Second, Luther's explication was of course theocentric, as distinct from the Buddhist sense of "awakening to the nonsubstantiality and the interdependence of everything in the universe" (31). While the deconstruction of Christianity, as here read through Nancy, will bring us closer to Abe's Buddhist point, I'm hoping to maintain a certain affective distinction from it.

70. Tranvik, "Translator's Introduction," 29.

71. Luther, *Freedom of a Christian*, 83.

72. Tranvik, "Translator's Introduction," 29.

73. Tranvik, editor's note in Luther, *Freedom of a Christian*, 49 n. 1.

74. Abe, "Kenotic God," 31.

75. Wolfson, summarizing Nietzsche's conclusions, "Cut that Binds," 150 n. 124.

76. See also Schneider, *Beyond Monotheism*, 162.

77. H. Richard Niebuhr, *Faith on Earth: An Inquiry into the Structure of Human Faith*, 1.

78. Roger Haight, presentation, Summer Seminar in Comparative Theologies, Union Theological Seminary, New York, June 2009. Haight contends that Christianity's doctrine of Spirit, since Augustine, has been concealed in its doctrine of grace.

79. Schneider, *Beyond Monotheism*, xi, 162.

80. In his sermon on the beatitude "Blessed are the poor in spirit," Meister Eckhardt describes this poverty of spirit, which he defines as wanting, knowing, and possessing nothing, even as it applies to his God concept: "The authorities say that God is a being, and a rational one, and that [God] knows all things. I say that God is neither being nor rational, and that [God] does not know this or that." Meister Eckhart, "Sermon 52: Beati Pauperes spiritu, quoniam ipsorum est regnum caelorum (Mt.5.3)," in *Meister Eckhart: The Essential Sermons, Commentaries, Treatises, and Defense*, 199–203.

81. Translated as "increase our faith," Luke 17:5 reads in Greek "*prostheses emin pistin.*"

82. Joanna Zylinska, "'The Future . . . Is Monstrous': Prosthetics as Ethics," 217–18.

83. Donna Haraway, *Simians, Cyborgs, and Women: The Reinvention of Nature*, 249.

84. David M. Halperin, *Saint Foucault: Towards a Gay Hagiography*, 66.

85. Vitor Westhelle. *The Scandalous God: The Use and Abuse of the Cross*, 41, 40.

86. Cited in Eberhard Bethge, *Dietrich Bonhoeffer: Eine Biographie*, 174.

87. David Wells, *Prosthesis*, 1.

88. Tyler Roberts, *Contesting Spirit: Nietzsche, Affirmation, Religion*, 70.

89. Roberts, *Contesting Spirit*, 73, 66, 68, 66.

90. Philip Sheldrake, *Spaces for the Sacred: Place, Memory and Identity*, 147.
91. Sheldrake, *Spaces for the Sacred*, 147.
92. Michel Foucault, "Friendship as a Way of Life," 136–37.
93. Foucault, "Friendship," 149–150.
94. Ronald Bogue, "The Minor," 115. The notion of "becoming-animal" echoes the sensibilities of some indigineous peoples who contend that humans must learn from the animals, our elders, which were born or learned to be content, to be at peace, with nature. Song and mask rituals enact this teaching.

A. B. "Liveability Ranking: Where the Livin' Is Easiest." *The Economist*, February 21, 2011. http://www.economist.com/blogs/gulliver/2011/02/liveability_ranking.

Abe, Masao. "Kenotic God and Dynamic Sunyata." In *The Emptying God: A Buddhist-Christian-Jewish Conversation*, ed. John B. Cobb, Jr. and Christopher Ives, 3–65. Maryknoll, N.Y.: Orbis, 1990.

Aitken, Ellen Bradshaw. *Jesus' Death in Early Christian Memory: The Poetics of the Passion*. Novum Testamentum et Orbis Antiquus 53. Gottingen: Vandenhoeck and Ruprecht, 2004.

Alexander, Bruce. *The Globalization of Addiction: A Study in Poverty of Spirit*. Oxford: Oxford University Press, 2008.

Allende, Isabel. *City of the Beasts*. Trans. Margaret Sayers Peden. New York: HarperCollins, 2002.

Althaus-Reid, Marcella. *Indecent Theology: Theological Perversions in Sex, Gender and Politics*. London and New York: Routledge, 2000.

———. "'A Saint and a Church for Twenty Dollars': Sending Radical Orthodoxy to Ayacucho." In *Interpreting the Postmodern: Responses to "Radical Orthodoxy,"* ed. Rosemary Radford Ruether and Marion Grau, 107–18. New York and London: T. and T. Clark International, 2006.

———. "*El Tocado* (*Le Toucher*): Sexual Irregularities in the Translation of God (The Word) in Jesus." In *Derrida and Religion: Other Testaments*, ed. Y. Sherwood and K. Hart, 393–405. London and New York: Routledge, 2004.

Amin, Ash, and Nigel Thrift. *Cities: Reimagining the Urban*. Cambridge: Polity Press, 2002.

Anidjar, Gil. "Secularism." *Critical Inquiry* 33 (2006): 52–77.

Appleyard, Frank. "Religion Faces Extinction in Canada: Social Pressure Contributing to Rise in Non-Affiliation in Several Western Countries." *Vancouver Sun*, March 23, 2011, B4.

Armstrong, Karen. *The Case for God*. New York: Anchor, 2010.

Asad, Talal. *Genealogies of Religion: Discipline and Reasons of Power in Christianity and Islam.* Baltimore: The Johns Hopkins University Press, 1993.

Augustine. *City of God.* Trans. Henry Bettenson. New York: Penguin, 1972.

Avila, Charles. *Ownership: Early Christian Teaching.* Maryknoll, N.Y.: Orbis, 1983.

Baker, Tom. "Health Insurance as Governance: Wellness Programs and the New Responsibility to Be as Healthy as You Can." Paper presented at Knowledge Brokers and Knowledge Formats: A Symposium, Inspired by the Work of Richard Ericson. Green College, University of British Columbia, Vancouver, September 24, 2011.

Bakhtin, Mikhail. *Rabelais and His World.* Trans. Helene Iswolsky. Cambridge, Mass: MIT Press, 1968.

Bakke, Ray. "Urbanization and Evangelism: A Global View." *Word and World* 19, no. 3 (1999): 225–35.

Barbedette, Gilles. "The Social Triumph of the Sexual Will: A Conversation with Michel Foucault." Trans. B. Lemon. *Christopher Street* 6, no. 4 (1982): 36–41.

Barker, Clare, and Stuart Murray. "Disabling Postcolonialism: Global Disability Cultures and Democratic Criticism." *Journal of Literary and Cultural Disability Studies* 4, no. 3 (2010): 219–36.

Barnes, Trevor J. "Placing Ideas: Genius Loci, Heterotopia and Geography's Quantitative Revolution." *Progress in Human Geography* 28, no. 5 (2004): 565–95.

Bartlett, Lawrence. "7-Billionth Person Expected this Fall: Baby Will Likely Be Born in Asia, Where Major Shift to Urban Areas Is Underway." *Vancouver Sun*, June 22, 2011, B5.

St. Basil the Great. *On the Holy Spirit.* Yonkers, N.Y.: St. Vladimir's Seminary Press, 1980.

Batstone, David, Edourdo Mendietta, Lynne Lorentzen, and Dwight D. Hopkins, eds. *Liberation Theologies, Postmodernity, and the Americas.* New York: Routledge, 1997.

Baudrillard, Jean. *The Ecstasy of Communication.* Trans. Bernard Schultze and Caroline Schultze. New York: Semiotext(e), 1988.

Bauckham, Richard. " 'Only the Suffering God Can Help': Divine Passibility in Modern Theology." *Themelios* 9, no. 3 (1984): 6–12.

Bauman, Zygmunt. *Globalization: The Human Consequences.* New York: Columbia University Press, 1998.

———. *Liquid Fear.* Cambridge: Polity, 2006.

———. *Liquid Modernity.* Cambridge: Polity, 2000.

———. *Wasted Lives: Modernity and Its Outcasts.* Cambridge: Polity, 2004.

Beasley, Chris, and Carol Bacchi. "Envisaging a New Politics for an Ethical Future: Beyond Trust, Care and Generosity Towards an Ethic of 'Social Flesh.'" *Feminist Theory* 8, no. 3 (2007): 279–98.

Beaverstock, Jonathan V., Peter J. Hubbard, and John Rennie Short. "Getting Away With It? The Changing Geographies of the Global Super-Rich." Research Bulletin 93, *Geoforum* 35, no. 4 (2004): 401–07.

Bennett, Jane. *Vibrant Matter. A Political Ecology of Things.* Durham, N.C.: Duke University Press, 2010.

Berg, Nate. "The Big Fix: Vancouver Aims to 'End' Homelessness." *The Atlantic Cities: Place Matters*, October 24, 2011, http://www.theatlanticcities.com /housing/2011/20/vancouver-aims.

Berger, Knute. "Righteous Rage: From Traffic-Circle Violence to Bike Rage, Trouble Is Breaking Out over Seattle's Best Intentions." *Seattle Magazine*, October 2008, 144.

Berges, Ulrich. "The Literary Construction of the Servant in Isaiah 40–55." *Scandinavian Journal of the Old Testament* 24, no.1 (2010): 28–38.

Berlant, Lauren. "Cruel Optimism." *Difference: A Journal of Feminist Cultural Studies* 17, no. 3 (2006): 20–36.

Beseliu, Ion, and Kees Doevendans. "Planning, Design and the Post-Modernity of Cities." *Design Studies* 23, no. 3 (2002).

Betcher, Sharon V. "Becoming Flesh of My Flesh: Feminist and Disability Theologies on the Edge of Posthumanist Discourse." *Journal of Feminist Studies in Religion* 26, no. 2 (2010): 107–39.

———. "Christianity as Path and Practice." *Canada Lutheran* 21, no. 2 (2006): 32–34.

———. "The Politics of Fear, the Path of Faith." In Trozzo, *Stand Boldly*, 33–60.

———. *Spirit and the Politics of Disablement.* Minneapolis: Fortress, 2007.

Bethge, Eberhard. *Dietrich Bonhoeffer: Eine Biographie.* 3rd ed. Munich: Kaiser, 1967.

Bibby, Reginald. *Restless Gods.* Toronto: Stoddart, 2002.

Bidini, Dave. "The Myths of Vancouver's Superiority Do the City a Disservice." *National Post*, June 25, 2011.

Black, Jay. "Hiding the Homeless: A History of Olympic Street-Sweep Laws." *Megaphone: Vancouver's Street Paper*, issue 45, December 29, 2009.

Blake, William. "The Tyger." In *The Complete Poetry and Prose of William Blake*, ed. David V. Erdman, commentary by Harold Bloom. New revised edition. New York: Random House Digital, 1982.

Blenkinsopp, Joseph. *Isaiah 40–55: A New Translation with Introduction and Commentary.* Anchor Bible, vol. 19a. New York: Doubleday, 2002.

Bloch, Robin. "The Metropolis Inverted: The Rise and Shift to the Periphery and the Remaking of the Contemporary City." Ph.D. dissertation, University of California–Los Angeles, 1994.

Bock, Charles. *Beautiful Children.* New York: Random House, 2008.

Boddy, Trevor, curator and producer. Vancouverism: Architecture Builds the City. Exhibit, January 16 to March 27, 2010. Woodwards Atrium,Vancouver.

Bogue, Ronald. "The Minor." In Stivale, *Gilles Deleuze*, 110–20.

Bond, George D. "Theravada Buddhism's Meditations on Death and the Symbolism of Initiatory Death." *History of Religions* 19, no. 3 (1980): 237–58.

Bonhoeffer, Dietrich. *Letters and Papers from Prison.* Ed. Eberhard Bethge. Trans. Reginald H. Fuller. London: SCM Press, 1953. Abridged ed., London: SCM Press, 2001.

Boo, Katherine. *Behind the Beautiful Forevers: Life, Death, and Hope in a Mumbai Undercity.* New York: Random House, 2012.

Borg, Marcus J. *Meeting Jesus Again for the First Time.* San Francisco: HarperSanFrancisco, 1994.

De Botton, Alain. *Religion for Atheists: A Non-Believer's Guide to the Uses of Religion.* New York: Pantheon Books, 2012.

Bowden, Charles. *Murder City: Ciudad Juarez and the Global Economy's New Killing Fields.* New York: Nation Books, 2010.

Boyer, M. Christine. "From Dreaming the Rational City." In Bridge and Watson, *Blackwell City Reader*, 39–45.

Bridge, Gary, and Sophie Watson, eds. *The Blackwell City Reader.* Malden, Mass.: Blackwell, 2002.

———. "Introduction to Part II: Reading Urban Economics." In Bridge and Watson, *Blackwell City Reader*, 105–6.

Brock, Rita Nakashima. *Journeys by Heart: A Christology of Erotic Power.* New York: Crossroad, 1992.

Brock, Rita Nakashima, and Rebecca Ann Parker. *Saving Paradise: How Christianity Traded Love of This World for Crucifixion and Empire.* Boston: Beacon, 2008.

———. *Proverbs of Ashes: Violence, Redemptive Suffering, and the Search for What Saves Us.* Boston: Beacon, 2001.

Brown, Nicholas. "Marxism and Disability: Review of *Aesthetic Nervousness: Disability and the Crisis of Representation* by Ato Quayson." *Meditations: Journal of the Marxist Literary Group* 23, no. 2 (2008): 187–92. www.meditations journal.org/articles/marxism-and-disability. Accessed March 9, 2009.

Brown, Peter. *Poverty and Leadership in the Late Roman Empire.* Hanover, N. H.: University Press of New England, 2002.

Brown, Wendy. *Regulating Aversion: Tolerance in the Age of Identity and Empire.* Princeton: Princeton University Press, 2006.

———. *States of Injury: Power and Freedom in Late Modernity.* Princeton: Princeton University Press, 1995.

———. "Wounded Attachments: Late Modern Oppositional Political Formations." In *States of Injury*, 52–76. Princeton: Princeton University Press, 1995.

Bruns, J. Edgar. *The Christian Buddhism of St. John.* Mahwah, N.J.: Paulist Press, 1971.

Buchanan, Ian. "The Problem of the Body in Deleuze and Guattari; or, What Can a Body Do?" *Body and Society* 3, no. 3 (1997): 73–91.

Bula, Frances. "Up Against the Wall." *Canadian Architect* 45, no. 9 (2000): 15–17.

Burnham, Clint. "Late Empire." In *Vancouver Art and Economies*, ed. Melanie O'Brian, 29–46. Vancouver: Arsenal Pulp, 2007.

Burrus, Virginia. "Augustine, Rosenzweig, and the Possibility of Experiencing Miracle." In *Material Spirit*, ed. Carl Good, Manuel Asensi, and Gregory Stallings. New York: Fordham University Press, forthcoming.

———. Response to Sharon V. Betcher, "Crip/tography: Of Karma and Cosmopolis." Presented at the Transdisciplinary Theology Conference, Drew University, October 30, 2007.

———. *Saving Shame: Martyrs, Saints, and Other Abject Subjects*. Philadelphia: University of Pennsylvania Press, 2008.

Burrus, Virginia, Mark D. Jordan, and Karmen MacKendrick, eds. *Seducing Augustine: Bodies, Desires, Confessions*. New York: Fordham University Press, 2010.

Burrus, Virginia, and Catherine Keller, eds. *Towards a Theology of Eros: Transfiguring Passion at the Limits of Discipline*. New York: Fordham University Press, 2006.

Butler, Judith. *Frames of War: When Is Life Grievable?* London: Verso, 2009.

———. *Giving an Account of Oneself*. New York: Fordham University Press, 2005.

———. "New Thoughts on Solidarity." Public address to the American Academy of Religion, San Francisco, November 20, 2011.

———. "Performativity, Precarity, and Sexual Politics." *AIBR: Revista de Antropologia Iberoamericana* 4, no. 3 (2009): i–xiii.

———. *Precarious Life: The Powers of Mourning and Violence*. New York: Verso, 2004.

Byassee, Jason. "The New Monastics." *Christian Century* 122, no. 21 (2005): 38–47.

Byers, Jim. "Vancouver Makes No Promises for Its Show." *Toronto Star*, August 13, 2008, News, A21.

Campbell, Colin. *The Romantic Ethic and the Spirit of Modern Consumerism*. Oxford: Alcuin Academics, 1987; 3rd ed. 2005.

Campbell, Fiona Kumari. *Contours of Ableism: The Production of Disability and Abledness*. New York: Palgrave Macmillan, 2009.

Canguilhem, Georges. "La monstruosité et le monstrueux." *Diogène* 40, no. 29 (1962): 28–43.

———. *The Normal and the Pathological*. New York: Zone Books, 1991.

Caputo, John D. *Against Ethics: Contributions to a Poetics of Obligation with Constant Reference to Deconstruction*. Bloomington: Indiana University Press, 1993.

———. "The Power of the Powerless." In *After the Death of God*, ed. Jeffrey W. Robbins, 114–60. New York: Columbia University Press, 2007.

———. "The Promise of the World: A Theology of the Event with Special Reference to Christianity." Guest lecture at Vancouver School of Theology, September 2008.

———. *The Weakness of God: A Theology of the Event*. Bloomington: Indiana University Press, 2006.

———. "Without Sovereignty, Without Being: Unconditionality, the Coming God and Derrida's Democracy to Come." *Journal of Cultural and Religious Theory* 4, no. 3 (2003): 9–26.

Caputo, John D., ed. *Deconstruction in a Nutshell: A Conversation with Jacques Derrida*. New York: Fordham University Press, 1997.

Caputo, John D., and Gianni Vattimo. *After the Death of God*, ed. Jeffrey W. Robbins. New York: Columbia University Press, 2007.

Carmi, T. "The Gate." In *At the Stone of Losses*, trans. Grace Schulman, 71. Philadelphia: Jewish Publication Society of America, 1983; Berkeley and Los Angeles: University of California Press, 1983.

Carson, Anne. *Decreation: Poetry, Essays, Opera*. New York: Knopf, 2005.

Carter, Warren. "Proclaiming (in/against) Empire Then and Now." *Word and World* 25 (2005): 149–58.

———. *Matthew and Empire: Initial Explorations*. Harrisburg, Penn.: Trinity Press International, 2001.

Cavadini, John C. "The Meaning and Value of Suffering: A Christian Response to Leora Batnitzky." In *Christianity in Jewish Terms*, ed. Tikva Frymer-Kensky, et al., 229–37. Boulder: Westview Press, 2000.

de Certeau, Michel. "Walking in the City: From *The Practice of Everyday Life*." In Bridge and Watson, *Blackwell City Reader*, 383–92.

Chambers, Iain. *Popular Culture: The Metropolitan Experience*. London: Methuen, 1986.

Chodron, Pema. *The Places that Scare You: A Guide to Fearlessness in Difficult Times*. Boston: Shambhala Classics, 2002.

———. *Start Where You Are: A Guide to Compassionate Living*. Boston: Shambhala Classics, 2001.

———. *When Things Fall Apart*. Boston: Shambhala Classics, 2000.

Chopp, Rebecca. "Introduction." In *The Disabled God: Toward a Liberation Theology of Disability* by Nancy L. Eiesland. Nashville: Abingdon, 1994.

Chopra, Deepak. *The Third Jesus: The Christ We Cannot Ignore*. New York: Three Rivers, 2009.

Chow, Rey. *The Protestant Ethnic and the Spirit of Capitalism*. New York: Columbia University Press, 2002.

Clines, David J. A. *I, He, We, and They: A Literary Approach to Isaiah 53*. Journal for the Study of the Old Testament Supplement Series, no. 1. Sheffield: JSOT, 1976.

Cobb, Jr., John B. *Spiritual Bankruptcy: A Prophetic Call to Action*. Nashville: Abingdon, 2010.

Cockburn, David. "Self, World and God in Spinoza and Weil." *Studies in World Christianity* 4, no. 2 (1998): 173–86.

Coetzee, J. M. *Disgrace*. London: Vintage, 2008.

Cohen, Hermann. *Religion of Reason Out of the Sources of Judaism*. Trans. Simon Kaplan. New York: Frederick Ungar, 1971.

"Compassion Deficit." *New York Times*, October 23, 2009, Editorial, A34. http://www.nytimes.com/2009/10/23/opinion/23fri4.html.

Connolly, William E. "Suffering, Justice, and the Politics of Becoming." *Culture, Medicine, and Psychiatry* 20, no. 3 (1996): 251–77.

———. "Suffering, Justice, and the Politics of Becoming." In *Why I Am Not a Secularist*, 47–72.

———. *Why I Am Not a Secularist*. Minneapolis: University of Minnesota Press, 1999.

———. *A World of Becoming*. Durham, N.C.: Duke University Press, 2011.

———. "A World of Becoming." In *Democracy and Pluralism: The Political Thought of William E. Connolly*, ed. Alan Finlayson, 222–35. London: Routledge, 2010.

Cooey, Paula. *Willing the Good: Jesus, Dissent, and Desire*. Minneapolis: Fortress, 2006.

de Coulanges, Fustel. *The Ancient City: A Study on the Religion, Laws, and Institutions of Greece and Rome*. Trans. Willard Small. Boston: Lothrop, Lee and Shepard, 1901.

Coupland, Douglas. *City of Glass: Douglas Coupland's Vancouver*. Vancouver: Douglas and McIntyre, 2000.

———. *Life after God*. New York: Washington Square Press, 1994.

Covino, Deborah Caslav. "Abject Criticism." *Genders* 32 (2000): section 12. http://www.genders.org/g32/g32_corvino.html. Accessed July 20, 2010.

Cox, Harvey. *The Future of Faith*. New York: HarperOne, 2009.

———. "The Myth of the Twentieth Century: The Rise and Fall of 'Secularization.'" In *The Twentieth Century: A Theological Overview*, ed. Gregory Baum, 135–43. Maryknoll, N.Y.: Orbis, 1999.

———. *The Secular City*. New York: MacMillan, 1965.

———. "The Secular City Twenty-five Years Later." *Christian Century*, Nov. 7, 1990, 1025–29.

Cox, Harvey, and D. Ikeda, eds. *The Persistence of Religion: Comparative Perspectives on Modern Spirituality*. New York: I. B. Tauris/Palgrave, 2009.

Cran, Gregory J. *Negotiating Buck Naked: Doukhobors, Public Policy, and Conflict Resolution*. Vancouver: University of British Columbia Press, 2006.

Crawford, Matthew B. *Shop Class as Soulcraft: An Inquiry into the Value of Work*. New York: Penguin Press, 2009.

Cresswell, Tim. *Place: A Short Introduction*. Malden, Mass.: Blackwell, 2004.

Crockett, Clayton. "Introduction." In *Religion and Violence in a Secular World: Toward a New Political Theology*, 1–19. Charlottesville: University of Virginia Press, 2006.

Crockett, Clayton, ed. *Secular Theology: American Radical Theological Thought*. London: Routledge, 2001.

Cross, John Dominic. *Jesus: A Revolutionary Biography*. San Francisco: HarperSanFrancisco, 1994.

Crowe, Benjamin D. "Nietzsche, the Cross, and the Nature of God." *Heythrop Journal* 48, no. 2 (2007): 243–59.

Czachesz, Istvan. "Metamorphosis and Mind: Cognitive Explorations of the Grotesque in Early Christian Literature." In *Metamorphosis: Resurrection, Body and Transformative Practice in Early Christianity (Ekstasis)*, ed. Turid Karlsen Seim and Jorunn Økland, 207–30. Berlin: DeGruyter, 2008.

Daley, Suzanne. "Chasing Riches from Africa to Europe and Finding Only Squalor." *New York Times*, May 25, 2011, A1.

Daly, Mary, and Jane Caputi. *Websters' First New Intergalactic Wickedary of the English Language*. San Francisco: HarperSanFrancisco, 1987.

Damasio, Antonio. *Descartes' Error: Emotion, Reason, and the Human Brain*. New York: Penguin, 1994.

Darwin, Charles. *On the Origin of Species*. Oxford: Oxford University Press, 1998. First published 1859 by John Murray.

Das, Lama Surya. *Awakening the Buddha Within: Tibetan Wisdom for the Western World*. New York: Broadway Books, 1998.

Davey, Andrew. *Urban Christianity and Global Order: Theological Resources for an Urban Future*. Peabody, Mass.: Hendrickson Publishers, 2002.

Davidson, Arnold I. "Spiritual Exercises and Ancient Philosophy: An Introduction to Pierre Hadot." *Critical Inquiry* 16, no. 3 (1990): 475–82.

Davis, Lennard J. *Bending Over Backwards: Disability, Dismodernism, and Other Difficult Positions*. New York: New York University Press, 2002.

———. "Nude Venuses, Medusa's Body, and Phantom Limbs: Disability and Visuality." In *The Body and Physical Difference: Discourses of Disability*, ed. David T. Mitchell and Sharon L. Snyder, 51–70. Ann Arbor: University of Michigan Press, 1997.

———. "Why Is Disability Missing from the Discourse on Diversity?" *Chronicle of Higher Education*, September 25, 2011.

Davis, Mike. "The Battle of Rio and the Future of the Slum." Public lecture, Urban Development and Sustainability Program, Simon Fraser University, Vancouver, September 26, 2011.

———. "From *City of Quartz: Excavating the Future in Los Angeles*." In Bridge and Watson, *Blackwell City Reader*, 323–32.

———. *Planet of Slums*. London: Verso, 2007.

Dederer, Claire. *Poser: My Life in Twenty-three Yoga Poses*. New York: Farrar, Straus and Giroux, 2010.

Delany, Paul. "'Hardly the Center of the World': Vancouver in William Gibson's 'The Winter Market.'" In *Vancouver: Representing the Postmodern City*, ed. Paul Delany. Vancouver: Arsenal Pulp, 1994.

Deleuze, Gilles. *Essays Critical and Clinical*. Trans. Daniel W. Smith and Michael A. Greco. Minneapolis: University of Minnesota Press, 1997.

———. *The Fold: Leibniz and the Baroque*. Trans. Tom Conley. Minneapolis: University of Minnesota, 1993.

———. "Nietzsche and Saint Paul, Lawrence and John of Patmos." In *Essays Critical and Clinical*, 36–53.

———. "To Have Done with Judgment." In *Essays Critical and Clinical*, 126–35.

Deleuze, Gilles, and Felix Guattari. *Anti-Oedipus: Capitalism and Schizophrenia*. Trans. Robert Hurley, Mark Seem, and Helen R. Lane. Minneapolis: University of Minnesota Press, 1983.

———. *What Is Philosophy?* Trans. Hugh Tomlinson and Graham Burchell. New York: Columbia University Press, 1994.

———. "What Is a Minor Literature?" In *Out There: Marginalization and Contemporary Cultures*, ed. Russell Ferguson, Martha Gever, Trinh T. Minh-ha, and Cornel West, 59–70. Cambridge, Mass.: MIT Press, 1990.

Derrida, Jacques. *Of Grammatology*. Ed. and trans. Gayatri Chakravorty Spivak. Baltimore: Johns Hopkins University Press, 1997.

Desai, Kiran. *The Inheritance of Loss*. New York: Atlantic Monthly Press, 2006.

DeShong, Scott. "The Nightmare of Health: Metaphysics and Ethics in the Signification of Disability." *Symploke* 15, no. 1–2 (2007): 268–86.

Deutsch, Elliot. *Advaita Vedānta: A Philosophical Reconstruction*. Honolulu: East-West Center Press, 1969.

Dierckes, Chris. Final paper for Process Theologies, 27 October 2008, Vancouver School of Theology.

Diprose, Roslyn. *Corporeal Generosity: On Giving with Nietzsche, Merleau-Ponty, and Levinas*. Albany: SUNY Press, 2002.

Dostoevsky, Fyodor. *The Idiot*. Trans. Allen Myers. Oxford: Oxford University Press, 2008. First published 1868.

Douglas, Mary. *Purity and Danger: An Analysis of the Concepts of Pollution and Taboo*. New York: Routledge, 1966.

Dreyfus, Hubert, and Sean Dorrance Kelly. *All Things Shining: Reading the Western Classics to Find Meaning in a Secular Age*. New York: Free Press/Simon and Schuster, 2011.

Dudley, Kathryn Marie. *The End of the Line: Lost Jobs, New Lives in Postindustrial America*. Chicago: University of Chicago Press, 1994.

Dunne, John S. *The City of the Gods: A Study in Myth and Morality.* New York: Macmillan, 1965.

Eckhart. "Sermon 52: Beati Pauperes spiritu, quoniam ipsorum est regnum caelorum (Mt.5.3)." In *Meister Eckhart: The Essential Sermons, Commentaries, Treatises, and Defense,* trans. Edmund Colledge and Bernard McGinn, 199–203. New York: Paulist Press, 1981.

Edgley, Charles. "Health Nazis and the Cult of the Perfect Body: Some Polemical Observations." *Symbolic Interaction* 13, no. 2 (1990): 257–79.

Ehrenreich, Barbara. "Is It Now a Crime to Be Poor?" *New York Times,* August 9, 2009, Opinion section, WK9.

Eiesland, Nancy. *The Disabled God.* Nashville: Abingdon, 1994.

Eisenstadt, Schmuel N. "The Axial Age: The Emergence of Transcendental Visions and the Rise of Clerics." *European Journal of Sociology* 23 (1982): 294–314.

Eisler, Colin. "The Athlete of Virtue: The Iconography of Asceticism." In *De Artibus Opuscula XL: Essays in Honor of Erwin Panofsky,* ed. Millard Meiss, 1: 82–97. New York: New York University Press, 1961.

Elgin, Duane. *Promise Ahead: A Vision of Hope and Action for Humanity's Future.* New York: William Morrow, 2000.

Eliade, Mircea. *Cosmos and History: The Myth of the Eternal Return.* Trans. Willard R. Trask. New York: Harper Torchbooks, 1959.

———. *The Sacred and the Profane: The Nature of Religion.* Trans. Willard R. Trask. New York: Harcourt Brace, 1959.

Elliott, Neil. "The Anti-Imperial Message of the Cross." In *Paul and Empire: Religion and Power in Roman Imperial Society,* ed. Richard A. Horsley, 167–83. Harrisburg, Penn.: Trinity Press International, 1997.

Erasmus, Desiderius. "Preparing for Death (*De Praeparatione ad mortem;* 1534). Translated and annotated by John Grant. In *Spiritualia and Pastoralia,* ed. John W. O'Malley, 389–450. Vol. 70 of *Collected Works of Erasmus.* Toronto: University of Toronto Press, 1998.

Erikson, Erik. *Young Man Luther: A Study in Psychoanalysis and History.* New York: W. W. Norton, 1958.

Estabrook, Barry. "Chemical Warfare." In *Tomatoland: How Modern Industrial Agriculture Destroyed Our Most Alluring Fruit,* 35–72. Kansas City, Mo.: Andrews McMeel Publishing, 2011.

Faber, Alyda. "*Dancer in the Dark:* Affliction and the Aesthetic of Attention." *Studies in Religion* 25, no. 1 (2006): 85–106.

———. "The Post-Secular Poetics and Ethics of Exposure in J. M. Coetzee's *Disgrace.*" *Literature and Theology* 23, no. 3 (2009): 303–16.

———. "'The Shock of Love' and the Visibility of 'Indecent' Pain: Reading the Woolf-Raverat Correspondence." In *Woolfian Boundaries: Selected Papers from the Sixteenth Annual International Conference on Virginia Woolf,* ed. Anna

Burrells, Steve Ellis, Deborah Parsons, and Kathryn Simpson, 58–64. Clemson, S.C.: Clemson University Digital Press, 2007.

Faber, Roland. "De-Ontologizing God: Levinas, Deleuze, and Whitehead." In *Process and Difference: Between Cosmological and Poststructuralist Postmodernisms*, ed. Catherine Keller and Anne Daniell, 209–34. Albany: SUNY Press, 2002.

———. "In the Wake of False Unifications: Whiteheadian Creative Resistance against Imperialistic Theologies." *Process Perspectives* 28, no. 1 (2005): 1–18.

———. "The Sense of Peace: A Para-Doxology of Divine Mulitiplicity." In Keller and Schneicer, *Polydoxy: Theology of Multiplicity and Relation*, 36–56.

Fainstein, Susan S., Lily M. Hoffman, and Dennis R. Judd. "Introduction." In Hoffman, Fainstein, and Judd, *Cities and Visitors*, 1–20.

Farley, Wendy. "'The Pain-Dispelling Draft': Compassion as a Practical Theology." *Perspectives in Religious Studies* 26, no. 3 (1999): 291–302.

Feder, Ellen K. "Tilting the Ethical Lens: Shame, Disgust, and the Body in Question." *Hypatia* 26, no. 3 (2011): 632–50.

Fitzgerald, F. Scott. *The Crack-Up*, ed. Edmund Wilson. New York: New Directions, 1956.

Flavin, Christopher. "Preface." In *State of the World 2007: Our Urban Future*, by Worldwatch Institute, ed. Linda Starke, xxiii–xxv. New York. W. W. Norton, 2007.

Flood, Gavin. *The Ascetic Self: Subjectivity, Memory, and Tradition*. New York: Cambridge University Press, 2004.

Foster, Roger. *Adorno. The Recovery of Experience*. Albany: SUNY Press, 2007.

Foucault, Michel. "The Ethic of Care for the Self as a Practice of Freedom: An Interview with Michel Foucault on January 20, 1984." In "The Final Foucault: Studies on Michel Foucault's Last Works," ed. James Bernauer and David M. Rasmussen. Special issue, *Philosophy and Social Criticism* 12, no. 2–3 (1987): 112–31.

———. "Friendship as a Way of Life." In *Ethics: Subjectivity and Truth*, ed. Paul Rabinow, 135–40. Vol. I of *The Essential Works of Foucault, 1954–1984*, ed. Paul Rabinow, et al. New York: New Press, 1994.

———. "Faire vivre et laisser mourir: La naissance du racisme." *Les Temps Modernes* 46, no. 535 (1991): 37–61.

———. *Madness and Civilization: A History of Insanity in the Age of Reason*. Trans. Richard Howard. New York: Vintage Press, 1965.

———. "Preface." In Deleuze and Guattari, *Anti-Oedipus: Capitalism and Schizophrenia*, xiii–xvi.

Frank, Adam. "The Anthropocene: Can Humans Survive a Human Age?" NPR blog *13:7: Cosmos and Culture*, June 21, 2011. http://www.npr.org/blogs/13.7/2011/06/21/137317694/the-anthropocene-can-humans-survive-a-human-age.

Friedman, Susan Stanford. *Mappings: Feminism and the Cultural Geographies of Encounter.* Princeton: Princeton University Press, 1998.

Frilingos, Christopher A. *Spectacles of Empire: Monsters, Martyrs, and the Book of Revelation.* Philadelphia: University of Pennsylvania Press, 2004.

Funke, Michael. "Ehrenreich Urges Economic Justice Movement." Portland Independent Media Center, November 21, 2002. http://portland.indymedia.org/en/2002/11/35157.shtml.

Futrell, Alison. *Blood in the Arena: The Spectacle of Roman Power.* Austin: University of Texas Press, 1997.

Gandhi, Mohandas K. *Vows and Observances.* Berkeley: Berkeley Hills Books, 1999.

Garcia-Rivera, Alejandro. *The Community of the Beautiful: A Theological Aesthetics.* Collegeville, Minn.: Liturgical Press, 1999.

———. "Endless Forms Most Beautiful." *Theology and Science* 5, no. 2 (2007): 125–35.

Gardner, Gary. *Invoking the Spirit: Religion and Spirituality in the Quest for a Sustainable World.* Worldwatch Paper 164. Washington, D.C.: Worldwatch Institute, 2002.

Garland-Thomson, Rosemarie. *Freakery: Cultural Spectacles of the Extraordinary Body.* New York: New York University Press, 1996.

———. "Misfits: A Feminist Materialist Disability Concept." *Hypatia* 26, no. 3 (2011): 591–609.

Gartner, Zsuzsi. "A Few Hundred Words from the Editor." In *Darwin's Bastards,* ed. Zsuzsi Gartner, 1–6. Vancouver: Douglas and McIntyre, 2010.

Gazzaniga, Michael. *Human: The Science behind What Makes Us Unique.* New York: HarperCollins, 2008.

Gebara, Ivone. *Longing for Running Water: Ecofeminism and Liberation.* Trans. David Molineaux. Minneapolis: Augsburg Fortress, 1999.

———. "Yearning for Beauty." *The Other Side* 30, no. 4 (July–August 2003): 24–25.

Gerrish, Brian A. "Atonement and 'Saving Faith.'" *Theology Today* 17, no. 2 (1960): 181–91.

Gibbs, Robert. "Unjustifiable Suffering." In *Suffering Religion,* ed. Robert Gibbs and Elliot R. Wolfson, 13–35. London: Routledge, 2002.

Gibson, William. *Burning Chrome.* New York: Arbor House, 1986.

———. "Dougal Discarnate." In *Darwin's Bastards,* ed. Zsuzsi Gartner, 231–41. Vancouver: Douglas and McIntyre, 2010.

———. "Life in the Meta City." In "Better, Greener, Smarter Cities." Special issue, *Scientific American* 305, no. 3 (2011): 88–89.

———. "The Winter Market." *Vancouver Magazine* 18, no. 11 (1985): 62–73, 108–14. Republished in Gibson, *Burning Chrome.*

Giddens, Anthony. *The Consequences of Modernity*. Palo Alto: Stanford University Press, 1990.

———. *Runaway World: How Globalization Is Reshaping Our Lives*. London: Profile, 1999.

Gillespie, Michael Allen. *The Theological Origins of Modernity*. Chicago: University of Chicago Press, 2008.

Glaeser, Edward. "Engines of Innovation." In "Better, Greener, Smarter Cities." Special issue, *Scientific American* 305, no. 3 (2011): 50–55.

———. *Triumph of the City: How Our Greatest Invention Makes Us Richer, Smarter, Greener, Healthier, and Happier*. New York: Penguin, 2011.

Gleeson, Brendan. "A Place on Earth: Technology, Space, and Disability." *Journal of Urban Technology* 5, no. 1 (1998): 87–109.

Glucklich, Ariel. *Sacred Pain: Hurting the Body for the Sake of the Soul*. Oxford: Oxford University Press, 2001.

Goldberg, Philip. *American Veda: From Emerson and the Beatles to Yoga and Meditation; How Indian Spirituality Changed the West*. New York: Harmony, 2010.

Goldstein, Rebbeca. *Mazel*. New York: Penguin, 1995.

Graham, Elaine, and Stephen Lowe. *What Makes a Good City? Public Theology and the Urban Church*. London: Darton-Longman and Todd, 2009.

Gram, Karen. "Philosophy: The Evolution of Movement; Yoga is Deeply Engrained in the West Coast Lifestyle, but Its Indian Roots Go Back Centuries." *Vancouver Sun*, July 4, 2011, D1.

Grosz, Elizabeth. "Bodies-Cities." In Bridge and Watson, *Blackwell City Reader*, 297–303.

Guattari, Felix. *Chaosmosis: An Ethico-Aesthetic Paradigm*. Trans. Paul Bains and Julian Pefanis. Bloomington: Indiana University Press, 1995.

Hacker, Andrew, and Claudia Dreifus. *Higher Education? How Colleges Are Wasting Our Money and Failing Our Kids—And What We Can Do about It*. New York: Times Books, 2010.

———. "Take Back the Liberal Arts." *Los Angeles Times*, August 17, 2011.

Hahn, Harlan. "Advertising the Acceptably Employable Image: Disability and Capitalism." In *The Disability Studies Reader*, ed. Lennard J. Davis, 172–86. London: Routledge, 1997.

———. "Can Disability Be Beautiful?" *Social Policy* 18 (1988): 26–32.

Haight, Roger. *The Future of Christology*. New York: Continuum, 2005.

———. Presentation, AAR/Luce Summer Seminar on Theologies of Religious Pluralism and Comparative Theologies.Union Theological Seminary, New York, June 2009.

Hall, Douglas John. *The Cross in Our Context: Jesus and the Suffering World*. Minneapolis: Fortress, 2003.

Halperin, David M. *Saint Foucault: Towards a Gay Hagiography*. Oxford: Oxford University Press, 1995.

Hampson, Daphne. "Luther on the Self: A Feminist Critique." *Word and World* 7, no. 4 (1988): 334–42.

Hanh, Thich Nhat. *The Miracle of Mindfulness*. Boston: Beacon Press, 1987.

Haraway, Donna. "Ecce Homo, Ain't (Ar'n't) I a Woman, and Inappropriate/d Others: The Human in a Post-Humanist Landscape." In *Feminists Theorize the Political*, ed. Judith Butler and Joan W. Scott, 86–100. London: Routledge, 1992.

———. *Modest Witness@Second Millennium. FemaleMan© Meets OncoMouse.*™ London: Routledge, 1997.

———. *Simians, Cyborgs, and Women: The Reinvention of Nature*. London: Routledge, 1991.

Hardt, Michael, and Antonio Negri. *Empire*. Cambridge, Mass.: Harvard University Press, 2000.

———. *Multitude: War and Democracy in the Age of Empire*. New York: Penguin, 2004.

Harnack, Adolf von. *The Mission and Expansion of Christianity in the First Three Centuries*. Vol. 1. Trans. James Moffatt. New York: G. P. Putnam's Sons, 1908.

Harrison, Beverly Wildung. "The Power of Anger in the Work of Love: Christian Ethics for Women and Other Strangers." In *Making the Connections: Essays in Feminist Ethics*, ed. Carol S. Robb, 3–21. Boston: Beacon Press, 1985.

Hart, David. *The Beauty of the Infinite: The Aesthetics of Christian Truth*. Grand Rapids, Mich.: Eerdmans, 2003.

Harvey, David. *Spaces of Hope*. Berkeley and Los Angeles: University of California Press, 2000.

———. "The Urban Process under Capitalism: A Framework for Analysis." In Bridge and Watson, *Blackwell City Reader*, 116–24.

Hassel, R. Chris, Jr. "Hamlet's 'Too, Too Solid Flesh.'" *Sixteenth Century Journal* 25, no. 3 (1994): 609–22.

Hedges, Chris. "City of Ruins." *The Nation*, November 22, 2010. http://www.thenation.com/print/ article/155801/city-ruins.

Heen, Erik M. Review of *Jesus' Death in Early Christian Memory: The Poetics of the Passion* by Ellen Bradshaw Aitken. *Review of Biblical Literature*, July 23, 2005. http://www.bookreviews.org/pdf/4729_4874.pdf.

Hengel, Martin. *The Atonement: The Origins of the Doctrine in the New Testament*. Philadelphia: Fortress, 1981.

Hengel, Martin, and Daniel P. Bailey. "The Effective History of Isaiah 53 in the Pre-Christian Period." In *The Suffering Servant: Isaiah 53 in Jewish and*

Christian Sources, ed. Bernd Janowski and Peter Stuhlmacher, trans. Daniel P. Bailey, 75–146. Grand Rapids, Mich.: Eerdmans, 2004.

Herbert, A. S. *The Book of the Prophet Isaiah: Chapters 40–66*. Cambridge: Cambridge University Press, 1975.

Hern, Matt. *Common Ground in a Liquid City: Essays in Defense of an Urban Future*. Edinburgh and Oakland, Calif.: AK Press, 2010.

Heuser, Sabine. *Virtual Geographies: Cyberpunk at the Intersection of the Postmodern and Science Fiction*. New York: Rodopi, 2003.

Hodgson, Peter. "Luther and Freedom." In *The Global Luther: A Theologian for Modern Times*, ed. Christine Helmer, 32–48. Minneapolis: Fortress, 2009.

Hoffman, Lily M., Susan S. Fainstein, and Dennis R. Judd, eds. *Cities and Visitors: Regulating People, Markets and City Space*. Malden, Mass.: Blackwell, 2003.

Hokusai09. "Mendicant—The One Who Gave Up Crown, Queen and Child." *Secret Lives of Words* (blog), April 4, 2009. http://hokusai09.wordpress.com /2009/04/04/mendicant-the-one-who-gave-up-crown-queen-and-child.

Holler, Linda. *Erotic Morality: The Role of Touch in Moral Agency*. New Brunswick, N.J.: Rutgers University Press, 2002.

Hollinghurst, Alan. *Line of Beauty*. New York: Bloomsbury, 2005.

Hollywood, Amy. "Performativity, Citationality, Ritualization." *History of Religions* 42, no. 2 (2002): 93–115.

———. "Towards a Feminist Philosophy of Ritual and Bodily Practice." In *Difference in Philosophy of Religion*, ed. Philip Goodchild, 73–83. Aldershot, Hampshire, U.K. and Burlington, Vt.: Ashgate, 2003.

Homer-Dixon, Thomas. *The Upside of Down: Catastrophe, Creativity, and the Renewal of Civilization*. Washington, D.C.: Shearwater Books/Island Press, 2006.

Hooker, Morna. *Jesus and the Servant: The Influence of the Servant Concept of Deutero-Isaiah in the New Testament*. London: SPCK Publishing, 1959.

Hooks, Bell. *Yearning: Race, Gender, and Cultural Politics*. Boston: South End Press, 1990.

Hooper, Barbara. "The Poem of Male Desires: Female Bodies, Modernity, and 'Paris, Capital of the Nineteenth Century.'" In *Making the Invisible Visible: A Multicultural History of Planning*, ed. Leonie Sandercock, 227–54. Berkeley and Los Angeles: University of California Press, 1998.

Horrell, David. "Between Conformity and Resistance: Beyond the Balch-Elliott Debate Towards a Postcolonial Reading of 1 Peter." In *Reading 1 Peter with New Eyes: Methodological Reassessments of the Letter of First Peter*, ed. R. L. Webb and B. J. Bauman-Martin, 111–43. London: T. and T. Clark, 2007.

Houle, Karen. "Micropolitics." In Stivale, *Gilles Deleuze*, 88–97.

Howe, P. David. "The Tail Is Wagging the Dog: Body Culture, Classification, and the Paralympic Movement." *Ethnography* 9, no. 4 (2008): 499–517.

Hrdy, Sarah Blaffer. "Infanticide as a Primate Reproductive Strategy." *American Scientist* 65, no. 1 (1977): 40–49.

Hughes, Bill. "The Constitution of Impairment: Modernity and the Aesthetic of Oppression." *Disability and Society* 14, no. 2 (1999): 155–72.

Hultgren, Arland. "Luther on Galatians." *Word and World* 20, no. 3 (2000): 232–38.

Hume, Stephen. "Never Say Never: Vancouverites Have a Long History of Rioting." *Vancouver Sun*, June 23, 2011. Westcoast News section, A9.

Ikeda, Daisaku. "The Age of the Internet: Interplay of Danger and Promise." In *The Persistence of Religion: Comparative Perspectives on Modern Spirituality*, ed. Harvey G. Cox and Daisuku Ikeda, 37–46. New York: I. B. Tauris, 2009.

Imrie, Rob. *Disability and the City: International Perspectives*. London: Paul Chapman Publishing, 1996.

Inge, John. *A Christian Theology of Place: Explorations in Practical, Pastoral and Empirical Theology*. Aldershot, Hampshire, U.K.: Ashgate, 2003.

Irigaray, Luce. *Between East and West: From Singularity to Community*. Trans. Stephen Pluhácek. New York: Columbia University Press, 2002.

———. *I Love to You: Sketch of a Possible Felicity in History*. Trans. Alison Martin. London and New York: Routledge, 1996.

Isaacs, Marie E. *The Concept of Spirit: A Study of Pneuma in Hellenistic Judaism and Its Bearing on the New Testament*. Heythrop Monographs 1. London: Heythrop College, 1976.

Isin, Engin. "Metropolis Unbound: Legislators and Interpreters of Urban Form." In *City Lives and City Forms: Critical Urban Research and Canadian Urbanism*, ed. Jon Caufield and Linda Peake, 98–127. Toronto: University of Toronto Press, 1996.

Iwamura, Jane Naomi. *Virtual Orientalism: Asian Religions and American Popular Culture*. Oxford: Oxford University Press, 2011.

Jacobs, Jane. *The Death and Life of Great American Cities*. Toronto: Random House, 1961.

Jacobs, Jane M. *Edge of Empire: Postcolonialism and the City*. London: Routledge, 1996.

Jaffe, Eric. "City Smog Linked to Cognitive Deficits in Children." *The Atlantic Cities: Place Matters*, October 31, 2011, http://www.theatlanticcities.com /arts-and-lifestyle/2011/10/city-smog-linked-cognitive-deficits-children /390/.

Jakobsen, Janet. "Can Homosexuals End Western Civilization as We Know It? Family Values in a Global Economy." In *Queer Globalizations: Citizenship and the Afterlife of Colonialism*, ed. Arnaldo Cruz-Malavé and Martin F. Manalansan IV, 49–70. New York: New York University Press, 2002.

James, William. *A Pluralistic Universe*. Charleston, S.C.: BiblioBazaar, 2006. First published 1909.

———. *The Varieties of Religious Experience: A Study in Human Nature*. New Orleans: Megalodon Entertainment, 2008. First published 1902.

Jayapal, Pramila. "India's Silent but Singing Revolution." *Yes! Magazine*, Winter 2001. http://www.yesmagazine.org/issues/a-new-culture-emerges/indias -silent-but-singing-revolution.

Jencks, Charles. *The Language of Post-Modern Architecture*. 4th ed. New York: Rizzoli Press, 1984.

Jencks, Charles, ed. *The Post-Modern Reader*. London: Academy Press, 1992.

Jenkins, Philip. *The Next Christendom: The Coming of Global Christianity*. 3rd ed. Oxford: Oxford University Press, 2011.

Jennings, Theodore W. "A God without Sovereignty." Spring convocation address, Chicago Theological Seminary, February 8, 2006. http://ctschicago .edu/pdf/convocation_06_Jennings.pdf. Accessed August 25, 2009.

de Jonge, Marinus. *God's Final Envoy: Early Christology and Jesus' Own View of His Mission*. Grand Rapids, Mich.: Eerdmans, 1998.

Kahlos, Maijastina. *Forbearance and Compulsion: The Rhetoric of Religious Tolerance and Intolerance in Late Antiquity*. London: Gerald Duckworth, 2009.

Kallos, Stephanie. *Broken for You*. New York: Grove, 2004.

Kant, Immanuel. *Critique of Judgment*. Trans. Werner S. Pluhar. Cambridge: Hackett, 1987.

Kataoka, Serena. "Vancouverism: Actualizing the Livable City Paradox." *Berkeley Planning Journal* 22 (2009): 42–56.

Katsnelson, Alla. "The Stress of Crowds." In "Better, Greener, Smarter Cities." Special issue, *Scientific American* 305, no. 3 (2011): 18–19.

Kearney, Richard. *Anatheism: Returning to God after God*. New York: Columbia University Press, 2010.

———. *The God Who May Be: A Hermeneutics of Religion*. Bloomington: Indiana University Press, 2001.

Kearns, Cleo McNelly. "Suffering in Theory." In *Suffering Religion*, ed. Robert Gibbs and Elliot R. Wolfson, 56–72. London: Routledge, 2002.

Kearns, Laurel, and Catherine Keller, eds. *EcoSpirit: Religions and Philosophies for the Earth*. New York: Fordham University Press, 2007.

Keller, Catherine. *Apocalypse Now and Then*. Boston: Beacon, 1996.

———. "Be a Multiplicity: Ancestral Anticipations." In Keller and Schneider, *Polydoxy*, 81–101.

———. *Face of the Deep: A Theology of Becoming*. London: Routledge, 2003.

———. *On the Mystery: Discerning God in Process*. Minneapolis: Fortress, 2008.

———. "Pluralism Is Not Enough" (home page). Polydoxy: Theologies of the Manifold (web site). Drew Transdisciplinary Theologies Conference, October 1–4, 2009. http://depts.drew.edu/tsfac/colloquium/2009/about.html.

Keller, Catherine, and Laurel C. Schneider. "Introduction." In Keller and Schneider, *Polydoxy*, 1–15.

Keller, Catherine, and Laurel C. Schneider, eds. *Polydoxy: Theology of Multiplicity and Relation*. London: Routledge, 2010.

Killen, Patricia O'Connell. "Memory, Novelty and Possibility in This Place." In Todd, *Cascadia: The Elusive Utopia*, 65–85.

Killen, Patricia O'Connell, and Mark Silk. *Religion and Public Life in the Pacific Northwest: The None Zone*. Walnut Creek, Calif.: AltaMira Press, 2004.

Kimmelman, Michael. "The Power of Place in Protest." *New York Times*, October 16, 2011, Sunday Review, News Analysis, SR1.

Kingwell, Mark. *Concrete Reveries: Consciousness and the City*. New York: Viking, 2008.

Kitamori, Kazoh. *Theology of the Pain of God*. Eugene, Ore.: Wipf and Stock, 2005. First published in Japan, 1946.

Kitchin, Rob. "'Out of Place,' 'Knowing One's Place': Space, Power and the Exclusion of Disabled People." *Disability and Society* 13, no. 3 (1998): 343–56.

Klima, Alan. "The Telegraphic Abject: Buddhist Meditation and the Redemption of Mechanical Reproduction." *Society for Comparative Study of Society and History* 43, no. 3 (2001): 552–82.

Knitter, Paul. *Introducing Theologies of Religions*. Maryknoll, N.Y.: Orbis, 2008.

Koester, Helmut. "The Memory of Jesus' Death and the Worship of the Risen Lord." *Harvard Theological Review* 91, no. 4 (1998): 335–50.

Kotkin, Joel. *The City: A Global History*. New York: Modern Library Chronicles Book, 2005.

Koyama, Kosuke. *Three Mile an Hour God*. Maryknoll, N.Y.: Orbis, 1980.

Kristeva, Julia. *New Maladies of the Soul*. Trans. Ross Guberman. New York: Columbia University Press, 1997.

———. *Powers of Horror: An Essay on Abjection*. Trans. Léon S. Roudiez. New York: Columbia University Press, 1982.

———. "Stabat Mater." Trans. Léon S. Roudiez. In *The Kristeva Reader*, ed. Toril Moi, 160–86.

———. *Strangers to Ourselves*. Trans. Léon S. Roudiez. New York: Columbia University Press, 1991.

Kunstler, James Howard. *The Long Emergency: Surviving the End of Oil, Climate Change, and Other Converging Catastrophes of the Twenty-First Century*. New York: Grove Press, 2006.

Kuppers, Petra. "Journey to the Holocaust Museum in Berlin, 2011." *Zombo.net* video, http://zomobo.net/Journey-To-The-Holocaust-Memorial-in-Berlin. Accessed December 9, 2011.

———. "Toward a Rhizomatic Model of Disability: Poetry, Performance and Touch." *Journal of Literary and Cultural Disability Studies* 3, no. 3 (2009): 221–40.

Kuppers, Petra, and James Overboe. "Introduction: Deleuze, Disability, and Difference." *Journal of Literary and Cultural Disability Studies* 3, no. 3 (2009): 217–20.

Kuschel, Karl-Joseph. *Born Before All Time? The Dispute over Christ's Origin.* New York: Crossroad, 1992.

Laeuchli, Samuel. "The Sexual Dilemma." In *Power and Sexuality: The Emergence of Canon Law at the Synod of Elvira.* Philadelphia: Temple University Press, 1972.

Lakoff, George. "How Occupy Wall Street's Moral Vision Can Beat the Disastrous Conservative Worldview." *Alternet*, October 20, 2011, http://www.alternet.org/story/152800/lakoff%3A_how_occupy_wall_street's_moral_vision_can_beat_the_disastrous_conservative_worldview.

Lefebrve, Henri. *The Production of Space.* Trans. D. Nicholson-Smith. Oxford: Blackwell, 1991.

Legge, Marilyn. "Inside Communities, Outside Conventions: What Is at Stake in Doing Theology?" *Studies in Religion* 29, no. 1 (2000): 3–18.

Lerner, Robert E. *The Heresy of the Free Spirit in the Later Middle Ages.* Berkeley and Los Angeles: University of California Press, 1972.

Lerro, Bruce. *From Earth Spirits to Sky Gods: The Socioecological Origins of Monotheism, Individualism, and Hyperabstract Reasoning from the Stone Age to the Axial Iron Age.* Lanham, Md.: Lexington Books, 2000.

Levinas, Emmanuel. *Difficile liberté: Essais sur le judaïsme.* Paris: Albin Michel, 1976.

———. *Difficult Freedom: Essays on Judaism.* Trans. Sean Hand. Baltimore: Johns Hopkins University Press, 1990.

———. "La souffrance inutile." In *Entre nous: Essais sur le penser-à-l'autre.* Paris: Bernard Grasset, 1991.

———. "Useless Suffering." In *Entre Nous: Essays on Thinking-of-the-Other.* Trans. Michael B. Smith and Barbara Harshav. New York: Columbia University Press, 1998.

Levine, Bruce E. "400% Rise in Anti-Depressant Pill Use: Americans Are Disempowered—Can the OWS Uprising Shake Us Out of Our Depression?" *AlterNet*, October 29, 2011, http://www.alternet.org/story/152873/400_rise_in_anti-depressant_pill_use%3A_americans_are_disempowered_--_can_the_ows_uprising_shake_us_out_of_our_depression/.

———. "Mass Society and Mass Depression." *The Ecologist* 37, no. 8 (2007): 48–51.

Levitt, Laura. "Letting Go of Liberalism." In *Postcolonialism, Feminism and Religious Discourse*, eds. Laura E. Donaldson and Kwok Pui-Lan, 161–79. New York: Routledge, 2002.

Little, Lester K. *Religious Poverty and the Profit Economy in Medieval Europe.* Ithaca: Cornell University Press, 1978.

Liu, I-ming (Liu I-ming). *Awakening to the Tao.* Trans. Thomas Cleary. Boston: Shambhala, 1988.

Longaker, Christine. *Facing Death and Finding Hope: A Guide to the Emotional and Spiritual Care of the Dying.* New York: Doubleday, 1998.

Lorey, Isabell. "Becoming Common: Precarization as Political Constituting." *e-flux journal* 17 (2010), http://worker01.e-flux.com/pdf/article_148.pdf. Accessed December 7, 2011.

Loy, David R. "The Religion of the Market." *Journal of the American Academy of Religion* 65, no. 2 (1997): 275–90.

Luther, Martin. *The Freedom of a Christian.* Trans. and with introduction by Mark D. Tranvik. Minneapolis: Fortress, 2008.

———. *Luther's Works.* Vol. 17, *Lectures on Isaiah 40–66,* ed. Hilton Oswald. St. Louis: Concordia, 1972.

———. *Luther's Works.* Vol. 26, *Lectures on Galatians, 1535, Chapters 1–4,* ed. Jaroslav Pelikan and Walter A. Hansen. St. Louis: Concordia, 1963.

———. *Luther's Works.* Vol. 27, *Lectures on Galatians, 1535, Chapters 5–6, 1519, Chapters 1–6,* ed. Jaroslav Pelikan and Walter A. Hansen. St. Louis: Concordia, 1964.

———. *Luther's Works.* Vol. 54, *Table Talk,* ed. Theodore G. Tappert and Helmut T. Lehman. Philadelphia: Fortress, 1967.

Lynch, Gordon. *After Religion? 'Generation X' and the Search for Meaning.* London: Darton-Longman and Todd, 2002.

———. *The New Spirituality: An Introduction to Progressive Belief in the Twenty-first Century.* London: I. B. Tauris, 2007.

Mabey, Richard. *Weeds: In Defense of Nature's Most Unloved Plants.* New York: HarperCollins, 2010.

MacKendrick, Karmen. *Counterpleasures.* Albany: SUNY Press, 1999.

Madsen, Anna. "Moral and Mortal Support: The Role of a Faith Community in Shaping Ethical Decisions." In Trozzo, *Stand Boldly.*

Magnusson, Warren. "Politicizing the Global City." In *Democracy, Citizenship and the Global City,* ed. Engin F. Isin, 289–306. London: Routledge, 2000.

Magnusson, Warren, and Karena Shaw, eds. *A Political Space: Reading the Global through Clayoquot Sound.* Minneapolis: University of Minnesota Press, 2002.

Maguire, Daniel. "Whom the Gods Would Destroy, They First Make Myopic: Religion and Ethics in Cross-Disciplinary Ecological Dialogue." *Union Seminary Quarterly Review* 63, no. 1–2 (2010): 67–83.

Makransky, John. *Awakening through Love.* Boston: Wisdom Publications, 2007.

Malcolm, Lois. "A Hidden God Revisited: Desecularization, the Depths, and God's Sort of Seeing." *Dialog* 40, no. 3 (2001): 183–91.

Manoussakis, John Panteleimon. *God after Metaphysics: A Theological Aesthetic.* Bloomington: Indiana University Press, 2007.

Marcuse, Herbert. "Liberation from the Affluent Society." In *The Dialectics of Liberation*, ed. David Cooper, 175–92. Baltimore: Penguin, 1968. Lecture presented at Dialectics of Liberation Conference, London, 1967.

Marovich, Beatrice. "Consent to Be Creature: The Politics of Creatureliness in Simone Weil's Theological Cosmology." Master's thesis, Vancouver School of Theology, May 2009.

Matousek, Mark. "Savage Grace: The Spirituality of Illness." *Utne Reader* 62 (1994): 104–11.

———. *When You're Falling, Dive: Lessons in the Art of Living*. New York: Bloomsbury, 2008.

May, Todd. *Gilles Deleuze: An Introduction*. Cambridge: Cambridge University Press, 2005.

McClure, John. *Partial Faiths: Postsecular Fiction in the Age of Pynchon and Morrison*. Athens: University of Georgia Press, 2007.

McDaniel, Jay. *Living from the Center: Spirituality in an Age of Consumerism*. St. Louis: Chalice, 2000.

McFague, Sallie. "Toward a New Cascadian Civil Religion of Nature." In Todd, *Cascadia*, 157–74.

———. "Where We Live: Urban Ecotheology." In *A New Climate for Theology: God, the World, and Global Warming*, 121–42. Minneapolis: Fortress, 2008.

McKenzie, Kwame. "Urbanization, Social Capital, and Mental Health," *Global Social Policy* 8, no. 3 (2008): 359–77.

McRuer, Robert. "Cripping Sex; or Globalizing Otherness." Public lecture. University of British Columbia, March 7, 2011.

Mengestu, Dinaw. *The Beautiful Things that Heaven Bears*. New York: Riverhead/Penguin, 2007.

Mercedes, Anna. "*Effluit Nobis*: Luther and Melanchthon on the Benefits of the Cross." In Trozzo, *Stand Boldly*, 85–111.

Mieville, China. *The City and the City*. New York: Ballantine, 2009.

Milbank, John, Graham Ward, and Edith Wyschogrod. *Theological Perspectives on God and Beauty*. Harrisburg, Penn.: Trinity Press, 2003.

Millard, Richard M. "Whitehead's Aesthetic Perspective." *Educational Theory* 11, no. 4 (1961): 255–68.

Miller, Susan B. *Disgust: The Gatekeeper Emotion*. Hillsdale, N.J.: Analytic Press, 2004.

Miller, William I. *The Anatomy of Disgust*. Cambridge, Mass.: Harvard University Press, 1997.

Minh-ha, Trinh T. "She, the Inappropriate/d Other." *Discourse* 8 (1986–87): 3–10.

Mitchell, David T. "Foreword." In Stiker, *A History of Disability*, vii–xiv.

Mitchell, Don. *The Right to the City*. New York: Guilford, 2003.

Moltmann, Jurgen. *The Spirit of Life: A Universal Affirmation.* Minneapolis: Fortress, 1992.

Moody, Nickianne. "Untapped Potential: The Representation of Disability/ Special Ability in the Cyberpunk Workforce." *Convergence: The International Journal of Research into New Media Technologies* 3 (1997): 90–105.

Moore, Stephen. *God's Beauty Parlor and Other Queer Spaces in and around the Bible.* Palo Alto: Stanford University Press, 2001.

Morgenstern, Julian. "The Suffering Servant—A New Solution." *Vetus Testamentum* 11, no. 3 (1961): 292–320.

Morris, David B. *The Culture of Pain.* Berkeley and Los Angeles: University of California Press, 1991.

Morton, Timothy. *Ecology without Nature: Rethinking Environmental Aesthetics.* Cambridge, Mass.: Harvard University Press, 2007.

Munzer, Stephen R. "Beggars of God: The Christian Ideal of Mendicancy." *Journal of Religious Ethics* 27, no. 2 (1999): 305–30.

Murdoch, Iris. *The Sovereignty of Good.* London: Routledge, 2001.

Mydans, Seth. "What Makes a Monk Mad: Karma Power." *New York Times,* September 30, 2007, Week in Review, 1, 14.

Nancy, Jean-Luc. *Being Singular Plural.* Trans. Robert D. Richardson and Anne E. O'Byrne. Palo Alto: Stanford University Press, 2000.

———. *Corpus.* Trans. Richard A. Rand. New York: Fordham University Press, 2008.

———. *The Creation of the World, or Globalization.* Trans. Francois Raffoul and David Pettigrew. New York: SUNY Press, 2007.

———. *Dis-Enclosure: The Deconstruction of Christianity.* Trans. Betinna Bergo, Gabriel Malenfant, and Michael B. Smith. New York: Fordham University Press, 2008.

———. "The Intruder." In *Corpus,* 161–170.

———. *The Muses.* Trans. Peggy Kamuf. Stanford: Stanford University Press, 1996.

Nandy, Ashis. *The Intimate Enemy: Loss and Recovery of Self under Colonialism.* Delhi: Oxford University Press, 1983.

Nasar, Sylvia. *A Beautiful Mind: A Biography of John Forbes Nash, Jr., Winner of the Nobel Prize in Economics, 1994.* New York: Simon and Schuster, 1998.

Neilson, Brett, and Ned Rossiter. "From Precarity to Precariousness and Back Again: Labour, Life and Unstable Networks." *Fibreculture Journal,* issue 5 (December 1, 2005), http://five.fibreculturejournal.org/fcj-022-from -precarity-to-precariousness-and-back-again-labour-life-and-unstable -networks/. Accessed November 25, 2011.

Newman, Paul. *Spirit Christology.* Lanham, Md.: University Press of America, 1987.

Niebuhr, H. Richard. *Faith on Earth: An Inquiry into the Structure of Human Faith*, ed. Richard R. Niebuhr. New Haven: Yale University Press, 1989.

Nietzsche, Friedrich. *The Gay Science*. Trans. Walter Kaufmann. New York: Random House, 1974.

Nixon, Rob. *Slow Violence and the Environmentalism of the Poor*. Cambridge, Mass.: Harvard University Press, 2011.

Norris, Kathleen. *Acedia and Me: A Marriage, Monks, and a Writer's Life*. New York: Riverhead Books, 2008.

———. *The Cloister Walk*. New York: Riverhead Books, 1997.

Nussbaum, Martha. *Hiding from Humanity: Disgust, Shame, and the Law*. Princeton: Princeton University Press, 2004.

O'Connell, Stephen. "Aesthetics: A Place I've Never Seen." *Canadian Review of Comparative Literature* 24, no. 3 (1997): 474–99.

O'Donnell, Darren. *Social Acupuncture: A Guide to Suicide, Performance and Utopia*. Toronto: Coach House Books, 2006.

Offer, Avner. *The Challenge of Affluence: Self-Control and Well-Being in the United States and Britain since 1950*. Oxford: Oxford University Press, 2006.

O'Kane, Martin. "Picturing 'The Man of Sorrows': The Passion-Filled Afterlives of a Biblical Icon." *Religion and the Arts* 9, no. 1–2 (2005): 62–100.

Oliver, Kelly. *Witnessing: Beyond Recognition*. Minneapolis: University of Minnesota Press, 2001.

Olson, Geoff. "The Future Isn't What It Used to Be: Measuring Cultural Change." *Common Ground* 192 (2007): 13.

Otto, Rudolph. *The Idea of the Holy: An Inquiry into the Non-Rational Factor in the Idea of the Divine and Its Relation to the Rational*. Oxford: Oxford University Press, 1958. First published in English by Oxford University Press, 1923.

Ouroussoff, Nicolai. "Inside His Exteriors: Toyo Ito Designs Buildings that Suggest the World Beyond." *New York Times*, July 12, 2009, Arts and Leisure, 1, 20–21.

Overboe, James. "'Difference in Itself': Validating Disabled People's Lived Experience." *Body and Society* 5, no. 4 (1999): 17–29.

Owen, David. *Green Metropolis: Why Living Smaller, Living Closer, and Driving Less Are the Keys to Sustainability*. New York: Riverhead Books, 2009.

———. "Manhattan is the Greenest City in North America." Lecture given on March 17, 2011, Playhouse Theatre, Vancouver. http://www.sala.ubc.ca/news/david-owen-lecture-why-manhattan-greenest-city-north-america.

Palwick, Susan. *The Necessary Beggar*. New York: Tor Books, 2005.

Panikkar, Raimon. *Initiation to the Vedas*. Ed. Milena Carrara Pavan. Delhi: Motilal Banarsidass Publishers, 2006.

Pannenberg, Wolfhart. *Toward a Theology of Nature: Essays on Science and Faith*. Louisville, Ky.: Westminster John Knox Press, 1993.

Parenti, Christian. *Tropic of Chaos: Climate Change and the New Geography of Violence.* New York: Nation Books, 2011.

Pascal, Blaise. "Prière pour demander a dieu le bon usage des maladies." In *Oeuvres complètes.* Ed. Louis Lafuma. Paris: Seuil, 1963.

Paton, Alan. *Cry, the Beloved Country.* New York: Scribner Classics, 2003. First published 1948 by Charles Scribner's Sons.

Pearson, Keith Ansell. *Germinal Life: The Difference and Repetition of Deleuze.* London: Routledge, 1999.

Penumaka, Moses P. P. "Luther and Shankara: Two Ways of Salvation in the Indian Context." *Dialog* 45, no. 3 (2006): 252–62.

Perkinson, James. "Beauty Born of Pain: Why Are We Afraid of Art? (Or, Blue Notes or Stopped Throats?)." In *Spirit of Fire: Faith, Art, and Action*, ed. Jim Wallis, Julie Polter, Rose Marie Berger, and Jim Rice, 25–27. Washington, D.C.: Sojourners, 2003.

———. "Theology and the City: Learning to Cry, Struggling to See." *Crosscurrents* 51, no. 1 (2001): 95–114.

Perpich, Diane. "*Corpus Meum:* Disintegrating Bodies and the Ideal of Integrity." *Hypatia* 20, no. 3 (2005): 75–91.

Pile, Steve. "Introduction: Opposition, Political Identities, and Spaces of Resistance." In *Geographies of Resistance*, ed. Steve Pile and Michael Keith, 1–32. London: Routledge, 1997.

Pippin, Robert. "Love and Death in Nietzsche." In *Religion after Metaphysics*, ed. Mark A. Wrathall, 7–28. Cambridge: Cambridge University Press, 2003.

———. "Nietzsche and the Melancholy of Modernity." *Social Research* 66, no. 2 (1999): 495–520.

Pirruccello, Ann. "Making the World My Body: Simone Weil and Somatic Practice." *Philosophy East and West* 52, no. 4 (2002): 479–97.

Pittenger, Norman. "Beauty in a World in Process." *Andover Newton Quarterly* 17 (1977): 243–49.

Poe, Edgar Allen. "Ligeia." 1838. In *The Portable Edgar Allan Poe*, 111–25. Ed. J. Gerald Kennedy. New York: Penguin, 2006.

Pottle, Adam. *Beautiful Mutants.* Halfmoon Bay, B.C.: Caitlin Press, 2011.

Powers, Daniel G. *Salvation through Participation: An Examination of the Notion of the Believers' Corporate Unity with Christ in Early Christian Soteriology.* Leuven: Peeters, 2001.

Price, Robert. "Practicing the Present (Eckhart Tolle, *The Power of Now: A Guide to Spiritual Enlightenment*)." In *Top Secret: The Truth behind Today's Pop Mysticisms.* Amherst, N.Y.: Prometheus Books, 2008.

"Punishing Poverty." New York Times, November 1, 2011, Opinion, A26. http://www.nytimes.com/2011/11/01/opinion/punishing-poverty.html.

Quayson, Ato. *Aesthetic Nervousness: Disability and the Crisis of Representation.* New York: Columbia University Press, 2007.

Rambachan, Anantanand. *The Advaita Worldview: God, World, and Humanity*. New York: SUNY Press, 2006.

Ratti, Carlo, and Anthony Townsend. "The Social Nexus." In "Better, Greener, Smarter Cities." Special issue, *Scientific American* 305, no. 3 (2011): 42–48.

Ravindra, Ravi. *Christ the Yogi: A Hindu Reflection on the Gospel of John*. Rochester, Vt.: Inner Traditions, 1990.

Ray, Darby. *Deceiving the Devil*. Cleveland: Pilgrim Press, 1998.

Rich, Adrienne. "Dreams Before Waking." In *Your Native Land, Your Life*. New York: W. W. Norton, 1986; 1993.

Rinpoche, Sogyal. *The Tibetan Book of Living and Dying*. Ed. Patrick Gaffney and Andrew Harvey. San Francisco: HarperSanFrancisco, 1993.

Robbins, Jeffrey W. "The Problem of Ontotheology: Complicating the Divide between Philosophy and Theology." *Heythorp* 43, no. 2 (2002): 139–51.

Roberts, Tyler T. *Contesting Spirit: Nietzsche, Affirmation, Religion*. Princeton: Princeton University Press, 1998.

Robinson, Andrew. "Precaritans of All Countries, Unite!" In Theory. *Ceasefire*, March 18, 2011, http://ceasefiremagazine.co.uk/new-in-ceasefire/in-theory-precarity/. Accessed November 25, 2011.

Rohr, Richard. "Mending the Breach." *Tikkun* 23, no. 3 (2007): 29.

Rolston, Holmes, III. "Does Nature Need to Be Redeemed?" *Zygon* 29 (1994): 205–29.

Rosenzweig, Franz. *The Star of Redemption*. Trans. William W. Hallo. Boston: Beacon, 1971.

———. *Der Stern der Erlösung*. In *Franz Rosenzweig: Der Mensch und sein Werk; Gesammelte Schriften*, vol. 2 The Hague: Martinus Nijhoff, 1976.

Roslin, Alex. "Japan's Fukushima Catastrophe Brings Big Radiation Spikes to B.C." *Georgia Straight* 45, no. 2276 (August 4–11, 2011): 13, 15.

Ross, Ellen M. *The Grief of God: Images of the Suffering Jesus in Late Medieval England*. Oxford: Oxford University Press, 1997.

Rubenstein, Mary-Jane. *Strange Wonder: The Closure of Metaphysics and the Opening of Awe*. New York: Columbia University Press, 2008.

Rushdie, Salman. *Midnight's Children*. New York: Knopf, 1981.

Russell, Marta. *Beyond Ramps: Disability at the End of the Social Contract; A Warning from an Uppity Crip*. Monroe, Me.: Common Courage Press, 1998.

Sacks, Robert. *A Geographical Guide to the Real and the Good*. New York: Routledge, 2003.

Said, Edward. *Culture and Imperialism*. New York: Vintage Books/Random House, 1993.

Samartin, Cecilia. *Tarnished Beauty: A Novel*. New York: Washington Square Press, 2009.

Sandercock, Leonie. *Cosmopolis II: Mongrel Cities of the Twenty-First Century*. London: Continuum, 2003.

———. *Towards Cosmopolis*. Chichester: John Wiley, 1998.

Sandilands, Catriona. "Between the Local and the Global: Clayoquot Sound and Simulacral Politics." In Magnusson and Shaw, *A Political Space*, 140–41.

Sands, Kathleen M. *Escape from Paradise: Evil and Tragedy in Feminist Theology*. Minneapolis: Fortress, 1994.

Sanford, Matthew. *Waking: A Memoir of Trauma and Transcendence*. New York: Holtzbrinck Publishers, 2006.

Sanguin, Bruce. *The Emerging Church: A Model for Change and a Map for Renewal*. Kelowna, B.C.: CopperHouse, 2008.

Sassen, Saskia. "From *Globalization and Its Discontents*." In Bridge and Watson, *Blackwell City Reader*, 161–70.

Saunders, Doug. *Arrival City: The Final Migration and Our Next World*. Toronto: Knopf, 2010.

Scarry, Elaine. *On Beauty and Being Just*. Princeton: Princeton University Press, 1999.

Schaap, Jessica. "Notes towards a Eucharistic Prayer." Paper given at Vancouver School of Theology, Vancouver, B.C., April 18, 2007.

Schaberg, Jane. *The Illegitimacy of Jesus: A Feminist Theological Interpretation of the Infancy Narratives*. San Francisco: Harper and Row, 1987.

Schipper, Jeremy. *Disability and Isaiah's Suffering Servant*. Oxford: Oxford University Press, 2011.

Schleiermacher, Friedrich. *The Christian Faith*. Ed. H. R. Mackintosh and J. S. Stewart. Edinburgh: T. and T. Clark, 1986.

Schneider, Laurel C. *Beyond Monotheism: A Theology of Multiplicity*. London: Routledge, 2008.

Schneiders, Sandra. *New Wineskins: Re-imagining Religious Life Today*. Mahwah, N.J.: Paulist Press, 1986.

Schoolman, Morton. "Series Editor's Introduction." In *Thoreau's Nature: Ethics, Politics, and the Wild* by Jane Bennett, vii. Walnut Creek, Cal.: AltaMira Press, 2000.

Schweik, Susan. "Begging the Question: Disability, Mendicancy, Speech and the Law." *Narrative* 15, no. 1 (2007): 58–70.

Scruton, Roger. *Beauty*. Oxford: Oxford University Press, 2009.

Sedgwick, Eve K. *Touching Feeling: Affect, Pedagogy, Performativity*. Durham, N.C.: Duke University Press, 2003.

Seigworth, Gregory J. "From Affection to Soul." In Stivale, *Gilles Deleuze*, 159–69.

Seigworth, Gregory J., and Melissa Gregg. "An Inventory of Shimmers." In *The Affect Theory Reader*, ed. Gregory J. Seigworth and Melissa Gregg, 1–25. Durham, N.C.: Duke University Press, 2010.

Seltzer, Sarah. "Elizabeth Warren Puts the Kibosh on GOP's 'Class Warfare': Nobody in This Country Got Rich on His Own." *Alternet*, September 21,

2011, http://www.alternet.org/newsandviews/article/669655/eliabeth_warren _puts_the _kibosh_on_gop.

Sennett, Richard. *The Conscience of the Eye: The Design and Social Life of Cities.* New York: Knopf, 1990.

———. *The Fall of Public Man.* New York: Knopf, 1977.

———. *Flesh and Stone: The Body and City in Western Civilization.* New York: W. W. Norton, 1994.

Sheldrake, Philip F. *Spaces for the Sacred: Place, Memory, and Identity.* Baltimore: Johns Hopkins University Press, 2001.

———. "Spirituality and Social Change: Rebuilding the Human City." Public lecture presented at Vancouver School of Theology, Vancouver, B.C., November 3, 2009.

———. "Spirituality and Social Change: Rebuilding the Human City." *Spiritus: Journal of Christian Spirituality* 9, no. 2 (2009): 137–56.

Sherman, Janette D., M.D., and Joseph Mangano. "Is the Dramatic Increase in Baby Deaths in the U.S. a Result of Fukushima Fallout?" *Progressive Radio Network*, June 13, 2011. http://prn.fm/health-headlines/2011/6/13 /janette-d-sherman-md-and-joseph-mangano-is-the-dramatic-increase-in -baby-deaths-in-the-us-a-result-of-fukushima-fallout-2/#axzz2GaboZBlP.

Sherwood, Yvonne. "Passion-Binding-Passion." In Burrus and Keller, *Toward a Theology of Eros*, 169–93.

Shibley, Mark A. "Secular but Spiritual in the Pacific Northwest." In Killen and Silk, *Religion and Public Life in the Pacific Northwest*, 139–67.

Shildrick, Margrit. "Unreformed Bodies: Normative Anxiety and the Denial of Pleasure." *Women's Studies* 34, no. 3–4 (2005): 327–44.

Shrift, Alan. "Logics of the Gift in Cixous and Nietzsche: Can We Still Be Generous?" *Angelaki: Journal of the Theoretical Humanities* 6, no. 2 (2001): 113–23.

Siebers, Tobin. "Aesthetics and the Disqualification of Disability." Paper presented at the Society for Disabilities Studies Annual Conference, San Jose, Calif., June 17, 2011.

———. "Disability Aesthetics." *Journal for Cultural and Religious Theory* 7, no. 2 (2006): 63–72.

———. *Disability Aesthetics.* Ann Arbor: University of Michigan Press, 2010.

———. "In the Name of Pain." In *Against Health: How Health Became the New Morality*, ed. Jonathan M. Metzl and Anna Kirkland, 183–94. New York: New York University Press, 2010.

———. "Kant and the Politics of Beauty." *Philosophy and Literature* 22, no. 1 (1998): 31–50.

Siebert, Charles. "Watching Whales Watching Us." *New York Times Magazine*, July 12, 2009, 26–35, 44–45.

Sigurdson, Ola. "The Christian Body as a Grotesque Body." In *Embodiment in Cognition and Culture*, ed. John Michael Krois, Mats Rosengren, Angela

Steidele, and Dirk Westerkamp, 243–60. Amsterdam: John Benjamins Publishing, 2007.

Silvers, Anita, and Leslie Pickering Francis. "Justice through Trust: Disability and the 'Outlier Problem' in Social Contract Theory." *Ethics* 116 (2006): 40–76.

Simons, Walter. *Cities of Ladies: Beguine Communities in the Medieval Low Countries, 1200–1565.* Philadelphia: University of Pennsylvania Press, 2001.

Singer, Peter. "Changing Ethics in Life and Death Decision Making." Symposium: The Shifting Ground of Life and Death. *Society* 38, no. 5 (2001): 9–15.

Sinha, Indra. *Animal's People.* New York: Simon and Schuster, 2007.

Sittler, Joseph. "A Theology for Earth." *Christian Scholar* 37 (1954): 367–74.

Sitton, John F. *Habermas and Contemporary Society.* New York: Palgrave Macmillan, 2003.

Smith, Charlie. "Sometimes, Is a Riot Normal?" *Georgia Straight* 45, no. 2270 (June 23–30, 2011): 19, 21.

Smith, Huston. "Western Philosophy as a Great Religion." In *Huston Smith: Essays on World Religions,* ed. M. Darrol Bryant, 205–23. New York: Paragon House, 1992.

Snell, Heather. "Assessing the Limitations of Laughter in Indra Sinha's *Animal's People.*" *Postcolonial Text* 4, no. 4 (2008): 1–15.

Snyder, Sharon L., and David T. Mitchell. *Cultural Locations of Disability.* Chicago: University of Chicago Press, 2006.

———. "The Eugenic Atlantic: Disability and the Making of an International Science." In Snyder and Mitchell, *Cultural Locations of Disability,* 100–32.

———. "Introduction: Ablenationalism and the Geo-Politics of Disability." *Journal of Literary and Cultural Disability Studies* 4, no. 2 (2010): 113–26.

———. *Narrative Prosthesis: Disability and the Dependence of Discourse.* Ann Arbor: University of Michigan Press, 2001.

Soelle, Dorothee. *The Silent Cry: Mysticism and Resistance.* Minneapolis: Fortress, 2001.

———. *Suffering.* Trans. Everett R. Kalin. Philadelphia: Fortress, 1975.

Soja, Edward. W. *Postmetropolis: Critical Studies of Cities and Regions.* Malden, Mass.: Blackwell, 2000.

———. "Seeing Nature Spatially." In *Without Nature: A New Condition for Theology,* ed. David Albertson and Cabell King, 181–202. New York: Fordham University Press, 2009.

Spencer, Richard. "Beijing Olympics: 'Ethnic' Children Revealed as Fakes in Opening Ceremony." *The Telegraph,* August 15, 2008. http://www.telegraph.co.uk/sport/olympics/2563786/Beijing-Olympics-Ethnic-children-revealed-as-fakes-in-opening-ceremony.html. Accessed August 17, 2008.

———. "Beijing Olympics: Faking Scandal over Girl who 'Sang' in Opening Ceremony." *The Telegraph,* August 12, 2008. http://www.telegraph.co.uk

/sport/olympics/2545387/Beijing-Olympics-Faking-scandal-over-girl-who
-sang-in-opening-ceremony.html. Accessed August 17, 2008.

Spivak, Gayatri Chakravorty. *A Critique of Postcolonial Reason: Toward a History of the Vanishing Present.* Cambridge, Mass.: Harvard University Press, 1999.

———. *Death of a Discipline.* New York: Columbia University Press, 2003.

———. "Globalicities: Terror and Its Consequences." *New Centennial Review* 4 (2004): 73–94.

———. *Human Rights, Human Wrongs: The Oxford Amnesty Lectures 2001.* Oxford: Oxford University Press, 2003.

———. "Righting Wrongs." *South Atlantic Quarterly* 103, no. 2/3 (2004): 523–81.

Stallybrass, Peter, and Allon White. "The City: The Sewer, the Gaze and the Contaminating Touch." In *The Politics and Poetics of Transgression*, ed. Peter Stallybrass and Allon White, 125–48. London: Methuen, 1986.

Steel, Carolyn. *Hungry City: How Food Shapes Our Lives.* London: Vintage Books, 2009.

Steingraber, Sandra. *Raising Elijah: Protecting Our Children in an Age of Environmental Crisis.* Cambridge, Mass.: A Merloyd Lawrence Book/Da Capo Press, 2011.

Stiegler, Bernard. "Derrida and Technology: Fidelity at the Limits of Deconstruction and the Prosthesis of Faith." In *Jacques Derrida and the Humanities*, ed. Tom Cohen, 238–70. Cambridge: Cambridge University Press, 2001.

Stiker, Henri-Jacques. *A History of Disability.* Trans. William Sayers. Ann Arbor: University of Michigan Press, 1999.

Stivale, Charles J. *Gilles Deleuze: Key Concepts.* Montreal, Qué. and Kingston, Ont.: McGill-Queen's University Press, 2005.

Stolow, Jeremy. "Religion, Globalization and Visibility: Some Problems of Definition." *Globalization and Autonomy Online Compendium*, http://www.globalautonomy.ca/global1/article.jsp?index=PP_Stolow_RGV.xml. Accessed July 27, 2010.

Strohmeyer, Sarah. *The Sleeping Beauty Proposal.* New York: New American Library/Penguin, 2008.

Swanson, Tod D. "To Prepare a Place: Johannine Christianity and the Collapse of Ethnic Territory." *Journal of the American Academy of Religion* 62, no. 2 (1994): 241–63.

Tanner, Jeremy. "Portraits, Power and Patronage in the Late Roman Republic." *Journal of Roman Studies* 90 (2000): 18–50.

Tanner, Kathryn. *Economy of Grace.* Minneapolis: Fortress, 2005.

———. "Incarnation, Cross, and Sacrifice: A Feminist-Inspired Reappraisal." *Anglican Theological Review* 86, no. 1 (2004): 35–56.

———. *Theories of Culture: A New Agenda for Theology.* Minneapolis: Fortress, 1997.

Taylor, Charles. *A Secular Age*. Cambridge, Mass.: Belknap/Harvard University Press, 2007.

Taylor, Mark C. *After God*. Chicago: University of Chicago Press, 2007.

Taylor, Mark Lewis. "Spirit and Liberation: Achieving Postcolonial Theology in the United States." In *Divinity and Empire: Postcolonial Theologies*, ed. Catherine Keller, Michael Nausner, and Mayra Rivera, 39–66. St. Louis, Mo.: Chalice Press, 2004.

Taylor, Timothy. *Stanley Park*. Toronto: Vintage Canada/Random House of Canada, 2001.

Tertullian. *On the Resurrection of the Flesh*. Trans. and Latin edited by Ernest Evans. London: SPCK Publishing, 1960.

Thiessen, Joel, and Lorne L. Dawson. "Is There a 'Renaissance' of Religion in Canada? A Critical Look at Bibby and Beyond." *Studies in Religion* 37, no. 3–4 (2008): 389–415.

Thistlethwaite, Susan Brooks. "Why Are Our Cities Dying?" *Theology Today* 51, no. 1 (1994): 17–26.

Thrush, Coll. *Native Seattle: Histories from the Crossing-Over Place*. Seattle: University of Washington Press, 2007.

Thurston, Bonnie. *Religious Vows, the Sermon on the Mount, and Christian Living*. Collegeville, Minn.: Liturgical Press, 2006.

Tillich, Paul. *Systematic Theology*, vol. 2. Trans. Arthur Wills. Chicago: University of Chicago Press, 1957.

Todd, Douglas. "As Metro's Ethnic Enclaves Expand, Will Residents' Trust Hold?" Part 5 of "Mapping Our Ethnicity." *Vancouver Sun*, October 20, 2011, Westcoast News, A15.

———. "Designing a Made-in-B.C. Spirituality: British Columbia Could Be Prime Ground for Starting a New Religion Rooted in a Local Vision." *Vancouver Sun*, July 4, 2009, Weekend Review, Issues and Ideas section, D4.

———. "We Need to Create a Common West Coast Vision." *Vancouver Sun*, May 9, 2009, section C4.

Todd, Douglas, ed. *Cascadia: The Elusive Utopia; Exploring the Spirit of the Pacific Northwest*. Vancouver: Ronsdale Press, 2008.

Tolle, Eckhart. *A New Earth: Awakening to Your Life's Purpose*. New York: Penguin, 2005.

———. *Living the Liberated Life and Dealing with the Pain Body*. Audio CD. Louisville, Colo.: Sounds True, 2001.

———. *The Power of Now*. Novato, Calif.: Namaste/New World Library, 1999.

Tombs, David. "Crucifixion, State Terror, and Sexual Abuse." *Union Seminary Quarterly Review* 53, no. 1–2 (1999): 89–119.

Torrey, Edwin Fuller, and Judy Miller. *The Invisible Plague: The Rise of Mental Illness from 1750 to the Present.* New Brunswick, N.J.: Rutgers University Press, 2002.

Tranvik, Mark D. "Preface." In Luther, *Freedom of a Christian*, vii–viii.

———. "Translator's Introduction: Martin Luther's Road to Freedom." In Luther, *Freedom of a Christian*, 1–30.

Trelstad, Marit. "Lavish Love: A Covenantal Ontology." In *CrossExaminations: Readings on the Meaning of the Cross Today*, ed. Marit Trelstad, 109–24. Minneapolis: Fortress, 2006.

———. "The Way of Salvation in Luther's Theology: A Feminist Evaluation." *Dialog* 45, no. 3 (2006): 236–45.

Tremain, Shelly. *Foucault and the Government of Disability.* Ann Arbor: University of Michigan Press, 2005.

Trozzo, Eric, ed. *Stand Boldly: Lutheran Theology Faces the Postmodern World.* Berkeley: Three Trees Press, 2009.

Turner, Chris. "Guerrilla Barley Growers Go Against the Grain." *Globe and Mail*, February 9, 2008, section F8.

Van Schaik, Carel P., Gauri R. Pradhan, and Marie A. van Noordwijk. "Mating Conflict in Primates: Infanticide, Sexual Harassment and Female Sexuality." Paper for Dominance, Leveling, and Egalitarianism in Primates and Other Animals: A Working Group at the Santa Fe Institute, 2004. http://tuvalu.santafe.edu/~bowles/Dominance/DominancePapers.htm.

Vattimo, Gianni. *After Christianity.* Trans. Luca D'Isanto. New York: Columbia University Press, 2002.

———. "Pain and Metaphysics." In *Nihilism and Emancipation: Ethics, Politics and Law*, ed. Santiago Zabala, trans. William McCuaig, 71–77. New York: Columbia University Press, 2004.

Vidler, Antony. "Bodies in Space/Subjects in the City." In Bridge and Watson, *Blackwell City Reader*, 46–51.

Vospers, Gretta. *With or Without God: Why the Way We Live Is More Important than What We Believe.* Toronto: HarperCollins, 2008.

de Waal, Frans. *The Age of Empathy: Nature's Lessons for a Kinder Society.* New York: Three Rivers, 2009.

Wallace, Mark I. "God is Underfoot: Pneumatology after Derrida." In *The Religious*, ed. John D. Caputo, 197–211. Malden, Mass.: Blackwell, 2002.

Ward, Graham. "Suffering and Incarnation." In *The Blackwell Companion to Postmodern Theology*, ed. Graham Ward, 192–208. Malden, Mass.: Blackwell, 2001.

———. "Bodies: The Displaced Body of Jesus." In *Radical Orthodoxy*, ed. John Milbank, Catherine Pickstock, and Graham Ward, 163–81. London: Routledge, 1999.

———. *Cities of God.* London: Routledge, 2000.

Waterfield, Bruno. "Ugly Food Tastes as Good as Pretty Food, So EU Ends Ban on the Bent and Knobbly." *Vancouver Sun*, November 12, 2008, D9.

Watters, Ethan. "The Americanization of Mental Illness." *New York Times Magazine*, January 10, 2010, 40–45.

Weil, Simone. *Gravity and Grace*. Trans. Emma Crawford and Mario von der Ruhr. London: Routledge, 1947; 2002.

———. "The Love of God and Affliction." In *Waiting for God*, 67–82.

———. "Meaning of the Universe." In *Gravity and Grace*, 140–144.

———. *The Notebooks of Simone Weil*, vol. 1. Trans. Arthur Wills. London: Routledge and Kegan Paul, 1956.

———. *Waiting for God*. Trans. Emma Craufurd. New York: Perennial Classics, 1951; 2001.

Wells, David. *Prosthesis*. Stanford: Stanford University Press, 1995.

Wenman, Mark. "William E. Connolly: Pluralism without Transcendence." *British Journal of Politics and International Relations* 10 (2008): 156–70.

Westhelle, Vitor. *The Scandalous God: The Use and Abuse of the Cross*. Minneapolis: Fortress, 2006.

Weyler, Rex. *The Jesus Sayings: The Quest for His Authentic Message*. Toronto: House of Anansi Press, 2009.

Whitehead, Alfred North. *Adventure of Ideas*. New York: Free Press/Simon and Schuster, 1967.

Wilber, Ken. "Boomeritis Buddhism." In *Integral Spirituality: A Startling New Role for Religion in the Modern and Postmodern World*, 103–18. Boston: Integral Books, 2007.

Wilfred, Fred. "Christianity and Religious Cosmopolitanism: Toward Reverse Universality." In *Pluralist Theology: The Emerging Paradigm*, ed. Luiz Carlos Susin, Andres Torres Queiruga, and Jose Maria Vigil. London: SCM Press, 2007.

Williams, Rowan. *Resurrection: Interpreting the Easter Gospel*. Cleveland: Pilgrim Press, 2003.

Wills, Lawrence M. "Ascetic Theology before Asceticism? Jewish Narratives and the Decentering of the Self." *Journal of the American Academy of Religion* 74, no. 4 (2006): 902–25.

Winch, Peter. *Simone Weil: "The Just Balance."* Cambridge: Cambridge University Press, 1989.

Winquist, Charles E. *Desiring Theology*. Chicago: University of Chicago Press, 1995.

Wolfson, Elliot R. "The Cut that Binds: Time, Memory, and the Ascetic Impulse." In *God's Voice from the Void: Old and New Studies in Bratslav Hasidism*, ed. Shaul Magid, 103–54. New York: SUNY Press, 2001.

Woolf, Virginia. *On Being Ill*. Introduction by Hermione Lee. Paris: Paris Press, 2002.

Worldwatch Institute. *State of the World 2007: Our Urban Future.* Ed. Linda Starke. New York: W. W. Norton, 2007.

Wrathall, Mark A. "Between the Earth and the Sky: Heidegger on Life after the Death of God." In *Religion after Metaphysics*, ed. M. A. Wrathall, 69–87. Cambridge: Cambridge University Press, 2003.

Wurmser, Leon. "The Superego as Herald of Resentment." *Psychoanalytic Inquiry* 29 (2009): 386–410.

Wyman, Leland C., ed. *Beautyway: A Navaho Ceremonial.* New York: Bollingen Foundation, 1957.

Young, Robert. *Colonial Desire: Hybridity in Theory, Culture and Race.* London: Routledge, 1995.

Yuan, David D. "Disfigurement and Reconstruction in Oliver Wendell Holmes's 'The Human Wheel, Its Spokes and Felloes.'" In *The Body and Physical Difference: Discourses of Disability*, ed. David T. Mitchell and Sharon L. Snyder, 71–88. Ann Arbor: University of Michigan Press, 1997.

Zabala, Santiago. "Christianity and the Death of God: A Response to Cardinal Lustiger." *Common Knowledge* 11, no. 1 (2005): 33–40.

Zachman, Randall C. *The Assurance of Faith: Conscience in the Theology of Martin Luther and John Calvin.* Louisville, Ky.: Westminster John Knox, 2005.

Zanker, Paul. *The Power of Images in the Age of Augustus.* Trans. Alan Shapiro. Ann Arbor: University of Michigan, 1990.

Zizoulas, John D. *Being in Communion: Studies in Personhood and the Church.* London: Darton, Longman and Todd, 1985.

Zukin, Sharon. *The Culture of Cities.* Malden, Mass.: Blackwell, 1995.

———. "From *Landscapes of Power: From Detroit to Disney World*." In Bridge and Watson, *Blackwell City Reader*, 197–207.

Zylinska, Joanna. "'The Future . . . Is Monstrous': Prosthetics as Ethics." In *Cyborg Experiments: The Extensions of the Body in the Media Age*, 214–36. London: Continuum, 2002.